INDUCTIVE REASONING

Without inductive reasoning, we couldn't generalize from one instance to another, derive scientific hypotheses, or predict that the sun will rise again tomorrow morning. Despite the prevalence of inductive reasoning, books on this topic are rare. Indeed, this is the first book on the psychology of inductive reasoning in twenty years. The chapters survey recent advances in the study of inductive reasoning and address questions about how it develops, the role of knowledge in induction, how best to model people's reasoning, and how induction relates to other forms of thinking. Written by experts in philosophy, developmental science, cognitive psychology, and computational modeling, the contributions here will be of interest to a general cognitive science audience as well as to those with a more specialized interest in the study of thinking.

Aidan Feeney is Senior Lecturer in Psychology at Durham University. He received his B.A. in psychology from Trinity College, Dublin, in 1992 and completed his Ph.D. at the Center for Thinking and Language at the University of Plymouth. He was appointed Lecturer in the Department of Psychology at Durham University in 1998 and became Senior Lecturer in 2005. Dr. Feeney's research has been supported by a number of grants from the Economic and Social Research Council (UK). He has published approximately thirty journal articles, book chapters, and papers on the psychology of hypothesis testing and reasoning.

Evan Heit is currently Professor of Psychology and Cognitive Science, and Founding Faculty, at the University of California, Merced. Previously, Dr. Heit was on the faculty in the Psychology Department of the University of Warwick, UK. He has undergraduate degrees in computer science and psychology from the University of Pennsylvania and a Ph.D. from Stanford University. He also carried out postdoctoral research at the University of Michigan and Northwestern University. Professor Heit has published more than fifty papers on the psychology of reasoning, memory, and categorization. His research has been funded by the National Science Foundation, the National Institutes of Health, the Economic and Social Research Council (UK), and the Biotechnology and Biological Sciences Research Council (UK). He is currently on the editorial board of *Memory and Cognition* and the *Journal of Experimental Psychology: Learning, Memory, and Cognition* and is Associate Editor of the *Journal of Memory and Language*.

Inductive Reasoning

Experimental, Developmental, and Computational Approaches

Edited by

AIDAN FEENEY

Durham University

EVAN HEIT

University of California, Merced

CAMBRIDGE
UNIVERSITY PRESS

CAMBRIDGE UNIVERSITY PRESS
Cambridge, New York, Melbourne, Madrid, Cape Town, Singapore, São Paulo, Delhi

Cambridge University Press
32 Avenue of the Americas, New York, NY 10013-2473, USA

www.cambridge.org
Information on this title: www.cambridge.org/9780521856485

First published 2007

Printed in the United States of America

A catalog record for this publication is available from the British Library.

Library of Congress Cataloging in Publication Data

Inductive reasoning : experimental, developmental, and computational approaches / edited by
Aidan Feeney and Evan Heit.
p.   cm.
Includes bibliographical references and index.
ISBN 978-0-521-85648-5 (hardback) – ISBN 978-0-521-67244-3 (pbk.)
1. Reasoning (Psychology)   2. Induction (Logic)
I. Feeney, Aidan, 1971–   II. Heit, Evan, 1965–   III. Title.
BF442.I53   2007
153.4′32–dc22   2007002735

ISBN   978-0-521-85648-5 hardback
ISBN   978-0-521-67244-3 paperback

Contents

List of Figures

List of Tables

List of Contributors

Jennifer Asmuth Department of Psychology, Northwestern University, 2029 Sheridan Road, Evanston, IL 60208-2710, USA

Sergey Blok Department of Psychology, 1 University Station A8000, University of Texas at Austin, Austin, TX 78712, USA

John D. Coley Department of Psychology, MS 0125 NI, Northeastern University, 360 Huntington Avenue, Boston, MA 02115-5000, USA

Aidan Feeney Department of Psychology, Durham University, Queen's Campus, Thornaby, Stockton-on-Tees, TS17 6BH, UK

Ulrike Hahn School of Psychology, Cardiff University, Tower Building, Park Place, Cardiff, CF10 3AT, UK

Brett K. Hayes School of Psychology, University of New South Wales, Sydney, NSW, Australia, 2052

Evan Heit School of Social Sciences, Humanities, and Arts, University of California, Merced, PO Box 2039, Merced, CA 95344, USA

Charles Kemp Department of Brain and Behavioral Sciences, 46-4053, Massachusetts Institute of Technology, 77 Massachusetts Avenue, Cambridge, MA 02139, USA

Douglas L. Medin Department of Psychology, Northwestern University, Swift Hall, 2029 Sherdian Road, Evanston, IL 60208-2710, USA

Gregory L. Murphy Department of Psychology, New York University, 6 Washington Place, New York, NY 10003, USA

Mike Oaksford School of Psychology, Birkbeck College London, Malet Street, London, WC1E 7HX, UK

Daniel Osherson Department of Psychology, Green Hall 3-S-12, Princeton University, Princeton, NJ 08544, USA

Bob Rehder Department of Psychology, New York University, 6 Washington Place, New York, NY 10003, USA

Lance J. Rips Psychology Department, Northwestern University, 2029 Sheridan Road, Evanston, IL 60208, USA

Brian H. Ross Beckman Institute, University of Illinois, 405 N. Mathews Ave., Urbana, IL 61801, USA

Patrick Shafto Department of Brain and Behavioral Sciences, 46-4053, Massachusetts Institute of Technology, 77 Massachusetts Avenue, Cambridge, MA 02139, USA

Steven Sloman Cognitive & Linguistic Sciences, Brown University, Box 1978, Providence, RI 02912, USA

Joshua B. Tenenbaum Department of Brain and Behavioral Sciences, 46-4015, Massachusetts Institute of Technology, 77 Massachusetts Avenue, Cambridge, MA 02139-4307, USA

Paul Thagard Philosophy Department, University of Waterloo, Waterloo, Ontario, Canada N2L 3G1

Anna Vitkin Department of Psychology, MS 0125 NI, Northeastern University, 360 Huntington Avenue, Boston, MA 02115-5000, USA

Sandra Waxman Department of Psychology, Northwestern University, Swift Hall, 2029 Sherdian Road, Evanston, IL 60208-2710, USA

Preface

Books on induction are rare; in fact, you are holding in your hands the first book devoted solely to the psychology of inductive reasoning in twenty years. And yet induction is a central topic in cognitive science, fundamental to learning, discovery, and prediction. We make inductive inferences every time we use what we already know to deal with novel situations. For example, wherever you found this book – in your university library, online, or in an academic bookshop – before picking it from the shelf or clicking on a link, you will have made some inductive inferences. Amongst other things, these inferences will have concerned the book's likely content given its title, its editors, its publisher, or its cover. Common to all of these inferences will have been the use of what you already know – about us, or the topic suggested by our title, or Cambridge University Press – to make predictions about the likely attributes of this book.

It is not only in publishers' catalogues that attention to induction has been scant. Despite its obvious centrality to an understanding of human cognition and behaviour, much less work has been carried out by psychologists on induction than on deduction, or logical reasoning. As a consequence, although there have been several edited collections of work on deduction and on decision making (Connolly, Arkes, & Hammond, 2000; Leighton & Sternberg, 2004; Gilovich, Griffin, & Kahneman, 2002; Manktelow & Chung, 2004), to the best of our knowledge there has never previously been an edited collection of papers on the psychology of inductive inference.

To attempt to redress the balance somewhat, in 2004 we organised a symposium on induction at the Fifth International Conference on Thinking, which was held in the historical setting of the University of Leuven in Belgium. The series of international conferences on thinking, of which the meeting in Leuven was part, has been primarily concerned with deductive inference, problem solving, and decision making. Our symposium was intended to raise the profile, in Europe particularly, of work on induction. Many, but not all, of the chapter authors for this book talked at the symposium, which took place on Saturday 24 July. Doug Medin, Pat Shafto, Paul Thagard, Brett Hayes, Josh Tenenbaum, Evan Heit, and Aidan Feeney all talked about their work on induction, and Steven Sloman was the discussant. John Coley, Mike Oaksford, and Bob Rehder were also present and contributed greatly on the day, and Lance Rips had also been vesting Leuven. The symposium went so well that we decided to press on with plans for a book. But what kind of book should it be?

The last book devoted wholly to the psychology of induction was Holland, Holyoak, Nisbett, and Thagard's landmark book on induction, which appeared in 1986. Broadly speaking, Holland and colleagues' book attempted to apply just one general explanatory framework to a variety of inductive phenomena including analogy, scientific discovery, generalisation, and rule learning. Since 1986 the field has changed and developed enormously. There have been great accomplishments in the study of how inductive reasoning develops, as well as a focus on precise mathematical modelling of induction throughout the 1990s, culminating in very powerful Bayesian models of inductive thinking that have emerged over the last few years. Other developments include a recent focus on the relationship between induction and deduction, widespread consideration of the role of categories and background knowledge in induction, and significant progress on questions about individual and cultural differences in inductive generalisation.

To emphasise how the field has changed since the mid-1980s, and because of the range of work on induction that has emerged in the intervening time, this book reverses the tactic employed by Holland and colleagues; instead of applying one approach to a variety of inductive phenomena, for the most part this book will focus on how a wide range of methodological and modelling approaches have increased our understanding of induction.

There is often a concern that edited books can lack coherence. Given that we wished to collect contributions on a wide range of approaches, this could have been a problem here. However, as most chapter authors presented at, or attended, the symposium in Leuven, we were all aware while writing our chapters of the concerns of other chapter authors. In addition, every chapter was read by two other chapter authors and every chapter was redrafted in the light of other authors' comments. Our goal throughout has been to achieve integration and overlap between chapters, and we hope that we have achieved coherence.

WHO IS THIS BOOK FOR?

This book is intended to be read by anyone interested in thinking. Our goal was to capture the current state of the art in our field. Thus all readers – be they psychologists, mathematical modellers, cognitive scientists, or philosophers – with even a passing interest in induction should find something to hold their attention here. Although we think that postgraduate students might be interested in most chapters, we also hope that undergraduates will find useful material. Whilst some of the chapters in this book focus in great detail on a very specific issue, others give very accessible overviews of big swathes of the literature. Although editors should probably refrain from favouring some contributions over others, because we think that all of the chapters in this book are excellent, we are happy to particularly recommend Chapters 1, 8, and 9 to undergraduates exploring the psychology of induction for the first time.

We also hope that many of our colleagues researching other forms of thinking such as deduction, decision making, analogy, and problem solving will be interested in this book. Whereas some of the issues, particularly those concerning development, culture, and individual differences, are likely to be similar across many forms of thinking, others are not. The particular issue that is distinctive to induction is that of knowledge; induction involves reasoning from all relevant belief. Whereas in some forms of reasoning it is an error to consider one's own beliefs, for inductive reasoning it is a necessity. Accordingly, to explain induction one has to consider how knowledge is structured, which type of knowledge is most relevant when, and how that knowledge is brought to bear on the premises of inductive arguments. Although these are not issues the literature on deduction, for example, has always highlighted, nevertheless we think that consideration of the role of different types of knowledge in reasoning might be very beneficial for researchers interested in deduction.

Finally, we think that Holland and colleagues were correct in suggesting that questions to do with induction are central to the study of cognitive science. How agents reuse previous experience stored in the form of knowledge is a key question for anyone interested in cognition. The diverse perspectives offered in this book should therefore be of interest to a wide range of researchers. Furthermore, we have tried very hard in this book to ensure coverage of molehills and mountains: molehills for the specialists and mountains for the general cognitive science reader.

ORGANISATION OF THE BOOK

When we drew up our list of invitees, the most important consideration was that we include a coherent set of contributions reflecting a range of approaches and methods important in contemporary cognitive science. These approaches are summarised in Chapter 1 by Evan Heit. Following a discussion of the differences between induction and deduction, the chapter uses the phenomenon of evidential diversity to explore approaches from philosophy, experimental psychology, mathematical modelling, and developmental science. After these introductory chapters, the book contains a further four sections, which we will briefly summarise.

The centrality of induction to cognitive development, and the centrality of the developmental approach to research on induction, can be seen in the chapters by Hayes and by Medin and Waxman. In Chapter 2 Brett Hayes provides a comprehensive overview of our current understanding of how inductive reasoning develops. He discusses the information that children use for inductive reasoning and presents the development of induction as being about the development of knowledge. Hayes also describes the uses to which developmental data may be put when evaluating theories of induction. Chapter 3, written by Doug Medin and Sandra Waxman, nicely illustrates how developmental data can constrain theory. Medin and Waxman concern themselves with asymmetries (preferences for arguments from certain categories over arguments from other categories) in children's reasoning. In contrast to Chapters 1 and 2, the chapter by Medin and Waxman is tightly focused on a single issue. However, by considering a range of possible explanations for asymmetries in the light of novel developmental evidence, some of which is cross-cultural, the authors are able to come down in favour of one account over all others.

The next three chapters all concern knowledge and induction. In Chapter 4, Bob Rehder makes a strong case for the importance of causal knowledge in induction. This chapter describes evidence that causal knowledge about a to-be-projected property affects its projectability, and it discusses the relationship between knowledge about similarity or taxonomic relations and knowledge about causal relations. Whereas the chapter by Rehder considers cases in which the two forms of knowledge are in competition, Chapter 5, contributed by Pat Shafto, John Coley, and Anna Vitkin, considers the role of availability in determining whether taxonomic or ecological knowledge dominates in induction. Shafto and colleagues consider two factors that might affect which type of knowledge is, or becomes, most available: context and experience. This framework proves a neat way of organising recent findings concerning the effects of content, property, expertise, and culture on inductive reasoning. Together these chapters demonstrate how far the field has moved beyond original attempts to model inductive inference using notions such as typicality and similarity.

Of course, similarity remains an extremely important construct in the literature on induction, and many inductive inferences will be based on similarity. One of the problems for models that have exploited similarity as an explanatory mechanism is the property that people are asked to project from members of one category to another. Typically, these models do not take account of the meaning of properties. In Chapter 6, Blok, Osherson, and Medin describe and experimentally verify a mathematical model of induction that takes as input (a) the similarity between the categories in the argument and (b) premise and conclusion probabilities. As the nature of the property determines the probability of the statements in an argument, this model can capture results for meaningful properties. Thus, it places similarity-based accounts on stronger footing.

The chapter by Blok and colleagues comes out of the very rich tradition of mathematical modelling in the literature on induction. So too does Chapter 7 on Bayesian models by Josh Tenenbaum, Charles Kemp, and Pat Shafto. The main contribution of this chapter is to show how certain assumptions about how knowledge is represented allow us to generate priors for a Bayesian belief-updating process. Thus, inductive reasoning can be given a comprehensive Bayesian treatment, which captures many of the knowledge effects discussed in previous chapters.

Chapter 8, by Greg Murphy and Brian Ross, offers an interesting perspective on Bayesian approaches to inductive reasoning. When generating a rating of argument strength, the models described by Tenenbaum and colleagues work through all of the hypotheses that are consistent with a particular inductive argument. Murphy and Ross show that, in many situations, people tend not to consider alternative hypotheses when evaluating inductive arguments. Murphy and Ross's chapter is problematic for the Bayesian view and asks questions about the link between normative and psychological models (as do Steven Sloman's comments in his integrative chapter), which researchers interested in Bayes would do well to address.

The volume closes with a set of chapters concerned with relations between induction and other forms of thinking. Paul Thagard outlines a theory of abductive reasoning, a form of induction in which one reasons to an explanation. This chapter touches on several themes in contemporary cognitive science as it posits an important role for the emotions and attempts to give a neuropsychologically plausible account of cognitive processes. Thagard was one of the authors of the 1986 book on induction, and his chapter brings an especially broad perspective to the study of thinking. As is apparent from this chapter, there are many types of thinking, and Thagard's comments on the likely frequency of deductive and inductive inference in everyday life are sobering.

Chapter 10, by Lance Rips and Jennifer Asmuth, although explicitly about a rarefied form of reasoning in mathematics, is ultimately concerned with the relationship between deduction and induction. Previous work (Rips, 2001) suggests that inductive and deductive reasoning are dissociated. Rips and Asmuth consider the case of mathematical induction, which they view as a form of deductive thinking. Interestingly, even quite advanced students of mathematics have problems with this form of reasoning.

Mike Oaksford and Ulrike Hahn in Chapter 11 argue for a probabilistic approach to argument evaluation. They claim that induction and deduction may be treated as belief-updating problems, although they do not rule out the possibility that some small amount of deduction takes place in the world. Because of its Bayesian character, this chapter is complementary to the chapter by Tenenbaum and colleagues. Also notable in this chapter is an attempt to get to grips with, from a Bayesian point of view, well-known informal reasoning fallacies, such as the argument from ignorance. Oaksford and Hahn demonstrate that some of these so-called fallacies may be justified from a Bayesian point of view.

In Chapter 12, Feeney takes a different perspective on the relationship between induction and other forms of thinking. Whereas Rips and Asmuth suggest that induction and deduction are different types of thinking, and Oaksford and Hahn suggest that, generally speaking, there is only one type of thinking, Feeney makes the argument that induction is no different from deduction in that both generally require the operation of two different types of thinking process. One of these is fast and associative whilst the other is slow and symbol manipulating (see Evans & Over, 1996; Sloman, 1996). The dual-process argument is not new, but its application here leads to a novel conception of inductive reasoning that is often thought of as involving only associative processes. Interestingly, however, causal knowledge is somewhat problematic for this dual-process view.

Finally, in Chapter 13, Steven Sloman comments on the other chapters in the book and draws together their common themes and implications in an interesting and provocative way. We do not want to spoil his punchlines here, but he has many interesting things to say about the relationship between types of thinking and about Bayesian approaches to induction. In many ways, this is the most important chapter in this book, as its role is to explicitly comment on the state of the field rather than merely describing and interpreting what is to be found in the literature.

ACKNOWLEDGMENTS

We wish to thank the organisers of the Fifth International Conference on Thinking for providing the forum for the meeting that led to this book. Darren Dunning helped us prepare the manuscript for submission to the publisher. Finally, we would like to thank all of the contributors to the symposium on induction, including Dinos Hadjichristidis, Fenna Poletiek, and Vinod Goel, and all of the contributors to this book.

References

Connolly, T., Arkes, H. R., & Hammond, K. R. (2000). *Judgement and decision making: An interdisciplinary reader.* Cambridge, UK: Cambridge University Press.

Evans, J. St. B. T., & Over, D. E. (1996). *Rationality and reasoning.* Hove, UK: Psychology Press.

Leighton, J. P., & Sternberg, R. J. (2004). *The nature of reasoning.* Cambridge, UK: Cambridge University Press.

Manktelow, K., & Chung, M. C. (2004). *Psychology of reasoning: Theoretical and historical perspectives.* Hove, UK: Psychology Press.

Rips, L. J. (2001). Two kinds of reasoning. *Psychological Science, 12,* 129–134.

Sloman, S. A. (1996). The empirical case for two systems of reasoning. *Psychological Bulletin, 119,* 3–22.

Editors
AIDAN FEENEY
Durham University
EVAN HEIT
University of California, Merced

1

What Is Induction and Why Study It?

Evan Heit

Why study induction, and indeed, why should there be a whole book devoted to the study of induction? The first reason is that inductive reasoning corresponds to probabilistic, uncertain, approximate reasoning, and as such, it corresponds to everyday reasoning. On a daily basis we draw inferences such as how a person will probably act, what the weather will probably be like, and how a meal will probably taste, and these are typical inductive inferences. So if researchers want to study a form of reasoning that is actually a pervasive cognitive activity, then induction is of appropriate interest.

The second reason to study induction is that it is a multifaceted cognitive activity. It can be studied by asking young children simple questions involving cartoon pictures, or it can be studied by giving adults a variety of complex verbal arguments and asking them to make probability judgments. Although induction itself is uncertain by nature, there is still a rich, and interesting, set of regularities associated with induction, and researchers are still discovering new phenomena.

Third, induction is related to, and it could be argued is central to, a number of other cognitive activities, including categorization, similarity judgment, probability judgment, and decision making. For example, much of the study of induction has been concerned with category-based induction, such as inferring that your next door neighbor sleeps on the basis that your neighbor is a human animal, even if you have never seen your neighbor sleeping. And as will be seen, similarity and induction are very closely related, many accounts of induction using similarity as their main currency (Heit & Hayes, 2005).

Finally, the study of induction has the potential to be theoretically revealing. Because so much of people's reasoning is actually inductive reasoning, and because there is such a rich data set associated with induction, and because induction is related to other central cognitive activities, it is possible to find out a lot about not only reasoning but cognition more generally by studying induction.

Induction is traditionally contrasted with deduction, which is concerned with drawing logically valid conclusions that must follow from a set of premises. The following section will consider possible definitions of induction by describing possible relations between induction and deduction. But first it is useful to briefly mention that the reasons for studying induction to some extent are linked to the differences between induction and deduction. That is, it could be argued that induction, in comparison to deduction, characterizes more of everyday reasoning, has the potential to be studied with a broader range of tasks and materials, and is closely related to other cognitive activities that help people manage uncertainty.

HOW IS INDUCTION RELATED TO DEDUCTION?

Although it might be natural to ask "how are induction and deduction different?" that would presuppose the conclusion that they are actually different. Although induction and deduction are traditionally considered alternatives to each other, as will be seen under some conceptions the similarities are much greater than the differences. Before assessing to what extent induction and deduction are similar or different, it is first important to consider just what kind of entities induction and deduction are. Although not always made explicit by researchers, there are two views on this issue, namely, the "problem view" and the "process view." According to the problem view, induction and deduction refer to particular types of reasoning problems. So from looking at a particular problem, say a question on a piece of paper in a psychological experiment on reasoning, it should be possible to say whether this is an induction problem or a deduction problem (or possibly it could be deemed debatable whether it is one or the other). In contrast, according to the process view, the locus of the question is not on the paper but in the head. That is, induction and deduction refer to psychological processes. For a given problem, it may be possible to answer it using induction processes or deduction processes. Likewise, we can investigate what is the relation between the two kinds of processing.

The problem view and the process view have to a large extent been confounded in the literature. That is, researchers who have studied problems that are traditionally thought of as induction have typically been interested in different psychological theories than researchers who have studied traditional deduction problems. However, for the sake of clarity it is better to treat the two views separately, namely, how problems of induction may differ from problems of deduction, and how inductive processes may differ (or not differ) from deductive processes. These two views will now be addressed in turn.

The Problem View

GENERAL AND SPECIFIC. It is sometimes said that induction goes from the specific to the general, and deduction goes from the general to the specific. For example, after observing that many individual dogs bark, one might induce a more general belief that all dogs bark. Alternately, having the general belief that all dogs bark, one might deduce that some particular dog will bark. However, there are difficulties with this version of the problem view. Consider the following arguments. (The statement above the line is a premise that is assumed to be true, and the task is to consider the strength of the conclusion, below the line.)

Dogs have hearts (1)

All mammals have hearts

All mammals have hearts (2)

Dogs have hearts

Dogs have hearts (3)

Wolves have hearts

Dogs have hearts (4)

At least some mammals have hearts

Argument (1) is a good example of an inductive argument going from specific to general, and likewise argument (2) is a good example of a deductive argument going from general to specific. Yet arguments (3) and (4) do not fit neatly into this scheme. Argument (3) is somewhat plausible but surely not deductively valid, so it is better thought of as an inductive argument. Yet it goes from specific to specific rather than specific to general. Finally, argument (4) seems to be deductively valid, yet it starts with a specific statement. Still, it is possible to disagree about these last two arguments. For argument (3), it could be said that there is an intervening general conclusion, such as "All mammals have hearts." For argument (4), it could be said that there is a hidden general premise, such as "All dogs are mammals." The key point is that one can't just look at the written form of an argument, in terms of whether it goes from specific to general or vice versa, and easily state whether it is inductive or deductive in nature.

DEFINING VALIDITY. Hence, it would seem profitable to take a more subtle approach to the problem view. Perhaps the most defensible version of the problem view is to define deductively valid arguments, and relate other kinds of arguments to those that are deductively valid. One standard definition of deductively valid arguments is that these are arguments following the rules of a well-specified logic. Assuming that one can specify the rules of one's preferred logic, say in terms of truth tables for various symbolic combinations, then it should be possible (if not easy) to determine whether any given argument is deductively valid or not. It might be seen as a small disadvantage of this approach that deductive validity is not defined in absolute terms but only relative to a logic. Different people might endorse different logics and hence disagree about which arguments are deductively valid. On the other hand, defining deductive validity relative to a logic could be seen as an advantage in terms of giving flexibility and in terms of appreciating that there is not a single true logic that is universally agreed.

A more serious problem with this version of the problem view is that it does not say much about inductive problems. Once the deductively valid arguments are defined, what remains are the deductively invalid ones. Presumably some of these are stronger than others, in terms of induction. For example, compare argument (1) above to argument (5) below.

Dogs have hearts (5)

All living things have hearts

It should be clear that neither (1) nor (5) is deductively valid, yet somehow (1) seems more plausible in terms of being a good inductive argument. Whatever rules of logic are used to define deductive arguments may not be too useful in determining that (1) is stronger than (5).

LEVELS OF CERTAINTY. Another approach to the problem view is to describe arguments in terms of the certainty of their conclusions (Skyrms, 2000). Consider argument (6).

Dogs have hearts (6)

Dogs have hearts

In this case, it seems absolutely certain that if the premise is taken to be true, then the conclusion must necessarily follow. This must be a perfectly valid argument. On the other hand, an argument such as (2) above might seem to have a very certain conclusion, perhaps 99.5% certain. This level of certainty could still be well over the threshold that is required for saying that an argument is deductively valid. Let's say, hypothetically, that arguments with conclusions below the 99% level of certainty will be called deductively invalid. Even among these arguments, this version of the problem view allows a great deal of differentiation. For example, argument (1) might be associated with 80% certainty and argument (5) might be associated with 10% certainty. Hence (1) would be considered a much stronger inductive argument in comparison to (5).

Perhaps the greatest appeal of this version of the problem view is that it allows for deduction and induction to be placed on a common scale of argument strength. In principle, any argument would have a place on this scale, and whether it is deductively valid, inductively strong, or inductively weak would be determined by the value on the scale. The most obvious problem, though, is that there is still a need for assessing the place of each argument on the scale. One nice idea might be an inductive logic, that is, some set of rules or operations that for a set of premises can assign a certainty value for a conclusion.

A subtler problem is that "certainty" itself would need to be defined better. For example, in argument (1), either the conclusion that all mammals have hearts is true or it is not, so the conversion from probability to certainty may not be obvious. For example, it would seem a little funny to assign a certainty level from 0% to 100% to a statement that is either true or false. (Perhaps certainty could be related to the proportion of mammals with hearts, rather than to whether it is true that all mammals have hearts.) Another issue to clarify is the distinction between argument strength and certainty of the conclusion. Argument (1) may seem strong simply because people believe the conclusion that all mammals have hearts. Now compare that argument to argument (7), below.

Lemons have seeds (7)

All mammals have hearts

Here is a situation where the two arguments have the same conclusion, which is equally certain in each case, but (1) seems much stronger than (7). It could be valuable to consider other ways of representing argument strength here, such as the conditional probability of the conclusion given the premise, or the difference between the unconditional probability of the conclusion and the conditional probability of the conclusion, given the premise.

MATTERS OF CONVENTION. A final perspective on the problem view is simply to be descriptive, that is, to enumerate what kinds of arguments are studied by researchers under the topics of induction and deduction. Induction is potentially a very broad topic and a variety of cognitive activities have been referred to as induction, including categorization, reasoning by analogy, and probability judgment. However, many of the chapters in this book focus on a more particular kind of induction, namely, category-based induction, involving arguments about categories and their properties. (Most of the examples in this chapter represent typical examples of category-based induction.) Research on adults' reasoning usually involves presenting arguments like these in written form; however, for children it is possible to present similar information with pictures. Studies of induction typically ask people to make judgments of argument strength, such as to judge which of two arguments is stronger, or with a single argument to make a continuous judgment of strength or probability.

In comparison to induction, research in deduction has used a narrower range of problems. One typical area of research within deduction is conditional reasoning – arguments involving ifs and thens, examining reasoning involving classic rules such as modus ponens and modus tollens. Another area of research within deduction is syllogistic reasoning – reasoning with arguments with statements like "All artists are beekeepers." Indeed, for syllogisms involving two premises, there are only sixty-four classical forms of syllogism. Research on deduction tends to ask people to assess logical validity of conclusions (a yes or no question) rather than make continuous judgments. Overall, the conventional approach is like other approaches to the problem view in that there is a relatively narrow range of arguments corresponding to deduction and a wider, somewhat ill-defined, range corresponding to induction. Yet even within the area of deduction research, there are lively debates about what exactly is a problem of deduction. For example, Wason's selection task, involving selecting cards to test a rule such as "If a card has a vowel on one side then it has an even number on the other side," has been variously argued to be a problem of deduction or induction (e.g., Feeney & Handley, 2000; Oaksford & Chater, 1994; Poletiek, 2001).

EVALUATION OF THE PROBLEM VIEW. Perhaps the most appealing aspect of the problem view is that it offers the possibility of defining induction and deduction in an objective way, in terms of the problem being solved or the question being asked. (The problem view is more impressive in terms of defining deduction in comparison to defining induction, though.) From the point of view of psychologists, this strength would also be the greatest weakness, namely, that the problem view does not itself refer to psychological processes. Just because one problem is defined as an induction problem and another is defined as a deduction problem does not guarantee that people will engage in inductive reasoning processes for one task and deductive reasoning processes for the other task. The same processes could be used for both, or the delimitation between types of psychological processes might not correspond at all to the agreed definition of problems, or any problem might engage a mixture of processes. In the terminology of memory research, there are no process-pure tasks. Of course, for computer scientists or logicians, reference to psychological processes may not be a priority. Still, it does seem desirable to consider the alternative of treating induction and deduction as possible kinds of psychological process. Hence, this chapter will next turn to the process view.

The Process View

According to the process view, comparing induction and deduction is a matter of specifying the underlying psychological processes. According to one-process accounts, the same kind of processing underlies both induction and deduction. Another way to describe this idea is that there is essentially one kind of reasoning, which may be applied to a variety of problems that could be considered either inductive or deductive in nature (Harman, 1999). In contrast, according to two-process accounts, there are two distinct kinds of reasoning. It is possible that these two kinds of reasoning directly correspond to induction and deduction. Alternately, the two kinds of reasoning might correspond to some other distinction, such as intuitive reasoning versus deliberative reasoning, that could be related to the distinction between induction and deduction. It should be acknowledged at the start that one-process and two-process accounts are somewhat poorly named. That is, at some level, reasoning surely involves many different psychological processes. The question, though, is whether the same processing account is applied to both induction and deduction, or whether two different processing accounts are applied. Some examples of one-process and two-process accounts will now be described, followed by the presentation of some experimental evidence aimed at assessing these accounts.

ONE-PROCESS ACCOUNTS. One of the most widely known theories of reasoning is mental model theory, which proposes that people solve reasoning problems extensionally by constructing models of possible states of the world and performing operations and manipulation on them (Johnson-Laird, 1983). Mental model theory is usually thought of as an account of deduction, and indeed it has been extensively applied to conditional-reasoning and syllogistic-reasoning problems. However, it has also been argued that mental model theory can be applied to problems of induction, namely, probabilistic reasoning tasks (Johnson-Laird, 1994; Johnson-Laird, Legrenzi, Girotto, Legrenzi, & Caverni, 1999). Hence, mental model theory is a one-process account, in the sense that it is aimed at giving a singular account for problems both of induction and deduction.

A newer alternative to mental model theory is the probabilistic account, which aims to account for a variety of reasoning phenomena, particularly traditional deduction problems in terms of probabilistic formulas, such as from Bayesian statistics (Chater & Oaksford, 2000; Oaksford & Chater, 1994). Essentially, the probabilistic account is saying that people solve deduction problems by means of induction processes. This account does not propose different kinds of processing for performing deduction, and hence the probabilistic account is also a one-process account.

The previous accounts are aimed mainly at problems of deduction. In contrast, other reasoning accounts have focused on problems of induction, such as category-based induction (Heit, 1998; Osherson, Smith, Wilkie, Lopez, & Shafir, 1990; Sloman, 1993). These accounts are aimed at predicting the judged strength of various inductive arguments, for example, that (1) above seems stronger or more plausible than (5). Typically, these accounts of induction are based on some measure of similarity or overlap between premise and conclusion categories, in terms of existing knowledge. In this example, there is more known overlap between dogs and mammals than between dogs and living things; hence the argument relating dogs and mammals seems stronger than the argument relating dogs and living things. Now refer back to argument (6). Here, there is perfect overlap between the premise category and the conclusion category – in this case the categories are both *dog*. Hence, there is perfect overlap between premise and conclusion categories, and these accounts of induction should predict that (6) is perfectly strong. In other words, accounts of induction can treat some deductively valid arguments as a special case rather than as being wholly different than inductively weak or strong arguments. The same processing mechanisms – for example, for assessing overlap – would be applied to problems of induction and deduction. In this way, these accounts of induction are one-process accounts. However, it should be made clear that these accounts of induction do not give complete accounts of deductive phenomena. For example, many deductively valid arguments in conditional and syllogistic reasoning could not be assessed simply in terms of feature overlap between premise and conclusion categories.

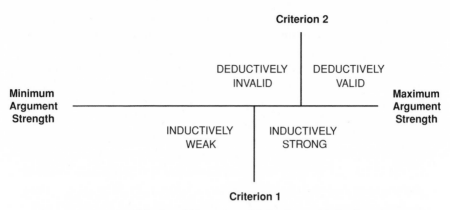

FIGURE 1.1. Criterion-shift account of deduction and induction.

In addition to these one-process accounts that specialize mainly in either deduction or induction problems, there is an alternative that does not give a detailed account of either deduction or induction but does offer a balanced view of how deduction and induction are related to each other. The criterion-shift account (described by Rips, 2001) is closely related to the levels-of-certainty version of the problem view and is illustrated in Figure 1.1. Under this account, assessing the strength of an argument involves finding its place on a one-dimensional scale ranging from minimum argument strength (the most unconvincing argument possible) to maximum strength (an utterly and completely compelling argument). To assess whether an argument should be considered inductively strong, its strength is compared to a criterion, such as criterion 1 in the figure. To assess whether an argument is deductively valid, the criterion is shifted to the right, to criterion 2. By this criterion, an argument would have to be judged extremely strong before it could be called deductively valid. The same reasoning mechanisms would be used for different argument types. The only difference between performing induction or deduction would be represented as a shift of the criterion.

TWO-PROCESS ACCOUNTS. In contrast to one-process accounts, other researchers have emphasized a distinction between two kinds of reasoning (e.g., Evans & Over, 1996; Sloman, 1996; Stanovich, 1999). In these two-process accounts there is one system that is relatively fast but heavily influenced by context and associations, and another system that is more deliberative and analytic or rule based. These two systems do not necessarily correspond directly to induction and deduction. That is, the traditional distinction between these two forms of reasoning may not be the best way to divide things in psychological terms. Still, it is plausible that induction would depend more on the first system, whereas deduction would depend more on the second system. These two-process accounts have been used to explain a variety of findings in reasoning, concerning individual differences, developmental patterns, and relations between reasoning and processing time. For example, in Stanovich's work there is a rich account of how reasoning in the more deliberative system is correlated with IQ, accounting for patterns of individual differences in a variety of problems that would rely more on one system or the other.

EVALUATING ONE-PROCESS AND TWO-PROCESS ACCOUNTS. How would it be possible to decide in favor of either one-process or two-process accounts? There is some neuropsychological evidence, based on brain imaging, for two anatomically separate systems of reasoning (Goel, Gold, Kapur, & Houle, 1997; Osherson et al., 1998). In the studies, subjects were given a set of arguments to evaluate. Half the subjects were asked to judge deductive validity and the other half were asked to judge inductive plausibility. Within each study, there were distinct brain areas implicated for deduction versus induction. What is particularly relevant for present purposes is that the problems were the same for the two conditions, but subjects were asked to perform either deduction or induction. Hence, this is a case of unconfounding the process view from the problem view – presumably all that varied between conditions was processes, unlike the situation in most previous studies of deduction, induction, or both, which used very different problems for one task or the other.

One does not require expensive brain imaging equipment to compare deduction versus induction instructions for a common set of problems. Rips (2001) used the same logic in a much cheaper pen-and-paper study, in which subjects were instructed to judge either deductive correctness or inductive strength for two types of arguments. One type of argument was deductively correct but causally inconsistent, such as "Jill rolls in the mud and Jill gets clean, therefore Jill rolls in the mud," and the other type was deductively incorrect but causally consistent, such as "Jill rolls in the mud, therefore Jill rolls in the mud and Jill gets dirty." In terms of the criterion-shift version of the one-process account, if one type of argument is stronger than another for deduction, then the same type of argument should be stronger for induction. In Figure 1.1, let the dots on the scale represent different types of argument. If one type is stronger, that is, further to the right end of the scale, then it should be stronger regardless of whether the induction or deduction criterion is used. Yet the results were that subjects in the deduction condition gave more positive judgments to the correct but inconsistent arguments, whereas subjects in the induction condition gave more positive judgments to the incorrect but consistent arguments. Rips concluded that these results contradicted the criterion-shift account, which predicted a monotonic ordering of arguments in the two conditions. (See Heit & Rotello, 2005, for further examinations of this kind, leading to the same conclusion.)

In sum, there is some evidence already that giving people deduction versus induction instructions leads to qualitatively different results. It would seem difficult to explain these results by assuming that deduction and induction processes are essentially the same, except that deduction involves a stricter criterion for giving a positive response. Yet at the same time, it seems too early to abandon the one-process accounts, which do provide detailed and accurate predictions about a range of phenomena, usually either concerning deductive or inductive problems. In contrast, the two-process view does not seem to be as well developed in terms of providing detailed process accounts and predictions. More experimentation, directly aimed at comparing the one- and two-process views and at further developing the two-process view, is clearly needed.

At a more general level, the process view itself seems to be a rich and worthwhile approach to studying induction. Certainly for psychologists, the problem view does not seem viable. It is a mistake to assume that people are performing deduction processes on designated deduction problems and induction processes on designated induction problems. Likewise, even for psychologists who are developing process level accounts of reasoning, it is important to keep in mind the wide range of possible reasoning problems. Assuming there is at least considerable overlap between deduction and in-duction processes, an ideal theory of reasoning would not be limited to either traditional problems of deduction or induction but would encompass both types of problem.

APPROACHES TO STUDYING INDUCTION: THE CASE OF THE DIVERSITY PRINCIPLE

Now that the position of induction with respect to deduction has been ex-plored, the next step will be to introduce the study of induction in more depth. Of course, this whole book is devoted to presenting research on in-duction, so the following material is intended to serve as a microcosm of the book rather than a complete review of induction research. The focus of the remainder of this chapter will be the diversity principle, namely, the idea that more diverse evidence seems to be stronger evidence than less diverse evidence. This principle seems to be ubiquitous in various forms of reasoning. For example, in social reasoning, seeing a person act in an extroverted way, in a variety of contexts, suggests that the person is truly extroverted by nature. In comparison, seeing a person repeatedly act in an extroverted way, but only in one context, does not give as good support for inferences that the person is truly extroverted. In legal reasoning, having two independent witnesses to a crime seems to be stronger evidence than two witnesses who may share a similar perspective, such as two members of the same family. Note that none of this represents anything like a deductively valid inference; however, there is still a sense of stronger evidence coming from more diverse observations.

The diversity principle has been an object of interest in terms of various approaches to induction, including the historical approach, the philosophical approach, the experimental approach, the developmental approach, and the model-based approach. These approaches will be reviewed in relation to how they have addressed the diversity principle.

The Historical Approach

The diversity principle has been historically important in science. Scientists have tended to favor testing a theory with a diverse set of experiments rather than repeatedly conducting the same experiment or close replications. Imagine two scientists who are testing their respective theories. One scientist essentially conducts the same experiment ten times, whereas the other conducts a variety of experiments assessing different aspects of the theory. Which theory will seem to have stronger support?

An early example of the diversity principle in action was in Bacon's *Novum Organum* (1620/1898), which cautioned scientists of the day against inferences drawn from narrow samples. Bacon illustrated this point with the concept of heat, listing twenty-eight different kinds of heat and hot things that would need to be observed in a study of heat. For example, Bacon listed the rays of the sun, fiery meteors, natural warm baths, hot vapor in furnaces, sparks, stacks of hay, and the insides of animals.

In a somewhat more modern example, Salmon (1984) described how early in the twentieth century, chemists and physicists had developed a wide variety of experimental methods for deriving Avogadro's number (6.02×10^{23}), the number of particles in a mole of any substance. These methods included Brownian movement, alpha-particle decay, X-ray diffraction, black-body radiation, and electrochemistry. Together, these techniques led to strong support for the existence of atoms and molecules because the existence of these particles was the basis of a unified explanation for a set of highly diverse results. Salmon argued that any one of these techniques taken alone, no matter how carefully applied, would not have been sufficient to convince scientists of that period to accept the atomic theory over its principal rival, known as energeticism, which conceived of matter as being continuous rather than being composed of particles.

More generally, it should be possible to study inductive reasoning by studying historical examples of reasoning, whether by scientists or others. One advantage of studying scientific reasoning is that the evidence and theories are usually explicit, in comparison to just studying everyday examples of reasoning. (See the previous book on induction, by Holland, Holyoak, Nisbett, and Thagard, 1986, as well as a more recent collection by Gorman, Tweney, Gooding, and Kincannon, 2005, for further examples.) There is an interesting parallel between the historical approach to the study of induction and the historical approach to the study of creativity (e.g., Weisberg, 1986). In each case, it seems that much can be learned about cognition by looking at paragon cases of thinking and reasoning, even outside the bounds of tightly controlled psychological studies.

The Philosophical/Normative Approach

This historical approach is complemented by attempts of philosophers and statisticians to argue that certain patterns of induction are normative or correct. The philosophical approach follows in the footsteps of Hume's (1777) problem of induction, namely, the problem of whether an inductive inference can ever be justified or considered valid. Without solving Hume's problem in absolute terms, it still might be possible to argue that performing induction in one way is better than another. As such, there have been various attempts to argue for or even prove the greater strength of diverse evidence in comparison to less diverse evidence.

For example, Nagel (1939) argued that a scientific theory should be derived from diverse observations to obtain more reliable estimates. He gave the example of inspecting the quality of coffee beans delivered on a ship. It would be better to inspect small samples of beans from various parts of the ship than to inspect a large number of beans from just one location. Carnap (1950) linked the collection of diverse evidence to the principle that scientific theories should make novel predictions rather than merely redescribe old data. Similarly, Hempel (1966) related the collection of diverse evidence to a falsifying research strategy, namely, it is better to test theories with a wide variety of challenging experiments.

These intuitive arguments did not lead directly to more formal proofs of the diversity principle. For example, Carnap (1950) promised a proof of the diversity principle in a future edition of his book that never did appear. More recently, however, there have been several attempts to formalize the advantage for following the diversity principle. As reviewed by Wayne (1995), there have been two approaches. The first approach compares correlated sources of evidence to independent sources of evidence, in statistical terms. For formal treatments of this correlation approach, linking similarity to probability theory, see Earman (1992) and Howson and Urbach (1993). The second approach is the eliminative approach. The idea behind the eliminative approach is that diverse data sets will be particularly useful for eliminating plausible but incorrect hypotheses, allowing stronger inferences to be drawn based on the remaining, contending hypotheses. In contrast, non-diverse data sets will likely be consistent with too many hypotheses to allow any strong inferences. For a formal treatment of this approach, including a geometric proof, see Horwich (1982), and see Heit (1998) and Tenenbaum and Griffiths (2001) for some psychological applications.

Moreover, there have been arguments that following the diversity principle is not normative. For example, using Earman's (1992) derivations of the diversity principle, Wayne (1995) showed that there can be exceptions, namely, that non-diverse observations can lead to strong inferences if this evidence is nonetheless very surprising. Wayne pointed to the case of the near-simultaneous discovery in 1974 of a previously unknown subatomic particle in two laboratories being a case of non-diverse evidence that still had strong implications for revision of theories in physics. Lo, Sides, Rozelle, and Osherson (2002) raised a related criticism of the normative status of the diversity principle. They too argued that what is crucial is not diversity of observations but rather surprisingness of observations. Lo et al. also suggested a set of exceptions, such as the following:

Squirrels can scratch through Bortex fabric in less than 10 seconds. (8)
Bears can scratch through Bortex fabric in less than 10 seconds.

All forest mammals can scratch through Bortex fabric in less than 10 seconds.

Squirrels can scratch through Bortex fabric in less than 10 seconds. (9)
Mice can scratch through Bortex fabric in less than 10 seconds.

All forest mammals can scratch through Bortex fabric in less than 10 seconds.

It seems intuitive that squirrels and bears are a more diverse pair than squirrels and mice. Yet Lo et al. argued that (9) is stronger than (8), because the evidence about squirrels and mice is more surprising than the evidence about squirrels and bears. That is, the knowledge that small animals are less capable of feats of strength than are large animals makes the evidence about squirrels and mice more surprising than evidence about squirrels and bears.

Heit, Hahn, and Feeney (2005) argued that these exceptions to the diversity principle, suggested by Wayne (1995) and Lo et al. (2002), are indeed exceptions, but they do not undermine the normative status of the diversity principle itself. In the example of the discovery of a new subatomic particle in 1974, physicists were influenced not only by diversity but also by many other sources of knowledge in particle physics. In the example of scratching through Bortex fabric, people would be influenced not only by diversity but also by other knowledge about animals and their strength. In other words, these exceptions as stated do not contain all the premises upon which the arguments are based. Reasoning about these arguments is also influenced by other hidden premises or background knowledge, so that diversity is not being assessed in isolation. Therefore, these counterexamples do not invalidate the diversity principle, because they are not pure tests of diversity. Rather, they show that people will use other knowledge when possible. Indeed, philosophers of science have not claimed that the diversity principle is the sole principle for assessing evidence. For example, Popper (1963, p. 232) listed diversity of supporting evidence as one of six criteria for assessing a scientific theory.

In more general terms, it should be possible to consider a variety of patterns in inductive reasoning in the light of the normative question, namely, what is good reasoning. For example, one of the most pervasive findings in psychological research on induction is the similarity effect, namely, that arguments such as (3) above concerning dogs and wolves are considered stronger than arguments such as (10).

Dogs have hearts. (10)

Bees have hearts.

Argument (10) seems much weaker, and this seems to be a consequence of the low similarity between dogs and bees. However, providing a proof of why it is normative to reason on the basis of similarity has been an elusive task for philosophers and psychologists (Goodman, 1972, but see Shepard, 1987).

The Experimental Approach

In addition to the normative perspective on the diversity principle, there has been a sustained effort by psychologists to document how well the diversity principle serves as a descriptive account of how people carry out informal, inductive reasoning. Osherson et al. (1990) documented diversity effects in adults by using written arguments like the following:

Hippos require Vitamin K for the liver to function. (11)
Rhinos require Vitamin K for the liver to function.

All mammals require Vitamin K for the liver to function.

Hippos require Vitamin K for the liver to function. (12)
Hamsters require Vitamin K for the liver to function.

All mammals require Vitamin K for the liver to function.

The subjects judged arguments like (12) to be stronger than arguments like (11), in response to the greater diversity of hippos and hamsters compared to hippos and rhinos. Indeed, there is a great deal of evidence that adults, mainly Western university students, follow the diversity principle when evaluating written arguments (see Heit, 2000, for a review).

However, when looking to other subject populations, and to evidence collected at a greater distance from the psychology lab, there seem to be exceptions to the diversity principle as a descriptive account. In their study of Itzaj-Mayan adults from the rainforests of Guatemala, Lopez, Atran, Coley, Medin, and Smith (1997) did not find evidence for diversity-based reasoning, using arguments with various living things and questions about disease transmission. Indeed, sometimes the Itzaj reliably chose arguments with non-diverse premise categories over arguments with diverse categories. It appears that they were using other knowledge about disease transmission that conflicted with diversity-based reasoning. For example, given a non-diverse argument that two similar kinds of tall palm trees get some disease, one person claimed it would be easy for shorter trees, located below, to get the disease as well. Giving further support to this idea that other strategies and knowledge can overrule diversity, Proffitt, Coley, and Medin (2000) reported that American adults who are tree experts (such as landscapers) did not show strong diversity effects when reasoning about trees and their diseases. The tree experts seemed to be relying on the knowledge that tree diseases tend to spread readily within tree families such as elms and maples.

Medin, Coley, Storms, and Hayes (2003) reported further exceptions to the diversity principle. One exception, referred to as non-diversity by property reinforcement, potentially makes a direct challenge to the diversity principle that is not as easily explained in terms of the use of other knowledge. The idea behind non-diversity by property reinforcement is that two diverse categories may nonetheless have some characteristic in common and tend to generalize only to other categories with this same characteristic. In the non-diversity by property reinforcement effect, "if an otherwise diverse set of premises shares a salient property not shared by the conclusion category, the reinforcement of the property might weaken that argument relative to a related argument with less diverse premises" (p. 523). This phenomenon is illustrated by the following example:

Polar bears have property X. (13)
Antelopes have property X.

All animals have property X.

Polar bears have property X. (14)
Penguins have property X.

All animals have property X.

When given a forced choice between polar bears and antelopes versus polar bears and penguins, subjects judged the two animals from the same biological class, polar bears and antelopes, to be more similar than the two animals from different biological classes, polar bears and penguins. However, when asked to assess the inductive strength of each argument, argument (14) was judged to be less convincing than argument (13). That is, argument (13) had less diverse evidence, yet it was the stronger argument. Intuitively, although polar bears and penguins are from different biological classes, they still share the characteristic of living in a cold climate. It might seem than property X does not apply to all animals but only to animals living in cold climates.

Heit and Feeney (2005) investigated the non-diversity by property reinforcement effect further and came to a somewhat different conclusion. Essentially, their subjects judged polar bears and penguins to be more similar than polar bears and antelopes. Hence, when argument (13) was judged to be stronger than argument (14), Heit and Feeney's subjects were showing a diversity effect rather than a non-diversity effect. Heit and Feeney concluded that the diversity effect was indeed robust, and their results suggest that exceptions may be hard to show consistently.

The Developmental Approach

The first experiment on diversity-based reasoning in induction was actually a developmental one by Carey (1985), comparing six-year-olds and adults. Carey looked at patterns of inductive projection given the premises that two diverse animals, dogs and bees, have some biological property. The purpose of this study was to see whether subjects reason that "if two such disparate animals as dogs and bees" have this property then "all complex animals must" (p. 141). Indeed, adults made broad inferences to all animals, extending the property not only to things that were close to the premises (other mammals and insects) but also to other members of the *animal* category (such as birds and worms). In contrast, the children seemed to treat each premise separately; they drew inferences to close matches such as other mammals and insects, but they did not use the diversity information to draw a more general conclusion about animals. Therefore in this first attempt there was evidence for effects of diversity in adults but not children. In a follow-up study, Carey looked at diversity effects based on the concept *living thing* rather than *animal*. The key comparison was that children were taught a biological fact either about dogs and bees or about dogs and flowers, with the latter being even more diverse than the former. Given a fact about dogs and flowers, children did tend to generalize fairly broadly, suggesting that children may have some sensitivity to diversity of premise categories. However, if anything they tended to overgeneralize, extending the property not only to other living things but often to inanimate objects as well. Hence, there was suggestive evidence for the impact of diversity of premise categories in this study, although children did not show the same pattern as adults.

Continuing along this line of research that looks for diversity effects in children, Lopez et al. (1992) found limited evidence for nine-year-olds and no evidence for five-year-olds. For the five-year-olds, choices in a picture-based task did not show any sensitivity to diversity of premise categories, even when the diversity was explicitly mentioned by the experimenter. However, nine-year-olds did show sensitivity to diversity of premises, but only for arguments with a general conclusion category such as *animal* rather than a specific conclusion category such as *kangaroo*. Gutheil and Gelman (1997) attempted to find evidence of diversity-based reasoning for specific conclusions in nine-year-olds, using category members at lower taxonomic levels which would presumably enhance reasoning. However, like Lopez et al. (1992), Gutheil and Gelman did not find diversity effects in nine-year-olds, although in a control condition with adults, there was robust evidence for diversity effects.

More recently, however, Heit and Hahn (2001) reported diversity effects in children younger than nine years in experiments that used pictures of people and everyday objects as stimuli rather than animals with hidden properties. For example, children were shown a diverse set of dolls (a china doll, a stuffed doll, and a Cabbage Patch doll), all being played with by a girl named Jane. Also children were shown a non-diverse set, three pictures of Barbie dolls, being played with by Danielle. The critical test item was another kind of doll, a baby doll, and the question was who would like to play with this doll. In another stimulus condition, there was a diverse set of hats worn by one person, and a non-diverse set worn by another person, and again, the critical question was whether another hat would belong to the person with diverse hats or the person with non-diverse hats. For 74% of these critical test items, children age five to eight years made the diverse choice rather than the non-diverse choice. It seems from the Heit and Hahn experiments that children can follow the diversity principle at some level. However, it will take further work to establish the critical differences that led the past studies to not find diversity effects in children. (See Lo et al., 2002, for additional results, and Gelman, 2003, for further discussion.)

The Model-Based Approach

The psychological study of inductive reasoning has benefited from the development of computational models. Perhaps what is most impressive about these models is that they systematize what is inherently unsystematic, namely, probabilistic inference. Furthermore, these models capture important empirical phenomena in inductive reasoning, such as the diversity effect. In general, modeling work and experimental work on induction have been closely linked. In the following section, there are brief, conceptual descriptions of some of the earlier models and how they address the diversity effect. Several chapters in this book present newer modeling work in more detail (see Heit & Hayes, 2005, for another review of models of induction).

OSHERSON ET AL. (1990). The most influential model of category-based induction was developed by Osherson et al. (1990). This model has two main components. The first component assesses the similarity between the premise category or categories and the conclusion category. For example, argument (3) seems fairly strong because of the high level of similarity between dogs and wolves. In comparison, argument (15) below seems weaker, due to the lower similarity between dogs and parrots.

Dogs have hearts. (15)

Parrots have hearts.

The second component of the model measures how well the premise categories cover the superordinate category that includes all the categories mentioned in an argument. For example, in arguments (11) and (12), the relevant superordinate category is *mammal*. Intuitively, hippos and rhinos are somewhat similar mammals that do not span the whole superordinate category. In comparison, hippos and hamsters cover a broader range of mammals. The Osherson et al. model formalizes the calculation of coverage based on the structure of the *mammal* category. In effect, different instantiations of *mammal* are considered, from mice to cows to elephants, with the model looking for matches between the premise categories and these instantiations. Hippos and rhinos are a fairly good match to elephants and other large mammals, but they will be a poor match to smaller mammals. In comparison, the diverse set, hippos and hamsters, gives good matches to both large mammals such as elephants and small mammals such as mice. The diverse set is considered to have greater coverage because it yields a wider range of good matches with members of the superordinate category. More generally speaking, the similarity and coverage components of this model can be used to explain not only the diversity effect but also a dozen other phenomena in induction.

SLOMAN (1993). This model was implemented as a connectionist network, and perhaps the most important difference from the Osherson et al. (1990) model is that it does not have a separate component for assessing coverage of a superordinate category. Indeed, the Sloman model is valuable because it shows how much can be accomplished without this second mechanism, indeed addressing many of the same phenomena as the Osherson et al. model but without coverage. In brief, the way this model works is that premises of an argument are encoded by training the connectionist network to learn associations between input nodes representing the features of premise categories and an output node for the property to be considered. Then the model is tested by presenting the features of the conclusion category and measuring the activation of the same output node. For example, after the network has been trained that dogs have hearts, it will give a strong response if the features of *dog* are presented again as input. In addition, the network would give a strong output signal to wolves, indicating that wolves have hearts, because the featural representations of dogs and wolves would have a lot of overlap. The model accounts for diversity effects because training on a diverse set of categories will tend to strengthen a greater number of connections than training on a narrow range of categories. For example, training the network that both hippos and hamsters have a certain property would activate a broad range of features that apply to various mammals, leading to a strong conclusion that all mammals have that property. That is, hippos and hamsters would activate different features and different connections. In contrast, training the network that hippos and rhinos have a property would activate only a narrow range of features and connections. Although this model does have a notion of breadth of features, there is no distinct component for assessing coverage of a super-ordinate category, and indeed the model does not even rely on knowledge about superordinate categories. Nonetheless, the Sloman model can account for not only diversity effects but a variety of other phenomena.

HEIT (1998). The final model to be discussed is the Bayesian model by Heit (1998). This model is linked to eliminative accounts of hypothesis testing and as such is a normative model of how to reason with a hypothesis space. In addition, this account is fairly successful as a descriptive account in the sense that it predicts most of the same psychological phenomena as the Osherson et al. (1990) and Sloman (1993) models. According to the Bayesian model, evaluating an inductive argument is conceived of as learning about a property, in particular learning for which categories the property is true or false. For example, upon learning that dogs have some novel property X, the goal would be to infer which other animals have property X and which do not. For example, do wolves have the property and do parrots have the property? The key assumption is that for a novel property such as in this example, people would rely on prior knowledge about familiar properties to derive a set of hypotheses about what the novel property may be like. People already know a relatively large number of properties that are true of both dogs and wolves, so if property X applies to dogs, then it probably applies to wolves too. On the other hand, people know a relatively small number of properties that are true of both dogs and parrots. Hence property X is relatively unlikely to extend to parrots.

How does the Bayesian model explain diversity effects? In brief, diverse categories bring to mind a very different set of hypotheses than non-diverse categories. If hippos and hamsters have some novel property X in common, one considers familiar properties that are shared by all mammals, such as warm-bloodedness. Hence, property X too seems to extend broadly to all mammals, assuming that it is distributed in a similar way as other properties that are brought to mind. In contrast, if hippos and rhinos have property X in common, it is easier to think of familiar properties that are shared by hippos and rhinos but not most other mammals, such as being large and having a tough skin. Property X, too, may be distributed in the same way, namely, only to large, thick-skinned mammals, and seems less likely to extend to all mammals.

In sum, this section has illustrated different modeling approaches to in-duction, which have subsequently developed in later work. Interestingly, these three models address a similar set of phenomena with different theoretical frameworks, namely, in terms of hierarchically structured categories (Osherson et al., 1990), features in a connectionist network (Sloman, 1993), and beliefs within a hypothesis space (Heit, 1998). Not only is it possible to systematize what is unsystematic by nature, namely, probabilistic inference, but there is more than one way of doing so.

CONCLUSION

This chapter should at the very least illustrate the richness of research on induction. Research on this topic might seem to face a lot of challenges. After all, the degree of overlap with deduction has not yet been determined, and some accounts of reasoning simply define induction in terms of not being deduction. By their very nature, inductive inferences do not have a "right answer" in the same way as deductive inferences. Yet there are still regularities, such as the diversity principle, which can be studied from a variety of perspectives, including historical, philosophical, experimental, developmental, and computational. By no means is this regularity completely deterministic; indeed, there are well-documented exceptions to the diversity principle that are themselves of interest.

The material in this chapter should be seen as an invitation to consider different approaches to induction and different phenomena in induction, including those presented in the subsequent chapters of this book. All of the chapters refer to the experimental approach to at least some extent. The chapters by Hayes and by Medin and Waxman focus on the developmental approach. The chapters by Tenenbaum and Blok, Osherson, and Medin largely take the modeling approach. The chapters by Rips and Asmuth, and by Thagard, involve the historical approach, and the chapters by Oaksford and Hahn, and by Thagard, involve the philosophical approach. Finally, several of the chapters (by Rehder, Rips & Asmuth, Oaksford & Hahn, Thagard, and Feeney) directly address the question of what induction is.

References

Bacon, F. (1620–1898). *Novum organum.* London: George Bell and Sons.

Carey, S. (1985). *Conceptual change in childhood.* Cambridge, MA: Bradford Books.

Carnap, R. (1950). *Logical foundations of probability.* Chicago: University of Chicago Press.

Chater, N., & Oaksford, M. (2000). The rational analysis of mind and behavior. *Synthese, 122,* 93–131.

Earman, J. (1992). *Bayes or bust? A critical examination of Bayesian confirmation theory.* Cambridge, MA: MIT Press.

Evans, J. St. B. T., & Over, D. E. (1996). *Rationality and reasoning.* Hove, UK: Psychology Press.

Feeney, A., & Handley, S. J. (2000). The suppression of q-card selections: Evidence for deductive inference in Wason's selection task. *Quarterly Journal of Experimental Psychology, 53A,* 1224–1242.

Gelman, S. A. (2003). *The essential child: Origins of essentialism in everyday thought.* New York: Oxford University Press.

Goel, V., Gold, B., Kapur, S., & Houle, S. (1997). The seats of reason: A localization study of deductive and inductive reasoning using PET (O15) blood flow technique. *NeuroReport, 8,* 1305–1310.

Goodman, N. (1972). *Problems and projects.* Indianapolis: Bobbs-Merrill.

Gorman, M. E., Tweney, R. D., Gooding, D. C., & Kincannon, A. P. (Eds.), (2005). *Scientific and technological thinking.* Mahwah, NJ: Lawrence Erlbaum Associates.

Gutheil, G., & Gelman, S. A. (1997). Children's use of sample size and diversity information within basic-level categories. *Journal of Experimental Child Psychology, 64,* 159–174.

Harman, G. (1999). *Reasoning, meaning, and mind.* Oxford: Oxford University Press.

Heit, E. (1998). A Bayesian analysis of some forms of inductive reasoning. In M. Oaksford & N. Chater (Eds.), *Rational models of cognition,* 248–274. Oxford: Oxford University Press.

Heit, E. (2000). Properties of inductive reasoning. *Psychonomic Bulletin & Review, 7,* 569–592.

Heit, E., & Feeney, A. (2005). Relations between premise similarity and inductive strength. *Psychonomic Bulletin & Review, 12,* 340–344.

Heit, E., & Hahn, U. (2001). Diversity-based reasoning in children. *Cognitive Psychology, 43,* 243–273.

Heit, E., Hahn, U., & Feeney, A. (2005). Defending diversity. In W. Ahn, R. Goldstone, B. Love, A. Markman, & P. Wolff (Eds.), *Categorization inside and outside of the laboratory: Essays in honor of Douglas L. Medin,* 87–99. Washington, DC: American Psychological Association.

Heit, E., & Hayes, B. K. (2005). Relations among categorization, induction, recognition, and similarity. *Journal of Experimental Psychology: General, 134,* 596–605.

Heit, E., & Rotello, C. M. (2005). Are there two kinds of reasoning? In *Proceedings of the Twenty-Seventh Annual Conference of the Cognitive Science Society.* Hillsdale, NJ: Lawrence Erlbaum Associates.

Heit, E., & Rubinstein, J. (1994). Similarity and property effects in inductive reasoning. *Journal of Experimental Psychology: Learning, Memory, and Cognition, 20,* 411–422.

Hempel, C. G. (1966). *Philosophy of natural science.* Englewood Cliffs, NJ: Prentice Hall.

Holland, J. H., Holyoak, K. J., Nisbett, R. E., & Thagard, P. (1986). *Induction: Processes of inference, learning, and discovery.* Cambridge, MA: MIT Press.

Horwich, P. (1982). *Probability and evidence.* Cambridge, UK: Cambridge University Press.

Howson, C., & Urbach, P. (1993). *Scientific reasoning: The Bayesian approach.* Chicago: Open Court.

Hume, D. (1777). *An enquiry concerning human understanding.* Oxford: Clarendon Press.

Johnson-Laird, P. (1983). *Mental models.* Cambridge, MA: Harvard University Press.

Johnson-Laird, P. N. (1994). Mental models and probabilistic thinking. *Cognition, 50,* 189–209.

Johnson-Laird, P. N., Legrenzi, P., Girotto, V., Legrenzi, M. A., & Caverni, J. P. (1999). Naive probability: A mental model theory of extensional reasoning. *Psychological Review, 106,* 62–88.

Lo, Y., Sides, A., Rozelle, J., & Osherson, D. (2002). Evidential diversity and premise probability in young children's inductive judgment. *Cognitive Science, 16,* 181–206.

Lopez, A., Gelman, S. A., Gutheil, G., & Smith, E. E. (1992). The development of category-based induction. *Child Development, 63,* 1070–1090.

Lopez, A., Atran, S., Coley, J. D., Medin, D. L., & Smith, E. E. (1997). The tree of life: Universal and cultural features of folkbiological taxonomies and inductions. *Cognitive Psychology, 32,* 251–295.

Medin, D. L., Coley, J. D., Storms, G., & Hayes, B. K. (2003). A relevance theory of induction. *Psychonomic Bulletin & Review, 10,* 517–532.

Nagel, E. (1939). *Principles of the theory of probability.* Chicago: University of Chicago Press.

Oaksford, M., & Chater, N. (1994). A rational analysis of the selection task as optimal data selection. *Psychological Review, 101,* 608–631.

Osherson, D. N., Smith, E. E., Wilkie, O., Lopez, A., & Shafir, E. (1990). Category-based induction. *Psychological Review, 97,* 185–200.

Osherson, D. N., Perani, D., Cappa, S., Schnur, T., Grassi, F., & Fazio, F. (1998). Distinct brain loci in deductive versus probabilistic reasoning. *Neuropsychologia, 36,* 369–376.

Poletiek, F. (2001). *Hypothesis testing behaviour.* Hove, UK: Psychology Press.

Popper, K. R. (1963). *Conjectures and refutations: The growth of scientific knowledge.* London: Routledge.

Proffitt, J. B., Coley, J. D., & Medin, D. L. (2000). Expertise and category-based induction. *Journal of Experimental Psychology: Learning, Memory, and Cognition, 26,* 811–828.

Rips, L. J. (2001). Two kinds of reasoning. *Psychological Science, 12,* 129–134.

Salmon, W. C. (1984). *Scientific explanation and the causal structure of the world.* Princeton, NJ: Princeton University Press.

Shepard, R. N. (1987). Towards a universal law of generalization for psychological science. *Science, 237,* 1317–1323.

Skyrms, B. (2000). *Choice and chance: An introduction to inductive logic.* (Fourth edition). Belmont, CA: Wadsworth.

Sloman, S. A. (1993). Feature-based induction. *Cognitive Psychology, 25,* 231–280.

Sloman, S. A. (1996). The empirical case for two systems of reasoning. *Psychological Bulletin, 119,* 3–22.

Stanovich, K. E. (1999). *Who is rational? Studies of individual differences in reasoning.* Mahwah, NJ: Lawrence Erlbaum Associates.

Tenenbaum, J. B., & Griffiths, T. L. (2001). Generalization, similarity, and Bayesian inference. *Behavioral and Brain Sciences, 24,* 629–641.

Wayne, A. (1995). Bayesianism and diverse evidence. *Philosophy of Science, 62,* 111–121.

Weisberg, R. W. (1986). *Creativity: Genius and other myths.* New York: Freeman.

2

The Development of Inductive Reasoning

Brett K. Hayes

From one perspective virtually every cognitive act carried out by young children involves induction. Compared to older children and adults, young children have little background knowledge about the world and have only a shaky grasp of the rules that govern propositional reasoning. They are continually faced with the task of making inferences based on their past observations and experience. This is true whether the child is trying to determine which kinds of animals have red blood cells, whether a specific tool can be used to assemble a bike, or whether the new kid who has moved next door is likely to be friendly. This chapter focuses on a particularly important aspect of the development of inductive reasoning – the way that children use their understanding of categories and category structure to generalize attributes from familiar to novel instances.

Category-based induction typically involves three components. First, observing that an inductive base or "premise" has the property P (e.g., that a shark has fins); second, deciding that X and a target or "conclusion" item Y are related in some way (e.g., that a shark and a trout are both fish); and third, inferring whether Y shares property P.[1] Investigating children's inductive reasoning allows us to determine when this reasoning ability first emerges and to chart important age-related changes in induction. It is also a valuable tool for understanding the development of children's category representations. In fact, some important theories of conceptual development (e.g., Carey, 1985) have been based, for the most part, on the results of studies of age changes in children's inductive generalizations.

This chapter will review and discuss work on the development of category-based induction from infancy through early and later childhood. The first part

---

[1] Throughout this chapter the terms "base" and "premise," and "target" and "conclusions" are considered synonymous and will be used interchangeably.

of the chapter will consider just what kinds of information infants and children use to decide whether the properties of one category generalize to other categories. To preface the main conclusions it will be argued that, by five years of age, children seem aware of a number of different ways in which two or more categories can be related, and they can use these different kinds of relations as a basis for inductive inference. In addition to relatively obvious relations such as the perceptual similarity of the inductive base and target, young children use taxonomic, hierarchical, and causal principles to guide property inferences. They are also sensitive to the fact that inferences often depend on the kind of property being considered. More complex heuristics that require the integration of information across multiple instances or premises (e.g., the premise diversity principle described in Chapter 1) may emerge somewhat later in development. However, even here recent evidence suggests that school-age children are better at using these principles than was once thought.

The second part of the chapter will examine the implications of this developmental research for general theories of induction, highlighting the ways that the developmental data can be used to evaluate and constrain competing theories. The third and final part will consider the best way of explaining developmental change in induction. Again, to preface the main argument, the current evidence suggests that many of the fundamental processes involved in inductive reasoning are developmentally stable from the preschool years and that the most significant age-related changes in induction may be due to the growth of more sophisticated knowledge about objects, object properties, and category structures.

I. PRINCIPLES THAT GUIDE CHILDREN'S INDUCTIVE INFERENCES

Perceptual Similarity

Classic theories of cognitive development emphasized the role played by perceptual similarity in determining early categorization and induction (e.g., Bruner, Olver, & Greenfield, 1966; Inhelder & Piaget, 1958; Vygotsky, 1934/1986). Subsequent work has confirmed that the influence of perceptual similarity on property inferences emerges at an early point in development. Baldwin, Markman, and Melartin (1993), for example, allowed infants aged between nine and sixteen months to inspect an object (the inductive base) that had an unusual and unexpected property (e.g., it wailed when it was shaken or tilted). Infants were then shown other toys that varied in their perceptual similarity to the base. In the critical test condition these were modified so that they could not generate the unexpected sound. Nevertheless, even the youngest infants persistently tried to reproduce the unexpected property with the toys that resembled the base. They rarely generalized the property to objects with a different colour or surface pattern (also see Graham, Kilbreath, & Welder, 2004; Rakison & Hahn, 2004).

This influence of perceptual similarity on induction continues throughout infancy and childhood (Farrar, Raney, & Boyer, 1992). Indeed, even most major theories of adult induction (e.g., Osherson et al., 1990; Sloman, 1993) acknowledge that similarity, in terms of the overlap in structural features between an inductive base and target, plays a major role in determining the strength of inductive inferences.

A more contentious issue though is whether perceptual similarity is the *primary* principle that governs early induction. Many early developmental theories assumed that young children's reasoning was "perceptually bound" in that perceptual similarity overshadowed consideration of logical or taxonomic relations (Inhelder & Piaget, 1958; Springer, 2001). Much of the work reviewed in the following sections challenges this view.

Taxonomic Relations

One of the most consistent themes in this book is that people are sensitive to the fact that the members of closely related categories are likely to share novel, non-obvious properties. It is important therefore to establish just when and how children first make use of shared taxonomic relations as a basis for inductive inference. The most common approach to studying this issue has been to examine whether infants and children are more likely to generalize a novel property from an inductive base to target when these are given the same noun label.

STUDIES WITH INFANTS. Welder and Graham (2001) examined the effects of verbal labels and perceptual similarity on induction by sixteen- to twenty-one-month-old infants. Infants were shown a base object with a novel property (e.g., a cloth-covered toy that squeaked when squeezed). This was presented together with either a novel noun label (e.g., "Look at this *blint*") or without a label (e.g., "Look at this *one*"). Infants were then shown test objects that varied in their similarity to the shape of the base, with the label present or absent. When there was no label infants relied on shape similarity in generalizing the property. In the shared label conditions generalization of the novel property depended on *both* shared labels and shape. This same pattern of inference has been shown with thirteen-month-olds who are just beginning to acquire productive language (Graham et al., 2004).

Many have interpreted such findings as evidence that infants understand that noun labels supply information about category membership and that members of the same categories are likely to share non-obvious properties (e.g., Gelman, 2003; Graham et al., 2004). An alternative view is that infants have simply learned that objects with the same label are usually similar in many other ways (Jones & Smith, 1993; Quinn & Eimas, 2000). It may also be that category labels simply count as additional perceptual features, albeit highly salient ones, when children compare base and target instances (Sloutsky & Fisher, 2004). In the latter cases the argument is that the use of shared labels in induction does not necessarily imply an understanding of the categorical implications of the label. This issue will be examined in more depth after reviewing relevant work with older children.

STUDIES WITH PRESCHOOLERS AND OLDER CHILDREN. One of the first suggestions that children look beyond surface similarity when doing induction came from the work of Carey (1985). Children aged from four to ten years, and adults, were shown a picture of a base item such as a person or other animal and were told that it had an unobservable novel property (e.g., "a spleen inside it"). Carey then presented a range of other objects, including dogs, bees, and flowers, as well as inanimate kinds like rocks, and asked people to decide which ones shared the novel property. Although children's inferences were often influenced by the similarity between the base and target items, Carey also found some important exceptions. For example, young children were more likely to generalize a biological property of humans to "bugs" than from bees to bugs. Carey explained this finding by arguing that humans were regarded by young children as a kind of ideal or prototypical animal, so that their properties were highly likely to be shared by other animals (see Chapter 3 by Medin and Waxman for further discussion).

In a series of studies spanning two decades, Susan Gelman and her colleagues have tried to systematically separate out the effects of taxonomic and perceptual factors on young children's induction (see Gelman, 2003, for a review). Gelman and Markman (1986), for example, used a triad task in which four-year-olds were taught a novel property about a base picture (e.g., a tropical fish) with a familiar category label ("fish") and shown two target pictures. One of these was perceptually similar to the base but had a different label (e.g., dolphin). The other looked less like the base but had the same label (e.g., a picture of a shark labelled as a "fish"). Children were asked to choose which of the targets was more likely to have the novel property. The majority of four-year-olds chose the taxonomic rather than the perceptual match. Subsequent work has found the same pattern of inference in children as young as two years of age (Gelman & Coley, 1990). Preschoolers' preference for inferences based on category labels over perceptual appearances has been found with realistic photographs as well as line drawings of animals (Deák & Bauer, 1996; Florian, 1994), and extends to artifact (Gelman, 1988) and social categories (e.g., Diesendruck, 2003; Heyman & Gelman, 2000a, b).

As we saw earlier there are at least two ways to interpret such findings. First, labels can have an indirect effect on inductive inferences by serving as a cue that the base and target instances belong to the same category. Alternatively, common labels could have a direct effect by serving as identical auditory features making the premise and conclusion items more perceptually similar.

A series of control studies support the argument that young children use shared category membership rather than just the perceptual aspects of shared labels as the basis for their inferences. Preschool children reliably generalize novel properties from premise to conclusion items with perceptually dissimilar but synonymous labels (e.g., "bunny" and "rabbit") (Gelman & Markman, 1986). Critically, however, preschool children *do not* use shared labels as a basis for induction when these labels lack information about category membership. Gelman and Coley (1990), for example, found that the presence of a shared label referring to a transient state like "is sleepy" did not promote the generalization of biological properties. Similarly, young children do not use shared proper names like "Anna" as a basis for generalizing behavioural traits, presumably because they recognize that such names refer to individuals rather than members of a social category (Heyman & Gelman, 2000a). Young children do not generalize properties on the basis of shared labels when these conflict with existing category knowledge (e.g., when catlike animals are labelled as "dogs") (Jaswal, 2004), or when they cross superordinate category boundaries (e.g., when the same label is given to animals and artifacts) (Davidson & Gelman, 1990).

In some cases labels may not be necessary for preschool children to generalize properties along taxonomic lines. Deák and Bauer (1996) presented young children with realistic photographs of premise objects (e.g., a panther) and conclusion alternatives from the same basic-level categories (e.g., a Tabby house cat) or a different category (e.g., a black horse). The different-category photo was always more similar in appearance to the premise than the same-category item. Even when no labels were given, children were more likely to generalize novel properties based on shared category membership than on overall perceptual appearance. Children used the information contained in the photographs to infer that the panther and cat belonged to the same biological category, and they used this relationship rather than appearance as a basis for property induction.

A final line of evidence suggesting that young children use taxonomic relations in induction is their understanding that typical category members support stronger inferences than less typical instances. López, Gelman, Gutheil, and Smith (1992) showed that kindergarten children were more likely to generalize a biological property from "dogs" to "animals" than from "bats" to "animals" (also see Carey, 1985, Lo et al., 2002). López et al. presented the "animal" category only verbally, so it is hard to see how this result could be explained in terms of the perceptual similarity of base and target items.[2]

Taken together, this is strong evidence that linguistic or structural cues suggesting the shared category membership of base and target items strengthens children's inductive inferences. Common noun labels can serve as a powerful cue to promote inference by promoting a belief in shared category membership.

Given the strong evidence that preschool children use labels as markers of category membership during induction, is there evidence that infants use labels in the same way? The kinds of controlled comparisons reviewed above that reveal the contexts in which children do or do not use shared labels for induction have yet to be carried out with infants. At least two kinds of evidence, however, suggest that by two years of age children have some grasp of the categorical implications of shared labels. First, two-year-olds understand that when adults use novel noun labels they are usually referring to classes of objects and that labels serve a different linguistic function from other kinds of utterances such as adjectives or expressions of personal preference (e.g., Henderson & Graham, 2005; Waxman & Booth, 2001). Second, studies of name extension suggest that, by eighteen months of age, infants understand that labels convey information about the kind of thing an object is. Booth, Waxman, and Huang (2005), for example, presented eighteen- and twenty-four-month-olds with a novel object called a "dax" together with vignettes that implied that daxes were either animals (e.g., "has a mommy who loves it very much") or artifacts (e.g., "was bought at a store"). Infants exposed to different vignettes attended to different kinds of perceptual features when generalizing the label to other objects. In other words infants were interpreting the label as implying membership of a particular global category and generalized the label accordingly.[3]

---

[2]   It should be noted that López et al. (1992) offer an alternative explanation of typicality effects, arguing that they can arise through an assessment of the similarity of the features of premise and conclusion items, without the activation of categorical information.

[3]   A little caution is required in drawing implications about the development of property inference from studies using a name extension paradigm. Adults and children usually distinguish names from other object properties and may generalize each in different ways (Markman & Ross, 2003). Nevertheless, the cited studies establish that infants understand the categorical implications of shared labels.

Hierarchical Relations

Taxonomic knowledge also entails an understanding that objects are embedded in hierarchies based on class inclusion relations. Daffodils are understood to be a kind of flower which is, in turn, a living thing. Like older children and adults, preschool children are most likely to generalize a novel property from a category to other items at the same hierarchical level, and they show decreasing generalization to test items located at more abstract levels (Carey, 1985; Gelman & O'Reilly, 1988; Inagaki & Hatano, 1996).

An important finding in other conceptual tasks like categorization and naming is that certain hierarchical levels are psychologically basic or "privileged" (Rosch, Mervis, Gray, Johnson, & Boyes-Braem, 1976). For example, children usually acquire the names of objects at intermediate levels of a hierarchy (e.g., apple) before they learn the names for things located at a more subordinate (e.g., Delicious apple) or superordinate level (e.g., fruit). In the case of induction the privileged level can be defined as the highest level in a hierarchy where there is a strong belief that the properties of objects at that level can be generalized to an immediate superordinate.

Coley, Hayes, Lawson, and Moloney (2004) examined the location of the privileged level within a biological hierarchy in five-year-olds, eight-year-olds, and adults. All groups were given two kinds of conceptual tasks; feature listing and inductive inference. In the first task participants listed the features they thought were shared by the members of each of four hierarchical levels (e.g., animals, birds, sparrows, house sparrows). In the induction task participants were taught a novel property about an instance from a given hierarchical level and asked whether this generalized to categories at the immediate superordinate level (e.g., from house sparrows to sparrows, from sparrows to birds, from birds to animals). The key finding was that, for eight-year-olds and adults, the location of the privileged level often differed across the two tasks. In feature listing the highest level in the hierarchy where objects were believed to share many features was the *life-form* (e.g., bird, fish, tree). For adults and, in many cases, for eight-year-olds, the privileged level for induction was the more specific *folk-generic* level (e.g., sparrow, maple). Adults and eight-year-olds generalized novel properties from very specific biological kinds such as house sparrow and sugar maple to sparrows and maples, respectively, but they were less likely to generalize from sparrows to birds or maples to trees. Five-year-olds showed a different pattern with the life-form level privileged for both feature listing and induction in the majority of biological categories.

The task discrepancies in the location of the basic level show that by eight years of age children often rely on different sorts of information for feature listing and induction. Feature listing reflects knowledge about category members. Adults and children knew more about the kinds of features shared by the members of life-form categories than they did about more specific categories. But their inferences reflected an *expectation* that features would cluster at the folk-generic level. One source of such expectations is the nomenclature for members of subordinate categories. In English (and most other languages) levels below the folk-generic are marked as subtypes by the use of compound names (e.g., desert oak). Coley et al. (2004) show that by eight years of age children recognize the implications of such subordination for inductive inference. An understanding of linguistic hierarchies alone, however, is unlikely to explain the emergence of a privileged level for induction. In a related study with adults, Coley, Medin, and Atran (1997) found that the privileged level for induction remained at the folk-generic level even when category labels contained a reference to the life-form level (e.g., goldfish, catfish). Expectations about feature clusters at the folk-generic level therefore may also reflect a more abstract belief that category members at this level share some underlying biological property that gives rise to those features.

More research is needed to clarify the factors that lead certain hierarchical levels to be privileged in children's induction. Nevertheless, the findings of Coley et al. (2004) highlight the importance of children's beliefs about category hierarchies in induction and indicate that these beliefs involve more than just an appreciation of the common and distinctive features of instances at different hierarchical levels.

Relations Involving Multiple Premises: Diversity and Monotonicity

When drawing inductive inferences adults are able to integrate information across more than one premise. Adult reasoners, for example, are sensitive to the effects of sample size or "premise monotonicity." In general, the more premise categories that share a particular property, the more likely it is that the property will be generalized to other members of the same superordinate category (Osherson et al., 1990). Adults are also sensitive to premise diversity. Cats and buffalos sharing some property, for example, is seen as a stronger basis for generalization to other animals than if the property was shared by cows and buffalos. The conventional explanation for this effect is that the more diverse set samples a greater range of the possible exemplars of the relevant superordinate and therefore provides a stronger base for induction (Osherson et al., 1990).

Intuitively, combining information across multiple premises seems to involve more complex processing than many of the inductive arguments discussed so far. Perhaps not surprisingly, therefore, early investigations of monotonicity- and diversity-based reasoning in children (e.g., Carey, 1985; Gutheil & Gelman, 1997; López et al., 1992) suggested that an understanding of these principles emerged rather late in development. López et al. (1992), for example, examined the generalizations made by five- and eight-year-olds presented with a variety of single- and multiple-premise arguments patterned after those used by Osherson et al. (1990). They found that young children were able to draw appropriate conclusions from certain kinds of arguments that included multiple premises. Five-year-olds, for example, judged that a property shared by horses and zebras was more likely to generalize to donkeys than to squirrels. Young children also exhibited "nonmonotonic" reasoning for some pairs of arguments. That is, adding a premise to an argument could weaken inductive strength if the added premise was not a member of the conclusion category (e.g., children were more likely to project a property from *lions* to *animals* than from *lions and apples* to *animals*). An appreciation of the role of premise monotonicity and premise diversity, however, took considerably longer to develop. Eight-year-olds, but not younger children, used monotonicity and premise diversity when the conclusion category was a more general one like "animals" that included the premise categories, but not when the conclusion was at the same level as the premises (e.g. generalizing from cats and buffalos to kangaroos) (also see Gutheil & Gelman, 1997; Lo, Sides, Rozelle, & Osherson, 2002).

Lopez et al. (1992) argued that the developmental progression from no understanding of monotonicity and diversity at age five, to an understanding of general-conclusion forms at around eight years, to an understanding of both general and specific forms in adulthood, fits well with Osherson et al.'s (1990) Similarity-Coverage model of induction. According to Osherson et al. understanding arguments involving premise-conclusion similarity involves a relatively straightforward computation of the similarity between the features of the premise and conclusion categories. Monotonicity and diversity, however, should be more difficult for young children because they require the additional process of "coverage" which involves computing the average maximum similarity of the premise categories to samples of the lowest-level category which includes both the premises and conclusions. In the general forms of these arguments the conclusion category is given in the argument. In the specific forms it has to be generated, a process that is likely to be particularly demanding for younger children (Markman & Callanan, 1984).

It is possible, however, that the negative conclusions regarding children's understanding of these more complex forms of induction may reflect their difficulties with the performance aspects of the tasks used by Lopez et al. (1992) and Gutheil and Gelman (1997). Heit and Hahn (2001) suggest that young children may have difficulty in applying principles like diversity and monotonicity to hidden or invisible properties (e.g., "has leucocytes inside"). Moreover, Lopez et al. (1992) required children to respond to a variety of inductive arguments (e.g., typicality, similarity, monotonicity, and diversity) administered in the same testing session. To perform well children would have to not only understand each kind of argument, but also switch between inductive strategies. Heit and Hahn (2001) tried to overcome these performance barriers by examining five- and nine-year-olds' generalization of concrete, observable properties from more or less diverse premise sets. For example, children were shown photographs of a diverse set of three dolls and told that they belonged to a girl named Jane. They were also shown a set of three very similar-looking dolls and told that they belonged to a girl named Danielle. They were then shown a new doll and asked who was the most likely owner. For observable properties, even five-year-olds reliably based their inferences on the diverse rather than the non-diverse premises. When hidden properties such as "has nuts inside" were used, only the nine-year-olds were sensitive to premise diversity.

In a similar vein Hayes and Kahn (2005) re-examined sensitivity to premise monotonicity in five- and nine-year-olds using items that always involved a choice between inferences based on a small or a large premise set. For example, children were presented with a small set of two grey turtles which shared a property such as "eats snails" or a larger set of six brown turtles that shared a different property such as "eats worms." The premises were presented with the cover story that they were samples from a larger inclusive category (i.e., both kinds of turtles came from the same zoo). Children were then asked to decide which property was most likely to be found in either another animal at the same hierarchical level (e.g., a turtle whose colour was unknown) or in most of the other animals of the same type at the zoo. Nine-year-olds were more likely to generalize the property of the larger set to both specific and general types of conclusions. Younger children did so only for the general conclusions (see Lo et al., 2002, for additional positive findings regarding children's use of monotonicity).

These data suggest that, by five years of age, children are able to use inductive heuristics like premise monotonicity and diversity. Exactly how they do this remains to be explained. One interpretation is that an ability to compute coverage develops by around five years of age. On the other hand it could be that Osherson et al.'s assumptions about how people process multiple premises in diversity and monotonicity tasks need to be revised. If young children have some understanding of these principles, as well as effects like premise-conclusion similarity and premise typicality, this may imply that similar kinds of computational processes subserve each of these phenomena. This possibility will be considered in more detail in Part II.

Property Knowledge

In all of the cases considered so far the focus has been on how children use various kinds of relations between premise and conclusion categories to draw inferences about properties. Unlike most of the items used in experimental induction tasks, however, most cases of everyday induction involve some knowledge of the properties to be inferred, as well as the relevant categories. Whether a property is generalized from one bird to another depends on whether the property is an internal organ, nesting pattern, or type of birdsong. There is plenty of evidence that adult inductive inference varies as a function of both knowledge about the categories *and* the predicate in question (e.g., Heit & Rubinstein, 1994; Nisbett, Krantz, Jepson, & Kunda, 1983). The evidence reviewed below suggests that preschool children, and possibly younger infants, are also sensitive to category-property interactions.

INFANT STUDIES. Infants' understanding of how certain properties might generalize across some categories but not others was examined by Mandler and McDonough (1996, 1998). Infants aged between nine and fourteen months were presented with instances of different superordinate categories (e.g., a dog and a car). Experimenters then modelled different kinds of actions for each instance (e.g. giving a drink to the dog or riding on the car). Infants as young as nine months of age generalized the actions observed with the base animal to other animals, and the actions observed with the base vehicle to other vehicles. However, they seemed to respect the boundaries between global categories and did not imitate "animal" actions in the presence of vehicles or vice versa. Furthermore, Mandler and McDonough (1998) found that fourteen-month-olds distinguished between actions that were appropriate to only animate or only inanimate kinds from those that are appropriate for both domains (e.g., being washed). They concluded that infants form global concepts of animals and vehicles and have some understanding of the characteristic properties within each domain.

These conclusions, however, have been challenged on both empirical and theoretical grounds (see McClelland & Rogers, 2003; Rakison & Hahn, 2004 for critiques). One problem is that Mandler and her colleagues may have underestimated the role played by perceptual similarity in driving induction.

Although the members of her global categories were perceptually diverse, it could be argued that the members of the animal category were still more similar to one another than they were to vehicles, and vice versa. Hence, the generalization to items from the same superordinate may in part be driven by perceptual similarity. Some aspects of Mandler's data are consistent with this argument. Although Mandler and McDonough (1998) found that domain-general properties like "being washed" were generalized to both animals and vehicles, the test object which infants imitated *first* was usually the one that was most similar in perceptual terms to the model.

Rakison and Hahn (2004) suggest that infants' inductive inferences are driven by their knowledge and expectations about the functional properties of object features rather than an understanding of the properties associated with different superordinate categories. In a variant on the Mandler and Mc-Donough (1998) procedure, eighteen-month-olds were shown models that moved along a non-linear path (thought to be characteristic of animate motion), or a linear path (thought to be characteristic of inanimate motion). Eighteen-month-olds generalized these actions based on a functional relationship with specific object parts rather than along taxonomic lines. For example, when the premise item was a cat who walked along a winding path, infants were more likely to imitate this action with an inanimate object that had a perceptual feature associated with walking (e.g., a bed with four legs) than with animals that lacked these features (e.g., a dolphin).

Such findings were seen to point to the primacy of perceptual features (i.e., object parts) over superordinate relations in infant induction (Rakison & Hahn, 2004). However, it needs to be noted that the infants in these studies were using perceptual information in a relatively sophisticated way. They understood that the ability to move in a particular way is causally dependent on having certain kinds of structural features like legs. Moreover, they used this knowledge as a basis for inductive inference. So by eighteen months of age infants are aware of differences in the generalizability of functional properties, although this awareness seems to be based on their knowledge of object parts rather than category membership.

STUDIES WITH PRESCHOOLERS AND OLDER CHILDREN. By three and a half to four years of age children are aware that certain properties are more generalizable than others. Children do not generalize transient properties like "is cold" or accidental properties like "fell on the floor this morning" even when the base and target have the same name and similar appearance (Gelman, 1988; Gelman & Markman, 1986, 1987; Springer, 1992). Young children believe that characters labelled with the same personality traits share novel behavioural properties such as "likes to play tibbits" but not transient properties such as "feeling thirsty" (Heyman & Gelman, 2000a).

Children also appear sensitive to certain kinds of specific property-category relations. In an ingenious study, Kalish and Gelman (1992) presented three- and four-year-olds with novel objects that had two labels, one that referred to object kind and one that described the material that the object was made from. In the critical experimental condition these labels supported different kinds of inferences. For example, whether "glass scissors" are judged to be fragile depends on which of the two labels is seen as more relevant to the judgment. Kalish and Gelman found that young children were sensitive to the kinds of labels that were relevant to generalizing different sorts of properties. When asked whether objects would share a novel dispositional property (e.g., "will fracture in water"), young children based their judgments on the material label. When asked whether they shared a novel functional property (e.g., "used for partitioning"), children used the object label.

Kelemen, Widdowson, Posner, Brown, and Casler (2003) have also shown that the direction of children's inferences within biological categories depends on the kind of property that is being generalized. Three- and four-year-olds based inferences about which animals had similar behavioural features (e.g., "fights off dangerous animals") on shared body parts relevant to this behaviour (e.g., having horns) rather than on overall perceptual similarity. This pattern reversed when children were generalizing a novel category label (cf. McCarrell & Callanan, 1995).

With age there appears to be an increasing appreciation of the role of category-property interactions in induction. Gelman (1988) presented four- and eight-year-olds with natural kinds such as *flowers* and artifacts such as *chairs*. Children were asked to decide whether the properties of these objects generalized to other natural kinds and artifacts. Some children were asked about properties which (from an adult perspective) were thought to be most generalizable within the domain of natural kinds (e.g., "needs CO_2 to grow"), while others were asked about properties thought to be more generalizable for artifacts (e.g., "you can loll with it"). Control conditions also examined properties thought to be generalizable to neither domain or to be equally generalizable to both. The older children were sensitive to the relations between categories and properties, being more likely to generalize "natural kind properties" to natural kind exemplars than to artifacts, and vice versa. Four-year-olds, however, did not discriminate between the properties typically associated with the two domains.

One way of interpreting the developmental trends described by Gelman (1988) is that sensitivity to category-property relations in induction increases as children learn more about the causal principles that operate in different conceptual domains and the specific properties associated with exemplars from each domain. Although a direct test of this developmental hypothesis has yet to be carried out, indirect support comes from studies of the effects of expertise on adult reasoning. Shafto and Coley (2003) found that fish experts used causal and ecological relations in generalizing familiar properties like "has disease X." When generalizing properties about which they knew little (e.g., "has sarca"), both experts and novices relied on similarity-based strategies. Hence, increasing domain knowledge is associated with greater use of inductive reasoning based on the interactions between specific categories and properties.

Causal Relations

The previous section showed that children's background knowledge of both categories and properties plays an important role in their inductive inferences. Exactly how does such knowledge interact with more "domain-general" principles such as premise-conclusion similarity, monotonicity, diversity, and so on? Recent studies with adults suggest that when people have some knowledge about the relations between premises this can override more general inductive principles. Medin, Coley, Storms, and Hayes (2003) showed that diversity-based reasoning is undermined when people perceive a salient or distinctive relation between the premises that is unlikely to be shared by a conclusion category. Adults, for example, judged that a novel property shared by *fleas* and *butterflies* was more likely to generalize to *sparrows* than a property shared by *dogs* and *fleas*, even though they saw the second set of premises to be more diverse. In other words, they were aware of the ecological relations between dogs and fleas and judged that this special relation was unlikely to generalize to other animals (but see Heit and Feeney, 2005, for a different interpretation).

An important goal for studies of the development of inductive reasoning is to specify how children integrate their causal knowledge with an understanding of more general inductive principles, and to examine whether this process changes as children develop more knowledge of the world. As a first step in this direction Thompson and Hayes (2005) devised a task in which five-year-olds, nine-year-olds, and adults were forced to choose between inductive inferences based on shared causal relations or featural similarity (cf. Lassaline, 1996). The basic procedure is illustrated in Figure 2.1. *Attribute base* items were fictional animals made up of three features that were not linked via explicit causal relations but which could plausibly co-exist. *Causal base* items

Attribute Base	*Causal Base*
The following are true of Animal A:	The following are true of Animal B:
• Has long fur • Has claw-like feet • Eats leaves from trees	• Has a large protective shell • Can stay in the sun without getting burned • The protective shell allows the animal to stay in the sun without getting burned

Target

The following facts are true of Animal C

• Has long fur
• Has claw-like feet
• Has a large protective shell

Induction Test

Animal C has one other feature. Do you think it:

Eats leaves from trees?

OR

Can stay in the sun without getting burned?

FIGURE 2.1. Schematic stimulus example from Thompson and Hayes (2005).

contained two features that could be linked by causal relations, together with a statement of the direction of causation. All features were illustrated with line drawings. After presentation of the bases, a target instance was described. As the table shows, this always had a higher featural similarity to the attribute base but contained the antecedent feature from the causal base. Participants had to predict which of two other properties was most likely to be found in the target, the third feature of the attribute base or the consequent feature from the causal base.

The main results are summarized in Figure 2.2. The proportion of "causal" choices at test exceeded chance for each age group. There was also a clear increase in the proportion of causal choices with age. When children's justifications for their choices were considered, there was even more robust evidence for the early development of an awareness of the role of causal relations in induction. Five-year-olds mentioned the causal relation in over forty percent of justifications. By comparison, explicit appeals to feature similarity as a basis for induction were relatively rare for all age groups. This shows that causal

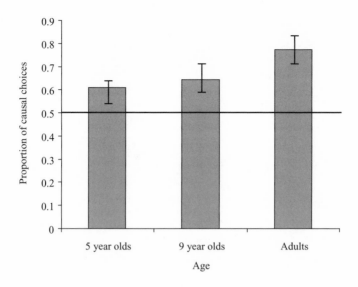

FIGURE 2.2. Mean proportion of causal choices on the Thompson and Hayes (2005) causal induction task.

relations between the features of premise and conclusion items can override featural similarity as a basis for induction, even in young children. It remains to be shown whether these results generalize to other category domains like artifacts and social kinds. Further work is also needed to establish just which aspects of causal relationships lead children to make stronger inductions.

Summary and Discussion

This review shows that, by the preschool years, children make inductive inferences based on a variety of premise-conclusion relations. As well as perceptual and taxonomic relations, children are sensitive to the role of hierarchical and causal relations, as well as the ways that these interact with certain kinds of property knowledge. There is some evidence that by five years children may use general heuristics like diversity and monotonicity. Even preverbal infants appear capable of going beyond perceptual similarity in their generalization of novel properties.

While these demonstrations of precocious induction are impressive, they need to be viewed within a broader perspective. An important agenda driving much of the research in this field has been to show that young children *are not* perceptually bound in their reasoning. To achieve this researchers often place perceptual cues in conflict with other cues like category labels and force children to choose one cue as a basis for inference. This approach can reveal the dominant cue for induction only in a given situation. It tells us little about how perceptual and conceptual cues might interact. Such interactions are likely to be important since in everyday induction it is not always easy to draw a clear distinction between "perceptual" and "conceptual" relations (Goldstone, 1994; Murphy, 2004). Moreover, the more perceptually obvious similarities between base and target items often provide useful clues to underlying causal or taxonomic relations (Gentner, 1988). As Madole and Oakes (1999) put it, "Objects that look like dogs also tend to sound like dogs, move like dogs, and smell like dogs. Moreover, they usually *are* dogs" (p. 270 [original emphasis]).

One implication is that although the various relations that influence children's induction have been treated separately in this review, this is not the way that they always appear in the child's (or even the adult's) world. Many of the more abstract or "conceptual" aspects of categorization involve understanding and explaining the links between observable features, such as why an object that has wings and feathers is likely to fly. Given this interdependence of perceptual and conceptual features, it makes little sense to ask whether children rely on "perceptual," "taxonomic," or "causal" relations when they do induction. In fact, adult studies that have manipulated both the number of features shared by base and target items and their causal relations have found that induction is influenced by *both* kinds of factors (e.g., Lassaline, 1996). Perhaps the best way of interpreting the studies reviewed here, therefore, is that they tell us about the kinds of cues that draw children's attention towards or away from the more observable or more abstract relations between bases/premises and targets/conclusions during induction.

II. IMPLICATIONS FOR THEORIES OF INDUCTION

In addition to revealing the origins and early developmental course of induction, developmental data may also be useful for evaluating competing process models of induction. The major inductive phenomena in infants and children reviewed so far are summarized in Table 2.1. How well do process models of induction, originally developed to explain adult data, account for these phenomena? The key issues here are whether existing models can explain the range of relations that children are capable of using as a basis for inductive inferences, and whether the models can predict the kinds of factors that direct children's attention to particular kinds of relations.

TABLE 2.1. *Summary of major category-based induction phenomena in infants and children*

Induction Phenomenon	By 18 months	By 5 years
Premise-conclusion similarity	Yes (Baldwin et al., 1993; Graham et al., 2004; Welder & Graham, 2001)	Yes (Carey, 1985; Gelman & Markman, 1986, 1987; Gelman, 1988; Sloutsky & Fisher, 2004)
Shared labels override perceptual similarity	Yes (Graham et al., 2004; Welder & Graham, 2001)	Yes (Deak & Bauer, 1996; Florian, 1994; Gelman, 1988; Gelman & Coley, 1990; Gelman & Markman, 1986, 1987; Heyman & Gelman, 2000a, b; Sloutsky & Fisher, 2004)
Similarity overrides shared labels		
• When labels conflict with existing knowledge	—	Yes (Davidson & Gelman, 1990; Jaswal, 2004)
• When adjective labels are used	—	Yes (Gelman & Coley, 1990; Gelman & Heyman, 1999)
• When labels are proper names	—	Yes (Heyman & Gelman, 2000a)
Conclusion homogeneity	—	Yes (Carey, 1985; López et al., 1992)
Premise Typicality	—	Yes (Lo et al., 2002; López et al., 1992)
Premise diversity: Specific conclusions	—	Yes (Heit & Hahn, 2001)

42

Phenomenon		
Premise diversity: General conclusions	—	No (Lo et al., 2002; López et al., 1992)
Premise Monotonicity (Sample size): Specific conclusions	—	No (Hayes & Kahn, 2005; López et al., 1992)
Premise Monotonicity: General conclusions	—	Yes (Hayes & Kahn, 2005; Lo et al., 2002)
Premise Nonmonotonicity: Specific conclusions	—	(Yes) (López et al., 1992)
Premise Nonmonotonicity: General conclusions	—	Yes (López et al., 1992)
Category-property interactions		
• Transient vs. entrenched properties	—	Yes (Gelman, 1988; Gelman & Coley, 1990)
• Property generalization depends on the category domain	(Yes) (Mandler & McDonough, 1996, 1998)	Yes (Carey, 1985; Gelman, 1988; Heyman & Gelman, 2000b; Kalish & Gelman, 1992)
Shared functional features promote inference	Yes (McCarrell & Callanan, 1995; Rakison & Hahn, 2004)	Yes (Kelemen et al., 2003)
Shared causal relations promote inference	—	Yes (Thompson & Hayes, 2005)

Note: Yes = Robust evidence for the phenomenon; (Yes) = Some positive evidence but some controversy still exists; No = Robust evidence against the phenomenon; — = No studies with the relevant age group.

The Similarity-Coverage Model (SCM)

As noted above, this model suggests that induction is driven by two principles, similarity and coverage. Arguments are perceived as strong or convincing to the extent that 1) the premise categories are similar to the conclusions and 2) the premises "cover" the lowest-level category that includes both premise and conclusion categories (Osherson et al., 1990). Because many of the induction phenomena that have been studied in children were derived from adult studies of the SCM (e.g., premise-conclusion similarity, typicality, nonmonotonicity), it is hardly surprising that these can be readily explained by that model.

Because the SCM model does not discriminate between "perceptual" and other forms of similarity, it is unclear whether it can explain competition between shared category labels and perceptual similarity in determining inductive generalization, although this may be possible if additional assumptions regarding similarity computations are added (Heit & Hayes, 2005). A more serious problem for the model is children's use of knowledge about the entrenchment or distribution of feature properties to promote or limit generalization (e.g., Gelman, 1988; Kelemen et al., 2003). The SCM model does not consider knowledge about specific properties and is unable to explain these effects. Further, because SCM focuses on the global similarity between categories, it is unable to explain children's induction based on causal relations shared by the premise and conclusion.

Feature-Based Induction Model (FBI)

Like SCM, Sloman's (1993) FBI model emphasizes the similarity of premise and conclusion categories as a basis for induction. However, it does so without the retrieval of superordinate categories. Instead, novel properties are generalized on the basis of the overlap between the known features of the premises and conclusions. Property generalization is proportional to the number of conclusion category features present in the premises. In terms of explaining induction in children, FBI shares many of the strengths and weaknesses of the Similarity-Coverage approach. It gives ready explanations of phenomena such as premise-conclusion similarity and typicality. By adding assumptions that shared causal features should be given more weight in similarity computations, it may also be able to account for the causal induction data of Thompson and Hayes (2005).

Generalization based on knowledge about the distribution of features within a category, however, lies outside of the scope of the model. Without additional assumptions, FBI also has difficulty in explaining children's sensitivity to nonmonotonicity effects. Moreover, the finding that children's featural knowledge does not always predict which hierarchical level will be privileged for induction (Coley et al., 2004) runs contrary to one of the model's key assumptions.

Similarity, Induction, Naming, and Categorization (SINC)

Sloutsky and Fisher (2004) proposed this model to explain developmental changes in induction, categorization, and naming. In the case of induction, the probability that a property will be generalized from a base to a target instance is a function of the similarity of these instances. Similarity is computed both in terms of the level of overlap in (visual) perceptual features and similarity in the labels attached to the premise and conclusion items. The relative salience of these two kinds of features is assumed to change with age, with similar labels being more salient for younger children. This model differs from other "similarity-based" models such as SCM and FBI in the different roles accorded to visual features and labels. It is also different in that the model focuses on induction over specific instances rather than categories.

So far SINC has been applied only to data from triad tasks like those developed by Gelman and Markman (1986). Moreover, it does not explain cases where young children fail to use shared labels as a basis for induction. It is also not clear how it would explain effects readily accounted for by other models, such as typicality, diversity, and monotonicity. Like other similarity-based models, it also offers no principled account of how children's knowledge about predicates influences inductive generalization. More generally, despite the claim that it differs from induction models like SCM that allow for the operation of taxonomic as well as perceptual relations, SINC makes many assumptions that parallel closely those made by other models. In particular, the constraint that shared labels should be given greater weight than shared visual features is common to many other models of inductive reasoning (Heit & Hayes, 2005).

Bayesian Models

Heit (1998) proposed a Bayesian model of induction such that generalization of a novel property from a premise to a conclusion category depends on prior knowledge about known properties shared by these categories. This knowledge is used to generate hypotheses about the projection of the novel property (e.g., whether it is shared by both the premises and conclusion categories or whether it is shared by the premises only). The information in the premise(s) is then used as evidence to evaluate these hypotheses using Bayesian rules (cf. McDonald, Samuels, & Rispoli, 1996). Heit (1998) showed that, with appropriate assumptions about knowledge of feature distribution, the Bayesian model could explain phenomena like premise-conclusion similarity, typicality, diversity, and monotonicity. An important finding supporting the Bayesian approach is that children's generalization of novel properties follows the same patterns as their generalization of familiar properties (Gelman, 1988). Because it accords a central role to property knowledge, the model can also explain children's sensitivity to differences in the generalizability of various features within and between categories. Moreover, the model posits the same basic processes to explain how people evaluate arguments involving premise-conclusion similarity, diversity, and monotonicity. It can therefore explain data suggesting that some understanding of premise diversity and monotonicity is present by age five.

The Bayesian model, however, has difficulty in explaining children's sensitivity to nonmonotonicity effects. Another limitation is that the validity of the model rests on its assumptions about children's and adult's prior knowledge about category features. So far, however, there have been no tests of these assumptions in real categories (see Chapter 7 by Tenenbaum, Kemp, and Shafto for a related approach).

Relevance Theory

With a view to explaining inductive phenomena in which people have varying levels of knowledge about inductive predicates, Medin et al. (2003) proposed a relevance framework such that people assume that the set of premises provided in inductive arguments are informative and will search for distinctive relations between them. For example, if told that *koalas, kangaroos,* and *wallabies* all shared some property, you might infer that the property had something to do with being an Australian animal (or more specifically, an Australian marsupial). Moreover, the activation of this distinctive relation can take place before considering the similarity between the premises and conclusions. If the conclusion category shared the distinctive relation (e.g., if it was another Australian animal), then the novel property is likely to be generalized. According to this approach, causal relations between premises are highly distinctive and therefore likely to influence induction.

A detailed process-model of relevance has yet to be described, so it is difficult to compare this approach with more explicit models like SCM and FBI. In general terms, however, this approach can explain why features that are believed to be causally linked to category membership (e.g., biological features in animal categories) are more likely to be generalized to other animals than transient behavioural features. It may also account for the fact that causal relations can override perceptual similarity in children's induction. In this approach an assessment of the featural similarity and taxonomic relations between premises and conclusions becomes the default if no more distinctive relations exist, so the approach can also account for the more "standard" induction phenomena such as premise-conclusion similarity, typicality, and so on.

Summary and Discussion

It appears that no existing process model gives an entirely satisfactory account of children's induction. Models like SCM and FBI provide detailed explanations of the cognitive processes that lead to effects that arise early in development, like premise-conclusion similarity and typicality, but fail to predict when children will or will not use labels as a basis for induction and to account for differences in inductive projection due to property knowledge. The Bayesian approach and Relevance theory on the other hand hold some promise of explaining children's induction with both blank and non-blank predicates within a single framework. Both of these approaches, however, currently lack detailed assumptions and processing constraints. Having said that, it seems that the broader perspective offered by the Bayesian and Relevance frameworks is likely to be necessary because children are able to flexibly employ a number of different premise-conclusion relations as a basis for property inference. The main goal for future theories of inductive development is to provide a more detailed process account of these multifaceted inferences and to specify the factors that lead certain kinds of relations to become more salient in specific induction contexts.

III. WHAT DEVELOPS IN INDUCTIVE REASONING?

Looking over Table 2.1, one might be struck by the degree of developmental continuity found in induction phenomena. By thirteen months of age children are sensitive to multiple relations between inductive bases and targets such as perceptual similarity and shared labels. From around five years of age children's inductive inferences seem to be influenced by the same broad range of cues and relations that influence adult judgments. Where there are age changes these seem to be mainly gradual and quantitative, with certain kinds of information (e.g., causal relations) being used more frequently and across a wider range of domains.

This final part of the chapter addresses two issues relating to this developmental pattern. First, how do children first acquire an understanding of the relations that can be used as a basis for induction? Second, where there are age-related changes in induction, can these simply be explained by the gradual expansion of children's background knowledge about categories, exemplars, and exemplar properties?

Early Acquisition of Inductive Potential

Two different kinds of answers have been proposed to explain the early emergence of induction and the early shifts in the kinds of relations used to make property inferences. Some have argued that cognitive architectures which track correlations between object parts, features, and labels can *learn* to group instances according to higher-order properties such as animacy (Loose & Mareschal, 1999; McClelland & Rogers, 2003; Rakison & Hahn, 2004). According to this "bottom-up" approach, learning about the inductive potential of categories requires only that infants perceive and interact with (lots of) objects over time. Hence, children shift from inferences based on appearances to inferences based on labels, not because they appreciate the conceptual significance of the labels, but because labels provide a more reliable basis of predicting the presence or absence of category features across exemplars (Loose & Mareschal, 1999).

A different kind of answer is that from a very early age children are biased or constrained to pay special attention to categorical cues like noun labels which imply a commonality of observed and hidden features (Keil, 1991; Gelman, 2003). Gelman (2003), for example, argues that from a very young age children hold essentialist beliefs about many categories; that is, they believe that there is some unobservable property or essence that causes things to be the way they are and that everyday categories reflect this essentialist structure.[4]

It is difficult to adjudicate between these competing approaches on the basis of empirical evidence alone. This is because much of the existing evidence on children's induction can be interpreted as in line with either account. Sloutsky and Fisher (2004), for example, showed that when taught a novel property about exemplars from an animal category like "cat," five-year-olds are less likely than eleven-year-olds and adults to spontaneously generalize this

---

[4] This of course begs the question as to the origins of essentialist biases or beliefs. See Gelman (2003) for a review of possible answers.

property to other category members. They also show that, with appropriate training, four-year-olds can readily learn to generalize in the same way as older children. Sloutsky and Fisher argue that their results show that young children do not have an a priori assumption that category members share hidden properties. However, the rapidity with which children learned to generalize along categorical lines could also be seen as consistent with a bias which favours category-based induction.

So far "bottom-up" models of category acquisition and induction have been applied to only a small part of the developmental induction data in Table 2.1. They can account for children's increasing reliance on labels as a basis for induction over time. However, it is unclear how they would explain why different kinds of labels have different effects on inductive inference, and why structural and functional features sometimes override labels as a basis for induction. Such models also offer no principled account of property-category interactions. It is too early to tell, therefore, whether these approaches will succeed without the incorporation of additional constraints like an essentialist bias. Nevertheless, the tension between these approaches has had a positive effect on the field by stimulating the development of more explicit models of the mechanisms involved in learning which object features are most important in promoting induction.

Are There Developmental Changes in Inductive Processes?

There seems little doubt that, in just about all conceptual domains, children's knowledge of perceptual, taxonomic, and causal relations, as well as the distribution of object properties, expands with age (Farrar et al., 1992). An important question is whether this expanding knowledge base is sufficient to explain the development of induction. Over and above these changes in knowledge, is there evidence of significant changes in the fundamental *processes* that children use to compare and integrate inductive premises and conclusions? So far two detailed accounts of such a change have been examined: Sloutsky and Fisher's (2004) proposal that there is a shift from treating labels as perceptual features to treating them as markers of category membership, and Lopez et al.'s (1992) argument that older children are more capable of computing the "coverage" components of the Similarity-Coverage model. Neither approach has been shown to give an adequate account of children's induction.

This should not, however, discourage us from the goal of devising more detailed process models of induction and applying these to the study of inductive development. In part, this will require some consideration of how the development of induction fits in with other kinds of age-related changes in children's reasoning and cognition. Developmental changes in children's ability to complete conditional or deductive reasoning tasks have been cited in support of more general models of developmental change in children's capacity to process more complex relations (e.g., Halford & Andrews, 2004). By contrast, there have been few attempts to explore the relationship between the processing mechanisms involved in children's category-based induction and those involved in the development of other kinds of reasoning. This is surprising given that other forms of reasoning are often subject to constraints that are similar to those that operate in induction. Like category-based induction, children's analogical reasoning is influenced by the similarity between the inductive base and target items and by children's level of knowledge of the causal relations involved in the analogy (Goswami, 2002). Some theories of analogical reasoning also posit developmental change in the factors that children attend to when drawing analogies. Gentner (1988), for example, suggests that young children are strongly influenced by the similarity between the surface features of base and target items but become more sensitive to the importance of shared relations as they grow older, a developmental change referred to as a *relational shift*. It would be interesting to examine the generality of this shift and, in particular, whether children's sensitivity to relational information in induction follows a similar developmental trajectory.

IV. CONCLUDING COMMENTS

This review of the development of category-based induction highlights the range and complexity of factors influencing children's judgements about whether and how far a property generalizes. Children draw inductive inferences based on a range of possible relations between premises and conclusions, as well as beliefs about the to-be-generalized property. Children derive information about each of these components from their perceptual analysis of object features, domain knowledge, and linguistic conventions. Describing the interaction between these components, and the way that this interaction changes with age, is a challenging but necessary goal for future models of induction.

ACKNOWLEDGMENTS

I would like to thank Susan Thompson and Tamara Cavenett for their valuable comments and assistance in the preparation of this chapter. The research described in the chapter was supported by Australian Research Council Grant DP0344436.

References

Baldwin, D. A., Markman, E. M., & Melartin, R. L. (1993). Infants' ability to draw inferences about nonobvious object properties: Evidence from exploratory play. *Child Development, 64,* 711–728.

Booth, A. E., Waxman, S. R., & Huang, Y. T. (2005). Conceptual information permeates word learning in infancy. *Developmental Psychology, 41,* 491–505.

Bruner, J. S., Olver, R. R., & Greenfield, P. M. (1966). *Studies in cognitive growth.* New York: Wiley.

Carey, S. (1985). *Conceptual change in childhood.* Cambridge, MA: MIT Press, Bradford Books.

Coley, J. D., Hayes, B., Lawson, C., & Moloney, M. (2004). Knowledge, expectations, and inductive reasoning within conceptual hierarchies. *Cognition, 90,* 217–253.

Coley, J. D., Medin, D. L., & Atran, S. (1997). Does rank have its privilege? Inductive inferences within folkbiological taxonomies. *Cognition, 64,* 72–112.

Davidson, N. S., & Gelman, S. A. (1990). Inductions from novel categories: The role of language and conceptual structure. *Cognitive Development, 5,* 151–176.

Deák, G. O., & Bauer, P. (1996). The dynamics of preschoolers' categorization choices. *Child Development, 67,* 740–767.

Diesendruck, G. (2003). Categories for names or names for categories? The interplay between domain-specific conceptual structure and language. *Language and Cognitive Processes, 18,* 759–787.

Farrar, M. J., Raney, G. E., & Boyer, M. E. (1992). Knowledge, concepts, and inferences in childhood. *Child Development, 63,* 673–691.

Florian, J. E. (1994). Stripes do not a zebra make, or do they? Conceptual and perceptual information in inductive inference. *Developmental Psychology, 30,* 88–101.

Gelman, S. A. (1988). The development of induction within natural kind and artifact categories. *Cognitive Psychology, 20,* 65–95.

Gelman, S. A. (2003). *The essential child: Origins of essentialism in everyday thought.* Oxford: Oxford University Press.

Gelman, S. A., & Coley, J. D. (1990). The importance of knowing a dodo is a bird: Categories and inferences in 2-year-old children. *Developmental Psychology, 26,* 796–804.

Gelman, S. A., & Markman, E. M. (1986). Categories and induction in young children. *Cognition, 23,* 183–209.

Gelman, S.A., & Markman, E. M. (1987). Young children's inductions from natural kinds: The role of categories and appearances. *Child Development, 8,* 157–167.

Gelman, S. A., & O'Reilly, A. W. (1988). Children's inductive inferences within super-ordinate categories: The role of language and category structure. *Child Development, 59,* 876–887.

Gentner, D. (1988). Metaphor as structure mapping: The relational shift. *Child Development, 59,* 47–59.

Goldstone, R. L. (1994). The role of similarity in categorization: Providing a groundwork. *Cognition, 52,* 125–157.

Goswami, U. (2002). Inductive and deductive reasoning. In U. Goswami (Ed.), *Blackwell handbook of cognitive development* (pp. 282–302). Oxford, UK: Blackwell.

Graham, S. A., Kilbreath, C. S., & Welder, A. N. (2004). 13-month-olds rely on shared labels and shape similarity for inductive inferences. *Child Development, 75,* 409–427.

Gutheil, G., & Gelman, S. A. (1997). Children's use of sample size and diversity information within basic-level categories. *Journal of Experimental Child Psychology, 64,* 159–174.

Halford, G., & Andrews, G. (2004). The development of deductive reasoning: How important is complexity? *Thinking and Reasoning, 23,* 123–145.

Hayes, B. K., & Kahn, T. (2005). *Children's sensitivity to sample size in inductive reasoning.* Paper presented at the 14th Biennial Conference of the Australasian Human Development Association, Perth, July.

Heit, E. (1998). A Bayesian analysis of some forms of inductive reasoning. In M. Oaksford & N. Chater (Eds.), *Rational models of cognition* (pp. 248–274). Oxford: Oxford University Press.

Heit, E., & Feeney, A. (2005). Relations between premise similarity and inductive strength. *Psychonomic Bulletin & Review, 12,* 340–344.

Heit, E., & Hahn, U. (2001). Diversity-based reasoning in children. *Cognitive Psychology, 47,* 243–273.

Heit, E., & Hayes, B. K. (2005). Relations between categorization, induction, recognition and similarity. *Journal of Experimental Psychology: General, 134,* 596–605.

Heit, E., & Rubinstein, J. (1994). Similarity and property effects in inductive reasoning. *Journal of Experimental Psychology: Learning, Memory, & Cognition, 20,* 411–422.

Henderson, A. M., & Graham, S. A. (2005). Two-year-olds' appreciation of the shared nature of novel object labels. *Journal of Cognition and Development, 6,* 381–402.

Heyman, G. D., & Gelman, S. A. (2000a). Preschool children's use of trait labels to make inductive inferences. *Journal of Experimental Child Psychology, 77,* 1–19.

Heyman, G. D., & Gelman, S. A. (2000b). Preschool children's use of novel predicates to make inductive inferences about people. *Cognitive Development, 15,* 263–280.

Inagaki, K., & Hatano, G. (1996). Young children's recognition of the commonalities between animals and plants. *Child Development, 67,* 2823–2840.

Inhelder, B., & Piaget, J. (1958). *The growth of logical thinking from childhood to adolescence.* New York: Basic Books.

Jaswal, V. (2004). Don't believe everything you hear: Preschoolers' sensitivity to speaker intent in category induction. *Child Development, 75,* 1871–1885.

Jones, S. S., & Smith, L. S. (1993). The place of perception in children's concepts. *Cognitive Development, 8,* 113–139.

Kalish, C. W., & Gelman, S. A. (1992). On wooden pillows: Multiple classifications and children's category-based inductions. *Child Development, 63,* 1536–1557.

Keil, F. (1991). The emergence of theoretical beliefs as constraints on concepts. In S. Carey & R. Gelman (Eds.), *The epigenesis of mind* (pp. 133–169). Hillsdale, NJ: Erlbaum.

Kelemen, D., Widdowson, D., Posner, T., Brown, A. L., & Casler, K. (2003). Teleo-functional constraints on preschool children's reasoning about living things. *Developmental Science, 6,* 329–345.

Lassaline, M. E. (1996). Structural alignment in induction and similarity. *Journal of Experimental Psychology: General, 22,* 754–770.

Lo, Y., Sides, A., Rozelle, J., & Osherson, D. (2002). Evidential diversity and premise probability in young children's inductive judgment. *Cognitive Science, 26,* 181–206.

Loose, J. J., & Mareschal, D. (1999). Inductive reasoning revisited: Children's reliance on category labels and appearances. In *Proceedings of the Twenty-First Annual Conference of the Cognitive Science Society* (pp. 320–325). Mahwah, NJ: Erlbaum.

López, A., Gelman, S. A., Gutheil, G., & Smith, E. E. (1992). The development of category-based induction. *Child Development, 63,* 1070–1090.

Madole, K. L., & Oakes, L. (1999). Making sense of infant categorization: Stable processes and changing representations. *Developmental Review, 19,* 263–296.

Mandler, J. M., & McDonough, L. (1996). Drinking and driving don't mix: Inductive generalization in infancy. *Cognition, 59,* 307–335.

Mandler, J. M., & McDonough, L. (1998). Studies in inductive inference in infancy. *Cognitive Psychology, 37,* 60–96.

Markman, A. B., & Ross, B. (2003). Category use and category learning. *Psychological Bulletin, 129,* 592–613.

Markman, E. M., & Callanan, M. A. (1984). An analysis of hierarchical classification. In R. Sternberg (Ed.), *Advances in the psychology of human intelligence,* Vol. 2 (pp. 325–366). Hillsdale, NJ: Erlbaum.

McCarrell, N. S., & Callanan, M. A. (1995). Form-function correspondences in children's inference. *Child Development, 66,* 532–546.

McClelland, J. L., & Rogers, T. T. (2003). The parallel distributed processing approach to semantic cognition. *Nature Reviews Neuroscience, 4*(4), 310–322.

McDonald, J., Samuels, M., & Rispoli, J. (1996). A hypothesis assessment model of categorical argument strength. *Cognition, 59,* 199–217.

Medin, D. L., Coley, J., Storms, G., & Hayes, B. K. (2003). A relevance theory of induction. *Psychonomic Bulletin & Review, 10,* 517–532.

Murphy, G. L. (2004). On the conceptual-perceptual divide in early concepts. *Developmental Science, 7,* 513–515.

Nisbett, R. E., Krantz, D. H., Jepson, C., & Kunda, Z. (1983). The use of statistical heuristics in everyday inductive reasoning. *Psychological Review, 90,* 339–363.

Osherson, D. N., Smith, E. E., Wilkie, O., López, A., & Shafir, E. (1990). Category-based induction. *Psychological Review, 97,* 185–200.

Quinn, P. C., & Eimas, P. D. (2000). The emergence of category representations during infancy: Are separate perceptual and conceptual processes required? *Journal of Cognition and Development, 1,* 55–61.

Rakison, D. H., & Hahn, E. (2004). The mechanisms of early categorization and induction: Smart or dumb infants? In R. Kail (Ed.), *Advances in child development and behavior,* Vol. 32 (pp. 281–322). New York: Academic Press.

Rosch, E., Mervis, C. G., Gray, W. D., Johnson, D. M., & Boyes-Braem, P. (1976). Basic objects in natural categories. *Cognitive Psychology, 8,* 382–439.

Shafto, P., & Coley, J. D. (2003). Development of categorization and reasoning in the natural world: Novices to experts, naive similarity to ecological knowledge. *Journal of Experimental Psychology: Learning, Memory, & Cognition, 29,* 641–649.

Sloman, S. A. (1993). Feature-based induction. *Cognitive Psychology, 25,* 231–280.

Sloutsky, V. M., & Fisher, A. V. (2004). Induction and categorization in young children: A similarity-based model. *Journal of Experimental Psychology: General, 133,* 166–188.

Springer, K. (1992). Children's awareness of the biological implications of kinship. *Child Development, 63,* 950–959.

Springer, K. (2001). Perceptual boundedness and perceptual support in conceptual development. *Psychological Review, 108,* 691–708.

Thompson, S., & Hayes, B. K. (2005). *Causal induction in adults and children.* Paper presented at 32nd Australasian Experimental Psychology Conference, Melbourne University, April.

Vygotsky, L. S. (1986). *Thought and language.* Cambridge, MA: MIT Press (original work published 1934).

Waxman, S. R., & Booth, A. E. (2001). Seeing pink elephants: Fourteen-month-olds' interpretations of novel nouns and adjectives. *Cognitive Psychology, 43,* 217–242.

Welder, A. N., & Graham, S. A. (2001). The influence of shape similarity and shared labels on infants' inductive inferences about nonobvious object properties. *Child Development, 72,* 1653–1673.

3

Interpreting Asymmetries of Projection in Children's Inductive Reasoning

Douglas L. Medin and Sandra Waxman

I. INTRODUCTION

Like adults, children use categories as a basis for inductive inference. Having learned that some property is true of some individual (e.g., "My dog, Magic, likes marshmallows"), a child might assume both that other members of the same category (dogs) share this property and that members of other, similar categories (e.g., cats) might also share this property. In short, inductive inference may be guided by and reflect categorical relationships, hence the term "category-based induction" or CBI. Cognitive and developmental researchers have used a category-based induction paradigm not only to study the use of categories in reasoning, but also to draw inferences from patterns of reasoning about the nature of conceptual structures themselves (Atran et al., 2001; Carey, 1985; Gelman & Markman, 1986; Gutheil, Bloom, Valderrama, & Freedman, 2004; Gutheil, Vera, & Keil, 1998; Hatano & Inagaki, 1994; Inagaki, 2002; Johnson & Carey, 1998; Medin & Smith, 1981; Ross, Medin, Coley, & Atran, 2003; Waxman, Lynch, Casey, & Baer, 1997).

One of the most influential examples of the use of inductive projections to draw inferences about conceptual organization comes from research in the domain of folkbiology involving categories of living things, including humans, nonhuman animals, and plants. Developmental evidence has revealed, in particular, certain systematic *asymmetries* in inductive strength among these categories. For example, researchers have found that children are more willing to project properties from humans to dogs than from dogs to humans. As we will see, one interpretation of this result is that children's biological knowledge is organized around humans as the prototype and that it is more natural to generalize or project from the prototype to its variants than from variants to the prototype (more about this later). There is even some evidence that young, urban children may violate the principle of similarity by generalizing more from humans to bugs than from bees to bugs (Carey, 1985).

In this chapter, our focus will be on asymmetries in children's inductive projections. We begin by describing Carey's studies and outlining the framework within which she interpreted her findings. Subsequent work has questioned the generality of Carey's findings across populations and procedures, but relatively little attention has been directed toward the theoretical basis for the asymmetries that she observed. We point out that although Carey's theoretical position is consistent with the observed asymmetries, it is not unique in this regard. We describe several other alternative interpretations and their associated claims about conceptual organization and processing principles. The upshot is that human-animal asymmetries underdetermine theoretical accounts, and that further empirical constraints are needed.

We next continue to examine asymmetries but broaden their range to include asymmetries involving humans, nonhuman mammals, plants, and insects. We also expand the empirical base by drawing on category-based induction in children from a range of cultures. The data show certain asymmetries that appear to hold across populations. These additional sources of evidence offer considerable leverage for evaluating alternative interpretations of asymmetries. To foreshadow, from this broader view, we find that the asymmetries in inductive inference are not well characterized as knowledge or typicality effects favoring humans, as Carey has suggested. Instead, these asymmetries seem to reflect the manner by which distinctive categories and features become activated by the comparison processes associated with inductive inferences. On this account, a major source of human-animal asymmetries is the ambiguous status of humans as members of the category "animal" *and* as members of a category "human" that is contrastive with animal. The distinctive features/categories account leads to further predictions that are supported by children's open-ended justifications of their responses. We close with a discussion of implications of this newer interpretation of asymmetries for the understanding of category structure, conceptual organization, and conceptual development.

II. ASYMMETRIES IN CATEGORY-BASED INDUCTION

An early source of evidence for asymmetries in young children's inductive reasoning comes from Carey's (1985) CBI task. In her task, she described a novel property (e.g., "has an omentum") that was attributed to a base (e.g., "human") and then tested children's willingness to project the property to various targets. She used "human," "dog," and "bee" as bases and multiple living and nonliving kinds as targets. The now-classic finding was that children from four to six years of age willingly project novel properties from humans to nonhuman animals but are reluctant to make the converse generalization from nonhuman animals to humans. More specifically, young children who were told that people have a little green thing inside them, called an omentum, were quite willing to assert that dogs also have an omentum. In contrast, when children were told that dogs have an omentum, they were reluctant to infer that people also have an omentum. In general, the youngest children were very reluctant to generalize from any base other than humans to other kinds. One striking consequence of this tendency is that the youngest children were more likely to generalize from humans to bugs than from bees to bugs, despite the stronger perceptual similarity and taxonomic relation between the latter than the former pair. Carey took this asymmetry as a reflection of the underlying conceptual structure of the young child's mind, in which biological knowledge is organized around humans as the prototype humans. Let's take a closer look.

An important assumption underlying Carey's interpretation of her results is that children's development can be understood in terms of domain-specific competences. At a minimum, one can distinguish between three domains in which children form naïve theories: physics, which is concerned with the physical principles that govern the actions of objects in the world (e.g., Spelke, 1990); psychology, which deals with beliefs, desires, and intentions (Leslie, 1984; Wellman & Gelman, 1992); and biology, which revolves around knowledge of plants and animals (Carey, 1985). One issue is whether these domains are present at birth and become elaborated with development, or whether they are wholly acquired. Carey and her colleagues argued that the pattern of findings on biological induction supports the view that young children do not have a distinct naïve biology, but rather their reasoning reflects a naïve psychology where humans are the prototypical psychological entity. Only later, when children are roughly seven to ten years of age, do they acquire a distinct biology, in which humans are seen as one animal among many. Older children do generalize from bases like "dog" and "bee," and at this developmental point the asymmetries in reasoning are no longer present. Notice that on this view, there is radical conceptual change, as children's biological reasoning shifts from an intuitive theory of psychology to a naïve biology.

There are, however, lingering questions concerning Carey's interpretation. One set of questions concerns the conditions under which these asymmetries in inductive reasoning arise. We touch on this only briefly in the current chapter (see Ross et al., 2003; Gutheil et al., 1998; and Atran et al., 2001, for a broader analysis of the generality of human animal asymmetries). More central to this chapter are the questions concerning the underlying basis of the asymmetries, whenever they do arise. In the next section, we outline a broad range of possibilities, focusing initially on the observed human–nonhuman mammal asymmetries. As will be seen, most of these alternative interpretations can straightforwardly account for the human–nonhuman mammal asymmetries. Ultimately, then, it will be necessary to broaden our focus to consider asymmetries among other categories of living things, including mammals, insects, and plants, and to use these additional sets of asymmetries to select among the alternatives.

III. ALTERNATIVE INTERPRETATIONS OF ASYMMETRIES

We will consider three broad classes of interpretations of the observed asymmetries in inductive inference. Within each class there are important variations. Our analysis begins with Carey's original interpretation and moves on to consider two others.

A. Typicality Effects

The explanations included in this section are consistent with the view espoused by Carey. In essence, the argument is that the asymmetries in inductive inference reflect an underlying conceptual structure in which humans are considered the prototypical entity. There are two variants of this general view, as described below, one relying on a central-tendency notion of typicality and the other on typicality as based on ideals.

1. Inductive Confidence Displays a Central-Tendency-Based Typicality Effect. Asymmetries in inductive confidence, which have been documented in adults, have often been attributed to differences in typicality (Osherson et al., 1990). On this view, inferences from typical to atypical category examples are stronger than the reverse direction of comparison. This typicality view was endorsed by Carey (1985) to account for the human–nonhuman animal asymmetries displayed by young children. Specifically, Carey suggests that young children treat humans as the prototypic animal, and that the asymmetries are just typicality effects.

To bolster this view, one would need independent, converging evidence that young children treat humans as the prototypical animal. It would also be beneficial to provide an account of how differences in typicality lead to asymmetries. First let's consider typicality. The most common reading of typicality is in terms of central tendency – being similar to other members of the same category and dissimilar to members of contrasting categories.

On the surface it does not appear that humans look more like other animals than, say, a dog does. But if we allow frequency of exposure to examples of the concept to bias typicality (see Barsalou, 1985, for evidence that frequency of instantiation as a member of the category is the more relevant variable), then humans *should* be the prototype, at least for urban children who may have little experience with other animals.

How might typicality effect induction? Let's examine how the similarity-coverage model (SCM) of Osherson et al. accounts for typicality effects. True to its name, the model has two components. The first is similarity. The greater the similarity between the base and the target, the greater the confidence that some novel property true of the base will be true of the target. The SCM assumes that similarity is symmetrical (the similarity of A to B is the same as the similarity of B to A), and therefore asymmetries do *not* arise from the similarity component. Instead, it is the coverage component that leads to typicality effects.

The coverage component works as follows: In addition to considering the similarity of the base and target categories, the model assumes that participants generate examples of the lowest-level category that encompasses both the base and target and then compute their similarity to the base. Because participants tend to generate typical examples (even if sampling is random, because a body of other work suggests that natural object categories have a typicality structure; see Rosch & Mervis, 1975; Smith, Shoben, & Rips, 1974, for evidence and Smith & Medin, 1981, for a review), on average they will be more similar to a typical than to an atypical base. Because inductive confidence is assumed to increase with similarity, typical bases will support stronger inductive inferences since they have greater similarity than atypical bases to the examples generated by the coverage component process. For example, consider an inference from penguins to cardinals compared to an inference from cardinals to penguins. Although the SCM treats similarity as symmetrical, the latter inference is predicted to be stronger than the former. The lowest-level superordinate in each case is "bird," and participants should think of specific (and typical) birds like robin, blue jay, and sparrow. Because these are more similar to cardinals than to penguins, cardinal will be stronger than penguin as an inductive base. In short, the SCM model predicts that inference will be stronger for typical bases than for atypical bases and that the coverage component of the model can generate asymmetries.

Although this coverage component accounts for asymmetries at a theoretical level, it is hard to see how it would account for the human asymmetries observed in young children. More specifically, it is difficult to see why "humans" would have better coverage than other mammals (e.g., "dog," "wolf") since humans are not especially similar to other mammals. We might need to amend the SCM model to allow frequency to strongly affect the category examples generated and then argue that young children tend to think of humans when generating examples of the superordinate category "animal." (We note, however, that recent evidence from our ongoing developmental studies suggests that this is not the case.) A different strategy is to conceptualize humans as a prototype in the ideal, rather than similarity, sense and to use something other than the similarity-coverage model to account for the asymmetries. We now turn to this option.

2. Asymmetries May Represent Ideal-Based Prototypicality Effects. An alternative view is that asymmetries derive from typicality effects but that these typicality effects are based on ideals rather than central tendency (Medin & Atran, 2004). To get on with developing this position, two related assumptions are needed, and both of them are drawn from Carey (1985). One is the assumption that because young children do not yet have a distinct naïve biology, their biological induction draws on an undifferentiated module (in which naïve psychology and naïve biology are fused) that is organized primarily by naïve psychology. The second and uncontroversial assumption is that humans are the prototypic psychological entity. If we adopt these assumptions, we can appeal to other research (Gleitman, Gleitman, Miller, & Ostrin, 1996), suggesting that it is more natural to compare the variant to the standard than vice versa. For example, when faced with a picture of a person, we notice that the picture has a likeness to the person rather than the person having a likeness to the picture. That is, what is relevant is that the picture has some aspects of, or similitude to, the person. In the same vein, comparing nonhuman animals to humans may be much more sensible and coherent for young children than the reverse comparison. As applied to induction, the claim is that in making an inductive inference, we act as if a comparison in the natural direction is more likely to involve a shared property than a comparison in the unnatural direction. (See Medin, Coley, Storms, & Hayes, 2003, for a relevance framework that seems generally compatible with this view.)

For this view to explain human–nonhuman animal asymmetries, we will need the idea that comparisons go from the target to the base. Hence when a nonhuman animal is a target and a human is the base, the nonhuman gets compared to the (prototypic ideal) human, and it is natural to assume that the property is shared. In the reverse direction, when the standard is being compared to the variant, differences become more accessible. This position has some testable consequences. To begin with, if humans aren't the prototype (as they may not be in some populations), then asymmetries should disappear. All we need is some independent index of prototypicality to tie things down. Once we have determined a typicality ordering, we should be able to predict a range of asymmetries. In summary, from this perspective, there is nothing special about humans with respect to generating asymmetries; the results follow from the (ideal-based) typicality of humans. If we can establish a ranking of idealness, then we should be able to predict a corresponding series of asymmetries.

B. Knowledge and Experience Effects

The explanations included in this section emphasize participants' knowledge about the base and target, focusing mainly on the base. In essence, the argument is that willingness to generalize from a given base to a given target depends on how much one knows about that base. We describe three main variants of this view.

1. Knowledge Increases Projection. The first notion is that the more a participant knows about some base, the more likely they are to project from it to some target. This idea is endorsed by Kayoko Inagaki and Giyoo Hatano (2001) and fits their observation that children who have experience raising goldfish use goldfish as well as humans as a good base for inductive generalization. The paradigm used by Inagaki and Hatano is somewhat different from that employed by Carey, so one has to be careful about their interrelationships. Inagaki and Hatano have shown that children who have knowledge of certain biological properties will extend those properties to near neighbors. We, however, do not know if we would find asymmetries if a novel property were attributed to goldfish versus, say, a turtle. That is, we don't know if an inference from goldfish to turtle would be stronger than an inference from turtle to goldfish. If such an asymmetry were found, it would provide strong support for knowledge of a base driving induction.

There is also some more direct evidence consistent with the idea that knowledge or familiarity with a base increases inductive projection (Atran et al., 2001), and in the limiting case of complete ignorance about the kind in question, it seems plausible. Nonetheless, an element is missing. It is not obvious that increased familiarity or certainty should lead to a greater tendency to generalize. After all, there is classic evidence from animal learning and conditioning to suggest that increased experience (in the form of discrimination training) tends to sharpen generalization gradients.

2. History of Successes and Failures of Induction Influences Inductive Confidence. There are both philosophical and psychological analyses of why some categories support induction better than others (Goodman, 1983; Shipley, 1993). The category of "blue things" probably does not permit much by way of inferences beyond the fact that they are things that are blue, but the category of "blue jays" is rich in the sense that the members share a large number of properties besides being blue. There may be innate or rapidly acquired biases for children to treat some categories as more "entrenched" or more powerful in inductive inferences than others (Gelman, 2003). Whether or not this is the case, categories and properties (or predicates) that have a history of successful inductive potential become further entrenched, or more powerful as inductive bases, over time. Therefore, based on this history, some categories and properties will come to support more and stronger inferences than others. In the variant that we consider here, the focus is once again on the categories and properties of the bases in inductive projections.

Projections are like predictions, and if they are supported by data, they become reinforced. Here the idea is that learners have made, seen, or heard previous successful inductive projections from humans to other animals but are much less likely to have done so from other animals to animals. If children have a more successful history projecting properties from humans to other animals than from other animals to humans or to other animals, then they should be more willing to project a novel property from humans than from some other animal. One straightforward way to obtain evidence bearing on this hypothesis would be to examine the input (this could be written text or speech corpora) to ascertain whether humans are preferred over nonhuman animals as a base in the comparisons that are available to children. To take this idea one step further, distinguishing between comparisons involving physical (biological) versus psychological properties should permit us to make more detailed predictions. In any event, this view falls into the projectability category given that the history of inductive inference may give rise to greater or lesser willingness to generalize from a particular base.

3. Differences in Prior Odds or Surprisingness of Predicates. In virtually all studies of induction, researchers use "blank" properties; that is, properties for which participants have no strong a priori beliefs. This design feature is important because participants' projection or generalization of the blank property cannot be guided by a simple application of their prior knowledge. Instead, the assumption is that their projection of a blank property must be guided by a genuine inductive inference. There is, however, a wrinkle in this assumption. Although it is usually assumed that blank properties have uniform prior odds, this may not be the case. Specifically, assuming that people are experts on people, they may have lower prior odds for novel (blank) properties attributed to people than for the same properties attributed to another base. That is, participants should be more surprised to hear that humans have an omentum inside (where omentum is a novel property) than to hear that a raccoon does.

Two factors (at least) appear to support this intuition. The first involves a "lack of knowledge inference" (Collins & Michalski, 1989). This would run something like the following: "If humans had omenta inside, then I would have heard about it, so it's unlikely that they do." The second and related idea is that there may be a bias for assuming that novel properties are associated with unfamiliar categories (Testa, 1975). If so, the asymmetries will follow directly for two reasons. First, because (by hypothesis) the priors are lower for humans than for other mammals, even if the premise (regarding the target) were ignored entirely and therefore had no effect whatsoever on beliefs about the target category, blank properties should be more broadly attributed when the target is a nonhuman mammal than when it is a human. (In the limiting case they might ignore the premise and simply base judgments on prior odds for the conclusion.) Second, it is generally assumed that the more informative or surprising a premise is, the greater its effect on a target (Osherson, Blok, & Medin, 2005). We suspect that it is more surprising to hear that humans have an omentum inside than to hear that some other mammal does. Taken together, then, these two factors suggest that inferences from humans to (other) mammals should be higher than inferences from mammals to humans.

C. Distinctive Categories and Features of the Target

The previous two accounts have focused primarily on the ways in which properties of the *bases* lead to asymmetric patterns of induction. Our third class of explanations brings into sharper focus the contribution of the *targets and the relationship between the target and the base*, and represents a strong departure from prior work. Specifically, it proposes that when bases and targets are compared, inferences are limited by distinctive properties of targets, relative to the base.

1. Different Patterns of Category-Label Activation. This explanation draws on the observation that, for most individuals living in the United States, humans have a dual status: they are considered members of the inclusive category "animal" (encompassing both human and nonhuman animals) and are also members of the more specific category "human" (contrasting with nonhuman animals).[1] In contrast, nonhuman animals do not have this dual status. It is important to point out that the inductive strength of a given target is diminished by salient categories it has that do not apply to the base. These observations are relevant to inductive inference in the following way: When a human is the base and a nonhuman animal is a target, the more inclusive category "animal" gets activated, which tends to prime the broad sense of "animal" that includes humans. In contrast, when a nonhuman animal is the base and a human is the target, the distinctive category of "human" gets activated in the target, and, as we noted above, this diminishes inductive confidence to nonhuman animals. (Later on we'll see that the same sort of asymmetry may arise for plants at a more superordinate level. We suspect that because animals may be prototypical living things, plants are more distinctive members of the superordinate category "living thing" than are animals. As a result, we suspect that when a plant is the base and an animal is a target, the more inclusive category "living thing" gets activated, but when an animal is the base and a plant is the target, the distinctive category of "plant" is more strongly activated, and this diminishes inductive confidence to animals.)

What might count as evidence for this proposal? First, if this proposal is correct, it should be evident in participants' justifications for their inductions. For example, participants should mention the distinctive feature of humans (e.g., "people aren't animals") as a justification more frequently when a human is a target than when it is a base for induction. A second piece of evidence involves cross-cultural comparisons. We know that there are cultures and languages in which the contrast between humans and animals is more clear-cut than in urban and suburban English-speaking communities in the United States. For example, in Indonesia these categories are kept quite distinct, and the Indonesian names are mutually exclusive (Anggoro, Waxman, & Medin, 2005). That is, the Indonesian term for "animal" cannot be applied to humans. In such cultural contexts, we would expect to find less inductive generalization between humans and nonhuman animals, and, as a consequence, the asymmetries should be diminished. See Anggoro et al. (2005) for evidence that this is the case.

2. *Different Patterns of Feature or Property Activation.* The argument here is parallel to the previous one, but the focus is on constituent properties rather than categories. As we have suggested, in urban and suburban communities

---

[1] A further complication is that "animal" sometimes is treated as equivalent to "beast" or "mammal" or even "quadruped."

in the United States, humans certainly can be considered animals, but they may also be considered to be a special case, namely, as animals with more distinctive features than other animals (e.g., humans are special because they talk, have beliefs, construct buildings, cook their food, etc.). The core idea, then, is that inductive inferences from nonhuman animals to humans should be diminished whenever the distinctive features of humans are activated, and such features are activated more when humans are the target than when they are the base. This follows from the idea that induction begins with a focus on the target category. By logic, the same should hold for any animal, human or nonhuman, whenever participants attribute more distinctive features to the target than to the base. In other words, there is nothing special about humans (save their distinctive features). If this is the case, then for any distinctive category (e.g., "goldfish" for Inagaki and Hatano's goldfish caretakers), generalizing a novel property (e.g., from goldfish to frogs) should be stronger than generalizations in the opposite direction (e.g., from frogs to goldfish). This would follow if the young goldfish caretakers knew more distinctive features about goldfish than about frogs.[2]

The account in terms of distinctive features of the target concept is not new. For example, Sloman's (1993) feature-based induction model assumes that distinctive features of the target category reduce inductive confidence more than the distinctive features of premise or base categories. Sloman (1993) also reports a variety of data from undergraduate populations, including asymmetries in inductive reasoning, supporting this assumption.

The feature-activation account shares similarities with the typicality account in that typicality is reduced by distinctive features. But note that the predictions are opposite in form – the feature activation story has it that distinctive features of the target category reduce induction, and this implies a reverse typicality effect. That is, when the premise or base is atypical and the target is typical, inductive confidence should be greater than in the reverse ordering.

3. Relevance and Distinctive Features. This position can be seen as a modest variation on either or both of the first two explanations in this class. The idea is that asymmetries of induction are not based on overall similarity but rather on matches and mismatches of a subset of features that appear to be

---

[2] Note that, as in the assumption for category activation above, we are attributing to this view the claim that the distinctive features of the target affect induction more than do distinctive features of the base. This is the opposite of Tversky's (1977) claim that it is the distinctive features of the base that receive more weight in asymmetries (in similarity judgment). This point is worth noting, but it is also worth noting that the induction paradigm is considerably different from a similarity-judgment paradigm.

most relevant in the experimental context. The motivating principle is that similarity comparisons are mainly focused on how things are similar rather than on how similar they are (Medin, Goldstone, & Gentner, 1993).

This position is compatible with the two others in this section, as long as one comes down on the side of distinctive features of the target being more important than those of the base. We cannot think of a compelling reason for why this should be the case, but, as we shall see, it appears to hold for our developmental data. In general, one would expect that if a salient property of some target is also a feature of the base, then inductive confidence should increase (and if it isn't, confidence should decrease). For example, an argument from "skunk" to "zebra" should be stronger than from "zebra" to "skunk" because the most distinctive property of zebras (being striped) is also shared by skunks (note that the reverse does not hold). This seems like a pretty strong (and perhaps incorrect) prediction in that a hypothesis-based model of induction (McDonald, Samuels, & Rispoli, 1996) would clearly make the opposite prediction – "skunk" should give rise to two hypotheses (odor, stripes) and "zebra" only one (stripes). To evaluate this position it would be important to obtain an independent measure of distinctive features.

Of course, relevant features of both the base and the target might well matter. There is good evidence that there are at least two different strategies for comprehending conceptual combinations (see Wisniewski, 1997, for a review) and that which of the two is more prominent depends on the similarity of the base and target (more technically on their alignability). In the case of induction the idea would be that for a base and target within the same lifeform, the base and target are aligned and induction is therefore limited by distinctive features of the base. For bases and targets that are from different lifeforms (and for humans versus other animals), attention would shift to salient properties and categories of the target. This idea is certainly testable.

4. Summary. We will stop with these three main classes of explanation for asymmetries in induction, though there certainly are others.[3] It should be

---

[3] Here are two additional possibilities:

1. Causal associations produce the asymmetry. Many causal relations have directional implications for induction. If Grass has Enzyme x, we are more sure that Cows have it than we are sure that Grass has Enzyme Y given that Cows have it (Medin et al., 2003). For this argument to work, the causal associations should be more likely in the human to (other) animal case than in the (other) animal to human case. One major problem with this explanation is that among populations of children where we see this sort of reasoning (see Ross et al., 2003, for details), the associations we see involving humans tend to have humans as an effect rather

clear that human–nonhuman animal asymmetries reported by Carey do not unambiguously implicate any one theoretical account over others.

IV. BROADENING THE VIEW: ANALYZING A WIDER RANGE OF CATEGORIES

We suggest that the most straightforward means of obtaining some leverage in choosing among the alternative accounts is to consider additional asymmetries in inductive reasoning. For example, if asymmetries are based on relative amounts of knowledge about bases and targets, then they should appear wherever there are demonstrable differences in knowledge, independent of whether humans are involved in the comparison. It seems uncontroversial that children being raised in urban and suburban communities in the United States know more about mammals than they do about plants, so one should expect mammal-plant asymmetries in which mammal to plant inductions are stronger than plant to mammal inductions. In this section we will look at data from an expanded analysis of asymmetries. We first describe a few cautionary notes to consider when comparing across different methods and populations, since a number of studies have examined the generality of Carey's results across populations and procedures (e.g., Atran et al., 2001; Ross et al., 2003) but have not followed Carey's procedure in every detail. Using this as a foundation, we go on to present evidence on a wider range of asymmetries.

A. Cautionary Notes in Comparing across Studies and Populations

First, although in Carey's original design the same kinds appear as both base and target,[4] in most recent instantiations of the category-based induction task this is not always the case. This difference in design may have consequences

---

than a cause (e.g., bees stinging humans). If this position has value, it may be in explaining why human-animal asymmetries are not found in some cases.

2. Asymmetries are mediated by size differences between base and target. There are two motivations for this idea. One is that both Itza' Maya and tree experts sometimes explicitly refer to relative size on induction tasks and argue that going from large to small (tree species) is more likely than going from small to large (Medin et al., 1997). The other impetus for worrying about size is that children may worry about it. Hatano and Inagaki (2003) observed that children sometimes deny that ants have hearts on grounds that they are too small to contain a heart. Note, however, that this example cuts the other way in that a property true of ants will fit into human dimensions, but the converse is not true. Still, it may be that, in induction, there is a big-to-small bias.

[4] Humans are the exception to this generalization. Although humans have consistently been presented as both bases and targets, the specific other mammal, insect, or plant that has been a base is rarely also a target.

on patterns of performance: A human–nonhuman animal asymmetry may be a consequence of differences in the similarity of the base versus target animals to humans (e.g., human to bears inferences may be stronger than squirrel to human inferences, not because of any inherent asymmetry but because bears and humans are more similar than bears and squirrels). Ideally, we would have studies where we equate for base and target similarity and have the same items as both base and target, at least across participants but ideally within participants. In our ongoing work, we have designed experiments in this way, but we do not yet have sufficient data to report on. Still, because we find that most of our findings consistently hold across studies, across populations, and across a variety of stimulus materials, the patterns of asymmetries reported below are sufficiently strong to support our main empirical claims.

There is a second difference between Carey's design and the more recent versions. In Carey's original version of the task, four- and six-year-olds were trained and tested on separate days, though this apparently was not done for older children and adults. On the first day, children were taught about "spleen" or "omentum" within the context of a review/probe of other, presumably more entrenched properties like "has lungs" or "has a heart." Moreover, the teaching was fairly elaborate. Children saw a diagram that indicated the location of the omentum, but there was no explicit appeal to other kinds that might or might not have that property. They were then tested on the novel property (e.g., "Does a dog have an omentum?") at a later date and within the context of the more familiar properties (e.g., "Does a dog have a heart?"). One consequence of this design difference is that children in Carey's study may have treated the probes regarding the novel property more as a test of knowledge than as an invitation to make an inductive inference. This raises the interesting possibility that there is a fundamental difference between spontaneous inference (as in Carey's task) versus prompted inference (as in Atran et al.'s and Ross et al.'s tasks). In this regard, we note that Inagaki and Hatano's work may be conceptually aligned to Carey's. In their work, they provided a group of young children with extensive experience with goldfish, and later examined children's spontaneous inferences (Inagaki, 2002). In any case, we suspect that if children view the probes as a test of knowledge, this would raise the threshold on their willingness to project from a base to a target – this account would still need to explain why this might happen for "dog" and "bee" as bases but not for "humans." A third difference between Carey's design and the more recent versions pertains to the inclusion criteria. Carey's analyses included only those children who correctly attributed the novel property (e.g., "omentum" or "spleen") to the base on which it was introduced.

Finally, and perhaps most interestingly, there are differences in the types of participants included in the original Carey task as compared to more recent work. Several recent studies have moved beyond the urban and suburban populations to examine how children raised in rural environments, who enjoy a more intimate contact with nature, reason about the biological world. We have found that children raised in rural environments sometimes appeal to "ecological reasoning," focusing on potential mechanisms of transmission of a property from one biological kind to another. For example, when they are told that "bees have sacra inside them," these children often infer that bears must also have sacra, and they justify their responses by mentioning that sacra could be transmitted when a bee stings a bear or when a bear eats honey (Ross et al., 2003).[5] The problem, however, is that when ecological reasoning is combined with procedures where base and target items are not counterbalanced, the problems loom larger. For example, "bee" may be a better base for supporting ecological reasoning than "fly." The bottom line is that skeptics might want to defer judgments about the claims we make in the next section.

B. Additional Asymmetries Help to Constrain the Alternative Theories

In this section we focus on the patterns of asymmetries produced by children and adults from a range of communities, in urban and rural U.S. settings and in rural Mexico. The primary data of interest, taken from Ross et al. (2003),[6] appear in Table 3.1. In this study children were told that humans, wolves, bees, or goldenrod had some novel biological property (e.g., "has sacra inside") and then were asked if they thought that other animals, plants, and inanimate things would also have sacra inside them. We refer the reader to the original article for methodological details, but we include the table here to permit readers to check our assertions about patterns of asymmetries. A number of the individual comparisons no doubt fall short of statistical reliability, but the trends are generally quite robust across populations.

---

[5] We should also note that in the causal-reasoning literature, there are some well-documented asymmetries in which it is easier to reason from cause to effect than vice versa (see Kahneman & Tversky, 1974, for asymmetries in causal judgment). In principle, at least some of the explanations that we have been considering might apply here as well.

[6] We also have considerable data from a study which follows up and expands on these studies with additional populations including Yukatek Maya children, majority culture and Menominee children from rural Wisconsin, and Chicago area urban and suburban children (see also Atran et al., 2001). In most cases we also have adult data but not always in sufficient quantity to be reported (yet). Although we do not present these data, they consistently support and expand the claims we make here from published data.

TABLE 3.1. *Ross et al. (2003) induction probabilities, indicating asymmetries*

	Ross et al. – Asymmetries							
Population	City		Rural			Menominee		
Age	7–9	9–11	5–7	7–9	9–11	5–7	7–9	9–11
Human-Mammal	0.70	0.73	0.52	0.58	0.80	0.58	0.70	0.72
Mammal-Human	0.33	0.35	0.24	0.16	0.47	0.42	0.47	0.52
Mammal-Mammal	0.96	0.90	0.76	0.78	0.92	0.75	0.82	0.88
Human-Insect	0.47	0.35	0.07	0.34	0.63	0.46	0.55	0.48
Insect-Human	0.31	0.08	0.28	0.20	0.53	0.63	0.35	0.38
Human-Plant	0.50	0.27	0.16	0.17	0.30	0.30	0.22	0.34
Plant-Human	0.13	0.12	0.10	0.12	0.30	0.42	0.41	0.38
Mammal-Insect	0.50	0.38	0.38	0.28	0.47	0.57	0.56	0.52
Insect-Mammal	0.50	0.56	0.38	0.25	0.56	0.56	0.56	0.56
Mammal-Plant	0.32	0.12	0.14	0.14	0.22	0.18	0.33	0.24
Plant-Mammal	0.32	0.38	0.24	0.25	0.42	0.50	0.42	0.46
Insect-Plant	0.40	0.44	0.26	0.30	0.58	0.46	0.40	0.42
Plant-Insect	0.31	0.62	0.24	0.34	0.33	0.29	0.41	0.43

Finding 1. Human to Nonhuman Mammal Asymmetries. As we noted before, studies on this topic have tended to use different mammals as base and target; humans are essentially the only kind that have appeared as both base and target. Despite this nontrivial concern, it nonetheless appears as if the human to nonhuman mammal asymmetry is fairly robust. The key finding is that this asymmetry never reverses. Although there may be cultural factors moderating the relationship (compare, for example, the evidence for this asymmetry in Ross et al., 2003, vs. Atran et al., 2001[7]), we suggest that the human–nonhuman mammal asymmetry is strong.

Finding 2. Human to Mammal vs. Mammal to Mammal Asymmetries. This result is not an asymmetry, but it constrains explanations of asymmetries. In Carey's view, young children lack a theory of folkbiology and rely instead on a theory of folkpsychology in which humans serve as the prototype. If this were the case, then inferences from humans to other nonhuman mammals should be stronger than from one nonhuman mammal (in our case: wolf, dog, peccary) to another. To the best of our knowledge, Carey is the only researcher who has found this pattern of results. The results of Table 3.1 reveal the opposite pattern. Although the absolute level of human to mammal

---

[7] The asymmetry was clear for "peccary" as a base but essentially absent with "dogs" as a base. This provides some support for knowledge or familiarity affecting induction. Nonetheless, familiarity will not account for the other asymmetries even within the Atran et al. data.

inferences ranges across groups, the (other) mammal to mammal inferences are always higher. This pattern of reverse typicality, apparent at each age and in all of our populations, strongly undermines the argument that humans serve as the prototypic animal for either young children or adults. On the contrary, the data suggest that throughout development, humans retain a somewhat atypical status within the animal category, and that it is something of a conceptual achievement when young children notice that humans are, in fact, also animals.

Finding 3. Human to Plant Asymmetries. In contrast to the previous result, here the asymmetries appear to vary across populations, and as a result, no clear overall pattern emerges. Urban children show a strong asymmetry favoring humans over plants as a base, rural children show little generalization and no asymmetry, and Menominee children show a reverse asymmetry. One possibility is that this pattern is a consequence of a shift to increasing use of ecological/causal reasoning across groups, but additional research is required to tie this down.

Finding 4. Mammal to Plant Asymmetries. A review of Table 3.1 reveals that the rate of generalization between mammals and plants is limited. However, we do see a consistent trend in favor of reverse asymmetries, with more inductive inferences from plants to mammals than from mammals to plants. This reverse asymmetry pattern holds for all but one (seven- to nine-year-old urban children show no difference) of the age and population samples.

Finding 5. Human to Insect Asymmetries. This set of comparisons is currently limited because the data are quite variable and in most cases include only one target insect (fly). In the Ross et al. (2003) data, asymmetries seem to be present for the urban children, but they are weak and in a few cases reversed for the rural and Menominee children. In the Atran et al. (2001) data, the asymmetries diminish with age and are sharply reversed in adults. This is consistent with the possibility that ecological reasoning (e.g., generalizing from a bee to a bear by suggesting that the property might be in honey, which the bear eats, or transmitted via a bee sting) increases with presumed intimacy of contact with nature. For more recent data with native and exotic bases intermixed, where we appear to have eliminated ecological reasoning, there is a pretty consistent asymmetry. This asymmetry appears to be larger for the exotic set of bases than the native set ("bee" versus "tarantula" as the base) for all but the Yukatek children.

Finding 6. Mammal to Insect Asymmetries. There's no reliable trend across populations and there are no really notable differences. Comparing human-insect arguments with mammal-insect arguments, the main difference is that insect to mammal inferences are higher than insect to human inferences. Note also that humans to insects inferences are consistently lower than mammals to insects inferences.

Finding 7. Insect to Plant Asymmetries. In the Ross et al. (2003) data, where the trends are a bit variable, there doesn't seem to be any clear overall asymmetry. For the newer data with mixed native and exotic bases there is a consistent pattern of reverse asymmetries (plant to insect being greater than insect to plant), though in several cases the effects are small because there is little overall generalization between insects and plants (especially compared to the generalization seen in Ross et al., 2003).

Other Asymmetries. A careful examination of other asymmetries in Table 3.1 reveals no consistent pattern across populations or age groups. As we noted earlier, we are suspicious of comparisons involving insects because base (bee) and target (fly) were not counterbalanced and may differ substantially in the availability of children's ecological/relational knowledge. In some follow-up studies we have unwittingly more or less eliminated ecological reasoning, and these induction data provide still stronger asymmetry constraints.

C. Bringing the Evidence from CBI to Bear on the Theoretical Alternatives

The results from this wider range of categories provide us with a stronger foundation from which to choose among the alternative theoretical accounts of the asymmetries in induction. With respect to potential for asymmetries (greater inductive confidence when the category is in the base position rather than the target position), we have an overall ordering of human and plant greater than insect and mammal (and insect greater than mammal when ecological reasoning is eliminated). In addition, we consistently find that mammal to mammal inferences are stronger than human to mammal inferences. As we'll see, these orderings place strong constraints on theories of induction. We'll now go through them, one by one.

1. Typicality Effects. Neither variant of typicality theory can explain these patterns of asymmetries. If humans are the prototype, then inferences from human to (nonhuman) mammal should be stronger than those from another mammal to mammals, and this was not the case. Instead, the ordering with respect to asymmetries may conform better to a reverse typicality gradient, suggesting that mammals are the most prototypical biological entity and humans the least. If typicality alone cannot account for the underlying basis for asymmetries, perhaps an account in which typicality is considered in conjunction with similarity would fare better. The proposal would be that humans are the ideal animal but, at the same time, are not especially similar to other mammals. But this account seems to add a new parameter for every data point it attempts to explain. Moreover, it provides no account of the plant to mammal asymmetry (and the simultaneous absence of a human to plant asymmetry). In short, the evidence from the broadened range of observations undermines the view that typicality effects can account for the human-animal asymmetries.

2. Knowledge/Familiarity Effects. The idea that inductive strength increases with knowledge about the base is also challenged by our observations. It is plausible to suggest that children know more about humans than other biological kinds, but it is extremely unlikely that they know more about plants than insects and more about insects than mammals. Therefore, none of the knowledge-based accounts would seem to predict the observed ordering.

3. Distinctive Features and Categories. The final class of explanations provides a nice account of the Ross et al. (2003) data. One can explain most of the results by claiming that "animal" (as opposed to "plant") is the most prototypical member of the category "living thing," and that most nonhuman mammals (as opposed to humans) are the most prototypical members of the category "animal." As a result, when reasoning about biological entities, humans are the most distinctive (either in terms of their features or in terms of categories), followed closely by plants. Insects and nonhuman mammals are less distinctive. Specifically, according to this account, when a base premise is given and a target suggested, participants compare the target to the base. Distinctive features or category memberships of the *target* reduce inductive confidence more than distinctive features of the base. So if (as we have suggested), with respect to distinctive features and categories, humans are equally or slightly more distinctive than plants, and if both are much more distinctive than insects or mammals, the following implications are straightforward:

1. Human to mammal should be stronger than mammal to human
2. Human to mammal should be weaker than other mammal to mammal
3. Plant to mammal should be stronger than mammal to plant

4. Plant to insect should be stronger than insect to plant
5. Human to insect should be stronger than insect to human
6. No clear human/plant asymmetry (trends should favor human to plant) or insect/mammal asymmetries (trends might favor insect to mammal).

This pattern conforms closely with the data. So far this looks very good for the distinctive features/categories position. The major limitation in what has been presented so far is that we have relied on intuitive notions of distinctive features and categories without providing any direct evidence bearing on them. Justification data, to be presented next, do provide some converging evidence for the distinctive features/categories account.

D. Bringing More Evidence to Bear: Justification Data

Children's justifications for their responses in the inductive inference task bear directly on the distinctive features/categories view. If the distinctive features/categories position is correct, then failures to generalize from a base to a target should be accompanied by justifications focusing on the distinctive features and categories of targets rather than bases. For example, a child should justify her failure to generalize from humans to raccoons by saying that raccoons have a tail or raccoons are animals. In contrast, a failure to generalize from squirrels to humans should bring with it comments that humans are not animals or that humans have two legs (and squirrels four).

At this point in our investigation, we have extensive justifications only from rural, majority culture children in Ross et al. (2003) (with a few additional justifications from Menominee children; they don't spontaneously offer justifications with sufficient frequency to justify reporting them). However, these justifications provide clear support for the distinctive features/categories account. The pattern about to be described holds for human-mammal and mammal-insect inferences. Both groups of rural children show the same qualitative trends. Furthermore, the younger and older rural, majority culture children show the same pattern, though the younger children focus relatively less on distinctive categories and relatively more on distinctive features.

First, we can also examine justifications to see if they focus on distinctive features/categories of the base versus those of the target. The answer is quite clear: The justifications overwhelmingly (95% or better, depending on the sample) focus on distinctive features and categories of the *target* object.[8]

---

[8] Importantly, this is true both for what one might call "alignable features" (Markman & Gentner, 1997) that reflect different values on a common dimension (e.g., number of legs) and for nonalignable features (e.g., presence versus absence of a tail). This not only points to the

We next consider the extent to which justifications focus on common versus distinctive features and categories. For this purpose we examined the relative numbers of common versus distinctive features and converted the numbers to proportions. For human to mammal inferences, the ratio of common to distinctive features is 0.64 for young children and 0.68 for older children. In other words, the majority of the time children mentioned common features. The corresponding ratio for mammal to human is 0.25 and 0.19 for the younger and older ages, respectively. That is, relatively speaking, children mention distinctive features much more often when humans are the target for induction than when they are the base.

The same pattern holds for shared versus distinctive categories. The ratio of common to distinctive categories for human to mammal is 0.23 and 0.77 for the younger and older ages, respectively. When the comparison shifts to mammal to human, these proportions drop to 0.12 and 0.43, respectively. Again, distinctiveness is more salient when humans are in the target position for induction. For mammal to insect inferences, exactly the same qualitative trends are observed in both age groups. For example, the young children show a common to distinctive features ratio of 0.22 in the insect to mammal case and a ratio of 0.00 in the reverse direction. The corresponding proportions for common to distinctive categories are 0.38 and 0.10, respectively. This pattern is noticeably absent for the human-insect justification data, where the young children give only distinctive features and distinctive categories regardless of the direction of comparison. Older children show a very slight tendency to have more common features and categories in the human to insect direction.

E. Summary

Overall, the induction data coupled with the justifications provide detailed support for the distinctive features/categories account (see also Sloman, 1993). They also highlight the importance of focusing on the target, the base, and the relation between them. On this view, we suggest that humans have the most distinctive features/categories, followed closely by plants, then insects and mammals. Note that other explanations for the pattern of asymmetries can, in principle, describe some of these trends, but they do so only by imposing some implausible assumptions. For example, consider the alternative view that differences in knowledge underlie the asymmetries. To capture the full range of data, this view would have to make the dubious claim that children

robustness of the focus on the target object but also undermines the idea that children might focus on the base for comparisons of alignable targets and the target for nonalignable targets. A further problem for this two-process account is that this same focus on the target category also holds for the mammal-mammal probes.

have more knowledge about plants than mammals. The same difficulty holds for accounts that appeal to ideals, histories of induction, or prior odds. Only the distinctive features/categories proposal can account for the ordering of asymmetries that emerge in the data.

V. IMPLICATIONS

What are the important implications of these findings? First, we suggest that the human-animal asymmetries that have been observed in category-based induction tasks do not bear on the status of bases as being either more familiar or better examples than targets. More generally, we suggest that accounts which focus primarily on the *base* are theoretically and empirically insufficient, for they cannot account for the range of asymmetries that emerge in children's inductive inferences about the biological world.

We have argued that the most promising explanation for the observed asymmetries in inductive inference is one that focuses on the target, the base, and the relation between them. More specifically, we suggest that such an account must incorporate not only the categories and features of the target, but also the distinctive categories and features that emerge when the target is compared with the base. This more inclusive view can account for the full pattern of asymmetries, the observation that nonhuman mammal to nonhuman mammal inferences are stronger than human to nonhuman mammal inferences, and the patterns of justification provided by children in category-based induction tasks. When it comes to categories, it appears that mammals are animals and little else, other than a specific kind of animal. Specific plants may be both plants (as a contrast with animals) and living things. Humans both contrast with and constitute animals. These categorical distinctions are paralleled by corresponding differences in distinctive features as a function of comparison direction.

A review of the literature reveals that, as is often the case, the seeds of this account are evident in previous work. For example, the idea that distinctive features of the target may be weighted more than distinctive features of the base is directly taken from Sloman's (1993) feature-based induction model. As another example, we point out that at least one earlier model of induction, the similarity-coverage model (Osherson et al., 1990), also drew on categories and relations among categories to account for patterns of inductive inference.

However, the account that we have offered here, the distinctive categories/features account, goes beyond its progenitors in (at least) three ways. First, it broadens the range of categories that are relevant for induction.

Second, it considers the relation between the coordinate categories in the target and base rather than relying on inclusion relations between bases and their superordinates. Third, our account highlights a role for language. We suggest that category names may play a more instrumental role in biological induction than previous accounts would suggest (see Waxman, 2005, for an amplification of this point and Anggoro et al., 2005, for an example involving Indonesian). Waxman has described the various inclusion and contrast classes associated with different biological kinds and outlined some of the ways in which these categories may influence children's learning about biological properties. Her results and ours suggest that the reasoning task provides a window on how different categories are conceptualized.[9]

The analysis that we have offered in this chapter is intriguing and appears to account well for the phenomena at hand. At the same time, however, the distinctive features/categories hypothesis would benefit from a fuller treatment of several issues. For example, it will be important to examine more closely the patterns of inference across different cultural and language groups. It will also be important to examine more closely the role of ecological reasoning in patterns of inductions. Although we have touched only briefly on this issue here, we do have data suggesting that intermixing native and exotic bases and targets largely eliminates ecological reasoning. In future work we would like to prime ecological reasoning and employ a design where categories appear as both base and target in order to examine the relationship between ecological reasoning and asymmetries more systematically. We also plan to explore ways of collecting independent evidence on the distinctive features and categories of bases and targets that arise in the comparison context.

In summary, we think that asymmetries in induction are theoretically significant, despite the fact that there are many contending, plausible accounts of human-animal asymmetries. As is often the case, broadening the set of empirical constraints allows us to gain leverage on these alternative theoretical explanations of asymmetries. The main theoretical implication of our work is that researchers should shift attention away from the inductive base alone in favor of examining the *relationship* between target and base. This relationship gives rise to distinctive features and categories and suggests new avenues for research on the interplay between categories and inductive reasoning. Finally,

---

[9] It may be possible to translate distinctive features/categories back into typicality language – in this view mammals are the typical biological organism, followed by insects and then plants and humans. Next you have to claim that comparing the variant to the standard yields a stronger induction than vice versa and that it's better (in terms of induction likelihood) to have distinctive properties in the base than in the target. Unless there's some obvious novel prediction that we're missing, this seems like a notational variation on the distinctive categories/features idea.

returning to Carey's original work, our data suggest that the human-animal asymmetries observed in the induction paradigm do not indicate that humans are typical or ideal animals. Instead the full range of evidence converges on the opposite conclusion – that humans are not singled out for their prototypicality as animals, but for their marked distinctiveness.

References

Anggoro, F., Waxman, S., & Medin, D. (2005). The effect of naming practices on children's understanding of living things. Paper presented at Cognitive Science 2005, Stresa, Italy.

Atran, S., Medin, D., Lynch, E., Vapnarsky, V., Ucan Ek', E., & Sousa, P. (2001). Folkbiology doesn't come from folkpsychology: Evidence from Yukatek Maya in cross-cultural perspective. *Journal of Cognition and Culture, 1,* 1–40.

Baillargeon, R. (1994). How do infants learn about the physical world? *Current Directions in Psychological Science, 3*(5), 133–140.

Barsalou, L. W. (1985). Ideals, central tendency, and frequency of instantiation as determinants of graded structure in categories. *Journal of Experimental Psychology: Learning, Memory, & Cognition, 11*(4), 629–654.

Carey, S. (1985). *Conceptual change in childhood.* Cambridge, MA: Bradford Books.

Collins, A., & Michalski, R. (1989). The logic of plausible reasoning: A core theory. *Cognitive Science, 13,* 1–49.

Gelman, S. A. (2003). *The essential child: Origins of essentialism in everyday thought.* New York: Oxford University Press.

Gelman, S. A., & Markman, E. M. (1986). Categories and induction in young children. *Cognition, 23*(3), 183–209.

Gleitman, L. R., Gleitman, H., Miller, C., & Ostrin, R. (1996). Similar, and similar concepts. *Cognition, 58*(3), 321–376.

Goodman, N. (1983). *Fact, fiction, and forecast.* New York: Bobbs-Merrill. (Original work published 1955.)

Gutheil, G., Bloom, P., Valderrama, N., & Freedman, R. (2004). The role of historical intuitions in children's and adults' naming of artifacts. *Cognition, 91*(1), 23–42.

Gutheil, G., Vera, A., & Keil, F. C. (1998). Do houseflies think? Patterns of induction and biological beliefs in development. *Cognition, 66*(1), 33–49.

Hatano, G., & Inagaki, K. (1994). Young children's naive theory of biology. *Cognition, 50*(1–3), 171–188.

Hatano, G., & Inagaki, K. (2003). The formation of culture in mind: A sociocultural approach to cognitive develoment. In J. Meheler, S. Carey, & L. L. Bonatti (Eds.), *Cognitive development and conceptual change.* Cambridge, MA: MIT Press.

Hatano, G., & Inagaki, K. (2002). *Young children's thinking about the biological world.* New York: Psychology Press.

Inagaki, K., & Hatano, G. (2001). Chidren's understanding of mind-body relationships. In M. Siegal & C. Peterson (Eds.), *Children's understanding of biology and health.* Cambridge, UK: Cambridge University Press.

Johnson, S., & Carey, S. (1998). Knowledge enrichment and conceptual change in folkbiology: Evidence from Williams syndrome. *Cognitive Psychology, 37*(2), 156–200.

Kahneman, D., & Tverksy, A. (1973). On the psychology of prediction. *Psychological Review, 80,* 237–251.

Leslie, A. M. (1984). Infant perception of a manual pick-up event. *British Journal of Developmental Psychology, 2*(1) (Mar 1984), 287–305.

Markman, A. B., & Gentner, D. (1997). The effects of alignability on memory. *Psychological Science 8*(4), 363–367.

McDonald, J., Samuels, M., & Rispoli, J. (1996). A hypothesis-assessment model of categorical argument strength. *Cognition, 59*(2), 199–217.

Medin, D. L., & Atran, S. (2004). The native mind: Biological categorization and reasoning in development and across cultures. *Psychological Review, 111*(4), 960–983.

Medin, D. L., Coley, J. D., Storms, G., & Hayes, B. K. (2003). A relevance theory of induction. *Psychonomic Bulletin & Review, 10*(3), 517–532.

Medin, D. L., Goldstone, R. L., & Gentner, D. (1993). Respects for similarity. *Psychological Review, 100*(2), 254–278.

Medin, D. L., Lynch, E. B., Coley, J. D, & Atran, S. (1997). Categorization and reasoning among tree experts: Do all roads lead to Rome? *Cognitive Psychology, 32,* 49–96.

Medin, D. L., & Smith, E. E. (1981). Strategies and classification learning. *Journal of Experimental Psychology: Human Learning & Memory, 7*(4), 241–253.

Osherson, D. N., Smith, E. E., Wilkie, O., Lopez, A., & Shafir E. (1990). Category-based induction. *Psychological Review, 97*(2), 185–200.

Rosch, E., & Mervis, C. B. (1975). Family resemblances: Studies in the internal structure of categories. *Cognitive Psychology, 7*(4), 573–605.

Ross, N., Medin, D., Coley, J. D., & Atran, S. (2003). Cultural and experimental differences in the development of folkbiological induction. *Cognitive Development, 18*(1), 25–47.

Shipley, E. F. (1993). Categories, hierarchies, and induction. *Psychology of Learning and Motivation, 30,* 265–301.

Sloman, S. A. (1993). Feature-based induction. *Cognitive Psychology, 25,* 231–280.

Smith, E. E., & Medin, D. L. (1981). *Categories and concepts.* Cambridge, MA: Harvard University Press.

Smith, E. E., Shoben, E. J., & Rips, L. J. (1974). Structure and process in semantic memory: A featural model for semantic decisions. *Psychological Review, 81*(3), 214–241.

Spelke, E. S. (1990). Principles of object perception. *Cognitive Science, 14*(1), 29–56.

Testa, T. J. (1975). Causal relationships and associative formation. *Dissertation Abstracts International, 35*(12-B, Pt 1), 6147.

Tversky, A. (1977). Features of similarity. *Psychological Review, 84*(4), 327–352.

Waxman, S. R. (2005). Why is the concept "Living Thing" so elusive? Concepts, languages, and the development of folkbiology. In W. Ahn, R. L. Goldstone, B. C. Love, A. B. Markman, & P. Wolff (Eds.), *Categorization inside and outside the laboratory: Essays in honor of Douglas L. Medin.* Washington, DC: American Psychological Association.

Waxman, S. R., Lynch, E. B., Casey, K. L., & Baer, L. (1997). Setters and samoyeds: The emergence of subordinate level categories as a basis for inductive inference in preschool-age children. *Developmental Psychology, 33*(6), 1074–1090.

Wellman, H. M., & Gelman, S. A. (1992). Cognitive development: Foundational theories of core domains. *Annual Review of Psychology, 43*(1), 337–375.

Wisniewski, E. J. (1997). When concepts combine. *Psychonomic Bulletin & Review, 4*(2), 167–183.

4

Property Generalization as Causal Reasoning

Bob Rehder

Induction – reasoning to uncertain conclusions – appears in many forms. In some cases one makes an uncertain inference about a specific object or event. Given a particular dog, one asks whether it is safe to pet it; given a particular berry, one asks if it is safe to eat it (e.g., see Chapter 8 by Murphy & Ross, this volume). But in other cases one makes *inductive generalizations* that are intended to characterize an entire class of situations or objects. On the basis of a finite number of medical cases, one might induce a general causal law, such as that unsafe sex can cause AIDS or that mosquitoes can cause malaria. Or, from a few examples one might make a generalization about a property being displayed by many or most members of a particular category, such as that koalas eat bamboo, Apple laptops have fire-prone batteries, or Madagascar Fire Ants have poisonous venom. This chapter is concerned with *category-based generalizations* such as these in which new properties are projected to an entire class of objects.

Let's consider a couple of examples intended to illustrate two different models of the reasoning processes which are supposed to underlie category-based generalizations. Suppose you are introduced to someone from Uzbekistan, the first person from that country you have ever met. During your otherwise pleasant conversation, you realize that this person has bad breath, and you are led to wonder whether bad breath is common among Uzbekistanis.[1] If you knew nothing about Uzbekistan, you'd probably be unlikely to jump to the conclusion that bad breath was a characteristic national trait.[2] But suppose

---

[1] No offense to the people of Uzbekistan, whose country was chosen at random from the too-long list of countries about which I know virtually nothing. The suggestion that Uzbekistani's have bad breath (or, as alleged below, that they eat salted fish, drink vodka, or don't wear business suits) is a figment of the author's imagination.

[2] Actually, you would be justified in thinking that its prevalence is slightly higher in Uzbekistan, because you do have a sample – albeit a very small one of size 1 – of people from Uzbekistan

that you actually know a little bit more about Uzbekistan. For example, imagine that you know how Uzbekistanis traditionally dress, some characteristic facial features, common religious beliefs, and so on. According to one prominent theory, you will be more likely to think that bad breath is frequent among Uzbekistanis if your new friend has many of these typical Uzbekistani traits, as compared to if he is, say, wearing a Western-style business suit, endorses a traditional western religion (e.g., Roman Catholicism), and so on.

Do you find this example compelling? Perhaps my intuitions have been ruined by reading too many papers about induction, but I can't say that I do. I might be *slightly* more willing to endorse the generalization about bad breath on the basis of typical or characteristic features, but not by much, and I think the reason has to do with the second model of category-based generalization illustrated by the next example. You're chatting with the Uzbekistani, but now, instead of knowing a few typical properties of people from that country, you know a few of the causes of bad breath. Let's say you know that eating salted fish causes bad breath, and so too does drinking vodka. You then learn from the Uzbekistani that salted fish is one of the staples of the Uzbekistani diet and that vodka is consumed at every meal. Now suddenly the idea that large numbers of Uzbekistanis frequently have bad breath doesn't seem so far fetched after all.

The first example suggesting that generalizations are based on an example's typicality is the province of the well-known *Similarity-Coverage Model* of category-based induction (Osherson, Smith, Wilkie, Lopez, & Shafir, 1990) discussed in numerous places throughout this volume (also see Sloman, 1993, for a related model). For example, according to the Similarity-Coverage Model (hereafter SCM), people will be more confident that all birds have some new property (e.g., sesamoid bones) when given an example of a sparrow with sesamoid bones as compared to a penguin, because sparrows are more typical birds than penguins (and thus, on this account, provide more "coverage" of the features of the bird category). Likewise, the model would predict that you would generalize bad breath to Uzbekistanis more strongly if your one example was typical and thus covers the "Uzbekistani" category more completely. In addition to coverage, the second component of the SCM – similarity – allows it to account for generalizations between categories that are not hierarchically nested. For example, people will be more confident that

with bad breath. After all, if bad breath is as uncommon in Uzbekistan as everywhere else, it is pretty surprising that the one Uzbekistani you get to meet just happens to be one of the few that have bad breath. But all depends on your beliefs regarding the prior distribution over the prevalence of bad breath. If you believe that either everybody in a country has bad breath or no one does, then the single example would be enough to conclude in favor of the former.

blackbirds have sesamoid bones given the fact that crows do as compared to sparrows, because (according to the SCM) blackbirds are more similar to crows than sparrows.

In contrast, the second mode of reasoning, referred to here as *generalization as causal reasoning* (hereafter GCR), focuses on the specific causal explanations which might lead one to believe that most or all members of a particular category display a particular property. Although it may be vague or incomplete, one often has at least some general idea of the type of causal mechanisms which produce or generate particular properties, and this knowledge can be used to estimate the prevalence of that property in some population (i.e., category of object). This view also explains why, despite the predictions of the SCM, the influence of typicality may be uncompelling in certain cases. For example, I usually attribute bad breath to a transient property – something consumed at a recent meal for instance – and this makes me reluctant to consider bad breath a stable property of even that individual person, to say nothing of the person's nationality, ethnicity, or any other group he or she might belong to. It also leads me to believe that the fact that the person is or is not displaying a typical property on some other dimension (their clothing style) is irrelevant to the question of generalizing bad breath. Of course, to be fair to the SCM, it was never intended to be a model of the mental processes that arise when one has knowledge of the causal mechanisms which might generate the to-be-generalized property. Famously, its predictions were intended to apply only to "blank properties" (like sesamoid bones) about which one has no prior knowledge. Nevertheless, the example illustrates how easy it may be for its similarity-based processes to be supplanted by explanation-based ones.

Moreover, it may often be the case that even when more typical examples *do* support stronger generalization, they do so not because of typicality per se, but rather because of the distinct pattern of reasoning that a typical example may support. For example, if you, unlike me, did think that a Uzbekistani dressed in traditional clothing justified a stronger generalization, I suspect you did so because you recognized that (a) bad breath can be attributed to a stable property such as the person's *diet*, (b) because diets and ways of dress covary, this diet (whatever it is) may be common to many Uzbekistanis, and therefore (c) so too is bad breath. But although this makes you a deeper reasoner than me, you are *reasoning* nonetheless, not just basing your judgment on some unanalyzed notion of typicality.

This chapter is divided into three sections. The first will present the current empirical evidence that people in fact engage in causal reasoning when generalizing properties. This evidence will come both from studies testing the effects of "background" causal knowledge – knowledge which subjects possess before the experiment starts – and from those which instruct subjects on causal knowledge as part of the experiment. The assumption is that both sorts of studies are useful. Establishing results with background knowledge helps provide some assurance that the reasoning processes involved are likely to be evoked in real-world contexts. Experimental materials, in turn, allow the controls necessary to distinguish specific hypotheses from one another. Two specific models of how causal knowledge influences category-based generalizations will be discussed.

The second section will address the relationship between causal reasoning and the similarity-based effects on property generalization. The claim here is not that similarity never influences generalizations, or that similarity-based processes are mischaracterized by the SCM, but rather that they and causal reasoning processes coexist side-by-side in the mental toolbox of processes which support induction. But when similarity and causality can each form the basis of a generalization, do people weigh (equally or unequally) both sources of information, or does one mode of reasoning override or suppress the other? I will review evidence suggesting that when causal information is available, it largely eliminates similarity-based influences.

The first two sections address the influence of the causal relations which directly relate existing category features and a to-be-generalized novel property. But what of the influence of causal relations not involving the novel property which relate features of the category to one another? The final section will discuss how such relations change the *coherence* of category, and by so doing promote the strength with which novel properties are generalized.

PROPERTY GENERALIZATION AS CAUSAL REASONING

There are now numerous sources of evidence that people reason causally in order to generalize properties. I first discuss the studies involving background causal knowledge, but, because recent reviews of this research already exist (Heit, 2000; Rips, 2001), only a few example will be covered here. I will then turn to more recent research testing causal relations which are provided as part of the experimental session.

Research with Background Causal Knowledge

One of the first studies suggesting that property generalization can depend on causal knowledge was conducted by Heit and Rubinstein (1994). Recall that, according to the SCM, a novel property will be generalized from one category to another to the extent that the categories are similar.[3] In particular, the SCM does not allow for how such generalizations might depend on the property itself, by virtue of, say, the specific causal mechanisms it is involved in. Heit and Rubinstein showed otherwise. They found, for example, that a behavioral property (e.g., travels in a zig-zag path) was generalized more strongly from tunas to whales as compared to from bears to whales. This result may have been expected on the basis of the fact that whales are more similar to tunas than bears. But when the novel property was biological rather than behavioral (e.g., a liver with two chambers that acts as one), it was generalized more strongly from bears to whales instead. Why should this reversal arise despite the fact that the categories involved (bears, tunas, and whales) were unchanged, and thus so too were the similarity relations? One explanation is that participants thought that bears and whales share biological properties (such as two-chambered livers), because such properties are likely to arise from causal mechanisms associated with their common biological category, that is, mammals. Tunas and whales, on the other hand, are more likely to share a survival behavior (traveling in a zig-zag path) because they are both prey animals living in a common ecology (also see Gelman & Markman, 1986, and Springer & Keil, 1989).[4]

Sloman (1994, 1997) has provided other examples of how a property will be more strongly generalized when the causal history which leads to a property in a base category is also present in the target. For example, he found that undergraduates were more willing to project a feature like "hired as bodyguard" from war veterans to ex-convicts, presumably because the underlying explanation (fighting experience makes for a good bodyguard) for war veterans also applies to ex-convicts. In contrast, they were less to willing to project the property "unemployed," apparently because the reasons for unemployment of war veterans (physical injury, PTSD) does not apply to ex-convicts. Note again that these different results obtained despite the fact that similarity was held constant (in both cases war veterans were the base and ex-convicts were the target).

Finally, Smith, Shafir, and Osherson (1993) also found that subjects apparently engaged in a form of causal reasoning when generalizing hypothetical

---

[3] Technically, according to the SCM generalizations between non-hierarchically nested categories are a function of not only their similarity but also the coverage the premise provides for the lowest-level superordinate category that includes both premise and target categories. This more precise definition is unimportant for what follows.

[4] Note that Heit and Rubinstein themselves attributed these results to subjects computing similarity between the base and target differently depending on whether the novel property was anatomical or behavioral. I'll return to this issue in the Discussion.

properties of familiar categories. For example, undergraduates were more likely to generalize the property "can bite through barbed wire" to German Shepherds from poodles than from Dobermans. This result obtained despite the fact that German Shepherds are more similar to Dobermans than to poodles. It seems that the participants were reasoning about the causal preconditions for the capacity to bite through barbed wire, and judged that a German Shepherd certainly could do so if a small dog like a poodle could, but not necessarily if the base category was another powerful dog (also see Osherson, Smith, Myers, & Stob, 1994).

Thus, there appears to be good reason to suspect that causal reasoning is intimately involved in the generalization of properties. But although suggestive, studies testing background knowledge are often correlational in nature, and thus there is always the possibility that the results arise due to factors other than causal knowledge itself. For this reason, some researchers have adopted a purely experimental approach in which subjects are presented with category members that display novel properties which are accompanied by a description of the (previously unknown) causal factors that led to their presence. The precision with which this approach allows causal knowledge to be manipulated has led to the first specific theories regarding how such knowledge affects property generalization, as I now describe.

Research with Experimentally-Provided Causal Knowledge

The theories which have been advanced thus far have been concerned with how a to-be-generalized property is related to a category's existing features. The first of these appeals to the notion of *feature centrality* (Hadjichristidis, Sloman, Stevenson, & Over, 2004). Features are more central to the extent they have many features which "depend on" them, or, equivalently, to the extent they are responsible for generating or producing many other features (Sloman, Love, & Ahn, 1998). One purported role for centrality is in determining a feature's importance to an object's category membership and its degree of typicality within a category. For example, a bird with all the characteristic features of robins except that it has unusual coloring is a more typical robin (and more likely to *be* a robin) than one with all the characteristic features of robin except for robin DNA. According to the centrality account, robin coloring is less central than robin DNA (and thus less important for establishing category membership) because coloring depends on DNA and not the other way around (Ahn, 1998; Ahn et al., 2000; see Rehder, 2003a, b; Rehder & Kim, 2006, for an alternative view).

Hadjichristidis et al. (2004) have proposed that the concept of centrality is also important to induction, suggesting that novel properties which are central are more likely to be generalized from one category to another. For example, suppose one person believes that many of a seal's physiological functions depend on a particular hormone, whereas another believes that only a few such functions depend on it. According to the centrality account, the hormone will be more central for the first person than the second. Hadjichristidis et al. suggest that the hormone will as a result not only be more important for identifying an animal as a seal for the first person, but he or she will also be more likely to generalize it to another category (say, dolphins). But they point out that the strength of generalization will also depend on whether the hormone is viewed as being central *in the target category*, which in turn depends on whether the hormone's "dependency structure" (e.g., the physiological functions) also appears in the target category. People will sometimes know enough about the target category to make this determination directly. But when they don't, Hadjichristidis et al. suggest that reasoners use the similarity between the base and target to estimate the amount of shared dependency structure. Thus, a hormone which is responsible for a seal's physiological functions is more likely to be present in dolphins than sparrows, because the similarity between seals and dolphins suggests they have many physiological functions in common (and thus also the hormone). In contrast, the dissimilarity between seals and sparrows suggests that they share many fewer physiological functions (and thus not the hormone).

Hadjichristidis et al. (2004, Experiment 2) tested this hypothesis by varying a novel property's centrality (e.g., a fictitious hormone was depended on by either many physiological functions, few such functions, or no information about dependency was provided) and the similarity of the base and target category (high, medium, or low). As predicted, central properties (with many dependents) were projected more strongly than less central properties (with few dependents), which in turn were stronger than properties with no dependents (Fig. 4.1). Also as predicted, Figure 4.1 also shows how the strength of this effect was moderated by the similarity of the two categories: Centrality had its greatest effect when the target category was very similar to the base category.

These findings provide one important illustration of how interfeature causal relations influence property generalization. However, one can ask if characterizing these results in terms of feature centrality alone artificially limits the scope of the effect of causal knowledge on such generalizations. This leads to the second theory of property generalization which treats such generalizations as an instance of causal reasoning (Rehder, 2006). According to this view, one computes whether a novel feature is likely to appear in a

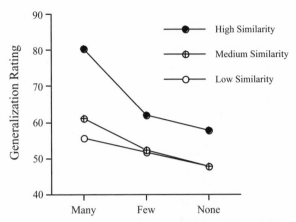

FIGURE 4.1. Number of dependents of novel property. Results from Hadjichristidis et al. (2004), Experiment 2.

target category not on the basis of any one characteristic of the feature (e.g., its centrality), but rather on the basis of one's beliefs about the causal laws which relate the feature to those of the target category.

The generalization as causal reasoning view (GCR) makes (at least) three predictions regarding how causal knowledge supports category-based generalizations. The first of these is that property generalization can be an instance of *diagnostic reasoning* in which one reasons from the presence of a novel property's effects to the presence of the novel property itself. The second prediction is that generalizations can reflect *prospective reasoning*, in which one reasons from the presence of the causes of a novel property to infer the presence of the property. The third prediction is that generalizations should exhibit the basic property of *extensional reasoning* in which a novel property will be more prevalent among category members to the extent its causes and/or effects are prevalent. As it turns out, each of these predictions has received empirical support.

EVIDENCE FOR DIAGNOSTIC REASONING. According to GCR, a property will be generalized to the extent that its presence can be inferred on the basis of the effects it is likely to produce. That is, generalization can be seen as that species of causal reasoning in which one "diagnoses" the presence of a property within category members on the basis of whether its "symptoms" (effects) are present in those objects.

The results from Hadjichristidis et al. (2004) just presented can be interpreted as just such a case of diagnostic reasoning. The fact that physiological functions "depend on" a hormone can be understood as the hormone causing or enabling those functions. Thus, the presence of one or more of the same physiological functions in another species "diagnoses" the presence of the hormone in that species. However, one complicating factor is the possibility that in the target species those physiological functions have different causes (e.g., different hormones). For this reason, the inference to the hormone is more certain when *multiple* of its "symptoms" (physiological functions) are present.[5] This situation is more likely to be true to the extent that the base and target categories are similar rather than dissimilar (Figure 4.1).

EVIDENCE FOR PROSPECTIVE REASONING. GCR not only reinterprets evidence in favor of the feature centrality view as a case of causal reasoning, it also makes new predictions which distinguish it from the feature centrality view. The second prediction of GCR is that a property will be generalized to the extent that the cause or causes which produce it are present in the target category. On this view, generalization can be seen an instance of prospective reasoning in which one reasons from causes to effects rather than from effects to causes.

To start, note that each of the demonstrations of the effect of background knowledge presented earlier implicates the role of the causal mechanisms which produce a novel property, such as when bears and whales are likely to posses the same kind of liver on the basis of the shared biological mechanisms of mammals (which presumably generate their internal organs). The prospective reasoning view also receives support from studies which manipulate causal knowledge experimentally. For example, Rehder (2006) instructed undergraduates on an artificial, but plausible, category, such as Romanian Rogos (a type of automobile). Rogos were described as having four characteristic features, each of which was described as occurring in 75% of category members: butane-laden fuel, loose fuel-filter gasket, hot engine temperature, and large amount of carbon monoxide in the exhaust. A single example of a Rogo was then presented with a novel property, and subjects were asked whether a second Rogo was likely to have that property. On some trials no causal explanation of the novel property was provided. For example, subjects would

---

[5] Whether one finds multiple versus few symptoms more diagnostic of an underlying common cause will depend on the details of the causal beliefs involved. If one believes there is no other possible causes of the symptoms, then even just one symptom is sufficient to infer the cause with certainty. Also relevant is whether the cause is deterministic (produces its effects with probability 1) or probabilistic. A deterministic cause invariably produces all of its effects, and thus the presence of the cause is ruled out if even one of its effects is absent. For a probabilistic representation of causality see Rehder (2003a, b) and Cheng (1997). For discussion of a deterministic versus probabilistic view of causaility, see Thagard (1999).

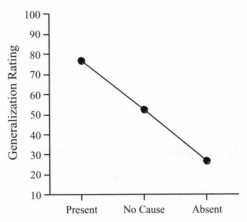

FIGURE 4.2. Cause of novel property. Results from Rehder (2006), Experiment 3.

be presented with a Rogo that had ceramic shocks, and then judged what proportion of all Rogos had ceramic shocks. Properties like ceramic shocks were chosen because they have no obvious causal connection with the other known properties of Rogos (e.g., butane-laden fuel, carbon monoxide in the exhaust, etc). But on other trials the novel property was described as being caused by one of the Rogo's characteristic features. For example, subjects would be presented with a Rogo which had a typical property (e.g., hot engine temperature) and a novel property (e.g., melted wiring) and told that the typical property caused the novel one ("The melted wiring is caused by the high-engine temperature"). A second Rogo was presented which either did or did not have high-engine temperature, and subjects were asked whether it had melted wiring.

The results, presented in Figure 4.2, shows that the novel property was generalized very strongly when its cause was present in the target Rogo, very weakly when it was absent, and with an intermediate rating when no information about causal mechanism was provided. The results were the same regardless of whether the category was an artifact (e.g., Rogos), a biological kind, or a nonliving natural kind. Clearly, subjects reason forward (prospectively) to infer a novel property's presence from the presence of its causes as readily as they reason backward (diagnostically) to infer a property's presence from its effects (also see Lassaline, 1996, and Wu & Gentner, 1998).

EVIDENCE FOR EXTENSIONAL REASONING. A third prediction of GCR is that generalizations should exhibit extentional reasoning in which the prevalence of a novel property depends on the prevalence of its causes and/or effects. For example, the prevalence of a hormone in a target category shouldn't depend on just the *number* of physiological functions it causes, but also how widespread those functions are amongst the population of target category members. Similarly, the prevalence of melted wiring caused by hot engines in a brand of automobile should depend on what proportion of those automobiles in fact have hot engines.

Maya Nair and I decided to test this prediction by explicitly manipulating the prevalence of a category feature which was the purported cause (or effect) of a novel property (Nair, 2005). The same categories as in Rehder (2006) were used (including Romanian Rogos), and subjects were asked what proportion of all Rogos had a novel property on the basis of a single example of a Rogo with that property. Two factors were manipulated as within-subjects variables. The first was the base rate of the characteristic feature. Two randomly chosen features of Rogos were described as occurring in 90% of Rogos, whereas the other two were described as occurring in 60%. The second orthogonal factor was whether the novel property was described as *caused by* or as the *cause of* one of the characteristic features. The characteristic features, the novel properties, and the causal relationships between the two are presented in Table 4.1 for Rogos. For example, some subjects would be presented with a Rogo which had all four characteristic features and a novel property (e.g., zinc-lined gas tank) and told that one of the typical properties caused the novel one. ("Butane-laden fuel causes a zinc-lined gas tank. The butane interacts with the chromium in the metal of the gas tank, which results in a thin layer of zinc on the inside of the tank.") Other subjects would be told that the novel property was the *cause of* the typical property. ("A zinc-lined gas tank causes the fuel to be butane-laden. The zinc prevents corrosion of the tank, but interacts chemically with gasoline to produce butane.") All subjects would then rate what proportion of all Rogos possessed the novel property. Each subject performed four generalization trials in which the four novel properties in Table 4.1 were each presented once, either as a cause and effect of a characteristic feature, and with the base rate of the characteristic feature (e.g., butane-laden fuel) described as either 90% or 60%.

Generalization ratings from this experiment are presented in Figure 4.3A as a function of whether the novel property was the cause or the effect and the base rate of the typical property. There was a strong effect of base rate, as subjects' generalization ratings were much higher when the novel property was causally related to a characteristic feature with a 90% versus a 60% base rate. Moreover, this result obtained regardless of whether the characteristic feature

TABLE 4.1. *Features and causal relationship for Romanian Rogos, an artifical category*

Characteristic Feature	Novel Feature	Characteristic Feature → Novel Feature	Novel Feature → Characteristic Feature
Butane-laden fuel	Zinc-lined gas tank	Butane-laden fuel causes a zinc-lined tank. The butane interacts with the chromium in the metal of the gas tank, which results in a thin layer of zinc on the inside of the tank.	A zinc-lined gas tank causes the fuel to be butane-laden. The zinc prevents corrosion of the tank, but interacts chemically with gasoline to produce butane.
Loose fuel filter gasket	Vibrations during breaking	A loose fuel filter gasket causes vibrations during braking. The fuel which leaks through the fuel filter gasket falls on one of the brake pads, causing abrasion which results in the car vibrating while braking.	Vibration during breaking causes a loose fuel filter. The rattling caused by the vibrations eventually leads to the fuel filter gasket becoming loose.
Hot engine temperature	Thin engine oil	Hot engine temperature causes thin engine oil. The oil loses viscosity after it exceeds a certain temperature.	Thin engine oil causes hot engine temperature. Thin oil does not provide sufficient lubrication for the engine's moving parts, and the engine temperature goes up as a result.
High amounts of carbon monoxide in the exhaust	Inefficient turbocharger	High amounts of carbon monoxide in the exhaust causes an inefficient turbocharger. As the exhaust leaves the engine it passes through the turbocharger. The lower density of carbon monoxide in the exhaust means that the turbocharger is not sufficiently pressurized.	An inefficient turbocharger causes high amounts of carbon monoxide in the exhaust. An inefficient turbocharger fails to inject enough oxygen into the engine, and so excess carbon does not undergo combustion.

A

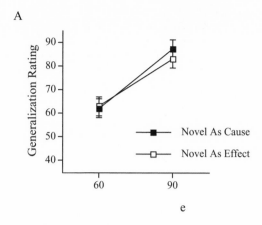

e

B

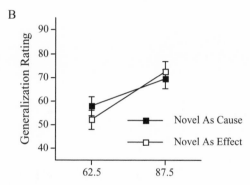

FIGURE 4.3. Observed base rate. Results from Nair (2005).

was the cause or effect of the typical property. In other words, subjects readily engage in the extensional reasoning which characterizes causal reasoning more generally.

In a follow-up experiment, we asked whether these results would obtain when the feature base rates were observed rather than given through explicit instruction. Informal post-experiment interviews in the first experiment revealed that the base rate manipulation was very powerful. Although generalization ratings were entered by positioning a slider on a computer-displayed scale which was not labeled numerically (one end was simply labeled "None," meaning that no Rogos have the novel property; the other end was labeled "All," meaning they all do), a number of subjects reported trying to position the marker at a point that they felt corresponded to 60% or 90%. That is, if a novel property was causally related to a typical property with a base rate

TABLE 4.2. *Category structure from Nair (2005),*
Experiment 2, consisting of eight Rogos (R1–8) and
eight non-Rogos (NR1–8).

	D1	D2	D3	D4
Rogos				
R1	1	1	0	1
R2	1	1	0	1
R3	1	1	0	1
R4	1	1	1	0
R5	1	1	1	0
R6	1	1	1	0
R7	0	1	1	1
R8	1	0	1	1
Non-Rogos				
NR1	0	0	1	0
NR2	0	0	1	0
NR3	0	0	1	0
NR4	0	0	0	1
NR5	0	0	0	1
NR6	0	0	0	1
NR7	1	0	0	0
NR8	0	1	0	0

of 90% (or 60%), many subjects felt that that property would be displayed by *exactly* 90% (or 60%) of Rogos. To determine if the extensional reasoning effect obtained only because the base rates were explicit, we performed a replication of the first experiment in which the feature base rates were learned implicitly through a standard classification-with-feedback task. In the first phase of the experiment subjects were asked to learn to distinguish Romanian Rogos from "some other kind of automobile." They were presented with the exemplars shown in Table 4.2, consisting of eight Rogos and eight non-Rogos. In Table 4.2, a "1" stands for a typical Rogo feature (e.g., loose fuel filter gasket, hot engine temperature, etc.), whereas each "0" stands for the opposite value on the same dimension (e.g., tight fuel filter gasket, cool engine temperature, etc.). The thing to note is that on two of the dimensions (Dimensions 1 and 2 in Table 4.1), the typical Rogo feature is very typical, because it occurs in seven out of eight Rogos (or 87.5%). On the other two dimensions (3 and 4), the characteristic feature is less typical, occurring in five out of eight Rogos (or 62.5%). The structure of the contrast category (the non-Rogos) is the mirror image of the Rogos.

The items in Table 4.2 were presented in a random order in blocks, subjects classified each and received immediate feedback, and training continued until subjects performed two blocks without error or reached a maximum of twenty blocks. They then performed the same generalization task as in the previous experiment in which whether the novel property was the cause or effect was crossed with the base rate of the typical Rogo feature (87.5% or 62.5%). The results of this experiment are presented in Figure 4.3B. The figure indicates that subjects in this experiment, just like those in the first one, took the base rate of the characteristic feature into account when generalizing the new property. They did this even though the difference in base rates between features was manifested in observed category members rather than provided explicitly. That is, people take into account the prevalence of that characteristic feature in the population of category members when generalizing the novel property, and they do so regardless of whether a novel property is the effect or cause of a characteristic feature. Note that in both experiments from Nair (2005), the results were unaffected by whether the category was a novel artifact, biological kind, or nonliving natural kind.

In summary, studies provide strong evidence that people are exhibiting some of the basic properties of causal reasoning when generalizing properties. When many of a novel property's effects are present in a category, people reason (diagnostically) to the presence of the property itself. People also reason (prospectively) to the presence of the property as a function of whether its causes are present or absent in the target. Finally, people are sensitive to how prevalent a novel property's cause (or effect) is among the population of category members.

WHEN CAUSALITY AND SIMILARITY COMPETE
IN PROPERTY GENERALIZATION

The preceding research firmly establishes the influence of causal explanations on how properties are generalized to categories. Another important question concerns how those explanations interact with the influences of similarity which have been formalized by the Similarity-Coverage model (SCM). Does each of these sources of evidence contribute (perhaps unevenly) to the generalization of a property, or do people choose to generalize on the basis of one source of evidence alone? As it turns out, research suggests that causal explanations not only influence generalizations, but they may also largely undermine, or supplant, similarity-based processes. Once again, I will first briefly review studies testing background knowledge, and then turn to the results from studies using experimentally-provided causal knowledge.

Research with Background Causal Knowledge

To investigate the role of causal knowledge in property generalization, a number of studies have compared how inductive reasoning varies across populations which differ in the nature and amount of background knowledge. For example, Lopez, Atran, Coley, Medin, and Smith (1997) studied category-based generalizations among the Itza' Maya (an indigenous population in central Guatemala), and found that the Itza' failed to exhibit standard *diversity effects*. Diversity refers to the fact that a more diverse set of base examples leads to stronger generalizations. All else being equal, people are more likely to conclude that all birds have sesamoid bones given that a dissimilar set of birds do (e.g., sparrows, hawks, and chickens) as compared to if the birds are more similar (e.g., sparrows, robins, and bluejays). Diversity effects are predicted by the SCM because less similar base categories provide better coverage of the target category. But Lopez et al. found that the Itza' failed to exhibit diversity effects, as they frequently appealed to specific causal mechanisms instead (e.g., judging that the prevalence of a disease in a species depended on the mechanisms which might spread that disease). In contrast, American undergraduates exhibited standard diversity effects on the same items (also see Bailenson, Shum, Atran, Medin, & Coley, 2002).

Of course, these findings could be attributed to some cultural difference between Americans and the Itza' other than domain knowledge (such as a difference in their default reasoning strategy). Contra this interpretation however, the dominance of causal explanations also holds for Americans who possess sufficient domain knowledge. Proffitt, Coley, and Medin (2000) tested three groups of North American tree experts (taxomomists, landscapers, and maintenance workers) to determine how they generalized a novel property of trees (an unspecified disease) as a function of the typicality and diversity of base categories (species of trees). Not only did two of the three groups of experts (the landscapers and maintenance workers) fail to exhibit diversity effects (just as the Itza' failed to), none of the groups exhibited standard typicality effects. Instead, the experts frequently reasoned in a manner which reflected their causal understanding of disease processes, such as the susceptibility or resistance of certain species to diseases, the geographic distribution of a tree species (more disperse species infect more trees), and the specific mechanisms by which diseases are transmitted from one tree to another (also see Bailenson et al., 2002; Shafto & Coley, 2003).

Finally, there is ample evidence that causal reasoning in support of induction is not limited to the rarefied world of domain experts (such as the Itza' or landscapers). Testing American undergraduates, Medin, Coley, Storms, and Hayes (2003) found, for example, that a more diverse set of premise categories consisting of a mammal and a bird (cats and sparrows) supported *weaker* generalizations (e.g., of a blank property "enzyme X") to lizards as compared to a less diverse set of two mammals (cats and rhinos). Apparently, the fact that cats eat sparrows suggested to subjects a possible causal mechanism by which enzyme X might be shared by them but not by lizards, which are in a different food chain. Similarly, the more diverse set of categories again consisting of a mammal and a bird (pigs and chickens) resulted in weaker generalization to cobras as compared to a less diverse set of two mammals (pigs and whales). It may have been that pigs and chickens were both recognized as farm animals, which suggested one or more candidate causes of the novel property (e.g., being injected with antibiotics). Inductions were then weaker because those candidate causes are absent in cobras.

These studies make a strong case that, in the presence of causal knowledge, similarity-based factors may become largely irrelevant to how people choose to generalize examples. Can we also find evidence for this conclusion when causal relations are manipulated experimentally?

Research with Experimentally Provided Causal Knowledge

To answer this question Rehder (2006) conducted a series of experiments which assessed how causal explanations moderate those effects of similarity on property generalization predicted by the SCM. Each experiment used a two-factor design in which one factor was the presence or absence of a causal explanation, and the second factor was either typicality, diversity, or similarity itself. This design of these experiments allowed a demonstration of SCM's standard similarity-based effects in the absence of causal explanations, and how those effects are moderated when such explanations are present.

CAUSAL EXPLANATIONS VERSUS TYPICALITY. American undergraduates were instructed on artificial categories like Romanian Rogos which possessed four characteristic features each described as occurring in 75% of category members. They were then presented with a particular Rogo that exhibited a novel property and asked to judge what proportion of all Rogos had that property. On some trials, the novel property was accompanied by a causal explanation (e.g., the Rogo was said to have melted wiring, which was caused by its hot engine temperature), whereas on other trials the novel property was "blank," that is, no explanation was provided (e.g., ceramic shocks). The second experimental factor was the typicality of the Rogo, which had either 1, 2, 3, or 4 characteristic features. A Rogo always possessed at least the characteristic feature which was described as the cause of a novel property (e.g., hot engine temperature in the case of melted wiring).

Based on the SCM, the prediction of course was that the generalization of blank properties would strengthen with the number of characteristic features. The critical question concerned whether typicality would also affect the generalization of novel properties when a causal explanation was present. The results are presented in Figure 4.4A as a function of whether a causal explanation was provided and the typicality of the exemplar. As expected, generalization ratings for blank properties increased as the exemplar's typicality (i.e., its number of characteristic features) increased, indicating that this experiment replicated SCM's standard typicality effect for blank properties. However, Figure 4.4A indicates that this effect of typicality was reduced when a causal explanation was provided.

One important question is whether the response pattern shown in Figure 4.4A is manifested consistently by all participants, or whether it arose as a result of averaging over individuals with substantially different response profiles. In fact, two subgroups of participants with qualitatively different responses were identified, shown in Figures 4.4B and 4.4C. The subgroup in Figure 4.4B produced higher induction ratings for the nonblank properties as compared to the blanks, that is, they were more willing to generalize a novel property when accompanied by a causal explanation. Importantly, however, whereas ratings for blanks properties were sensitive to typicality, typicality had no effect on the generalization of the nonblanks. In contrast, the second subgroup in Figure 4.4C did not generalize nonblanks more strongly than blanks, and both types of properties were equally sensitive to typicality. In other words, when reasoners chose to base their responses on the causal explanations (as evidenced by the nonblank's higher ratings in Figure 4.4B), there was no effect of typicality; when they chose to base their responses on typicality, there was no effect of causal explanations (Figure 4.4C). Apparently, the use of a causal explanation versus typicality is an all-or-none matter, with reasoners using one strategy or the other, but not both.

CAUSAL EXPLANATIONS VERSUS DIVERSITY. In a second experiment, Rehder (2006) also assessed how the presence of a causal explanation for a novel property moderates the diversity effect. Diversity was manipulated by presenting two category members with five stimulus dimensions with the same novel property. The two category members exhibited either low diversity (i.e., they shared all five features) or high diversity (they shared only one feature). (The

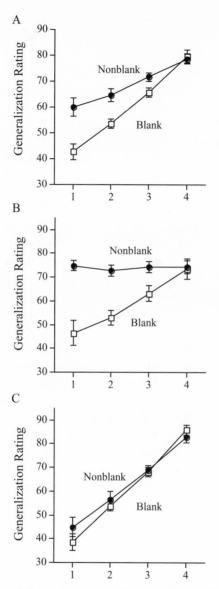

FIGURE 4.4. Number of features in source example. Results from Rehder (2006), Experiment 1.

two exemplars were chosen so that both always had three features, so that their typicality was held constant across low- and high-diversity trials.) Whether the novel property had a causal explanation was manipulated orthogonally. On the basis of the SCM, the prediction was that the generalization of blank novel properties would be stronger when displayed by more diverse pairs of exemplars. The critical issue concerned the effect of causal explanations on the diversity effect.

In contrast to the previous experiment in which all subjects exhibited a typicality effect with blank properties, only half of the subjects in this experiment exhibited a diversity effect with blank properties. This result is in keeping with the literature demonstrating the diversity heuristic's general lack of robustness relative to typicality (Lopez, Gelman, Gutheil, & Smith, 1992; see Heit, 2000, for a review). The important result, however, is that when a causal explanation for a novel property was provided, any effect of diversity disappeared entirely. That is, just as in the previous experiment, the presence of a causal explanation can eliminate the effect of one of the SCM's similarity-based heuristic (in this case, diversity). Apparently, explanations direct attention away from features which would normally contribute to how well a category is "covered" by the exemplar(s) displaying a novel property. When this occurs, the typicality or diversity of those exemplars becomes irrelevant to the generalization.

CAUSAL EXPLANATIONS VERSUS SIMILARITY. As mentioned, the SCM predicts that generalizations between items that are not hierarchically nested will be influenced by their similarity. To determine how causal explanations affect the influence of similarity, Rehder (2006, Experiment 3) asked participants to generalize a property from one category member to another. One experimental factor was whether the base and target exemplars shared three of four features (high similarity condition) or only one (low similarity condition). (The base and target were chosen so that they always possessed three and two characteristic features, respectively, so that their typicality was held constant over similarity conditions.) The other factor was whether a causal explanation was provided for the novel property. For blank properties, SCM's prediction was that the generalization will be stronger for high versus low similarity targets. The critical question concerned the influence of similarity on nonblank properties.

The results are presented in Figure 4.5 as a function of the similarity between the base and target exemplar, and whether the novel property was blank or nonblank (and, if nonblank, whether the cause feature was present or absent in the target). As predicted by the SCM, blank properties were more strongly projected when the target exemplar was more similar to the base exemplar. Also as expected, nonblank properties were more strongly projected when the cause of that property appeared in the target exemplar versus when it

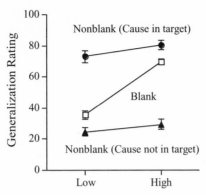

FIGURE 4.5. Similarity of source and target. Results from Rehder (2006), Experiment 3.

did not appear. The important finding is that the projection of nonblank properties was much less sensitive to the similarity of the base and target exemplar. (Unlike the previous two experiments, the group-level pattern of responding, shown in Figure 4.5, was exhibited by virtually all participants.) Once again, it appears that the effect of causal explanations is to draw attention away from features not involved in the explanation, with the result that the two exemplars' similarity becomes largely irrelevant to how strongly a novel property is generalized from one to the other.[6]

At first glance it may seem that these results conflict with those from Hadjichristidis et al. (2004) which showed that novel properties were projected more strongly as a function of the similarity between the base and target (Figure 4.1). Recall however that Hadjichristidis et al.'s claim is that similarity will be used to estimate dependency structure when its presence in the target category is otherwise uncertain. This situation was manifested in their experiments by referring to a hormone's dependents as nameless "physiological functions," making it impossible to determine whether those specific functions were present in the target category. In contrast, in the current experiment subjects were told exactly which category features were causally related to the novel feature, a situation which apparently invited them to largely ignore how the base and target might be similar on other dimensions.

---

[6] Note that in this experiment the effect of similarity was not *completely* eliminated (as the effects of typicality and diversity were eliminated in the first two experiments), as the generalization rating of nonblank properties was on average 6 points higher (on a 100 point scale) when the base and target were similar as compared to dissimilar, a difference which reached statistically significance. Nevertheless, note that the magnitude of this similarity effect is vastly lower than it is for blank properties (34 points). (See Lassaline, 1996, for related results.)

In summary then, these three experiments support the claim that when a causal explanation for a novel property is available, it often supplants similarity as the basis for the generalization of that property. First, in the first experiment all participants exhibited an effect of typicality for blank properties, but half of those participants showed no sensitivity to typicality when the novel property was accompanied with a causal explanation (nonblanks). Second, in the second experiment half the participants exhibited sensitivity to diversity for blank properties, but that sensitivity was completely eliminated for nonblanks for all participants. Finally, in the third experiment virtually all participants exhibited sensitivity to similarity for blanks, but this effect was (almost) completely eliminated for nonblanks. Apparently, when people note the presence of a causal explanation for a novel property, it often draws attention away from the exemplars' other features, making their similarity (or typicality or diversity) largely irrelevant to the inductive judgment.

PROPERTY GENERALIZATION AND CATEGORY COHERENCE

The preceding studies have addressed how the causal relations in which a novel property is directly involved influence the generalization of that property. But what of causal relations not involving the property itself, such as those between the category's existing features? For example, we know not only that birds have wings, fly, and build nests in trees, but also that they build nests in trees because they can fly and fly because they have wings. We know not only that automobiles have gas, spark plugs, and produce carbon monoxide, but also that gas and spark plugs interact to produce the carbon monoxide. How does the *coherence* a category gains by these causal relations affect the degree to which it supports the generalization of new blank properties, such as sesamoid bones (for birds) or ceramic brakes (for automobiles)? Once again, light on this question has been shed by studies testing both background and experimentally provided causal knowledge.

Research with Background Causal Knowledge

Numerous studies have demonstrated that natural categories differ in systematic ways in the degree to which they support generalization. In one study, Gelman (1988) found that second graders, but not preschoolers, were more likely to generalize new properties to natural kinds rather than to artifacts. She attributed this result to folk theories about the coherence of natural kinds acquired by the older children. On this account, the coherence provided by emerging theories of biological kinds led the older children to expect such kinds to be more structured and constrained, and hence more homogenous. Novel properties of biological kinds are generalized more strongly because this expectation of homogeneity extends to new properties in addition to existing one (also see Gelman et al., 1988; Shipley, 1993).

Additional evidence comes from studies investigating which level in a taxonomic hierarchy supports the strongest inductions. Coley, Medin, and Atran (1997) presented both American undergraduates and the Itza' with a subspecies (e.g., black vultures) that exhibited an unspecified disease and then tested the degree to which that disease was generalized to vultures (a category at the *species* or *folk-generic level*), birds (the *life form level*), or all animals (the *kingdom level*). They found that for both groups the strength of generalizations dropped substantially when the target category was at the life form level or higher. Again, biological species appear to be especially potent targets of inductive generalizations (also see Atran, Estin, Coley, & Medin, 1997).

One notable aspect of these latter findings is the fact that American undergraduates, like the Itza', treated the species level as inductively privileged despite the well-known result that for these individuals the *basic level* is normally one level higher in the hierarchy, namely, at the level of life form (e.g., tree or bird) rather than species (e.g., oak or robin) (Rosch, Mervis, Gray, Johnson, & Boyes-Braem, 1976). One explanation that Coley et al. offer for this discrepancy is that whereas the *explicit* knowledge that the American students possess (which is tapped, for example, by the various tasks used by Rosch et al., such as feature listing) is sufficient only for life forms to emerge as identifiable feature clusters, their *expectations* are nevertheless that individual species are those biological categories with the most inductive potential. (In contrast to the Americans, for the Itza' the species level is both basic and inductively privileged, a result Coley et al. suggest reflects their greater explicit ecological knowledge as compared to the Americans.) They further suggest that these expectations reflect an *essentialist bias* in which species are presumed to be organized around a causally potent essence which determines not only category membership, but also the degree to which category members are likely to share (known and to-be-discovered) features (Gelman, 2003; Medin & Ortony, 1989).

Can studies which experimentally manipulate the knowledge associated with a category shed any light on the details of how interfeature theoretical knowledge promotes generalizations? In particular, can we find direct evidence that a category based on an underlying cause (i.e., an essence) promotes generalizations?

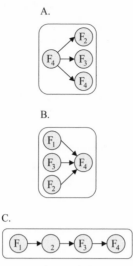

FIGURE 4.6. Network topologies tested in Rehder and Hastie (2004), Experiment 2. A. Common cause network. B. Common effect network. C. Chain network.

Research with Experimentally Provided Causal Knowledge

Rehder and Hastie (2004) addressed this question by manipulating the causal relations between known category features in order to create a laboratory analog of the essentialist knowledge associated with real-world categories. Once again, subjects were instructed on artificial but plausible categories like Romanian Rogos. In these experiments, however, the Rogos' characteristic features were described as causally related to one another rather than to a to-be-generalized property. In one condition the causal links formed a *common cause* topology in which one characteristic feature (F_1) was the cause of the three remaining ones (F_2, F_3, and F_4), as shown in Figure 4.6A. For example, for Romanian Rogos subjects would be told that butane-laden fuel (F_1) caused the other three characteristic features (e.g., loose fuel-filter gasket, hot engine temperature, etc.). They were then presented with a series of Rogos which each possessed a blank novel property (e.g., ceramic brakes) and judged what proportion of all Rogos possessed that property. The particular combination of characteristic features that the Rogos possessed was varied.

The question of interest was whether the presence of a common cause causal structure, which was intended to mimic that of a category organized around a causally potent essence (a common cause), would result in the same enhanced inductive potential exhibited by biological species. However, we felt it important also to ask whether any such enhancement required the specific common-cause causal structure. For example, one alternative hypothesis is that categories support stronger generalizations when they are organized around any central feature or theme, regardless of whether that feature is a cause or an effect. Another is that generalizations may be stronger as a result of the global coherence afforded by interfeature relations, regardless of the specific arrangement of the causal links. To assess these possibilities, we also tested a *common-effect network* in which one feature (F_4) is caused by the other three features (F_1, F_2, and F_3) (Figure 4.6B), and a *chain network* in which feature F_1 causes F_2 which in turn causes F_3 which in turn causes F_4 (Figure 4.6C). We expected that only a common-cause network would result in stronger generalizations if they are promoted by a single underlying generative cause, both the common-cause and common-effect networks would do so if they are promoted by any central theme, and all three networks would do so if inductions are promoted by any category exhibiting overall coherence provided by interfeature causal relations.

The results are presented in Figure 4.7 for each causal network as a function of the particular combination of characteristic feature that the Rogo with the to-be-generalized property possessed. Each panel in Figure 4.7 also includes the results from a control condition which presented no causal links between characteristic features. There were two notable results. First, Figure 4.7A shows that, as predicted, common-cause categories supported stronger inductive generalizations relative to the control condition, but only when the Rogo was typical (i.e., possessed all four characteristic features, as denoted by "1111"). When the Rogo was atypical (e.g., when it possessed the common cause F_1 but not the other three features, as denoted by "1000"), generalizations were *weaker* than in the control condition. Note that in the common cause condition this Rogo is not just atypical because it is missing three characteristic features (F_2, F_3, and F_4); it is *incoherent* in the light of the category's causal laws (the common cause F_1, butane-laden fuel, is present but its three effects are absent).

The second important finding is that these effects were not unique to a common-cause network, because the results were essentially the same for categories with a common-effect network (Figure 4.7B) or a chain network (Figure 4.7C). Each network supported stronger generalizations, so long as the category member with the novel property was typical (1111). But when the category member was incoherent, generalization were weaker than in the control condition. Exemplar 0001 is incoherent in the common effect condition because the common effect F_4 is present even though its causes F_1, F_2, and F_3 are all absent. Exemplar 0101 is incoherent in the chain condition because F_2 and F_4 are present even though their causes F_1 and F_3 are absent

B. Rehder

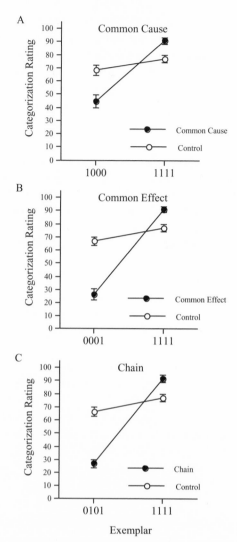

FIGURE 4.7. Generalization ratings from Rehder and Hastie (2004), Experiment 1.

(and because F_3 is absent even though its causes F_2 is present). In other words, it is not coherent *categories* that support stronger generalizations but rather coherent *category members*, and this effect holds regardless of the topology of the causal relations which make them coherent.[7] As in my other studies

---

[7] In a different phase of the experiment, Rehder and Hastie (2004) also asked the subjects to estimate the degree of category membership of the same exemplars which displayed the novel properties. Like the generalization ratings, category membership ratings for the most typical

reported in this chapter, these results held not just for artifacts like Rogos, but also for biological kinds and for nonliving natural kinds.

These results have three implications for the received view that biological kinds promote inductions because of the presumed presence of an essence. First, it may not be a presumption of a single common cause (an essence) which promotes inductions but rather a presumption of coherence, that is, causal relations which link category features regardless of the specific topology of those links. Second, this effect of coherence is not limited to biological kinds but will apply equally well to other kinds (e.g., artifacts) when generalizers have reason to believe that one of those kinds is coherent. Third, this effect can be reversed when the *specific* category member which displays a novel feature is *incoherent* in the light of the category's causal laws.

Of course, it should be noted that our failure to discover any special inductive potential of a common cause network as compared to the other two networks may have obtained because our experimental materials failed to fully elicit our subjects' essentialist intuitions. For example, perhaps such intuitions depend on the underlying nature of a category remaining vague (e.g., even young children have essentialist intuition, even though they know nothing of DNA; see Gelman, 2003), but in our categories the common cause was an explicit feature (e.g., butane-laden fuel for Rogos). Or, perhaps those explicit features clashed with our adult subjects' own opinions about the nature of the "essence" of a brand of automobile (the intention of the automobile's designer; see Bloom, 1998) or a biological species (DNA). Nevertheless, these results raise the possibility that the inductive potential of categories thought to arise from folk essentialism about biological kinds may in fact arise from a more general phenomenon, namely, theoretical coherence, which potentially applies to kinds of categories in addition to biological kinds.

DISCUSSION

This chapter has reviewed three sorts of evidence related to how causal knowledge is involved in property generalization. The first section presented

exemplars (i.e., 1111) were higher in the causal conditions than in the control condition, and ratings for incoherent exemplars (e.g., 1000, 0001, and 0101 in the common cause, common effect, and chain conditions, respectively) were lower than in the control condition. That is, the causal knowledge which makes exemplars appear more (or less) coherent is reflected in their perceived degree of category membership in addition to their propensity to support generalizations. Overall, the correlations between generalization and category membership ratings were .95 or higher.

evidence that people can go beyond the similarity-based heuristics formalized by the Similarity-Coverage model and generalize on the basis of causal reasoning. The second section addressed how causal reasoning and the similarity-based heuristics interact, and it showed that subjects which showed an effect of causal relations exhibited virtually no effect of similarity, whereas those which showed no effect of causal relations exhibited a sensitivity to similarity. Apparently, the use of a causal explanation versus similarity is an all-or-none matter, with reasoners using one strategy or the other, but not both. The third section reviewed evidence suggesting that categories presumed to be based on an underlying cause seem to be the target of strong generalizations, and it found that stronger generalizations may not be the responsibility of a single generative essence but rather of the presumed coherence that a category gains from the causal knowledge which interrelates existing features.

The evidence in support of these claims came from studies testing both natural and artificial categories, approaches which have complimentary strengths and weaknesses. For example, a critic could dismiss the studies testing artificial categories on the grounds that the causal knowledge was provided to participants as part of the experimental session rather than coming from a participants' own background knowledge, a practice which was likely to have made that knowledge especially salient and available (bypassing the need for the reasoner to retrieve it from their semantic memory). However, this criticism is blocked by the numerous studies testing natural categories, which show that it is common for reasoners to use causal knowledge in the service of generalizations. The benefit of testing artificial categories, in turn, is that it has made it possible to test specific claims regarding how causal knowledge influences generalization. One view is that properties are more generalizable to the extent they are more central (i.e., have more dependents in the base and target categories) (Hadjichristidis et al., 2004). My own view is, in contrast, that people engage in a kind of causal reasoning in which they evaluate whether a property is likely to appear in a target category. Data were presented showing that people can reason forwards from the presence of to-be-generalized property causes to the property itself (prospective reasoning) as well as they can reason from the property's effects or dependents (diagnostic reasoning). Additional experiments also showed that people will judge a new property to be more prevalent in a population of category members to the extent that its causes and/or effects are present in that population.

Although this chapter's central claim is that properties are often generalized on the basis of causal reasoning, it is important to consider whether some of the results could be explained by a more sophisticated version of similarity.

For example, recent progress has been made in extending similarity-based models to account for some results with nonblank properties, such as the GAP2 model proposed by Blok, Osherson, and Medin (this volume). In addition, one component of Medin et al.'s (2003) *relevance theory* of induction is that similarity emerges from a process of comparing the premise and conclusion categories. For example, comparing skunks and zebras would yield stripedness as a highly relevant feature, whereas comparing skunks and onions would yield strong odor (or, equivalently, stripedness becomes *available* in the context of skunks and zebras whereas strong odor is available in the context of skunks and onions; Shafto, Coley, & Vitkin, this volume). However, by themselves neither the GAP2 model nor comparing premise and conclusion categories are able to account, for example, for the Heit and Rubinstein (1994) study presented earlier because similarity doesn't change as a function of the property involved. The import of the Heit and Rubinstein results, however, is just that the relative strength of generalization (between, say, bears and whales as compared to tunas and whales) varied as a function of whether the property was anatomical or behavioral.

Heit and Rubinstein themselves proposed that their results could be explained in terms of similarity, but that similarity was computed flexibly, that is, in a manner which is influenced by the to-be-generalized property. Indeed, they showed that judgments regarding the generalization of anatomical and behavioral properties were well predicted by the rated similarity of the base and target categories when those ratings were made *with respect to* anatomy or behavior, respectively. Heit and Rubinstein suggested that anatomy and behavior may be two of a small number of fixed similarity measures which people can compute, or that people might use the theoretical knowledge invoked by the to-be-generalized property to dynamically select which dimensions along which similarity between base and target should be computed. The latter account can also explain some of the results from Rehder (2006) presented in the second section. For example, there I showed that the presence of a causal explanation linking the to-be-generalized property to an existing feature in the base resulted in reasoners being very sensitive to whether that feature was present in the target and insensitive to whether the base and target were similar on other dimensions (Figure 4.5). I described these results as indicating that the explanation drew attention away from the other dimensions, which of course is equivalent to saying that it determined the (single) dimension along which base-target similarity was computed.

Nevertheless, these more sophisticated views of similarity fail to explain, for instance, the diagnostic reasoning which apparently occurs during some cases of generalization. In the Hadjichristidis et al. (2004) study, subjects were asked to generalize a fictitious hormone from one category to another (e.g., from seals to dolphins). According to Heit and Rubinstein, the fact that the novel property is a hormone might induce reasoners to adopt an anatomical notion of similarity. But this fails to explain why the hormone was projected more strongly from seals to dolphins when it was responsible for many versus few physiological functions, because in both cases the base category (seals), the target category (dolphins), and the property (the hormone) are the same, and thus so too is (anatomical) similarity. Clearly, to explain these results one must also make reference to the causal network in which the hormone is involved. The view I promote is that generalizers reasoned backward (diagnostically) from the presence of the many physiological functions to the presence of the hormone.

As mentioned, testing artificial categories has made it possible to begin to develop specific computational theories of how causal knowledge influences generalization. But while a start has been made, my own work has considered only the causal knowledge which interrelates a category's features. But categories are also related by causal relations to one another, and research reviewed above documented the influence of one type of inter-category causal link – ingestion – on induction (e.g., a property displayed by both cats and sparrows will be attributed to the fact that cats eat sparrows). Indeed, in addition to comparison-based similarity, a second component of Medin et al.'s (2003) relevance theory is the assumption that causal relations between premise and conclusion categories will often form the basis of induction. Progress in providing a computational account of the influence of ingestion relations as one type of inter-category relation is reported by Tenenbaum, Kemp, and Shafto (this volume). In this research, subjects were trained to memorize a particular "food web" consisting of a number of animal species which prey on one another. For example, one food web included the facts that sand sharks eat herring which eat kelp; another that lions eat wolves which eat squirrels. Subjects were then asked to generalize a disease property "D" from one species to another in the same food web. Their judgments were well-predicted by a Bayesian model which computed the probability with which the disease was transmitted through the web from the base species to the target. Interestingly, when the property was "gene XR-23," the food-web model performed poorly, and it was a Bayesian model which operated on a taxonomic representation of the species that performed well instead. This result is reminiscent of Heit and Rubinstein's suggestion that the nature of the to-be-generalized property influences the mental processes responsible for induction, but it suggests that this influence amounts to recruiting different complex knowledge structures (a food-web versus a taxonomic hierarchy) rather than just different ways of computing similarity.

More work is needed, because of course diseases can spread in ways other than ingestion (e.g., physical proximity; see Proffitt et al., 2000). And the generalization of other types of properties might depend on yet other types of inter-category relations (properties might be shared between substances based on their common origin, e.g., between sand and glass; Medin et al., 2003). But one common thread between the causal reasoning view I have advocated here and that of Tenenbaum et al. (this volume) is the emphasis on domain-general reasoning processes. For example, one striking aspect of the results from Rehder (2006) and Rehder and Hastie (2004) testing artificial categories is the consistency of the results across biological kinds, nonliving natural kinds, or artifacts. Such results suggest that domain differences found with natural categories arise from differences in the type and amount of knowledge associated with those domains. Of course, this is not to suggest that such differences are theoretically unimportant, because one can always ask what causes them to exist. For example, it may be that young children make unique assumptions about the organization of biological kinds (e.g., that they are based on some kind of essence, or, as I prefer, that they are presumed to be coherent). Even so, it is causal reasoning which directly mediates whether or not a property is generalized to an entire class of objects.

References

Ahn, W. (1998). Why are different features central for natural kinds and artifacts? The role of causal status in determining feature centrality. *Cognition, 69,* 135–178.

Ahn, W., Kim, N. S., Lassaline, M. E., & Dennis, M. J. (2000). Causal status as a determinant of feature centrality. *Cognitive Psychology, 41,* 361–416.

Atran, S., Estin, P., Coley, J. D., & Medin, D. L. (1997). Generic species and basic levels: Essence and appearance in folk biology. Journal of Ethnobiology, 17(1), 22–45.

Bailenson, J. N., Shum, M. S., Atran, S., Medin, D. L., & Coley, J. D. (2002). A bird's eye view: Biological categorization and reasoning within and across cultures. *Cognition, 84,* 1–53.

Bloom, P. (1998). Theories of artifact categorization. *Cognition, 66,* 87–93.

Cheng, P. (1997). From covariation to causation: A causal power theory. *Psychological Review, 104*(2), 367–405.

Coley, J. D., Medin, D. L., & Atran, S. (1997). Does rank have its privilege? Inductive inference within folkbiological taxonomies. *Cognition, 64,* 73–112.

Gelman, S. A. (1988). The development of induction within natural kinds and artifact categories. *Cognitive Psychology, 20,* 65–95.

Gelman, S. A. (2003). *The essential child: The origins of essentialism in everyday thought.* New York: Oxford University Press.

Gelman, S. A., & Markman, E. M. (1986). Categories and induction in young children. *Cognition, 23*, 183–208.

Gelman, S. A., & O'Reilly, A. W. (1988). Children's inductive inferences with superordinate categories: The role of language and category structure. *Child Development, 59*, 876–887.

Hadjichristidis, C., Sloman, S. A., Stevenson, R., & Over, D. (2004). Feature centrality and property induction. *Cognitive Science, 28*(1), 45–74.

Heit, E. (2000). Properties of inductive reasoning. *Psychonomic Bulletin & Review, 7*(4), 569–592.

Heit, E., & Rubinstein, J. (1994). Similarity and property effects in inductive reasoning. *Journal of Experimental Psychology: Learning, Memory, and Cognition, 20*(2), 411–422.

Lassaline, M. E. (1996). Structural alignment in induction and similarity. *Journal of Experimental Psychology: Learning, Memory, and Cognition, 22*(3), 754–770.

Lopez, A., Atran, S., Coley, J. D., Medin, D. L., & Smith, E. E. (1997). The tree of life: Universal and cultural features of folkbiological taxonomies and inductions. *Cognitive Psychology, 32*(3), 251–295.

Lopez, A., Gelman, S. A., Gutheil, G., & Smith, E. E. (1992). The development of category-based induction. *Child Development, 63*, 1070–1090.

Medin, D. L., Coley, J. D., Storms, G., & Hayes, B. K. (2003). A relevance theory of induction. *Psychonomic Bulletin & Review, 10*(3), 517–532.

Medin, D. L., & Ortony, A. (1989). Psychological essentialism. In S. Vosniadou & A. Ortony (Eds.), *Similarity and analogical reasoning* (pp. 179–196). Cambridge: Cambridge University Press.

Nair, M. (2005). *The role of causal reasoning in category-based generalizations.* Unpublished honors thesis. New York University.

Osherson, D., Smith, E. E., Myers, T. S., & Stob, M. (1994). Extrapolating human probability judgment. *Theory and Decision, 36*, 103–126.

Osherson, D. M., Smith, E. E., Wilkie, O., Lopez, A., & Shafir, E. (1990). Category-based induction. *Psychological Review, 97*, 185–200.

Proffitt, J. B., Coley, J. D., & Medin, D. L. (2000). Expertise and category-based induction. *Journal of Experimental Psychology: Learning, Memory, and Cognition, 26*(4), 811–828.

Rehder, B. (2003a). Categorization as causal reasoning. *Cognitive Science, 27*(5), 709–748.

Rehder, B. (2003b). A causal-model theory of conceptual representation and categorization. *Journal of Experimental Psychology: Learning, Memory, and Cognition, 29*(6), 1141–1159.

Rehder, B. (2006). When similarity and causality compete in category-based property induction. *Memory & Cognition, 34*, 3–16.

Rehder, B., & Hastie, R. (2004). Category coherence and category-based property induction. *Cognition, 91*(2), 113–153.

Rehder, B., & Kim, S. W. (2006). How causal knowledge affects classification: A generative theory of categorization. *Journal of Experimental Psychology: Learning, Memory, & Cognition, 32*, 659–683.

Rips, L. J. (2001). Necessity and natural categories. *Psychological Bulletin, 127*(6), 827–852.

Rosch, E. H., Mervis, C. B., Gray, W., Johnson, D., & Boyes-Braem, P. (1976). Basic objects in natural categories. *Cognitive Psychology, 8*, 382–439.

Shafto, P., & Coley, J. D. (2003). Development of categorization and reasoning in the natural world: Novices to experts, naive similarity to ecological knowledge. *Journal of Experimental Psychology: Learning, Memory, and Cognition, 29*(4), 641–649.

Shipley, E. F. (1993). Categories, hierarchies, and induction. In D. Medin (Ed.), *The psychology of learning and motivation* (Vol. 30, pp. 265–301). New York: Academic Press.

Sloman, S. A. (1993). Feature-based induction. *Cognitive Psychology, 25,* 231–280.

Sloman, S. A. (1994). When explanations compete: The role of explanatory coherence on judgments of likelihood. *Cognition, 52,* 1–21.

Sloman, S. A. (1997). Explanatory coherence and the induction of properties. *Thinking and Reasoning, 3*(2), 81–110.

Sloman, S. A., Love, B. C., & Ahn, W. (1998). Feature centrality and conceptual coherence. *Cognitive Science, 22*(2), 189–228.

Smith, E. E., Shafir, E., & Osherson, D. (1993). Similarity, plausibility, and judgments of probability. *Cognition, 49,* 67–96.

Springer, K., & Keil, F. C. (1989). On the development of biologically specific beliefs: The case of inheritance. *Child Development, 60,* 637–648.

Thagard, P. (1999). *How scientists explain disease.* Princeton, NJ: Princeton University Press.

Wu, M. L., & Gentner, D. (1998). *Structure in category-based induction.* Paper presented at the 20th Annual Conference of the Cognitive Science Society, Madison, WI.

5

Availability in Category-Based Induction

Patrick Shafto, John D. Coley, and Anna Vitkin

Induction can be supported by many kinds of knowledge. To be effective, reasoning should be context sensitive; different kinds of knowledge should be selectively deployed in different situations. For example, in the domain of biology, when reasoning about the distribution of novel internal properties over species, taxonomic knowledge should be recruited since we know that taxonomic membership is not only related to perceptual similarity but is also a good predictor of shared unobservable anatomical features such as four-chambered hearts. However, when reasoning about the distribution of environmental toxins, ecological knowledge should be recruited since such a toxin would plausibly spread through an ecosystem. In this chapter, we address the factors that influence the recruitment of different kinds of knowledge in different contexts. We propose that different kinds of knowledge are differentially available across contexts. Using this concept of availability, we will address an array of experimental results, arguing for availability as a way to unite and explain a broad range of phenomena in category-based induction.

In a classic paper, Tversky and Kahneman (1973) discuss *availability* as a heuristic "by which people evaluate the frequency of classes or the likelihood of events" (p. 207). This involves estimating frequency or probability "by the ease with which instances or associations are brought to mind" (p. 208). As such, availability on this view is essentially a metacognitive heuristic by which information is judged more likely or plausible based on an estimate of the effort involved in retrieving the information; indeed, Tversky and Kahneman argue that "to assess availability it is not necessary to perform the actual operations of retrieval or construction. It suffices to assess the ease with which these operations could be performed" (p. 208). Our goal in this chapter is to use the spirit of this concept of availability – if not the letter – to unify a set of seemingly disparate findings on category-based inductive reasoning.

We see inductive inference as a process by which knowledge of relations among concepts is used to assess the likelihood that members of two categories will share a novel property. We will argue that the ease with which specific knowledge of conceptual relations comes to mind predicts the likelihood that such knowledge will be used to guide inductive inference. Below, we will present evidence that the availability of different kinds of knowledge to inform induction depends on two factors: acute (short-term) influences of context on availability and chronic (long-term) effects of experience, reflected in baseline differences in the availability of different knowledge structures. In this sense, availability can be thought of as a dynamic property of knowledge in memory that provides a ranking of the likelihood that different kinds of knowledge will be accessed in a given context (e.g., Horowitz et al., 1966; Pearlstone & Tulving, 1966).

Thus, like Tversky and Kahneman (1973), we argue that availability is a variable that mediates between prior knowledge and behavior via the relative accessibility of different kinds of knowledge in a particular situation. Here we part ways with Tversky and Kahneman because for our purposes an *estimate* of the ease with which information might be accessed is not sufficient. Because specific knowledge must be brought to mind to guide or assess inductive inference, it *is* necessary to "perform the actual operations of retrieval or construction."

The structure of this chapter will be as follows. First, we will discuss the effects of two kinds of context on availability. We will then turn to how experience influences availability and interacts with context. Finally, we will relate this approach to other frameworks, and discuss novel predictions motivated by availability.

AVAILABILITY IN CATEGORY-BASED INDUCTION

A central problem in the psychology of induction is what kinds of knowledge we use to guide a particular inductive inference. Given all that we may know about a concept, which knowledge is relevant to a particular problem? This problem is beyond the scope of many previous models of inductive reasoning, which rely on a single kind of knowledge in a domain (though some recent progress has been made toward models supporting multiple kinds of knowledge, see Shafto, Kemp et al., 2005; Shafto et al., in prep). We propose a framework for understanding reasoning in rich domains, explicitly linking the acute effects of immediate context and the chronic effects of long-term experience via the *availability* of different kinds of knowledge. We suggest that inductive generalizations are guided by the knowledge that is most available in a particular context, given past experience. Moreover, availability is dynamic in that changes in availability arise from one of two sources: changes in context or changes in underlying knowledge.

Context plays a crucial role in acute changes in availability. For any given inductive task, the presence of a biasing context can change the relative availability of different kinds of knowledge. For example, if you learn of a new *environmental toxin* affecting *frogs*, ecological knowledge about who may be exposed or causal knowledge about how the toxin might be transmitted may become more available, leading you to expect that *herons* might be at risk (because they share a habitat with and eat frogs). In contrast, if you learn of a new *enzyme* discovered in frogs, you might expect the same enzyme to be present in *toads*, due to their close biological affinity, and never consider herons as a plausible candidate for the enzyme. Even if we know nothing about the nature of the property in question, any known examples that possess it may influence the availability of knowledge. For example, if told about a property that cows, chickens, and pigs have, knowledge about domesticated animals may become more available.

In the case where context does not provide a bias, availability reduces to a default way of thinking about a domain, which reflects the knowledge that has been rendered chronically most available by experience. Experience may lead to multiple kinds of knowledge all becoming equally available or a single kind of knowledge becoming available over time. For example, the relative salience of the ecological versus taxonomic knowledge that inform the inferences about *frog* might differ for an ecologist working for Greenpeace, a molecular biologist, or a relatively uninformed undergraduate participant in a psychology experiment. The chronic effects of experience are manifest in baseline availability of default knowledge in a domain.

Importantly, acute and chronic changes in availability can interact, which can have important implications for reasoning in a domain. If, at baseline, multiple kinds of knowledge are equally available, reasoning will be highly sensitive to acute changes in availability as a result of context. However, if at baseline one kind of knowledge is a highly available default, much stronger context will be required to elicit reasoning based on the less-available knowledge. Thus, the interaction between acute and chronic changes in availability has an important impact on the kinds of knowledge that are available to guide reasoning.

In the following sections, we will consider several studies that demonstrate that context and experience result in important changes in inductive reasoning. Most important, we will consider studies that show interactions between experience and context in inductive reasoning. We will argue that these effects are best understood in terms of acute and chronic changes in the availability of different kinds of knowledge.

Context-Based Changes in Availability

We suggest that the context provided by an inductive argument results in acute changes in the availability of different kinds of knowledge and different patterns of reasoning. In this section, we will consider a range of previous results investigating reasoning in knowledge-rich domains. We will reconsider this evidence in the light of availability, particularly looking for qualitative changes in reasoning based on immediate inductive context. We consider two sources of context in these category-based induction tasks: the property in question, and the set of categories given in the problem.

Property Effects on Induction. One source of context in an inductive problem is the property to be generalized from premise to conclusion. Knowing something about the nature of this property can be informative as to what relations are recruited for making guesses about the distribution of that property. For example, if we are told that chickens have sesamoid bones we might conclude that other flightless birds might share a physiological, internal property such as bone structure. On the other hand, if we knew that chickens had the sesamoid flu we might reconsider having chicken for dinner for fear of catching it ourselves. Although in each example the premise category is *chicken*, the conclusion categories we believe to share a property can change dramatically depending on what that property is. The systematic use of different kinds of knowledge to inform induction has been termed *inductive selectivity*. On our view, the immediate context provided by the property of an inductive argument can produce acute changes in the availability of different kinds of knowledge for inductive generalizations.

Heit and Rubinstein (1994, exp. 1 & 2) proposed that different relations between premise and conclusion categories determined the strength of an inductive inference depending on the property a premise and conclusion were said to share. In their study they asked participants to make estimates of the probability that a pair of animal categories might share a property. Pairs of animals were chosen to be related by shared anatomy (e.g., *whale* and *bear*) or behavior (e.g., *whale* and *tuna*). Participants were asked about the likelihood of such pairs sharing an anatomical property like having two chambers in their liver that act as one, or a behavioral property such as traveling in a back-and-forth or zigzag trajectory. Heit and Rubinstein found that participants made the highest probability estimates for items where the relation between a pair of animals matched the kind of property they were asked to reason about (e.g., whales and bears have two-chamber livers, whales and tuna travel in zigzag trajectories). These results suggest that the property of projection influenced the kind of knowledge that was recruited to support inductive inferences: anatomical properties made anatomical knowledge more available, whereas behavioral properties made behavioral knowledge more available.

Ross and Murphy (1999) have shown similar effects of property on the selective use of conceptual relations to guide inferences in the domain of food. They established that most participants cross-classified food into two major knowledge structures – taxonomic, based on shared features or composition, and script, based on what situations a food is consumed in. Participants in their study were asked to make biochemical or situational inferences about triplets of food. Participants were taught that the target food, such as bagels, had a biochemical property (enzyme) or situational property (eaten at an initiation ceremony). They were then asked to project the property to one of two alternatives, a taxonomic alternative such as crackers, or a script alternative such as eggs. Ross and Murphy found that participants made more taxonomic choices for biochemical properties and more script choices when considering situational properties. It seems that the nature of the property increased the availability of relevant knowledge about shared composition or situational appropriateness of a food, ultimately producing different patterns of induction for different kinds of properties.

Recent evidence also suggests that, like adults, children's inductive generalizations are sensitive to the property in question. Using a similar triad method to that of Ross and Murphy (1999), Nguyen and Murphy (2003) found that in the domain of food, seven-year-old children (but not four-year-olds) made more taxonomic choices when reasoning about a biochemical property and more script choices when reasoning about a situational property. That is, they thought that a bagel would be more likely to share an enzyme with crackers but be more likely to be eaten at a ceremony with eggs. This suggests that the context provided by a property begins to mediate the differential availability of knowledge from an early age.

Further evidence of children's selective use of knowledge based on property comes from the domain of biology. Coley and colleagues (Coley, 2005; Coley, Vitkin, Seaton, & Yopchick, 2005; Vitkin, Coley, & Kane, 2005) asked school-aged children to consider triads of organisms with a target species, a taxonomic alternative (from the same superordinate class but ecologically unrelated), and an ecological alternative (from a different taxonomic class but related via habitat or predation). Children were taught, for example, that a banana tree had a property (either a disease or "stuff inside") and asked to choose if a calla lily (taxonomic match) or a monkey (ecological match) shared the property. Results clearly indicate that children were sensitive to the kind of property they were asked about, choosing taxonomic matches at above-chance levels when reasoning about insides, and choosing ecological matches at above-chance levels when reasoning about diseases that might plausibly spread through an ecosystem. In another task, children were asked to make open-ended predictions about what kinds of things might come to share properties (Vitkin, Coley, & Hu, 2005). They were taught that a pair of animals either had a disease or "stuff inside," and they were then asked to project what other things might share this property and explain their reasoning. Children's responses were characterized as being based on similarity (taxonomy, shared features, etc.) or interaction (contact through ecosystems). Children made more responses rooted in similarity when thinking about internal substances and more interaction-based responses when asked to consider diseases. Consistent with availability, this pattern of response demonstrated that children's generalizations were guided by different kinds of knowledge depending on what properties they were reasoning about.

Overall, we have seen that the property projected in an inductive task provides context for inferences, changing the kinds of information that are used make generalizations. Specifically, the property being projected provides useful clues about what kinds of conceptual relations (disease transmitted through ecology, biochemical composition shared by taxonomic food classes, etc.) might support the generalization of such a property. This has been demonstrated in at least two different domains of knowledge (food and biology) and in both children and adults. These results are consistent with the idea that the property being projected is one factor that influences the relative availability of different kinds of knowledge to support inductive reasoning.

Relations Among Premise and Conclusion Categories. Another line of evidence compatible with the proposal that availability mediates the basis of inductive reasoning examines the effects of relations among premise categories, or among premise and conclusion categories, as influencing the availability of different kinds of knowledge for guiding inductive inference. Work by Medin, Coley, Storms, and Hayes (2003) identified several effects associated with the relationship between categories presented in the premises and conclusions, under the rubric of *relevance effects*. One key component of the relevance framework, as well as our availability framework, is the idea that salient relations among premise categories, or between premise and conclusion categories, may guide or constrain the inference supported by those premises.

Medin et al. (2003) examine this idea with respect to two broad classes of phenomena, *causal relations* and *property reinforcement*. We concentrate on the latter. Medin et al. (2003) present several examples where increasing the salience of specific relations among categories in an inductive argument leads to violations of normative logic or of the predictions of similarity-based models of inductive reasoning.

The first of these is *non-diversity via property reinforcement*, which predicts that an argument with less diverse premises might be perceived to be stronger than an argument with more diverse premises if the premise categories of the more diverse argument reinforce a salient relation not shared by the conclusion category. For example, consider the following arguments:

A. Polar Bears have Property X.
    Antelopes have Property X.
    All Animals have Property X.

B. Polar Bears have Property X.
    Penguins have Property X.
    All Animals have Property X.

From a strictly taxonomic point of view, *polar bears* (a mammal) and *penguins* (a bird) provide better coverage of the conclusion category *animal* than polar bears and antelopes, which are both mammals. Thus, a model based only on taxonomic knowledge must predict Argument B to be stronger. However, the salient property shared by polar bears and penguins – namely, adaptation to a cold climate – renders plausible the possibility that Property X is related to life below zero, and therefore might weaken the inference that all animals would share the property. Indeed, Medin at al. (2003) find that subjects in the United States, Belgium, and Australia on average rated arguments like A stronger than arguments like B.[1] This suggests that the salient property shared by the premise categories in B cancels out the greater coverage they provide of the conclusion category.

A second related phenomenon discussed by Medin et al. (2003) is *conjunction fallacy via property reinforcement*, which predicts that arguments with a single conclusion category might be perceived to be weaker than arguments with an additional conclusion category (a violation of normative logic because a conjunctive statement cannot be more probable than one of the component statements) if the second conclusion category reinforces a salient relation shared by all categories. For example, consider the following arguments:

---

[1] Though recent evidence suggests that this effect may not be particularly robust (Heit & Feeney, 2005).

C. <u>Chickens have Property X.</u>
   Cows have Property X.

D. <u>Chickens have Property X.</u>
   Cows have Property X.
   Pigs have Property X.

Normative logic requires that "cows have Property X" must be more likely than "cows and pigs have Property X," but Medin et al. (2003) found that participants reliably rated arguments like D as more likely than arguments like C. The addition of *pigs* might serve to increase the availability of the knowledge about farm animals, and therefore strengthens Argument D relative to Argument C.

Finally, Medin et al. (2003) discuss *non-monotonicity via property reinforcement*. Monotonicity is the idea that all else being equal, adding premise categories that are proper members of the same superordinate as a conclusion category should strengthen the argument (see Osherson et al., 1990). Medin et al. (2003) predict that adding premises might weaken an argument if the added categories reinforce a relation shared by premise categories but not the conclusion category. For example, consider the following arguments:

E. <u>Brown Bears have Property X.</u>
   Buffalo have Property X.

F. Brown Bears have Property X.
   Polar Bears have Property X.
   Black Bears have Property X.
   <u>Grizzly Bears have Property X.</u>
   Buffalo have Property X.

Monotonicity predicts that Argument F should be at least as strong as Argument E because the premise categories in F necessarily cover the lowest inclusive category *mammals* at least as well as the premise of E, and are at least as similar to *buffalo*. However, Medin et al. (2003) find that – contrary to the principle of monotonicity – arguments like E are consistently given stronger ratings than arguments like F, presumably because the premises of F reinforce the relation of *being a bear*, and therefore make plausible the inference that Property X is particularly ursine in nature, and therefore unlikely to be true of buffalo.

Together, these results suggest that manipulation of relations among premise and/or conclusion categories can result in violations of normative logic (in the case of the conjunction fallacy) or violations of predictions derived from similarity-based models (in the case of non-diversity

TABLE 5.1. *Sample items from adult open-ended projection study*

Ecological	Taxonomic Distance	
Relation	Near	Far
Related	*Heron, Duck*	*Hawk, Field Mouse*
Unrelated	*Otter, Deer*	*Chipmunk, Bullfrog*

or non-monotonicity). We propose that these manipulations can be seen as manipulations of the availability of specific conceptual relations. By rendering specific relations such as *polar animals, farm animals,* or *bears* highly available, these manipulations serve to overcome more general default approaches to the evaluation of inductive arguments.

Using a more natural paradigm that allows participants to generate their own conclusions given a set of premises, Baker and Coley (2005) (see also Coley, Baker, & Kemp, 2004) have investigated whether spontaneous and relatively unconstrained inductive projections are sensitive to manipulations of relations among premise categories. In this study, thirty college undergraduates were given pairs of premise species, taught a novel property said to be shared by the pair, and asked what other species might have the property, and why. Premise pairs were either drawn from the same superordinate category (taxonomically near pairs) or from different superordinates (taxonomically far pairs). Pairs were also ecologically related (via habitat, predator-prey relation, or ecological niche) or unrelated. See Table 5.1 for sample items.

Reponses were coded according to the relationship between the given premise pair and the conclusion categories generated by the participants. The basis of an inference was judged to be *taxonomic* if participants' explanations emphasized that premise and conclusion categories belonged to the same class or kind, were similar in appearance, or similar in general. Responses were coded as *ecological* if participants' explanations relied on an interaction between premise and conclusion categories that highlighted a non-taxonomic relation such as a predator/prey relation, shared diet, or shared habitat.

Results suggest that projections were sensitive to salient relations among premise categories. Specifically, taxonomic inferences were more frequent for taxonomically near pairs than for taxonomically far pairs, and were also more frequent for ecologically unrelated than for ecologically related pairs. Likewise, ecological inferences were more frequent for ecologically related pairs than for unrelated pairs, although frequency of ecological inferences was not affected by taxonomic distance among premise categories. In sum, relations among premise categories appear to influence the knowledge recruited to support generalizations.

These findings suggest that relations among premise categories may impact the availability of different kinds of knowledge for guiding spontaneous inferences. Premise categories that share salient taxonomic relations render such knowledge available and thereby increase the likelihood of taxonomic generalizations. Likewise, premise categories that share salient ecological relations increase the availability and likelihood of ecological inferences.

Availability, Experience, and Default Domain Knowledge

Availability, as we have described it, depends on prior knowledge and context. In the previous section, we considered acute changes in availability due to the nature of the property being projected and relations among categories in an argument. In this section, we present evidence that increased knowledge and experience in a domain can lead to chronic changes in the relative availability of different kinds of knowledge for inductive reasoning. We will argue that experience-related changes in underlying knowledge – such as accrual of more facts, changes in the frequency with which different knowledge is used, and even fundamental changes in conceptual structure – are accompanied by changes in the baseline availability of different kinds of knowledge, and also by an increased sensitivity to context. In brief, we argue that the concept of availability is useful in explaining observed effects of experience on inductive reasoning.

Experience-Related Changes in Availability of Different Kinds of Knowledge.
By definition, experts in a given domain know more than novices. However, in addition to the accrual of facts, expertise may also result in changes to the relative availability of different kinds of knowledge. We argue above that taxonomic knowledge may be a default guide for novices when reasoning about a given domain. However, several lines of evidence suggest that taxonomic relations consistently fail to predict expert reasoning to the same extent. For instance, López et al. (1997) show that when forced to choose the stronger of two inductive arguments about local mammals species, University of Michigan undergraduates' responses are almost unanimously in accord with the Osherson et al. (1990) taxonomically based similarity-coverage model. In contrast, responses of Itza' Maya participants – indigenous people of Guatamala who live in close contact with nature and depend largely on hunting and swidden agriculture for subsistence, and who therefore possess extensive knowledge of local flora and fauna – were at chance when evaluated against predictions of the Similarity-Coverage Model. Instead of relying on taxonomic relations, the Itza' recruited specific causal-ecological knowledge

to evaluate the arguments. Follow up work by Proffitt, Coley, and Medin (2000) revealed a pattern of induction among Chicago-area tree experts that was remarkably similar to that of the Itzá, suggesting that domain-specific experience, rather than language or culture, is the driving factor. Indeed, this same general finding – increase in the relative salience of non-taxonomic relations for guiding induction – has been reported for commercial fishermen, professional musicians, and even undergraduates reasoning about alcohol (see Coley, Shafto, Stepanova, & Baraff, 2005, for a review).

Not only does experience in general change the relative availability of different kinds of knowledge, but specific kinds of expertise also appear to lead to differential salience of knowledge among experts. For instance, Proffitt et al. (2000) report that of three different groups of experts (taxonomists, landscapers, and maintenance workers), only taxonomists' patterns of induction relied on taxonomic knowledge. Taxonomists were also more likely to explain their inferences by referring to taxonomic factors such as typicality, family size, or diversity of premise species. Taxonomists, with their focus on knowledge about genealogical relations among species, tend to apply taxonomic knowledge even when reasoning about diseases among trees. However, landscapers and maintenance workers, who have other concerns, were more likely to apply other kinds of knowledge to the same task. Converging evidence comes from studies of categorization; Medin, Lynch, Coley, and Atran (1997) found that these same groups of experts tended to sort tree species on the basis of relations specific to their area of expertise. For example, taxonomists tended to utilize botanical families, landscapers utilized categories like *specimen tree* that reflected a species' typical use in landscape design, and maintenance workers tended to use categories like *weed tree*, which reflected the ease of caring for different species. Thus, within a single domain, differential experience can render different knowledge available. These effects demonstrate how extensive experience can elicit chronic changes in availability.

Culture is another source of differential experience that could impact the availability of knowledge for induction. A striking example of culturally induced changes in availability can be found in the work of Choi, Nisbett, and Smith (1997). They investigated reasoning about biological and social categories among Americans and Koreans. Some have argued that western individualist cultures tend to process information analytically and generally attend to categories and rules, whereas eastern collectivist cultures tend to consider problems holistically, attending to categories in terms of interactions in a setting (see Nisbett, Peng, Choi, & Norenzayan, 2001, for a review). One interesting exception to this is in the domain of social categories and roles, which are argued to be particularly salient and important to eastern collectivist cultures. Based on these cultural differences, Choi et al. (1997) predicted that manipulations of taxonomic category salience (specific versus general conclusions) would have a differential effect on American and Korean peoples' reasoning about biological and social categories. Specifically, they predicted that because taxonomic categories in general are less culturally salient to members of a collectivist culture, manipulations of salience should have a more pronounced effect on Koreans' biological inferences than on Americans', for whom taxonomic knowledge is already highly salient. In contrast, they predicted the opposite effect for social categories, where taxonomic knowledge is argued to be more salient for Koreans than for Americans. Consistent with these predictions, they found that when reasoning about biological categories, Koreans preferred taxonomic responses to arguments with general conclusions than to those with specific conclusions, whereas this manipulation had no effect on Americans' responses. Conversely, when reasoning about social categories, Americans preferred taxonomic responses to arguments with general conclusions than to those with specific conclusions, whereas this manipulation had no effect on Koreans' responses. These results are consistent with the claim that culture can be viewed as a kind of experience that may result in chronic changes in the availability of different kinds of knowledge in a domain.

In sum, experimental results consistently reveal differential use of taxonomic versus other knowledge in experienced versus novice populations. We propose that these differences can be understood as reflecting chronic changes in the relative availability of different kinds of knowledge that accompany the acquisition of expertise.

Experience-Related Changes in Sensitivity to Context. In this section, we focus on experience-based differences in the availability of knowledge to guide induction as a function of context. We argue that general changes in baseline availability of different kinds of knowledge also lead experts to be more sensitive to context. In other words, because more kinds of knowledge become available with experience, experts can draw on the most appropriate relation to guide a given inference. Below we present evidence that domain-specific experience is associated with increased inductive selectivity and with increased sensitivity to relations among premise categories.

EXPERIENCE-RELATED CHANGES IN INDUCTIVE SELECTIVITY. Recent evidence suggests that experience leads to an increase in inductive selectivity. For example, Shafto and Coley (2003) demonstrate experience-related changes in inductive selectivity by contrasting how experts (commercial fishermen) and novices (university undergraduates) reasoned about marine creatures. In this experiment, participants were given either a novel blank property ("has a property called sarca") or a novel disease ("has a disease called sarca") to reason about. Participants were given examples of creatures that had the property and then were asked to infer which other creatures (from a broad array of fish, sharks, whales, and crustaceans) would have the property. Results indicated marked differences in inductive selectivity between novices and experts. When told about blank properties, experts tended to generalize to taxonomically related creatures. However, when told about diseases, experts tended to generalize to creatures related in the food web, specifically by making directional inferences from prey to predators. In contrast, novices tended to generalize to taxonomically related creatures regardless of the property. This result is notable because although novices were unlikely to have the detailed knowledge about marine food web relations on which commercial fishermen depend for their livelihood, they undoubtedly possessed some rudimentary knowledge of marine food web relations (e.g., that sharks eat fish and not the other way around). This constitutes enough knowledge to make rough inferences based on food web information. Nevertheless, we observed no such reasoning among novices.

We interpret these results as suggesting that for novices, knowledge about food web relations is generally less available and that the context provided in this experiment (essentially, *disease*) did not create enough of a change in the availability of food web knowledge to overcome their taxonomic default. On the other hand, for experts who rely heavily on knowledge of food web relations among these creatures on a daily basis, taxonomic and food web knowledge have relatively similar baseline availabilities, and the experimental context (*disease* versus *property*) was enough to manipulate the availability of the different kinds of knowledge.

Stepanova and Coley (2003) (see also Coley, Shafto, Stepanova, & Baraff, 2005; Stepanova, 2004) also contrasted reasoning by individuals with extensive or limited experience in a domain. However, rather than comparing experts and novices reasoning about a single domain, they compared a single population (U.S. college undergraduates) reasoning about a domain they have extensive experience with (alcoholic drinks) versus a domain with much less relevance to their daily lives (animals), on the assumption that for the typical college student, alcohol possesses greater relevance and cultural importance than animals, and undergraduates are likely to have more first-hand experience of, more frequent exposure to, and richer and more abundant folk theories about alcohol than animals. The task required participants to choose which of two pairs of premise categories provided better evidence for a generalization to *any alcohol* (or *any animal*). Sets of premise categories were chosen so that one would clearly be stronger via diversity. In addition to being randomly assigned to the animal or alcohol conditions, participants were also randomly assigned to evaluate arguments about a chemical component or about getting sick. Results showed clear evidence for inductive selectivity when undergraduates were reasoning about alcohol. Specifically, participants reasoning about alcohol showed differential use of taxonomic knowledge as a function of property; these participants were more likely to make diversity-based inferences about getting sick than about a chemical component. Moreover, participants reasoning about alcohol also provided different explanations for their choices as a function of property; they were more likely to offer causal explanations for inferences about getting sick, but more likely to offer taxonomic explanations for inferences about a chemical component. In contrast, there was no evidence of inductive selectivity when participants were reasoning about animals; neither the relative frequency of diversity-based choices nor the type of explanations provided for those choices varied for inferences about a chemical versus getting sick. These results are in close accord with those of Shafto and Coley (2003) just described, and they suggest that greater domain-specific experience may increase the potential availability of multiple conceptual relations and therefore increase inductive selectivity as a function of property being projected.

EXPERIENCE-RELATED CHANGES IN SENSITIVITY TO PREMISE RELATIONS. Recent developmental work also suggests that domain-specific experience may increase children's sensitivity to relations among premise categories as potential constraints on induction. In the Vitkin, Coley, and Hu (2005) study described earlier under "Property effects on induction" relations between premises as well as property effects were investigated using open-ended inductive projections among elementary school children from urban communities and rural communities. Relations among animal pairs were manipulated in a two-by-two design such that each pair was either taxonomically close (from the same superordinate) or taxonomically far (from different superordinates) and either ecologically related (via habitat or predator-prey relations) or ecologically unrelated. Responses were coded as being based on similarity (taxonomy, shared features, etc.) or interaction (contact through ecosystems). If experience increases sensitivity to context, then the greater opportunity for direct interaction with plants and animals in relatively intact ecosystems afforded by a rural environment may lead to increased sensitivity to relations among premise categories among rural children.

Indeed, urban and rural children differed strikingly with respect to their sensitivity to relations among premise categories. Rural children showed consistent sensitivity to differential relations among premise categories.

Specifically, rural children made more similarity-based projections for taxonomically close pairs than for taxonomically far pairs. They also made more interaction-based projections for ecologically related pairs than for unrelated pairs, and for taxonomically far pairs than for taxonomically close pairs. None of these effects were evident for urban children. These results suggest that experience may mediate the availability of different conceptual relations for guiding children's spontaneous inferences. For biologically experienced rural children, relations among premise pairs was sufficient context to render taxonomic and ecological knowledge differentially available to inform inductive projections. In contrast, for biologically inexperienced urban children, this was not the case.

Taken together, these results suggest that the influence of experience on inductive reasoning can be thought of in terms of changes in the relative availability of different kinds of knowledge. Experience can be seen as increasing the relative availability of non-default knowledge for guiding induction, as in the cases of fishermen reasoning about marine creatures and undergraduates reasoning about alcohol. Because multiple kinds of knowledge are equally available, expert reasoning is highly sensitive to context. In contrast, because one kind of knowledge is a highly available default for novices, much stronger context is required to elicit reasoning based on the less-available knowledge. Thus, changes in chronic availability result in increased sensitivity to context among experts relative to novices.

Summary: Availability in Category-Based Induction

Previous research has demonstrated two main factors that influence recruitment of different kinds of knowledge in category-based induction: experimental context and prior experience. We argue that these factors are best understood as manipulations of the *availability* of different kinds of knowledge.

We have reviewed previous work demonstrating that people's inductive generalizations are sensitive to the property to be projected. We find that different properties can lead to qualitatively different patterns of generalization, such as in the domain of foods where biochemical properties lead to taxonomic reasoning and situational properties lead to script-based reasoning. We propose that properties that are consistent with a particular kind of knowledge will increase the availability of that kind of knowledge. For example, reasoning about what foods would be eaten together at an initiation ceremony activates script knowledge about what foods typically co-occur, therefore increasing the likelihood of script-based inferences by rendering that knowledge temporarily available. Thus, the property of projection can lead to an acute change in availability of knowledge and characteristically different patterns of generalizations.

Similarly, we propose that relations between premise and conclusion categories are also able to elicit changes in availability. In cases such as *nonmonotonicity via property reinforcement* as well as open-ended induction, the presence of known relations among the premises results in characteristically different patterns of generalization. For example, if you learn a new fact that is true of turtles and lizards, you might generalize it to other reptiles, whereas if you learn a new fact that is true of turtles and ducks, you might generalize it to pond creatures instead. We suggest that presenting information about categories that are united by a particular kind of knowledge leads to an acute increase in the availability of that kind of knowledge and an increased likelihood of an inference based on that knowledge.

More compelling evidence derives from the role of experience. In our framework, availability depends on context and prior knowledge accrued through experience. We have reviewed research with experts suggesting that experience can change the baseline availability of different kinds of knowledge. People tend to use knowledge that they have a deep understanding of and that has proven useful in the past. For example, evidence from tree experts suggests that a person's experiential background leads to chronic changes in the kinds of knowledge that are available for reasoning; by default, tree taxonomists tend to think about trees in terms of scientific taxonomies, whereas maintenance workers tend to think about trees in terms of maintenance concerns. This evidence suggests that experience can lead to chronic changes in the availability of different kinds of knowledge.

However, we think the most compelling evidence is manifest in interactions between experience and context. People are more likely to demonstrate robust inductive selectivity in domains where they have extensive experience. For example, when reasoning about marine creatures, commercial fishermen demonstrated more inductive selectivity than university undergraduates; university undergraduates demonstrated more inductive selectivity when reasoning about alcohol than when reasoning about animals. We propose that experience facilitated inductive selectivity in these studies by causing an increase in the availability of non-default knowledge, essentially "leveling the playing field" and allowing for an increased sensitivity to context.

In sum, we see availability as a promising explanation for both context and experience effects in category-based induction. However, at this point, much of our case remains circumstantial. Though availability seems an apt explanation of previous results, one might ask, what do we gain by thinking about these effects in terms of availability?

CONNECTIONS AND EXTENSIONS

Traditional models of inductive reasoning have focused on a single kind of knowledge in a domain, eschewing the effects of context. For example, the similarity-coverage model (Osherson et al., 1990) focused on taxonomic knowledge in the domain of biology, using similarity between premises and conclusions as well as a taxonomic coverage to predict inductive generalizations. These models account for phenomena such as taxonomic diversity, that is, the fact that people rate an anatomical property true of diverse premises such as *robins* and *ostriches* more likely to be shared by *all birds* than a property shared by *robins* and *doves* and are generally in remarkably close accord with novices generalizations of anatomical properties.[2] Though able to capture reasoning based on taxonomic knowledge, the similarity-coverage model does not account for reasoning based on other kinds of knowledge and thus does not naturally extend to the kinds of reasoning we have been discussing here (see Smith et al., 1993, for an account of some property effects). Some context effects, such as inferences about behavioral and anatomical inferences in Heit and Rubinstein (1993), can be handled by allowing similarity to be defined context sensitively; however, no similarity-based models can account for the kinds of asymmetric causal inferences in Shafto and Coley (2003).

Sloman's feature-based induction model (1993) also predicts inferences about taxonomic properties, but it differs from the similarity-coverage model in not assuming a taxonomic structure over objects. Under (the geometric interpretation of) this model, prior knowledge is represented by an object-feature matrix, and inferences are generated by considering the proportion of shared properties between the premise and conclusion, relative to the total number of properties for the premise. There are many potential ways to extend the feature-based model to handle context effects, including adding context-specific feature weights. However, all extensions require the addition of abstract knowledge not present in the original model.

Rather than focusing on the fact that these models do not account for property effects, we think it worthwhile to emphasize commonalities between the similarity-coverage and feature-based models and our availability-based approach. The success of both of these models in predicting undergraduates' judgments suggests that knowledge about taxonomic relations is central to undergraduates' conceptualization of biological kinds. We have suggested

---

[2] The authors also propose that category members may be differentially available; for example, suggesting that robins are more available members of the category *bird* than turtledoves.

that taxonomic knowledge is chronically more available to undergraduates, and therefore relied on as a default strategy, while taxonomic and ecological knowledge are both chronically available to experts (such as commercial fishermen). However, neither the similarity-based nor the feature-based model includes a means to explain the effects of properties on reasoning, or a natural way to explain how experience influences reasoning.

Some interesting parallels can be drawn between the availability framework and some previous work that has addressed aspects of induction discussed under our approach. Our notion of availability in inductive reasoning is analogous to Barsalou's (1982) distinction between *context-independent* and *context-dependent* properties of concepts.[3] Context-independent properties (e.g., basketballs *are round*) "are activated by the word for a concept on all occasions" (p. 82), whereas context-dependent properties (e.g., basketballs *float*) "are only activated by relevant contexts in which the word appears" (p. 82). Barsalou demonstrates that, for example, priming with relevant context facilitates the verification of context-dependent properties but has no effect on the verification of context-independent properties. This distinction can be applied to our analysis of availability in category-based induction by granting that relations among concepts, as well as properties of individual concepts, may vary in their context dependence. Thus, what we have called acute changes in availability correspond to priming a relevant context, whereas chronic changes in availability corresponds to representational changes in the context dependence of classes of relations among concepts (e.g., predator-prey relations). It remains to be seen whether any class of relations is truly context independent, but taxonomic relations may be one candidate (e.g., Coley, Shafto et al., 2005).

Our notion of availability as applied to category-based induction also fits nicely into Medin et al.'s (2003) "relevance framework." A central claim of the relevance framework is that relations among premise categories, or between premise and conclusion categories, guide or constrain an inductive inference to the degree that such relations are deemed *relevant*. Relevance, in turn, is conceptualized in terms of *effort* and *effect*. The less effort needed to access or construct a relation, the more likely it is to be deemed relevant to a particular inference. Conversely, premises that have greater cognitive effect (in the sense of potentially leading to conceptual changes or allowing the derivation of novel conclusions) are more likely to be deemed relevant. On this view, our notion of availability can be seen as a more detailed way to think about the effort component of the relevance framework. Specifically, the effort associated with a given

---

[3] We are grateful to Brett Hayes for pointing out this connection.

conceptual relation reflects the availability of that knowledge; all else being equal, more available knowledge requires less effort to access and use. Thus, both the acute and chronic changes in availability reviewed above reflect – from the perspective of relevance – acute and chronic changes in the effort required to access a given set of conceptual relations.

In the spirit of both Barsalou (1982) and Medin et al. (2003), availability makes two distinctions: chronic changes in availability of different kinds of knowledge grounded in experience, and acute changes in availability as a result of context. Chronic changes in availability account for why taxonomic knowledge is less effortful than ecological knowledge for biological novices and taxonomists but not for fishermen. Acute changes in availability reflect the fact that context manipulates effort to access different knowledge (cf. Heit & Bott, 2000). The interaction between chronic and acute changes in availability determines the degree to which people show inductive selectivity.

Though we believe availability provides a coherent framework uniting expertise and property differences in induction, we think that the true merit of thinking about category-based induction in terms of availability will be in the guidance it provides in moving research forward. In the next section, we describe some recent work inspired by availability, and derive additional novel (but yet untested) predictions from this proposal.

Availability in Action

We see two major challenges in the development of an availability-based framework. The first is to identify what kinds of predictions can be generated by understanding the relationship between knowledge and reasoning in terms of availability, and to begin to test those predictions. The second is to explain how chronic changes in availability arise with experience. In this section, we will outline some initial studies addressing the first challenge and some preliminary ideas which address the second.

To be useful, any framework must generate new hypotheses as well as describe existing results. In a recent set of studies, we investigated availability as a possible explanation for the lack of inductive selectivity in novice populations (Shafto, Coley, & Baldwin, 2005). To implicate availability, it is important to show that having knowledge is not sufficient for inductive selectivity. Previous research (Shafto & Coley, 2003) suggests that context (*novel diseases* and *novel properties*) did not elicit the selective use of taxonomic and ecological knowledge in biological novices. One reason novices may not have demonstrated inductive selectivity was a baseline difference in the availability of taxonomic and ecological knowledge. In a series of experiments (Shafto, Coley, & Baldwin, 2005), we provided support for this claim by investigating the effects of context on novices' use of taxonomic and ecological knowledge, focusing on ecological relations that were familiar to novices. Pre-testing ensured that the novices knew the taxonomic and ecological relations in question. However, despite demonstrated knowledge of ecological relations, participants consistently rated inductive generalizations between taxonomically related species stronger than generalizations between ecologically related species. This was true regardless of whether they were reasoning about a blank property, disease, or toxin. In other words, possessing requisite knowledge of ecological relations was not sufficient for the selective use of that knowledge to guide induction. As Shafto and Coley (2003) found, the property manipulation did not render ecological knowledge sufficiently available to novices.

In two subsequent experiments, we provided evidence that taxonomic knowledge was more available than ecological knowledge in this population. First, we contrasted primed and unprimed similarity judgments for pairs of taxonomically or ecologically related species (following Ross & Murphy, 1999, exp. 4). If ecological knowledge was chronically less available, then priming ecological categories should increase the availability of ecological knowledge, resulting in increased similarity ratings for ecological pairs in the primed versus the unprimed condition. In contrast, if taxonomic knowledge was already highly available, then taxonomic priming should elicit no change in similarity ratings. As predicted, priming was found to increase similarity ratings for ecologically related pairs but not taxonomically related pairs, consistent with the suggestion that ecological knowledge is less available than taxonomic knowledge.

A second experiment provided further evidence by contrasting inductive judgments with and without time pressure. We predicted that time pressure would decrease access to less available knowledge by curtailing memory search but would not affect use of knowledge that was already highly available. In line with this prediction, likelihood ratings for ecological inferences decreased under time pressure relative to unspeeded judgments, whereas ratings for taxonomic inferences remained unchanged. These results show that for novices in the domain of biology, taxonomic knowledge is chronically more available than ecological knowledge and suggest that differences in availability may impede inductive selectivity. More generally, this series of studies is one example of how the notion of availability can be used to generate novel predictions about the use of knowledge in category-based induction.

Apart from generating testable hypotheses about inductive reasoning, another important challenge for the availability framework is to elucidate the mechanisms by which experience elicits changes in availability of different kinds of knowledge. One route through which chronic changes may be elicited is the frequency with which knowledge is accessed. Naturally, we expect information that gets used frequently in a particular context to be more available (Horowitz et al., 1966). This assumption reflects the fact that our past experience should provide a useful reference in the future, a basic principle of memory (Anderson & Milson, 1989). Extending this idea to availability merely implements this assumption as a means to sort out what knowledge is deemed appropriate for a particular inference given our experience and the current context.

A second potential mechanism for eliciting chronic change in availability is representational efficiency. Availability should increase with increased representational efficiency. Here representational efficiency reflects a compromise between the accumulation of facts and a means to summarize the facts efficiently. For example, one reason that taxonomic knowledge may be highly available for biological reasoning is the fact that it provides a succinct summary of a large amount of factual knowledge. Taxonomic knowledge encompasses genetic information, anatomical information, information about shape, behavior, environment, and so forth. On the other hand, knowledge valued by experts such as ecological knowledge does not have the same immediate payoff that taxonomic knowledge does. Taxonomic structures provide a simple way of encompassing all living kinds in a representational structure that is scale invariant; all subsections of the taxonomy are branching trees. Perhaps an increase in availability of ecological knowledge for experts represents an increase in the efficiency with which ecological relations capture relevant knowledge. However, these proposals are speculations that will require extensive empirical research.

We suggest that the problem of reasoning in knowledge-rich domains is crucial to understanding human intelligence. We have focused on one aspect of this problem, how experience is brought into contact with context in informing inductive reasoning. We have argued that in any given context, different kinds of knowledge are more or less available, and that availability predicts how likely the knowledge is to be used in reasoning. Though much of our evidence at this stage is preliminary, the notion of availability unites existing work on knowledge and context-specific reasoning and may provide a useful framework from which to investigate how knowledge is deployed in specific situations to guide category-based induction.

References

Anderson, J. R., & Milson, R. (1989). Human memory: An adaptive perspective. *Psychological Review, 96,* 703–719.

Baker, A., & Coley, J. D. (2005). *Taxonomic and ecological relations in open-ended induction.* Paper presented at the 27th Annual Conference of the Cognitive Science Society, Stresa, Italy.

Barsalou, L. W. (1982). Context-independent and context-dependent information in concepts. *Memory & Cognition, 10,* 82–93.

Choi, I., Nisbett, R. E., & Smith, E. E. (1997). Culture, category salience, and inductive reasoning. *Cognition, 65,* 15–32.

Coley, J. D. (2005). *Relational properties in folk biological induction.* Paper presented at the Biennial Meetings of the Society for Research in Child Development, Atlanta, GA.

Coley, J. D., Baker, A., & Kemp, C. (2004). *Taxonomic and ecological relations in open-ended induction.* Paper presented at the 45th Annual Meeting of the Psychonomic Society, Minneapolis, MN.

Coley, J. D., Shafto, P., Stepanova, O., & Baraff, E. (2005). Knowledge and category-based induction. In W. Ahn, R. L. Goldstone, B. C. Love, A. B. Markman, & P. Wolff (Eds.), *Categorization inside and outside the laboratory: Essays in honor of Douglas L. Medin* (69–86). Washington, DC: American Psychological Association.

Coley, J. D., Vitkin, A. Z., Seaton, C. E., & Yopchick, J. E. (2005). *Effects of experience on relational inferences in children: The case of folk biology.* Paper presented at the 27th Annual Conference of the Cognitive Science Society, Stresa, Italy.

Heit, E., & Bott, L. (2000). Knowledge selection in category learning. *Psychology of Learning and Motivation, 39,* 163–199.

Heit, E., & Feeney, A. (2005). Relations between premise similarity and inductive strength. *Psychonomic Bulletin & Review, 12,* 340–344.

Heit, E., & Rubinstein, J. (1994). Similarity and property effects in inductive reasoning. *Journal of Experimental Psychology: Learning, Memory & Cognition, 20,* 411–422.

Horowitz, L. M., Norman, S. A., & Day, R. S. (1966). Availability and associative symmetry. *Psychological Review, 73,* 1–15.

López, A., Atran, S., Coley, J. D., Medin, D., & Smith, E. E. (1997). The tree of life: Universal and cultural features of folkbiological taxonomies and inductions. *Cognitive Psychology, 32,* 251–295.

Medin, D., Coley, J. D., Storms, G., & Hayes, B. (2003). A relevance theory of induction. *Psychonomic Bulletin and Review, 10,* 517–532.

Medin, D. L., Lynch, E. B., Coley, J. D., & Atran, S. (1997). Categorization and reasoning among tree experts: Do all roads lead to Rome? *Cognitive Psychology, 32,* 49–96.

Nguyen, S. P., & Murphy, G. L. (2003). An apple is more than just a fruit: Cross-classification in children's concepts. *Child Development, 6,* 1783–1806.

Nisbett, R. E., Peng, K., Choi, I., & Norenzayan, A. (2001). Culture and systems of thought: Holistic versus analytic cognition. *Psychological Review, 108,* 291–310.

Osherson, D. N., Smith, E. E., Wilkie, O., Lopez, A., & Shafir, E. (1990). Category-based induction. *Psychological Review, 97*(2), 185–200.

Pearlstone, Z., & Tulving, E. (1966). Availability versus accessibility of information in memory for words. *Journal of Verbal Learning and Verbal Behavior, 5,* 381–391.

Proffitt, J. B., Coley, J. D., & Medin, D. L. (2000). Expertise and category-based induction. *Journal of Experimental Psychology: Learning, Memory & Cognition, 26,* 811–828.

Ross, B. H., & Murphy, G. L. (1999). Food for thought: Cross-classification and category organization in a complex real-world domain. *Cognitive Psychology, 38,* 495–553.

Shafto, P., & Coley, J. D. (2003). Development of categorization and reasoning in the natural world: Novices to experts, naïve similarity to ecological knowledge. *Journal of Experimental Psychology: Learning, Memory & Cognition, 29,* 641–649.

Shafto, P., Coley, J. D., & Baldwin, D. (2005). *Availability in inductive reasoning.* Paper presented at the 46th Annual Meeting of the Psychonomic Society, Toronto.

Shafto, P., Kemp, C., Baraff, E., Coley, J. D., & Tenenbaum, J. B. (2005). *Context-sensitive induction*. Paper presented at the 27th Annual Conference of the Cognitive Science Society, Stresa, Italy.

Shafto, P., Kemp, C., Baraff, E., Coley, J. D., & Tenenbaum, J.B. (in prep). Inductive reasoning with causal knowledge.

Sloman, S. A. (1993). Feature-based induction. *Cognitive Psychology, 25*, 231–280.

Smith, E. E., Shafir, E., & Osherson, D. N. (1993). Similarity, plausibility, and judgments of probability. *Cognition, 49*, 67–96.

Stepanova, O., & Coley, J. D. (2003). *Animals and alcohol: The role of experience in inductive reasoning among college students.* Paper presented at the 44th Annual Meeting of the Psychonomic Society, Vancouver, British Columbia.

Stepanova, O. (2004). *Vodka and vermin: Naïve reasoning about animals and alcohol.* Unpublished doctoral dissertation, Northeastern University.

Tversky, A., & Kahneman, D. (1973). Availability: A heuristic for judging frequency and probability. *Cognitive Psychology, 5*, 207–232.

Vitkin, A. Z., Coley, J. D., & Hu, R. (2005). *Children's use of relevance in open-ended induction in the domain of biology.* Paper presented at the 27th Annual Conference of the Cognitive Science Society, Stresa, Italy.

Vitkin, A., Coley, J. D., & Kane, R. (2005). *Salience of taxonomic and ecological relations in children's biological categorization.* Paper presented at the Biennial Meetings of the Society for Research in Child Development, Atlanta, GA.

6

From Similarity to Chance

Sergey Blok, Daniel Osherson, and Douglas L. Medin

In reality, all arguments from experience are founded on the similarity which we discover among natural objects, and by which we are induced to expect effects similar to those which we have found to follow from such objects. . . . From causes which appear similar we expect similar effects.

> David Hume, *An Enquiry Concerning Human Understanding* (1772)

1. SIMILARITY AND INFERENCE

1.1 The Property Problem

Ever since Goodman's (1972) warnings about the "false friend" similarity, psychologists have been cautious about explaining inductive inference in terms of resemblance. Innumerable shared properties unite any pair of objects, inviting their dubious certification as similar along with the inference that some further property is also shared. Genuine resemblance appears to be a three-place predicate, relating two objects only in the context of a set S of properties (often implicit) that determine the *respects* in which objects may be compared.[1]

When it is plausible that the same set S is brought to mind in judging similarity and inductive strength, it can be revealing to explain the latter in terms of the former. Thus, famous Linda resembles the average feminist bank teller more than the average bank teller; and whatever properties support this judgment are likely also in place when people judge her chance of being one

---

[1] See also Goodman (1955), Quine (1960). In the psychology literature, the matter has been rehearsed by Tversky & Gati (1978), Osherson, Smith, & Shafir (1986), Medin, Goldstone, & Gentner (1993), and Keil, Smith, Simons, & Levin (1998), among others.

or the other.[2] Indeed, the probabilities people assign in Linda-like problems are accurately predicted from the relevant similarities rated independently (Shafir, Smith, & Osherson, 1990).

A radical means of inclining S to remain constant between similarity and inference is to limit attention to arguments involving "blank" predicates like *requires biotin for hemoglobin synthesis.* The blankness consists in the difficulty of evaluating the relative credibility of the predicate's application to different objects.[3] The blank-predicate argument

Bears require biotin for hemoglobin synthesis.

Wolves require biotin for hemoglobin synthesis.

evokes a vaguely physiological context but not much more. Thus, one may have the intuition that cameras and computers do not require biotin but no *a priori* sense of whether bears and wolves do. Nonetheless, the assertion that bears require biotin, coupled with the similarity of wolves to bears, accords strength to the foregoing argument. Theories that incorporate similarity as a basis for induction – such as the SIMILARITY-COVERAGE model – have been able to account for a range of reasoning phenomena.[4]

SIMILARITY-COVERAGE is unsuited to non-blank predicates like that figuring in the following arguments;

(1) (a) $\dfrac{\text{Fieldmice often carry the parasite Floxum.}}{\text{Housecats often carry the parasite Floxum.}}$

    (b) $\dfrac{\text{Tigers often carry the parasite Floxum.}}{\text{Housecats often carry the parasite Floxum.}}$

---

[2] Linda was born in Tversky & Kahneman (1983). For recent debate about the fallacy she illustrates, see Kahneman & Tversky (1996), Gigerenzer (1996), and Tentori, Bonini, & Osherson (2004), along with references cited there.

[3] A more cautious formulation would relativize blankness to a particular judge and also to the objects in play. Degrees of blankness would also be acknowledged, in place of the absolute concept here invoked. In what follows, we'll rely on rough formulations (like the present one) to convey principal ideas.

[4] See Osherson, Smith, Wilkie, López, & E. Shafir (1990). An alternative account is offered in Sloman (1993). Blank predicates first appear in Rips (1975). For examination of SIMILARITY-COVERAGE type phenomena in the context of natural category hierarchies, see Coley, Atran, & Medin (1997) and Medin, Coley, Storms, & Hayes (2003). Developmental perspectives on SIMILARITY-COVERAGE are available in López, Gelman, Gutheil, & Smith (1992), Heit & Hahn (1999), and Lo, Sides, Rozelle, & Osherson (2002). Similarity among biological categories may be more resistant to contextual shifts than is the case for other categories (Barsalou & Ross, 1986). This would explain their popularity in many discussions of inductive inference.

Many people find (1)a to be stronger than (1)b, no doubt because the relational property *characteristically ingests* readily comes to mind (probably evoked by mention of parasites). In contrast, ingestion is unlikely to be salient when judging the similarity of fieldmice to housecats, preventing similarity from predicting strength. The root of the problem is the difference in causal theories that may occur to the reasoner when diverse sets of properties are evoked in the two settings.[5]

For another limitation of Similarity-Coverage, consider the conclusion that Labradors can bite through wire (of a given thickness and composition) given the alternative premises (a) Collies can, versus (b) Chihuahuas can. More people think that (b) provides better evidence for the conclusion than does (a), despite the fact that Labradors are more similar to Collies than to Chihuahuas (Smith, Shafir, & Osherson, 1993). This intuition likely derives from the belief that Chihuahuas are less powerful than Collies, hence (b) is less likely to be true. The example therefore suggests that a model of induction based solely on similarity will fail when the probability of predicate-application is not uniform across the objects in play.

The aim of the chapter is to show how the prior probabilities of statements might be incorporated into a similarity-based model of induction.[6] We attempt to achieve this by elaborating a new version of the "Gap Model" advanced in Smith et al. (1993). We also suggest how probabilities and similarities can be exploited to construct joint distributions over sets of propositional variables. The first step in our endeavor is to characterize a class of predicates that are neither blank nor epistemically too rich.

1.2 Towards Non-Blank but Manageable Predicates

In the space between blank and Floxum-like predicates are those that are meaningful yet mentally evoke the same set S of properties when people judge similarity compared to argument strength. Let us use Qo to abbreviate the attribution of a predicate Q to an object or category o, and $\neg Qo$ for the denial of this attribution. An argument composed of statements like these will be termed *stable* just in case the same set of properties come to

---

[5] The Floxum example is based on López, Atran, Coley, Medin, & Smith (1997). It is exploited in Lo et al. (2002) to argue that the "diversity principle" does not have the normative status often assumed by psychologists. For the role of causal theories in commonsense reasoning, see Ahn, Kalish, Medin, & Gelman (1995) and Lassaline (1996), along with the theoretical discussions in Ortiz (1993) and Turner (1993).

[6] Reservations about the role of similarity in theories of reasoning are advanced in Sloman & Rips (1998). Overviews of theories of inductive reasoning are available in Heit (2000), Sloman & Lagnado (2005).

mind when judging the strength of the argument compared to judging the similarity of the objects figuring in it. To test the stability of an argument, the mental potentiation of various predicates would need to be measured during similarity judgment and inference. We do not offer a recipe for such measurement but observe that stability is not circularly defined in terms that guarantee the success of any particular model of inference (like ours, below). Call a predicate "stable" if it gives rise to stable arguments.

For a further distinction, suppose that a is Dell Computer Corporation, and c is HP/Compaq. If Q is *increases sales next year*, then Qa will strike many reasoners as confirmatory of Qc, whereas if Q is *increases market share next year*, then Qa will seem disconfirmatory of Qc. The similarity of a and c can be expected to have different effects in the two cases. To mark the difference, we qualify a predicate Q as *monotonically increasing* [respectively *decreasing*] for objects $O = \{o_1 \cdots o_n\}$ just in case $\mathrm{Prob}\,(Qx : Qy) \geq \mathrm{Prob}\,(Qx)$ [respectively, $\mathrm{Prob}\,(Qx : Qy) \leq \mathrm{Prob}\,(Qx)$] for all $x, y \in O$; and call Q *monotonic* for O if Q is either monotonically increasing or decreasing for O.

Let us illustrate these ideas. The authors expect that for many people the following predicates are monotonically increasing, and yield stable arguments over the class of mammal species[7]:

> has trichromatic vision
> can suffer muscle damage through contact with poliomyelitis
> (2) brain/body mass ratio is 2 percent or more
> requires at least 5 hours of sleep per day for normal functioning
> sex drive varies seasonally

We are now in a position to define a circumscribed yet vast class of arguments.

> (3) DEFINITION: An argument A is *elementary* just in case:
>   (a) A has the form $\pm Qa \,/\, \pm Qc$ or $\pm Qa, \pm Qb \,/\, \pm Qc$, where a, b, c occupy the same hierarchical level;
>   (b) A is stable; and
>   (c) Q is monotonic for the objects appearing in A.

The notation $\pm Qo$ represents either Qo or $\neg Qo$.

How often do elementary arguments embody a person's reasoning? The authors refrain from exaggerated appraisal. We are uncertain, for example, of the stability of the predicate "can bite through wire," discussed earlier. Let it

---

[7] For another example, susceptibility to disease is usually perceived to be shared for species of the same genus (Coley, Atran, & Medin, 1997).

merely be noted that few explicit, testable theories of inductive strength for non-trivial classes of arguments are presently on offer. The stable predicates in (2) suggest the richness of the class of elementary arguments. Success in predicting their strength is thus a challenging endeavor and may point the way to more general models.

1.3 Theoretical Goals

The next section advances a theory of the strength of elementary arguments. Given such an argument, let $\text{Prob}\,(\pm Qc : \pm Qa)$ or $\text{Prob}\,(\pm Qc : \pm Qa, \pm Qb)$ be the conditional probability assigned by a given judge to the argument's conclusion given its premises. We attempt to predict these numbers from (a) the absolute probabilities the judge assigns to premises and conclusion individually, and (b) the similarities among the objects appearing in the argument. Letting $\text{sim}(x, y)$ represent the judge's perceived similarity of x to y, our theory takes the form of a function with the following inputs and outputs:

	type of elementary argument	inputs		output
(4)	$\pm Qa / \pm Qc$	$\text{Prob}\,(\pm Qc)$ $\text{Prob}\,(\pm Qa)$ $\text{sim}(a, c)$		$\text{Prob}\,(\pm Qc : \pm Qa)$
	$\pm Qa, \pm Qb / \pm Qc$	$\text{Prob}\,(\pm Qc)$ $\text{Prob}\,(\pm Qa)$ $\text{Prob}\,(\pm Qb)$ $\text{sim}(a, c)$ $\text{sim}(b, c)$ $\text{sim}(a, b)$		$\text{Prob}\,(\pm Qc : \pm Qa,$ $\pm Qb)$

Similarity judgments are assumed to lie in the unit interval (identity corresponding to 1), and to be symmetric.[8] Beyond this, our model makes no assumptions about how similarity assessments are generated; in particular, complex processes of "feature alignment" may be involved (as in Gentner & Markman, 1997; Goldstone, 1994). Nor do we require that reasoners know whether an argument is elementary, specifically, whether its predicate is stable. Our theory applies when stability holds; other cases lie outside the boundary

---

[8] Claims for asymmetry appear in Tversky (1977) but seem to arise only in unusual circumstances; see Aguilar & Medin (1999). The assumption $\text{sim}(o_i, o_j) \in [0, 1]$ is substantive; in particular, dissimilarity might be unbounded. This possibility is ignored in what follows. For a review of ideas concerning asymmetries in inductive reasoning, see Chapter 3 by Medin & Waxman in the present volume.

conditions. The reliance on absolute probabilities as inputs to the theory [Prob $(\pm Qc)$, etc.] underlines the fundamental character of such judgments. For analysis of their provenance, see Juslin and Persson (2002), which adapts the classification model of Medin and Schaffer (1978).

The "Gap" model described by Smith, Shafir, and Osherson (1993) was designed for stable predicates but required strong hypotheses about the featural decomposition of objects and predicates. The present theory is free of such assumptions and captures the insights of the Gap model in a different way. Given the family history of these ideas, we refer to the present model as "GAP2."

After presentation of the theory, we describe an initial experimental test and its results. A second approach to exploiting similarity for predicting inductive judgments is then advanced.

2. A THEORY OF ELEMENTARY ARGUMENTS

Our theory takes the form of equations that determine the outputs of (4) from the inputs. For simplicity in what follows, we consider only predicates that are monotonically increasing. The decreasing case is presumed to be parallel. As a preliminary, we list some qualitative conditions that any candidate theory seems required to satisfy. The conditions express aspects of common sense for a typical reasoner.

2.1 Qualitative Requirements: The One-Premise Case

Let an elementary argument $Qa \; / \; Qc$ be given, and consider Prob $(Qc : Qa)$. We expect the latter quantity to approach 1 as $\text{sim}(a, c)$ does. For if $\text{sim}(a, c) \approx 1$ then Prob $(Qc : Qa) \approx$ Prob $(Qc : Qc) = 1$. To illustrate, the conditional probability that pigs have trichromatic vision given that the hogs do is close to 1 given the similarity of these creatures.

On the other hand, Prob $(Qc : Qa)$ should go to Prob (Qc) as $\text{sim}(a, c)$ goes to 0, This is because $\text{sim}(a, c) \approx 0$ signals the unrelatedness of a and c, rendering Qa irrelevant to the estimation of Qc.

Further conditions arise from purely probabilistic considerations. Thus, Prob $(Qa) \approx 1$ should imply Prob $(Qc : Qa) \approx$ Prob (Qc). (Consider the probability that newborn rats typically weigh at least one ounce assuming that the same is true for newborn elephants.) Conversely, and other things equal, as Prob (Qa) decreases, Prob $(Qc : Qa)$ should increase. Our equations should also respect the familiar fact that as Prob (Qc) goes to 1, so does Prob $(Qc : Qa)$, and similarly for zero.

Related requirements apply to arguments of the forms (i) $\neg Qa \ / \ Qc$, (ii) $Qa \ / \ \neg Qc$, and (iii) $\neg Qa \ / \ \neg Qc$. For example, Prob $(Qc : \neg Qa)$ and Prob $(\neg Qc : Qa)$ should both approach 0 as $\text{sim}(a, c)$ approaches 1, whereas Prob $(\neg Qc : \neg Qa)$ should approach 1.

2.2 Qualitative Requirements: The Two-Premise Case

Now let a two-premise elementary argument $Qa, Qb \ / \ Qc$ be given. Common sense suggests a large number of constraints on Prob $(Qc : Qa, Qb)$. To begin, as either $\text{sim}(a, c)$ or $\text{sim}(b, c)$ approach 1, Prob $(Qc : Qa, Qb)$ should also approach 1. To illustrate, the conditional probability that pigs have trichromatic vision given that the hogs and squirrels do is close to 1 in view of the similarity of pigs and hogs.

If both $\text{sim}(a, c)$ and $\text{sim}(b, c)$ go to 0, then Prob $(Qc : Qa, Qb)$ should go to Prob (Qc) (since zero similarity signals irrelevance of the conditioning events). On the other hand, if just $\text{sim}(a, c)$ approaches 0, then Prob $(Qc : Qa, Qb)$ should approach Prob $(Qc : Qb)$; likewise, if just $\text{sim}(b, c)$ approaches 0, then Prob $(Qc : Qa, Qb)$ should approach Prob $(Qc : Qa)$. For example, the probability that wolves are fond of garlic given that the same is true of bears and bees is close to the probability that wolves are fond of garlic given than bears are.

Next, as $\text{sim}(a, b)$ goes to 1, Prob $(Qc : Qa, Qb)$ should go to Prob $(Qc : Qa)$ [equivalently, Prob $(Qc : Qa, Qb)$ should go to Prob $(Qc : Qb)$]. For $\text{sim}(a, b) \approx 1$ indicates that Qa, Qb record nearly identical facts. Thus, the probability that otters can hear ultrasounds given that porpoises and dolphins can should be close to the probability that otters can hear ultrasounds given that porpoises can. On the other hand, as $\text{sim}(a, b)$ approaches 0, the strength of $Qa, Qb \ / \ Qc$ should increase (the "diversity effect"). We therefore expect Prob $(Qc : Qa, Qb) >$ Prob $(Qc : Qa)$, Prob $(Qc : Qb)$ (except at the extremes). To illustrate, the probability that geese have a magnetic sense given that sparrows and eagles do exceeds the probability that geese have a magnetic sense given that sparrows do, without reference to eagles.

Additional conditions on Prob $(Qc : Qa, Qb)$ involve only probability. They include the following:

(a) As Prob (Qa) approaches 1, Prob $(Qc : Qa, Qb)$ approaches Prob $(Qc : Qb)$. Likewise, as Prob (Qb) approaches 1, Prob $(Qc : Qa, Qb)$ approaches Prob $(Qc : Qa)$.

(b) As Prob (Qa) and Prob (Qb) both approach 1, Prob $(Qc : Qa, Qb)$ approaches Prob (Qc).

(c) Other things equal, as $\text{Prob}(Qa)$ and $\text{Prob}(Qb)$ both decrease, $\text{Prob}(Qc : Qa, Qb)$ increases.

(d) As $\text{Prob}(Qc)$ approaches 1, so does $\text{Prob}(Qc : Qa, Qb)$; as $\text{Prob}(Qc)$ approaches zero, so does $\text{Prob}(Qc : Qa, Qb)$.

Similar constraints apply to the seven types of two-premise arguments with negated premises or conclusion; their formulation is left to the reader.

2.3 Formulas for One-Premise Arguments

Consider again the elementary argument $Qa \ / \ Qc$. We propose that $\text{Prob}(Qc : Qa)$ is governed by

(5) $\text{Prob}(Qc : Qa) = \text{Prob}(Qc)^{\alpha}$, where

$$\alpha = \left(\frac{1 - \text{sim}(a, c)}{1 + \text{sim}(a, c)} \right)^{1 - \text{Prob}(Qa)}$$

The reader can verify that (5) satisfies the qualitative conditions reviewed above for $Qa \ / \ Qc$. To illustrate, as $\text{sim}(a, c)$ goes to 1, $\frac{1 - \text{sim}(a,c)}{1 + \text{sim}(a,c)}$ goes to 0, hence α goes to 0, so $\text{Prob}(Qc)^{\alpha}$ goes to 1 [hence, $\text{Prob}(Qc : Qa)$ goes to 1]. For another example, as $\text{Prob}(Qa)$ goes to 1, α goes to 1, so $\text{Prob}(Qc)^{\alpha}$ goes to $\text{Prob}(Qc)$, hence $\text{Prob}(Qc : Qa)$ goes to $\text{Prob}(Qc)$ as desired. Of course, (5) is not unique with these properties, but it is the simplest formula that occurs to us [and restricts $\text{Prob}(Qc : Qa)$ to the unit interval]. In the next section, (5) will be seen to provide a reasonable approximation to $\text{Prob}(Qc : Qa)$ in an experimental context. It can be seen that our proposal is meant for use with monotonically increasing predicates inasmuch as it guarantees that $\text{Prob}(Qc : Qa) \geq \text{Prob}(Qc)$.

The following formulas are assumed to govern one-premise elementary arguments with negations. They satisfy commonsense requirements corresponding to those discussed above.

(6) $\text{Prob}(Qc : \neg Qa) = 1.0 - (1.0 - \text{Prob}(Qc))^{\alpha}$, where

$$\alpha = \left(\frac{1 - \text{sim}(a, c)}{1 + \text{sim}(a, c)} \right)^{\text{Prob}(Qa)}$$

(7) $\text{Prob}(\neg Qc : Qa) = 1.0 - \text{Prob}(Qc)^{\alpha}$, where

$$\alpha = \left(\frac{1 - \text{sim}(a, c)}{1 + \text{sim}(a, c)} \right)^{1 - \text{Prob}(Qa)}$$

(8) $\text{Prob} (\neg Qc : \neg Qa) = (1.0 - \text{Prob} (Qc))^{\alpha}$, where

$$\alpha = \left(\frac{1 - \text{sim}(a, c)}{1 + \text{sim}(a, c)} \right)^{\text{Prob}(Qa)}$$

The formulas also guarantee that $\text{Prob} (Qc : Qa) + \text{Prob} (\neg Qc : Qa) = 1$ and $\text{Prob} (Qc : \neg Qa) + \text{Prob} (\neg Qc : \neg Qa) = 1$.

We do not assume that people perform the calculations corresponding to Equations (5)–(8). Our claim is merely that the formulas approximate whatever underlying process gives rise to judgments about conditional probability.

2.4 Formulas for Two-Premise Arguments

Two-premise arguments likewise require distinguishing multiple cases, all variations on the same theme. We consider only arguments with positive conclusions; negated conclusions are handled similarly (and none of our experiments involve them). We rely on the following concept:

(9) DEFINITION: The *confirmation* exhibited by an argument of form Qa / Qc is

$$\frac{\text{Prob} (Qc : Qa) - \text{Prob} (Qc)}{1 - \text{Prob} (Qc)}.$$

The *confirmation* exhibited by an argument of form $\neg Qa / Qc$ is

$$\frac{\text{Prob} (Qc) - \text{Prob} (Qc : \neg Qa)}{\text{Prob} (Qc)}.$$

Given an argument $\pm Qa, \pm Qb / Qc$, the *dominant premise* is $\pm Qa$ if the confirmation exhibited by $\pm Qa / Qc$ exceeds the confirmation exhibited by $\pm Qb / Qc$; otherwise, $\pm Qb$ is the dominant premise.

Confirmation is the impact of an argument's premise on the credibility of its conclusion. The measure suggested above normalizes by the potential impact allowed by the prior credibility of the conclusion (namely, the distance to unity for positive premises and the distance to zero for negative). A variety of confirmation measures are analyzed in Eells and Fitelson (2002). In Tentori, Crupi, Bonini, and Osherson (2007), they are compared for their ability to predict shifts of opinion in an experimental setting involving urns. The dominant premise in a two-premise argument is the one that yields the one-premise argument of greatest confirmation. The one-premise probabilities are derived from the theory of one-premise arguments offered above. We now present our theory of two-premise arguments.

(10) CASE 1. Arguments of form $Qa, Qb / Qc$ with Qa dominant.

Prob $(Qc : Qa, Qb) =$ Prob $(Qc : Qa) +$
$[(1 - \text{sim}(a, b)) \times (1 - \text{Prob}\,(Qc : Qa)) \times (\text{Prob}\,(Qc : Qb) - \text{Prob}\,(Qc))].$

Arguments of form $Qa, Qb / Qc$ with Qb dominant are treated similarly.

In words, (10) claims that Prob $(Qc : Qa, Qb)$ is given by the probability of the dominant argument increased by a fraction of the probability $1 -$ Prob $(Qc : Qa)$ that the dominant argument "leaves behind." The size of this fraction depends on two factors, namely, the similarity between a and b (to avoid redundancy), and the impact of the nondominant premise on the credibility of Qc.

The constraints outlined earlier are satisfied by (10). For example, the formula implies that Prob $(Qc : Qa, Qb) \approx 1$ if $\text{sim}(a, c) \approx 1$. Note that our proposal ensures that strength increases with extra premises, that is, Prob $(Qc : Qa, Qb) \geq$ Prob $(Qc : Qa)$, Prob $(Qc : Qb)$. This feature is plausible given the restriction to monotonically increasing predicates.

We now list the other two-premise cases. They are predictable from (10) by switching the direction of similarity and "the probability left behind" as appropriate.

(11) CASE 2. Arguments of form $\neg Qa, Qb / Qc$ with $\neg Qa$ dominant.

Prob $(Qc : \neg Qa, Qb) =$ Prob $(Qc : \neg Qa) +$
$[\text{sim}(a, b) \times (\text{Prob}\,(Qc : \neg Qa)) \times (\text{Prob}\,(Qc : Qb) - \text{Prob}\,(Qc))].$

Arguments of form $Qa, \neg Qb / Qc$ with $\neg Qb$ dominant are treated similarly.

(12) CASE 3. Arguments of form $\neg Qa, Qb / Qc$ with Qb dominant.

Prob $(Qc : \neg Qa, Qb) =$ Prob $(Qc : Qb) +$
$[\text{sim}(a, b) \times (1 - \text{Prob}\,(Qc : Qb)) \times (\text{Prob}\,(Qc : \neg Qa) - \text{Prob}\,(Qc))].$

Arguments of form $Qa, \neg Qb / Qc$ with Qa dominant are treated similarly.

(13) CASE 4. Arguments of form $\neg Qa, \neg Qb / Qc$ with $\neg Qa$ dominant.

Prob $(Qc : \neg Qa, \neg Qb) =$ Prob $(Qc : \neg Qa) +$
$[(1 - \text{sim}(a, b)) \times (\text{Prob}\,(Qc : \neg Qa)) \times (\text{Prob}\,(Qc : \neg Qb) - \text{Prob}\,(Qc))].$

Arguments of form $\neg Qa, \neg Qb / Qc$ with $\neg Qb$ dominant are treated similarly.

In summary, GAP2 – our theory of elementary arguments – consists of formulas (5)–(8), and (10)–(13). For a blank predicate Q, we set Prob (Qo) to a fixed constant for any object o (.5 will often be a reasonable choice). Then GAP2 still makes intuitively sound predictions, allowing it to be applied to elementary arguments with blank predicates as a limiting case.

3. EXPERIMENTAL TEST OF THE THEORY

3.1 Stimuli and Procedure

To test GAP2 quantitatively we chose a domain about which undergraduates were likely to have opinions and interest, namely, post-graduation salaries from different colleges and universities. The following institutions served as objects:

(14)	(a) Connecticut State University	(b) Oklahoma State University
	(c) Arkansas State University	(d) Yale University
	(e) Harvard University	(f) Harvard Divinity School
	(g) Texas Technical Institute	(h) Texas Bible College

The following predicate was employed:

graduates [of a given institution] earned an average salary of *more* than $50,000 a year in their first job after graduation.

Its negation was taken to be the following:

graduates [of a given institution] earned an average salary of *less* than $50,000 a year in their first job after graduation.

Considering just objects (14)a – e, there are twenty arguments of form Qa / Qc, and sixty of form Qa, Qb / Qc. Nine undergraduates were recruited to assess the inputs and outputs in (4) for all twenty arguments of form Qa / Qc, and half of the sixty arguments of form Qa, Qb / Qc. Another nine did the same for all twenty arguments of form Qa / Qc, and the other half of the sixty arguments of form Qa, Qb / Qc.[9]

---

[9] The predicate was slightly (but inessentially) different for these eighteen participants. Note that we distinguish the order of two conditioning events; otherwise, there would be only thirty probabilities of form Prob $(Qc : Qa, Qb)$ based on five objects. No student received two arguments differing just on premise order. The order in which information is presented is an important variable in many reasoning contexts (Johnson-Laird, 1983) but there was little impact in the present study.

Considering just objects (14)e–h, there are twelve arguments of form Qa / Qc and twelve of form $\neg Qa$ / Qc. Forty-one additional students evaluated the inputs and outputs for all twenty-four arguments of these two forms. The same objects give rise to ninety-six two-premise arguments of form Qa, Qb / Qc or $\neg Qa, Qb$ / Qc or $Qa, \neg Qb$ / Qc or $\neg Qa, \neg Qb$ / Qc. A third group of forty-seven students evaluated inputs and outputs for different halves of these ninety-six arguments (each argument was evaluated by either twenty-three or twenty-four people).

All participants were undergraduates at Northwestern University. Data were collected using a computerized questionnaire. Similarity judgments were elicited first, followed by absolute probabilities, then conditional probabilities. Within these categories, stimuli were individually randomized.

3.2 Results

Overall, the inputs and outputs for 200 different arguments were evaluated, each by nine, eighteen, twenty-three, twenty-four, or forty-one undergraduates. The analysis that follows is based on the mean estimates for each input and output.

We computed the Pearson correlation between the values obtained for $\text{Prob}(Qc : \pm Qa)$ or $\text{Prob}(Qc : \pm Qa, \pm Qb)$ with the values predicted by GAP2. The result is $r = 0.94$. The regression line has slope $= 0.874$, and intercept $= 0.094$. See Figure 6.1. To gauge the role of the prior probability $\text{Prob}(Qc)$ in GAP2's performance, we computed the correlation between the observed probabilities $\text{Prob}(Qc : \pm Qa)$ and $\text{Prob}(Qc : \pm Qa, \pm Qb)$ versus the predictions of GAP2 with $\text{Prob}(Qc)$ subtracted out. The correlation remains substantial at $r = 0.88$ (slope $= 0.811$, intercept $= 0.079$).

Twenty arguments of form Qa / Qc were evaluated using objects (14)a–e, and another twelve using (14)e–h. In thirty-one of these thirty-two cases, the average probabilities conform to the monotonicity principle $\text{Prob}(Qc : Qa) \geq \text{Prob}(Qc)$ thereby agreeing with GAP2. The situation is different in the two-premise case. An argument of form Qa, Qb / Qc exhibits monotonicity if the average responses yield the following:

(15) $\text{Prob}(Qc : Qa, Qb) \geq \max\{\text{Prob}(Qc : Qa), \text{Prob}(Qc : Qb)\}$.

In our experiment, objects (14)a–e figured in sixty arguments of form Qa, Qb / Qc, with the same participants also evaluating Qa / Qc and Qb / Qc. In these sixty cases, (15) was violated fifty-one times ($p < .001$ via a binomial test).

These results suggest modifying our theory by *averaging* the impact of individual premises in a two-premise argument. Let us be cautious, however,

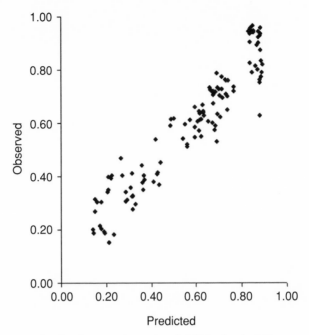

FIGURE 6.1. Predicted versus observed probabilities for the 200 arguments.

about backing off GAP2's monotonicity in this way. Averaging depicts the reasoner as strangely insensitive to the accumulation of evidence, which becomes an implausible hypothesis for larger premise sets. Also, the prevalence of nonmonotonic responding may be sensitive to procedural details. A preliminary study that we have conducted yields scant violation of monotonicity when premises are presented sequentially rather than two at a time.

3.3 Second Test of the Model

To assess the generality of the foregoing results, we constructed sixteen one-premise and sixteen two-premise arguments using the following objects and predicate.

Objects:

bears	wolves	cows
sheep	cougars	lions

Predicate: "have at least 18% of their cortex in the frontal lobe"

The sixteen one-premise arguments were equally divided among the forms Qa / Qc, $Qa / \neg Qc$, $\neg Qa / Qc$, and $\neg Qa / \neg Qc$. The sixteen two-premise arguments were equally divided among $Qa, Qb / Qc$ and $Qa, \neg Qb / Qc$. Objects

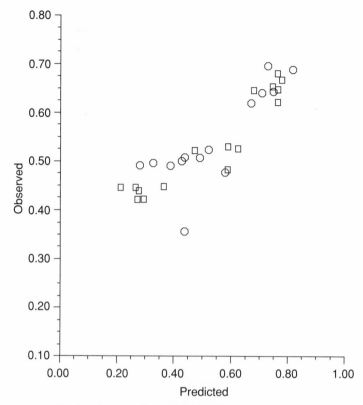

FIGURE 6.2. Predicted versus observed probabilities for thirty-two arguments.

(i.e., the six mammals) were assigned to the thirty-two arguments so as balance their frequency of occurrence. Twenty college students at Northwestern
University rated the similarity of each of the fifteen pairs of objects drawn
from the list above. A separate group of twenty students estimated the conditional probabilities of the thirty-two arguments plus the probabilities of the
six statements Qa. Data were collected via computer interface.

Since the similarity and probability estimates were collected from separate
groups of subjects there could be no contamination of one kind of judgment
by the other. The data from each group were averaged. The fifteen similarity
averages plus six averages for unconditional probabilities were then used
to predict the thirty-two average conditional probabilities via GAP2. The
correlation between predicted and observed values was .89. The results are
plotted in Figure 6.2.

More thorough test of GAP2 (and comparison to rivals) requires experimentation with a range of predicates and objects. The arguments described in

here are *homogeneous* in the sense that the same predicate figures in each. We expect GAP2 to apply equally well to *heterogeneous* collections of elementary arguments (involving a multiplicity of predicates).

4. EXTENSIONS OF GAP2

It is easy to envision extensions of GAP2 beyond elementary arguments [as defined in (3)]. For example, the conditional probability associated with a general-conclusion argument like

Rats have retractable claws.
Squirrels have retractable claws.

All rodents have retractable claws.

might be computed as the minimum of the conditional probabilities for

Rats have retractable claws.
Squirrels have retractable claws.

X have retractable claws.

according to GAP2, where X ranges over the rodent species that come to the reasoner's mind.[10] Another extension is to arguments in which neither the object nor predicate match between premise and conclusion. The goal would be to explain the strength of arguments like the following:

Howler Monkeys will eat cheddar cheese.

Spider Monkeys will eat Swiss cheese.

Both these extensions still require that the argument's predicate(s) be stable and monotonic for the single-premise case. Escaping this limitation requires understanding how the same predicate can evoke different associations when assessing strength compared to similarity. Specific causal information may often be responsible for such a state of affairs. We acknowledge not (presently)

[10] A "coverage" variable could also be added to the theory, in the style of the Similarity-Coverage Model. Coverage for specific arguments is motivated by asymmetry phenomena such as the greater strength of 'Qcats / Qbats' compared to 'Qbats / Qcats' (see Carey, 1985; Osherson et al., 1990). GAP2 does not predict this phenomenon for any predicate Q such that $\mathsf{Prob}(Qcats) = \mathsf{Prob}\,(Qbats)$ (e.g., when Q is blank). Asymmetry is known to be a weak effect, however (see Hampton & Cannon, 2004). If it is robust enough to merit modeling, this could also be achieved by positing asymmetry in sim.

knowing how to incorporate causal judgments into an explicit model of induction.

5. CONSTRUCTING JOINT PROBABILITY DISTRIBUTIONS USING SIMILARITY

Theories like GAP2 might help to automate the collection of subjective probabilities for artificial expert systems, especially since it is conditional probabilities that are typically needed (Pearl, 1988; Russell & Norvig, 2003). A more general approach to generating large sets of probability estimates for use in A.I. would construct an entire joint distribution from simple inputs involving similarities and probabilities. The remainder of the chapter advances one method for this purpose.

We limit attention to the following kind of context. Let n propositions $Q(o_1) \cdots Q(o_n)$ be given, where the o_i are n objects at the same hierarchical level, and Q is a stable predicate (in the sense of Section 1.2, above). In the present setting the requirement that predicates be monotonic is no longer needed. Thus, for $n = 6$, the $Q(o_i)$ might correspond to the following:

(16)
Hawks have muscle-to-fat ratio at least 10-to-1.
Eagles have muscle-to-fat ratio at least 10-to-1.
Parakeets have muscle-to-fat ratio at least 10-to-1.
Cardinals have muscle-to-fat ratio at least 10-to-1.
Geese have muscle-to-fat ratio at least 10-to-1.
Ducks have muscle-to-fat ratio at least 10-to-1.

Closing the six statements under boolean operators yields logically complex statements like the following:

(17) (a) Eagles and Cardinals have muscle-to-fat ratio at least 10-to-1.[11]
    (b) Ducks but not Geese have muscle-to-fat ratio at least 10-to-1.
    (c) Either Hawks or Parakeets (or both) have muscle-to-fat ratio at least 10-to-1.

Pairs of statements represent conditionals such as the following:

(18) (a) Cardinals have muscle-to-fat ratio at least 10-to-1 assuming that Parakeets do.

---

[11] A more literal rendition of closure under boolean conjunction would be "Eagles have muscle-to-fat ratio at least 10-to-1 and Cardinals have muscle-to-fat ratio at least 10-to-1." We assume throughout that the official logical structure of statements is clear from the abbreviations that make them more colloquial. Note also that negation of predicates may often be expressed without "not." Thus, "have muscle-to-fat ratio below 10-to-1" serves as the negation of "have muscle-to-fat ratio at least 10-to-1."

(b) Eagles have muscle-to-fat ratio at least 10-to-1 assuming that Geese don't.

(c) Ducks and Geese have muscle-to-fat ratio at least 10-to-1 assuming that Hawks do.

Judgments about chance begin to fade in the face of increasing logical complexity, but many people have a rough sense of probability for hundreds of complex and conditional structures like those in (17) and (18). We claim

(19) Estimates of the chances of complex and conditional events defined over $Q(o_1) \cdots Q(o_n)$ are often mentally generated from no more information than:

(a) probability estimates for each of $Q(o_1) \cdots Q(o_n)$; and

(b) the pairwise similarity of the n objects o_i to each other.

Just as for GAP2, we here make no claim about the probabilities of $Q(o_1) \cdots Q(o_n)$. The focus is rather on sentences involving logical connectives and conditionalization, predicting their perceived chance on the basis of (19)a,b. The next section describes an algorithm whose inputs are the probabilities of $Q(o_1) \cdots Q(o_n)$ along with the pairwise similarities of the o_i, and whose output is the probability of every complex and conditional statement over $Q(o_1) \cdots Q(o_n)$. In support of (19), experimental data will be presented to show that the algorithm's output is a fair approximation of human intuition about statements simple enough to be evaluated.

The algorithm is not intended as a performance model, that is, as an account of the processes whereby people convert the algorithm's inputs into outputs. The algorithm lends credence to (19) only by demonstrating the sufficiency of its inputs as a basis for generating its output. The human method for effecting the same transformation is doubtless different.

Finally, consider a person whose estimates of probability are to be predicted. We use $Ch(\cdot)$ and $Ch(\cdot : \cdot)$ to denote the chances that the person assigns to statements and conditional statements. It is not assumed that Ch is a total function since the person may have no opinion about the probability of highly complex statements. As before, we let $sim(\cdot, \cdot)$ denote the person's similarity function over pairs of objects. It is assumed that $sim(o_i, o_j) \in [0, 1]$, with 1 representing identity and 0 maximal dissimilarity. For simplicity, we again assume that sim is symmetric in its two arguments.

The goal of our algorithm may now be stated concisely. It is to predict the values of Ch from sim along with just the values of Ch on $Q(o_1) \cdots Q(o_n)$. We begin by reviewing elements of subjective probability (for more ample discussion, see Jeffrey, 1983; Nilsson, 1986; and Skyrms, 2000, among other sources). Then an overview of the algorithm is presented, followed by details.

5.1 Subjective Probability

Let $Q(o_1) \cdots Q(o_n)$ be given, where each statement $Q(o_i)$ is called a *variable*. By a *complete conjunction* we mean a sentence of the form $\pm Q(o_1) \wedge \cdots \wedge \pm Q(o_n)$, where each $\pm$ is either blank or the negation symbol $\neg$. For $n = 3$, one complete conjunction is $\neg Q(o_1) \wedge Q(o_2) \wedge \neg Q(o_3)$. A complete conjunction relative to (16) might be expressed in English as

Hawks and Eagles and Parakeets but neither Cardinals nor Geese nor Ducks have muscle-to-fat ratio at least 10-to-1.

When there are n variables, there are 2^n complete conjunctions. By a *probability distribution over* $Q(o_1) \cdots Q(o_n)$ is meant a function that maps each complete conjunction to a nonnegative number so that all the numbers sum to one. Such a distribution is extended as follows to the class of boolean formulas constructed from $Q(o_1) \cdots Q(o_n)$. Given a distribution *Prob* and a formula φ, Prob (φ) is defined to be

$$\sum \{ \text{Prob}\,(\alpha) : \alpha \text{ is a complete conjunction that logically implies } \varphi \}.$$

Prob is extended again to pairs (φ, ψ) of formulas such that Prob $(\psi) > 0$; specifically:

$$\text{Prob}\,(\varphi, \psi) = \frac{\text{Prob}\,(\varphi \wedge \psi)}{\text{Prob}\,(\psi)}.$$

Conforming to the usual convention, we write Prob (φ, ψ) as Prob $(\varphi : \psi)$ (the conditional probability of φ assuming ψ). To summarize, any procedure mapping the complete conjunctions into nonnegative numbers that sum to one also assigns probabilities and conditional probabilities to formulas of arbitrary complexity.

The function *Ch* is called *(probabilistically) coherent* if there is some distribution *Prob* such that (a) for all formulas φ, if $Ch(\varphi)$ is defined then $Ch(\varphi) = \text{Prob}\,(\varphi)$, and (b) for all pairs φ, ψ of formulas, if $Ch(\varphi : \psi)$ is defined then $Ch(\varphi : \psi) = \text{Prob}\,(\varphi : \psi)$. It is widely recognized that human estimates of chance are easily led into incoherence.[12] Since our algorithm makes its predictions through construction of a (coherent) distribution, its accuracy is limited by whatever incoherence is manifested in *Ch*.

---

[12] See the references in note 2. Incoherence can be "fixed" via a method described in Batsell, Brenner, Osherson, Vardi, & Tsvachidis (2002).

5.2 Overview of the Algorithm

The algorithm is based on a function f, defined below, that maps binary conjunctions of form $\pm Q(o_i) \wedge \pm Q(o_j)$ $(i < j)$ into the unit interval. Given a complete conjunction α over n variables, $f(\alpha)$ is defined to be the average of $f(\pm Q(o_i) \wedge \pm Q(o_j))$ for all binary conjunctions $\pm Q(o_i) \wedge \pm Q(o_j)$ whose conjuncts occur in α $(i < j \leq n)$. To illustrate, if $n = 3$, then the complete conjunction $\neg Q(o_1) \wedge Q(o_2) \wedge \neg Q(o_3)$ includes three binary conjunctions, namely, $\neg Q(o_1) \wedge Q(o_2)$, $\neg Q(o_1) \wedge \neg Q(o_3)$, and $Q(o_2) \wedge \neg Q(o_3)$. f maps each of them into $[0, 1]$; and f maps $\neg Q(o_1) \wedge Q(o_2) \wedge \neg Q(o_3)$ into the average of the latter three numbers. Use of average reflects the difficulty of evaluating long conjunctions directly; the binary conjunctions serve as estimates of the compatibility of all the conjuncts in a given complete conjunction.

We conceive of f as assigning "provisional chances" to the set of complete conjunctions generated from $Q(o_1) \cdots Q(o_n)$. Such provisional chances may not define a probability distribution since there is no guarantee that

$$\sum \{ f(\alpha) : \alpha \text{ is a complete conjunction} \} = 1.$$

After the provisional chances are generated via f, the goal of the algorithm is to build a genuine distribution that comes as close as possible to respecting them, subject to the constraints imposed by the rated probability $Ch(Q(o_i))$ of each variable. We therefore solve the following *quadratic programming problem*:

(20) Find a probability distribution *Prob* such that

$$\sum \{ (f(\alpha) - \text{Prob}(\alpha))^2 : \alpha \text{ is a complete conjunction} \}$$

is minimized subject to these constraints:

(a) $\text{Prob}(Q(o_i)) = Ch(Q(o_i))$ for $i \leq n$,
(b) $\text{Prob}(\alpha) \geq 0$ for all complete conjunctions α, and
(c) $\sum \{ \text{Prob}(\alpha) : \alpha \text{ is a complete conjunction} \} = 1$.

The last two constraints embody the requirement that *Prob* be a probability distribution. It can be shown (Luenberger, 1984) that the solution *Prob* to (20) is unique. It is taken to be the output of our algorithm.

We note that (20) can be supplemented with any other equalities $\text{Prob}(\varphi) = Ch(\varphi)$ or $Prob(\varphi : \psi) = Ch(\varphi : \psi)$ where φ, ψ are arbitrary formulas; the only requirement is that the set of equalities appearing in (20) be coherent. The resulting quadratic program yields a distribution that honors these constraints while minimizing discrepancy with similarity-based estimates of the chances of complete conjunctions. Thus, our method may be applied to situations in which the agent has particular information about the probabilities of various events and conditional events.[13]

5.3 The Function f

Let c be the conjunction $\pm Q(o_i) \wedge \pm Q(o_j)$ $(i < j \leq n)$. We define $f(c)$ via four cases, depending on the polarity of the two conjuncts of c.

CASE 1: $c = Q(o_i) \wedge Q(o_j)$. As $\mathrm{sim}(o_i, o_j)$ approaches unity, $Q(o_i)$ and $Q(o_j)$ become the same proposition, hence $Ch(c)$ should approach $\min\{Ch(Q(o_i)), Ch(Q(o_j))\}$.[14] As $\mathrm{sim}(o_i, o_j)$ approaches zero, $Q(o_i)$ and $Q(o_j)$ bear no relation to each other, hence should be probabilistically independent, so that $Ch(c)$ approaches $Ch(Q(o_i)) \times Ch(Q(o_j))$. Linear interpolation between these extremes yields

$$f(Q(o_i) \wedge Q(o_j)) = [\mathrm{sim}(o_i, o_j) \times \min\{Ch(Q(o_i)), Ch(Q(o_j))\}]$$
$$+ [(1 - \mathrm{sim}(o_i, o_j)) \times Ch(Q(o_i)) \times Ch(Q(o_j))].$$

CASE 2: $c = \neg Q(o_i) \wedge \neg Q(o_j)$. Substituting $1 - Ch(Q(o_i))$ for $Ch(Q(o_i))$, and similarly for $Q(o_j)$, transforms this case into the prior one. We therefore define

$$f(\neg Q(o_i) \wedge \neg Q(o_j)) = [\mathrm{sim}(o_i, o_j) \times \min\{1 - Ch(Q(o_i)), 1 - Ch(Q(o_j))\}]$$
$$+ [(1 - \mathrm{sim}(o_i, o_j)) \times (1 - Ch(Q(o_i))) \times (1 - Ch(Q(o_j)))].$$

CASE 3: $c = Q(o_i) \wedge \neg Q(o_j)$. As $\mathrm{sim}(o_i, o_j)$ approaches unity, $Q(o_i)$ and $Q(o_j)$ become the same proposition, hence c becomes a contradiction and $Ch(c)$ should approach zero. As $\mathrm{sim}(o_i, o_j)$ approaches zero, $Q(o_i)$ and $\neg Q(o_j)$ bear no relation to each other, hence should be probabilistically independent. Linear interpolation yields

$$f(Q(o_i) \wedge \neg Q(o_j)) = (1 - \mathrm{sim}(o_i, o_j)) \times Ch(Q(o_i)) \times (1 - Ch(Q(o_j))).$$

---

[13] More generally, the constraints may be weak inequalities rather than equalities.

[14] As $\mathrm{sim}(o_i, o_j)$ approaches unity, $Ch(c)$ should also approach $\max\{Ch(Q(o_i)), Ch(Q(o_j))\}$. Prior to reaching the limit, however, the maximum might exceed $Ch(c)$, which is probabilistically incoherent. No such incoherence is introduced by the minimum.

CASE 4: $c = \neg Q(o_i) \wedge Q(o_j)$. This case is parallel to the preceding one. Hence

$$f(\neg Q(o_i) \wedge Q(o_j)) = (1 - \text{sim}(o_i, o_j)) \times (1 - Ch(Q(o_i))) \times Ch(Q(o_j)).$$

The foregoing definition of f seems to be among the simplest ways to assign reasonable probabilities to conjunctions, based on just similarity and the chances attributed to variables.

Let us denote by QPf the algorithm just described, involving quadratic programming and the use of f to assign provisional chances to the set of complete conjunctions generated from $Q(o_1) \cdots Q(o_n)$.

5.4 Test of the Algorithm QPf

Materials. As objects o_i we chose the following sets of avian categories:

(21) (a) hawk, eagle, parakeet, cardinal, goose, duck
     (b) robin, sparrow, chicken, bluejay, pigeon, parrot.

For predicates Q we chose the following:

(22) (a) have muscle-to-fat ratio at least 10-to-1
     (b) have detectable testosterone blood levels throughout the year.

Based on no more than intuition, we expected that the predicates would be stable and monotonic for our subjects. Applying each predicate to each group yields four sets of six variables $Q(o_1) \cdots Q(o_6)$.

Similarity was assessed by measuring the distance between each kind of bird in Figure 1 of Rips, Shoben, and Smith (1973, p. 10). The latter figure displays the multidimensional scaling solution among the twelve categories in (21)a,b.[15] These distances are shown in Table 6.1. To compute $\text{sim}(o_i, o_j)$, we divided each distance by the largest value in the associated matrix, and subtracted this number from 1. The most separated pair in a given subset is thus assigned 0, whereas 1 is reserved for self-identity.

Note that the same similarity function is used for all participants in the study. Since similarity questions were not posed, there is no possibility of respondents interpreting similarity queries as disguised requests for conditional probability.

---

[15] The raw data for the multidimensional scaling algorithm were rated semantic similarities for each pair of categories. Distance in the output reflects dissimilarity. (Included in the ratings was semantic similarity to the superordinate concept *bird*.)

TABLE 6.1. *Distances (in millimeters) in Figure 1 of Rips, Shoben, & Smith (1973)*

	robin	sparrow	chicken	bluejay	pigeon
sparrow	4.0				
chicken	39.0	38.5			
bluejay	10.3	6.4	38.1		
pigeon	17.5	17.4	21.5	18.6	
parrot	15.5	16.0	23.5	17.9	2.3

	hawk	eagle	parakeet	cardinal	goose
eagle	4.8				
parakeet	41.0	43.0			
cardinal	36.2	36.9	13.4		
goose	40.0	44.8	34.1	42.6	
duck	40.5	44.9	31.5	40.5	3.2

Note: To illustrate, sim(robin, parrot) = 1.0 − (15.5/39.0)

Statements. Each of the four combinations available from (21) and (22) gives rise to a set of variables $Q(o_1) \cdots Q(o_6)$. Thirty-six complex statements were generated from the variables. The logical forms of the complex statements were the same across the four sets of stimuli; they are shown in Table 6.2. To illustrate, relative to (21)a and (22)a, the complex statement of form $Q(o_6) \wedge \neg Q(o_5)$ is (17)b, above. For the same set of stimuli, the form $Q(o_2)|\neg Q(o_5)$ is (18)b. In this way, each of the four stimulus-sets was associated with forty-two statements (six variables plus thirty-six complex statements).

Procedure. Forty Princeton undergraduates assessed the probabilities of the forty-two statements associated with one of the four sets of stimuli. It was explained that "probability" was to be interpreted in the sense of personal conviction. Brief explanation was also provided for the logical connectives. Probabilities were collected via a computer interface, which presented the forty-two statements in individualized random order.

Three data sets were discarded without further analysis; two manifested stereotyped answers (one or two values chosen for almost all questions), the other included a majority of extreme responses (either zero or one). Of the remaining thirty-seven participants, ten worked with the stimuli (21)a, (22)a, ten with (21)a, (22)b, nine with (21)b, (22)a, and eight with (21)b, (22)b.

5.5 Results

The average estimates for the variables are shown in Table 6.3. The algorithm (20) was used to derive a separate distribution *Prob* for each participant.

TABLE 6.2. *The 36 Complex Statements Figuring in the Experiment*

Structure	#	Formulas		
$p \wedge q$	7	$Q(o_1) \wedge Q(o_2)$ $\quad Q(o_5) \wedge Q(o_6)$ $\quad Q(o_1) \wedge Q(o_5)$ $Q(o_1) \wedge Q(o_6)$ $\quad Q(o_2) \wedge Q(o_5)$ $\quad Q(o_2) \wedge Q(o_6)$ $Q(o_3) \wedge Q(o_4)$		
$p \wedge \neg q$	7	$Q(o_1) \wedge \neg Q(o_3)$ $\quad Q(o_1) \wedge \neg Q(o_4)$ $\quad Q(o_2) \wedge \neg Q(o_5)$ $Q(o_2) \wedge \neg Q(o_6)$ $\quad Q(o_6) \wedge \neg Q(o_1)$ $\quad Q(o_1) \wedge \neg Q(o_2)$ $Q(o_6) \wedge \neg Q(o_5)$		
$\neg p \wedge \neg q$	7	$\neg Q(o_4) \wedge \neg Q(o_3)$ $\quad \neg Q(o_6) \wedge \neg Q(o_3)$ $\quad \neg Q(o_6) \wedge \neg Q(o_5)$ $\neg Q(o_2) \wedge \neg Q(o_1)$ $\quad \neg Q(o_6) \wedge \neg Q(o_1)$ $\quad \neg Q(o_2) \wedge \neg Q(o_5)$ $\neg Q(o_3) \wedge \neg Q(o_5)$		
$p \vee q$	3	$Q(o_2) \vee Q(o_3)$ $\quad Q(o_4) \vee Q(o_5)$ $\quad Q(o_6) \vee Q(o_4)$		
$p : q$	5	$Q(o_1) : Q(o_2)$ $\quad Q(o_2) : Q(o_3)$ $\quad Q(o_3) : Q(o_2)$ $Q(o_4) : Q(o_1)$ $\quad Q(o_5) : Q(o_2)$		
$p : \neg q$	4	$Q(o_1) : \neg Q(o_5)$ $\quad Q(o_2) : \neg Q(o_6)$ $Q(o_3) : \neg Q(o_4)$ $\quad Q(o_6) : \neg Q(o_5)$		
$\neg p : q$	3	$\neg Q(o_4) : Q(o_3)$ $\quad \neg Q(o_5) : Q(o_1)$ $\quad \neg Q(o_6) : Q(o_3)$		

Note: Indices are relative to the orderings in (21)a, b. The symbols $\wedge$ and $\vee$ denote conjunction and disjunction, respectively; $\neg$ denotes negation. Conditional probabilities are indicated with a colon (:).

We then compared *Prob* to the subject's thirty-six assignments of chance to complex statements.[16] The median correlations obtained for the four sets of stimuli appear in the first column of Table 6.4. Next, for a given stimulus set we averaged the probabilities assigned to each of the forty-two statements, and repeated the analysis for this "average subject." (There was thus one average subject for each stimulus-set; its forty-two "judgments" were the mean responses from the eight, nine, or ten subjects who worked with those stimuli.) The correlations between predicted and observed values for the four average subjects are shown in the second column of Table 6.4; scatter plots are provided in Figure 6.3. When random numbers are substituted for the provisional chances provided by f, the quadratic program (20) yields correlations reliably lower than those shown in Figure 6.3 ($p < .05$); see the third column of Table 6.4.

Recall that our algorithm returns a genuine distribution of probability. Its predictive success thus requires a modicum of coherence in the input estimates of chance. Allowing a 10% margin of error, we counted the number

---

[16] *Prob* perfectly "predicts" the probabilities assigned to $Q(o_1) \cdots Q(o_6)$ since the quadratic programming problem (20) takes the latter values as constraints on the solution.

TABLE 6.3. *Average Probabilities Assigned to Variables*

#	(21)a, (22)a ($N = 10$)	(21)a, (22)b ($N = 10$)	(21)b, (22)a ($N = 9$)	(21)b, (22)b ($N = 8$)
1	.79	.75	.54	.35
2	.79	.74	.61	.43
3	.39	.36	.30	.53
4	.45	.42	.61	.40
5	.28	.59	.40	.44
6	.29	.47	.48	.36

Note: The numbers under # are relative to the orderings in (21)a,b.

of times the inputs violated the following consequences of the probability calculus[17]:

(23) (a) $\mathsf{Prob}\,(\varphi) + \mathsf{Prob}\,(\psi) - 1.05 \leq \mathsf{Prob}\,(\varphi \wedge \psi) \leq \mathsf{Prob}\,(\varphi) + .05, \mathsf{Prob}\,(\psi) + .05$

(b) $\mathsf{Prob}\,(\varphi) - .05, \mathsf{Prob}\,(\psi) - .05 \leq \mathsf{Prob}\,(\varphi \vee \psi) \leq \mathsf{Prob}\,(\varphi) + \mathsf{Prob}\,(\psi) + .05$

(c) $\mathsf{Prob}\,(\varphi \wedge \psi)/\mathsf{Prob}\,(\psi) - .05 \leq \mathsf{Prob}\,(\varphi : \psi) \leq \mathsf{Prob}\,(\varphi \wedge \psi)/\mathsf{Prob}\,(\psi) + .05.$

All twenty-four complex, absolute statements (see Table 6.2) are either conjunctions or disjunctions, hence accountable to one of (23)a,b. Only four of the twelve conditional statements could be tested against (23)c since in eight cases the required conjunction $\varphi \wedge \psi$ does not figure among the absolute statements. For the averaged data, there are few violations of 23a,b – 6, 0, 1, and 1, respectively, for the four stimulus sets. In contrast, (23)c was violated all four times in each stimulus set (averaged data), confirming the well documented incomprehension of conditional probability by college undergraduates (see, e.g., Dawes, Mirels, Gold, & Donahue, 1993). Incoherence was greater when tabulated for each subject individually. Participants averaged 10.3 violations of 23a,b out of 24 possible, and 3.8 violations of (23)c out of 4 possible.

Our results support Thesis (19) inasmuch as the only inputs to the algorithm are similarities and the chances of variables. The algorithm's predictions are not perfect, however, and suggest that revised methods might prove more successful. In particular, accuracy may improve when similarities are elicited from respondents to the probability questions, instead of derived globally from an ancient text (Rips et al., 1973).

---

[17] For their derivation, see Neapolitan (1990).

TABLE 6.4. *Correlations Between Predicted and Observed Probabilities*

	(1) Median individual correlation	(2) Correlation for the average subject	(3) Correlations with random provisional chances	(4) Correlations based on 32 provisional chances
(21)a, (22)a	.811	.915	.757	.795
(21)a, (22)b	.763	.899	.539	.872
(21)b, (22)a	.609	.753	.531	.601
(21)b, (22)b	.595	.773	.238	.754

Note: Each correlation involves the set of 36 complex observations. All coefficients in columns (1), (2), and (4) are reliable ($p < .01$). Column (3) shows the correlation between predicted and observed probabilities when random numbers in the unit interval are substituted for the provisional chances provided by f in the quadratic program (20), using averaged data. In each case, the correlations in columns (2) and (3) differ reliably ($p < .05$). The correlations in the column (4) are the average of six computations with 32 randomly chosen complete conjunctions.

The construction of a (coherent) probability distribution over the set of complete conjunctions renders our algorithm unrealistic psychologically, but enhances its potential role in the design of autonomous, intelligent agents. Indeed, the probability calculus provides an attractive canonical form for reasoning, and is often considered to be the "faithful guardian of common sense" (Pearl, 1988).

5.6 Application to the Design of Autonomous Intelligent Agents

Our algorithm allows numerous probabilities to be computed from a small reservoir of stored values. For example, a distribution for thirty variables of form $Q(o_i)$ requires more than a billion probabilities but is specified by only 465 numbers within the scheme described here (namely, 30 probabilities for variables plus 435 pairwise similarities). The empirical results described above suggest that the 465 numbers can be chosen in a way that generates reasonable – that is human-like – estimates of chance. Moreover, the bulk of these numbers (namely, the similarity coefficients) will be of potential use for other purposes, for example, when the agent must decide whether one object can be substituted for another in pursuit of a larger goal.

Although 465 numbers suffice to define a distribution involving thirty variables, recovering the distribution via our algorithm requires quadratic programming with a billion-dimensional matrix [see (20), above]. To avoid such computations, a small random sample of complete conjunctions can

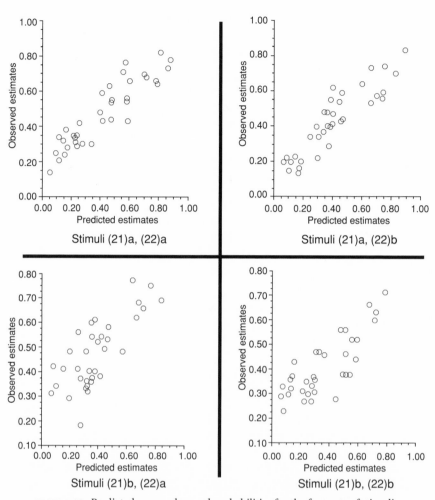

FIGURE 6.3. Predicted versus observed probabilities for the four sets of stimuli.

be chosen to carry all positive probabilities, and quadratic programming undertaken just with them. At least one sampled complete conjunction must imply each variable in order for the variables' estimated chances to be preserved in the solution; but this condition on samples is easy to check.

To assess the potential of the foregoing scheme, for each set of stimuli we drew six samples of thirty-two complete conjunctions, out of the sixty-four that are generated by six variables.[18] The resulting quadratic program – which

---

[18] A few times it was necessary to draw a new sample because one of the variables was not implied by any of the chosen complete conjunctions.

is one quarter the size of the original – was then used to predict the subjects' average estimates of chance. The last column in Table 6.4 shows the mean of the six correlations produced for each set of stimuli. Comparing these values to the second column reveals some loss of predictive accuracy; substantial correlations nonetheless remain. In a sophisticated implementation of our algorithm, loss of accuracy could be partially remedied by applying quadratic programming to several samples of complete conjunctions and averaging the results.

6. CONCLUDING REMARKS

Both GAP2 and QPf rely on similarity to predict the probabilities assigned to complex statements. We hope that the performance of the models demonstrates that similarity can play an explanatory role in theories of induction provided that attention is limited to stable predicates. Extension beyond the confines of stability is not trivial but might be facilitated by comparison to the simpler case.

The importance of similarity to estimates of probability was already articulated in the 17th and 18th century (see Cohen, 1980; Coleman, 2001). Bringing quantitative precision to this idea would be a significant achievement of modern psychology.

ACKNOWLEDGMENTS

Thanks to Robert Rehder for careful reading and helpful suggestions. Research supported by NSF grants 9978135 and 9983260. Contact information: osherson@princeton.edu, blok@psy.utexas.edu, medin@northwestern.edu.

References

Aguilar, C. M., and D. L. Medin (1999). "Asymmetries of comparison," *Psychonomic Bulletin & Review, 6,* 328–337.

Ahn, W., C. W. Kalish, D. L. Medin, & S. A. Gelman (1995). "The role of covariation versus mechanism information in causal attribution," *Cognition, 54,* 299–352.

Barsalou, L. W., and B. H. Ross (1986). "The roles of automatic and strategic processing in sensitivity to superordinate and property frequency," *Journal of Experimental Psychology: Learning, Memory, & Cognition, 12*(1), 116–134.

Batsell, R., L. Brenner, D. Osherson, M. Vardi, and S. Tsvachidis (2002). "Eliminating incoherence from subjective estimates of chance," *Proceedings of the Ninth International Workshop on Knowledge Representation.* Morgan Kaufmann.

Blok, S. V. (2004). "Modeling induction as conditional probability judgment," *Dissertation Abstracts International, 65*(1), 457, Northwestern University.

Carey, S. (1985). *Conceptual change in childhood,* MIT Press, Cambridge MA.

Cohen, L. J. (1980). "Some historical remarks on the Baconian conception of probability," *Journal of the History of Ideas, 61,* 219–231.

Coleman, D. (2001). "Baconian probability and Hume's theory of testimony," *Hume Studies,* 27(2), 195–226.

Coley, J. D., S. Atran, and D. L. Medin (1997). "Does rank have its privilege? Inductive inference within folk biological taxonomies," *Cognition, 64,* 73–112.

Dawes, R., H. L. Mirels, E. Gold, and E. Donahue (1993). "Equating inverse probabilities in implicit personality judgments," *Psychological Science, 4*(6), 396–400.

Eells, E., and B. Fitelson (2002). "Symmetries and asymmetries in evidential support," *Philosophical Studies, 107*(2), 129–142.

Gentner, D., and A. Markman (1997). "Structure mapping in analogy and similarity," *American Psychologist, 52*(1), 45–56.

Gigerenzer, G. (1996). "Reply to Tversky and Kahneman," *Psychological Review, 103*(3), 592–593.

Goldstone, R. (1994a). "Similarity, interactive activation, and mapping," *Journal of Experimental Psychology: Learning, Memory, & Cognition, 20*(1), 3–28.

Goldstone, R. L. (1994b). "The role of similarity in categorization: Providing a groundwork," *Cognition, 52,* 125–157.

Goodman, N. (1955). *Fact, fiction, and forecast,* Bobbs-Merrill, Indianapolis IN.

Goodman, N. (1972). "Seven strictures on similarity," in *Problems and projects.* Bobbs-Merrill, New York NY.

Hampton, J., and I. Cannon (2004). "Category-based induction: An effect of conclusion typicality," *Memory & Cognition, 32*(2), 235–243.

Heit, E. (2000). "Properties of inductive reasoning," *Psychonomic Bulletin & Review, 7,* 569–592.

Heit, E., and U. Hahn (1999). "Diversity-based reasoning in children age 5 to 8," in *Proceedings of the Twenty-First Annual Conference of the Cognitive Science Society,* Erlbaum, Mahawah NJ.

Jeffrey, R. C. (1983). *The logic of decision* (2nd edition). The University of Chicago Press, Chicago IL.

Johnson-Laird, P. N. (1983). *Mental models.* Harvard University Press, Cambridge MA.

Juslin, P., and M. Persson (2002). "PROBabilities from EXemplars (PROBEX): A 'lazy' algorithm for probabilistic inference from generic knowledge," *Cognitive Science, 26,* 563–607.

Kahneman, D., and A. Tversky (1996). "On the reality of cognitive illusions," *Psychological Review, 103*(3), 582–591.

Keil, F., W. C. Smith, D. J. Simons, and D. T. Levin (1998). "Two dogmas of conceptual empiricism: Implications for hybrid models of the structure of knowledge," *Cognition, 65,* 103–135.

Lassaline, M. E. (1996). "Structural alignment in induction and similarity," *Journal of Experimental Psychology : Learning, Memory, and Cognition, 22,* 754–770.

Lo, Y., A. Sides, J. Rozelle, and D. Osherson (2002). "Evidential diversity and premise probability in young children's inductive judgment," *Cognitive Science, 26,* 181–206.

López, A., S. Atran, J. Coley, D. Medin, and E. Smith (1997). "The tree of life: Universal and cultural features of folkbiological taxonomies and inductions," *Cognitive Psychology, 32,* 251–295.

López, A., S. A. Gelman, G. Gutheil, and E. E. Smith (1992). "The development of category-based induction," *Child Development, 63,* 1070–1090.

Luenberger, D. G. (1984). *Linear and nonlinear programming* (2nd edition), Addison-Wesley, Reading MA.

Medin, D. L., J. D. Coley, G. Storms, and B. K. Hayes (2003). "A relevance theory of induction," *Psychonomic Bulletin & Review 10*(3), 517–532.

Medin, D. L., R. L. Goldstone, and D. Gentner (1993). "Respects for similarity," *Psychological Review, 100,* 254–278.

Medin, D. L., and M. M. Schaffer (1978). "Context model of classification learning," *Psychological Review, 85,* 207–238.

Neapolitan, R. (1990). *Probabilistic reasoning in expert systems: Theory and algorithms.* John Wiley & Sons, New York NY.

Nilsson, N. (1986). "Probabilistic logic," *Artificial Intelligence, 28*(1), 71–87.

Ortiz, C. L. (1999). "A commonsense language for reasoning about causation and rational action," *Artificial Intelligence, 111,* 73–130.

Osherson, D., E. E. Smith, and E. Shafir (1986). "Some origins of belief," *Cognition, 24,* 197–224.

Osherson, D., E. E. Smith, O. Wilkie, A. López, and E. Shafir (1990). "Category-based induction," *Psychological Review, 97*(2), 185–200.

Pearl, J. (1988). *Probabilistic reasoning in intelligent systems.* Morgan Kaufmann, San Mateo, CA.

Quine, W. V. O. (1960). *Word and Object.* MIT Press, Cambridge MA.

Rips, L. (1975). "Inductive judgments about natural categories," *Journal of Verbal Learning and Verbal Behavior, 14,* 665–681.

Rips, L., E. Shoben, and E. Smith (1973). "Semantic distance and the verification of semantic relations," *Journal of Verbal Learning and Verbal Behavior, 12,* 1–20.

Russell, S. J., and P. Norvig (2003). *Artificial intelligence: A modern approach* (2nd edition). Prentice Hall, Upper Saddle River NJ.

Shafir, E., E. Smith, and D. Osherson (1990). "Typicality and reasoning fallacies," *Memory and Cognition,* 18(3), 229–239.

Skyrms, B. (2000). *Choice & chance: An introduction to inductive logic,* Wadsworth, Belmont CA.

Sloman, S. A. (1993). "Feature based induction," *Cognitive Psychology, 25,* 231–280.

Sloman, S. A., and D. Lagnado (2005). "The problem of induction," in *Cambridge handbook of thinking & reasoning,* ed. by K. Holyoak and R. Morrison. Cambridge University Press, Cambridge.

Sloman, S. A., and L. J. Rips (1998). "Similarity as an explanatory construct," *Cognition,* 65, 87–101.

Smith, E. E., E. Shafir, and D. Osherson (1993). "Similarity, plausibility, and judgments of probability," *Cognition, 49,* 67–96.

Tentori, K., N. Bonini, and D. Osherson (2004). "The conjunction fallacy: A misunderstanding about conjunction?" *Cognitive Science, 28*(3), 467–477.

Tentori, K., V. Crupi, N. Bonini, and D. Osherson (2007). "Comparison of confirmation measures," *Cognition,* 103, 107–119.

Turner, H. (1999). "A logic of universal causation," *Artificial Intelligence, 113,* 87–123.

Tversky, A. (1977). "Features of similarity," *Psychological Review, 84,* 327–352.

Tversky, A., and I. Gati (1978). "Studies of similarity," in *Cognition and categorization,* ed. by E. Rosch and B. Lloyd. Erlbaum, Hillsdale NJ.

Tversky, A., and D. Kahneman (1983). "Extensional versus intuitive reasoning: The conjunction fallacy in probability judgment," *Psychological Review, 90,* 293–315.

7

Theory-Based Bayesian Models of Inductive Reasoning

Joshua B. Tenenbaum, Charles Kemp, and Patrick Shafto

1. INTRODUCTION

Philosophers since Hume have struggled with the logical problem of induction, but children solve an even more difficult task – the practical problem of induction. Children somehow manage to learn concepts, categories, and word meanings, and all on the basis of a set of examples that seems hopelessly inadequate. The practical problem of induction does not disappear with adolescence: adults face it every day whenever they make any attempt to predict an uncertain outcome. Inductive inference is a fundamental part of everyday life, and for cognitive scientists, a fundamental phenomenon of human learning and reasoning in need of computational explanation.

There are at least two important kinds of questions that we can ask about human inductive capacities. First, what is the knowledge on which a given instance of induction is based? Second, how does that knowledge support generalization beyond the specific data observed: how do we judge the strength of an inductive argument from a given set of premises to new cases, or infer which new entities fall under a concept given a set of examples? We provide a computational approach to answering these questions. Experimental psychologists have studied both the process of induction and the nature of prior knowledge representations in depth, but previous computational models of induction have tended to emphasize process to the exclusion of knowledge representation. The approach we describe here attempts to redress this imbalance by showing how domain-specific prior knowledge can be formalized as a crucial ingredient in a domain-general framework for rational statistical inference.

The value of prior knowledge has been attested by both psychologists and machine learning theorists, but with somewhat different emphases. Formal analyses in machine learning show that meaningful generalization is not possible unless a learner begins with some sort of inductive bias: some set of constraints on the space of hypotheses that will be considered (Mitchell, 1997). However, the best known statistical machine-learning algorithms adopt relatively weak inductive biases and thus require much more data for successful generalization than humans do: tens or hundreds of positive and negative examples, in contrast to the human ability to generalize from just one or few positive examples. These machine algorithms lack ways to represent and exploit the rich forms of prior knowledge that guide people's inductive inferences and that have been the focus of much attention in cognitive and developmental psychology under the name of "intuitive theories" (Murphy & Medin, 1985). Murphy (1993) characterizes an intuitive theory as "a set of causal relations that collectively generate or explain the phenomena in a domain." We think of a theory more generally as any system of abstract principles that generates hypotheses for inductive inference in a domain, such as hypotheses about the meanings of new concepts, the conditions for new rules, or the extensions of new properties in that domain. Carey (1985), Wellman and Gelman (1992), and Gopnik and Meltzoff (1997) emphasize the central role of intuitive theories in cognitive development, both as sources of constraint on children's inductive reasoning and as the locus of deep conceptual change. Only recently have psychologists begun to consider seriously the roles that these intuitive theories might play in formal models of inductive inference (Gopnik & Schulz, 2004; Tenenbaum, Griffiths, & Kemp, 2006; Tenenbaum, Griffiths, & Niyogi, in press). Our goal here is to show how intuitive theories for natural domains such as folk biology can, when suitably formalized, provide the foundation for building powerful statistical models of human inductive reasoning.

Any familiar thing can be thought about in a multitude of ways, and different kinds of prior knowledge will be relevant to making inferences about different aspects of an entity. This flexibility poses a challenge for any computational account of inductive reasoning. For instance, a cat is a creature that climbs trees, eats mice, has whiskers, belongs to the category of felines, and was revered by the ancient Egyptians – and all of these facts could potentially be relevant to an inductive judgment. If we learn that cats suffer from a recently discovered disease, we might think that mice also have the disease; perhaps the cats picked up the disease from something they ate. Yet if we learn that cats carry a recently discovered gene, lions and leopards seem more likely to carry the gene than mice. Psychologists have confirmed experimentally that inductive generalizations vary in such ways, depending on the property involved. Our computational models will account for these phenomena by positing that people can draw on different prior knowledge structures – or different intuitive theories – within a single domain, and by showing how very different patterns of inference can arise depending on which of these theories is triggered.

Our models aim for both predictive and explanatory power. As in any mathematical modeling, we seek accounts that can provide close quantitative fits to human judgments across a range of different tasks or contexts, with a minimum number of free parameters or ad hoc assumptions. At the same time, we would like our models to explain why people make the inductive generalizations that they do make, and why these judgments are mostly successful in the real world – how people can reliably come to true beliefs about the world from very limited data. In the spirit of rational analysis (Anderson, 1990; Oaksford & Chater, 1998), or Marr's (1982) computational-theory level of analysis, we will assume that people's inductive capacities can be characterized as approximations to optimal inferences, given the structure of the environments and the task contexts that they have adapted to over the course of evolution and development. Our mission as modelers is then to characterize formally the nature of the optimal inference mechanism, the relevant aspects of environmental structure and task context, and the interaction between these components.

Our core proposal has two components. First, domain-specific knowledge that supports induction in different contexts can be captured using appropriate families of probabilistic models defined over structured representations: in particular, relational systems of categories such as taxonomic hierarchies or food webs. These structured probabilistic models are far from being complete formalizations of people's intuitive domain theories; they are minimalist accounts, intended to capture only those aspects of theories relevant for the basic inductive inferences we study. Second, knowledge in this form can support inductive generalization by providing the prior probabilities for a domain-general Bayesian inference engine. Both of these claims are necessary for explaining how people's inductive inferences can be so successful, and perhaps approximately optimal, with respect to the world that we live in. The structured representations of intuitive domain theories are important because the world contains genuine structure: a tree-structured representation of biological species is useful, for example, because it approximates the structure of the evolutionary tree. Bayesian inference is important because it provides a normative and general-purpose procedure for reasoning under uncertainty. Taking these two components together – rational domain-general statistical inference guided by appropriately structured intuitive domain theories – may help explain the uniquely human capacity for learning so much about the world from so little experience.

Our work goes beyond previous formal models of induction, which either do not address the rational statistical basis of people's inferences or find it difficult to capture the effects of different kinds of knowledge in different inductive contexts, or both. In one representative and often-cited example, the similarity-coverage model of Osherson, Smith, and colleagues, the domain-specific knowledge that drives generalization is represented by a similarity metric (Osherson et al., 1990). As we will see below, this similarity metric has to be defined in a particular way in order to match people's inductive judgments. That definition appears rather arbitrary from a statistical point of view, and arbitrarily different from classic similarity-based models of other cognitive tasks such as categorization or memory retrieval (Nosofsky, 1986; Hintzman et al., 1978). Also, the notion of similarity is typically context independent, which appears at odds with the context-dependent nature of human inductive reasoning. Even if we allow some kind of context-specific notion of similarity, a similarity metric seems too limited a representation to carry the richly structured knowledge that is needed in some contexts, or even simple features of some reasoning tasks such as the strong asymmetry of causal relations. In contrast, the knowledge that drives generalization in our theory-based Bayesian framework can be as complex and as structured as a given context demands.

The plan of this chapter is as follows. Section 2 provides a brief review of the specific inductive tasks and phenomena we attempt to account for, and Section 3 briefly describes some previous models that have attempted to cover the same ground. Section 4 introduces our general theory-based Bayesian framework for modeling inductive reasoning and describes two specific instantiations of it that can be used to model inductive reasoning in two important natural settings. Section 5 compares our models and several alternatives in terms of their ability to account for people's inductive judgments on a range of tasks. Section 6 discusses the relation between our work and some recent findings that have been taken to be problematic for Bayesian models of induction. Section 7 concludes and offers a preview of ongoing and future research.

2. PROPERTY INDUCTION

This section reviews the basic property induction task and introduces the core phenomena that our models will attempt to explain. Following a long tradition (Rips, 1975; Carey, 1985; Osherson et al., 1990; Sloman, 1993; Heit, 1998), we will focus on inductive arguments about the properties of natural categories, in particular biological species categories. The premises of each argument state that one or more specific species have some property, and the conclusion (to be evaluated) asserts that the same property applies to either another specific species or a more general category (such as all mammals). These two kinds of arguments are called *specific* and *general* arguments, respectively, depending only on the status of the conclusion category.

We use the formula $P_1, \ldots P_n \xrightarrow{prop} C$ to represent an *n*-premise argument where P_i is the *i*th premise, C is the conclusion, and *prop* indicates the property used. We will often abbreviate references to these components of an argument. For example, the argument

> Gorillas have T4 hormones
> Squirrels have T4 hormones
> ――――――――――――――――――――
> All mammals have T4 hormones

might be represented as *gorillas, squirrels* $\xrightarrow{T4}$ *mammals*.

The most systematic studies of property induction have used so-called "blank properties." For arguments involving animal species, these are properties that are recognized as biological but about which little else is known – for example, anatomical or physiological properties such as "has T4 hormones" or "has sesamoid bones." As these properties are hardly "blank" – it is important that people recognize them as deriving from an underlying and essential biological cause – we will instead refer to them as "generic biological properties."

For this class of generic properties, many qualitative reasoning phenomena have been described: Osherson et al. (1990) identify thirteen and Sloman (1993) adds several others. Here we mention just three. *Premise-conclusion similarity* is the effect that argument strength increases as the premises become more similar to the conclusion: for example, *horses* $\xrightarrow{T4}$ *dolphins* is weaker than *seals* $\xrightarrow{T4}$ *dolphins*. For general arguments, *typicality* is the effect that argument strength increases as the premises become more typical of the conclusion category. For example, *seals* $\xrightarrow{T4}$ *mammals* is weaker than *horses* $\xrightarrow{T4}$ *mammals*, since seals are less typical mammals than horses. Finally, *diversity* is the effect that argument strength increases as the diversity of the premises increases. For example, *horses, cows, rhinos* $\xrightarrow{T4}$ *mammals* is weaker than *horses, seals, squirrels* $\xrightarrow{T4}$ *mammals*.

Explaining inductive behavior with generic biological properties is a challenging problem. Even if we find some way of accounting for all the phenomena individually, it is necessary to find some way to compare their relative weights. Which is better: an argument that is strong according to the typicality criterion, or an argument that is strong according to the diversity criterion? The problem is especially difficult because arguments that are strong according to one criterion may be weak according to another: for example, $seals, squirrels \xrightarrow{T4} mammals$ has premises that are quite diverse but not very typical of the conclusion. For this reason, rather than trying to account for isolated qualitative contrasts between pairs of arguments, we will assess the performance of computational models in terms of how well they can predict relative argument strengths across multiple datasets each containing a large number of arguments of the same form.

The strength of an argument depends critically on the property involved, because changing the property will often alter the inductive context. Many researchers have described related effects (Gelman & Markman, 1986; Heit & Rubinstein, 1994; Shafto & Coley, 2003; Smith et al., 1993), and we mention just three of them. Gelman and Markman (1986) showed that children reason differently about biological properties (e.g., "has cold blood") and physical properties (e.g., "weighs one ton") – for example, $brontosaurus \xrightarrow{coldblood} triceratops$ is relatively strong, but $brontosaurus \xrightarrow{oneton}$ $triceratops$ is relatively weak. Heit and Rubinstein (1994) showed that anatomical or physiological properties and behavioral properties are treated differently by adults. While anatomical or physiological properties typically support default, similarity-like patterns of inductive reasoning, behavioral properties may depend less on generic similarity and more on shared ecological roles. Finally, Shafto and Coley (2003) argue that disease properties may draw on causal knowledge about predator-prey interactions, and thus may be treated differently from arguments about generic biological properties. For example, $salmon \xrightarrow{leptospirosis} grizzlybears$ may be judged stronger than $grizzlybears \xrightarrow{leptospirosis} salmon$, where $leptospirosis$ stands for "carry leptospirosis bacteria." This asymmetry has no justification in terms of the similarity between salmon and grizzly bears, which is presumably symmetric or nearly so, but it seems sensible from the perspective of causal reasoning: knowing that grizzly bears eat salmon, it seems more likely that grizzly bears would catch some disease from salmon than that any specific disease found in grizzly bears necessarily came from the salmon that they eat.

Our aim has been to develop a unifying computational framework that can account for many of the phenomena mentioned above. We will focus in this chapter on modeling reasoning about two kinds of properties: the classic setting of generic biological properties, and causally transmitted properties such as diseases (Shafto & Coley, 2003) that give rise to very different patterns of judgment. Before introducing the details of our framework, we summarize several existing models of property induction and describe how we hope to improve on them.

3. PREVIOUS MODELS

The tradition of modeling property induction extends at least as far back as the work of Rips (1975). Here we summarize a few of the more prominent mathematical models that have been developed in the intervening thirty years.

3.1 Similarity-Coverage Model

The similarity-coverage model (SCM) of Osherson et al. (1990) is perhaps the best known mathematical model of property induction. It predicts the strength of inductive arguments as a linear combination of two factors, the similarity of the conclusion to the premises and the extent to which the premises "cover" the smallest superordinate taxonomic category including both premises and conclusion. The SCM has some appealing properties. It makes accurate predictions for generic biological properties, and it uses a simple equation that predicts many different kinds of judgments with a minimum of free parameters. Yet the SCM has two major limitations. First, it can only use domain knowledge that takes the form of pairwise similarities or superordinate taxonomic categories. The model is therefore unable to handle inductive contexts that rely on knowledge which cannot be expressed in this form. Second, the SCM lacks a principled mathematical foundation: the accuracy of its predictions depends critically on certain arbitrary choices which specify the mathematical form of the model.

This arbitrariness shows up most clearly in the formal definition of coverage: the average over all instances i in the superordinate class of the *maximal* similarity between i and the examples in the premise set. We refer to this (standard) version of SCM as "MaxSim." Osherson et al. (1990) also consider a variant we call "SumSim," in which coverage is defined by averaging the *summed* similarity to the examples over all instances of the superordinate class. Generalization based on the summed similarity to exemplars or weight traces is the foundation for many other successful models of categorization, learning, and memory (Nosofsky, 1986; Kruschke, 1992; Hintzman et al., 1978) and can be interpreted in rational statistical terms as a version of nonparametric density estimation (Ashby & Alfonso-Reese, 1995; Silverman, 1986). Yet despite these precedents for using a summed-similarity measure, Osherson et al. (1990) advocate MaxSim, or some weighted combination of MaxSim and SumSim – perhaps because SumSim performs dramatically worse than MaxSim in judging the strength of general arguments (see Section 5). Since Osherson et al. (1990) do not explain why different measures of setwise similarity are needed in these different tasks, or why SumSim performs so much worse than MaxSim for inductive reasoning, the SCM is less principled than we might like.

3.2 Feature-Based Models

As Goodman (1972) and Murphy and Medin (1985) have argued, similarity is a vague and elusive notion, and it may be meaningless to say that two objects are similar unless a respect for similarity has been specified. Instead of founding a model directly on similarity judgments, an alternative is to start with a collection of object features, which might plausibly be observable perceptually or have been previously learned.[1] In some settings, it will be necessary to assume that the features are extracted from another kind of input (linguistic input, say), but in general the move from similarity to features is a move towards models that can learn directly from experience.

The feature-based model of (Sloman, 1993) computes inductive strength as a normalized measure of feature overlap between conclusion and example categories. Sloman (1993) presents a quantitative comparison with the SCM: the results are not conclusive but suggest that the model does not predict human judgments as accurately as the SCM. The model, however, predicts some qualitative phenomena that the SCM cannot explain. More recently, Rogers and McClelland (2004) have presented a feature-based approach to semantic cognition that uses a feedforward connectionist network with two hidden layers. This connectionist approach is more ambitious than any of the others we describe, and Rogers and McClelland (2004) apply their model to a diverse set of semantic phenomena. One of the applications is a property induction task where the model makes sensible qualitative predictions, but there has been no demonstration so far that the model provides good quantitative fits to human judgments.

From our perspective, both feature-based models share the limitations of the SCM. Despite the range of applications in Rogers and McClelland (2004), it is not clear how either model can be extended to handle causal settings or other inductive contexts that draw on sophisticated domain knowledge. Both models also include components that have been given no convincing

---

[1] Note that a feature-based version of the SCM is achieved if we define the similarity of two objects as some function of their feature vectors. Section 5 assesses the performance of this model.

justification. The model of Sloman (1993) uses a particular mathematical measure of feature overlap, but it is not clear why this should be the right measure to use. Rogers and McClelland (2004) provide no principled explanation for the architecture of their network or their strategy for computing the strength of inductive arguments, and their model appears to rely on several free parameters.

3.3 A Bayesian Analysis

Heit (1998) presented a computational theory where property induction is modeled as Bayesian inference. This inference engine is essentially the same as we describe later in Section 4.1. Applying a Bayesian analysis to any specific case of property induction requires a prior distribution over hypotheses about the extension of the property in question. Heit does not specify a formal method for generating priors, nor does he test his model quantitatively against any specific judgments. He shows that it captures several qualitative phenomena if it is supplied with the right kinds of priors, and that appropriate priors could allow it to handle both blank and non-blank properties. He also suggests how priors could be extracted from long-term memory: the probability of a hypothesis could be proportional to the number of familiar features that can be retrieved from memory and that have the same extension as that hypothesis. But it is far from clear that this suggestion would, if implemented, yield appropriate priors; as we show below, a simple version of this idea does not perform nearly as well as the SCM's gold standard in predicting human judgments.

Our framework adopts a Bayesian approach to inference like Heit's, but we emphasize the importance of modeling the form and the origins of appropriate priors. A formal account of how the learner's prior is structured and where it comes from provides two distinct advantages. First, it leads to strong quantitative models, predicting people's inductive judgments as well or better than any previous approach. More important, it adds genuine explanatory power. Most of the knowledge that supports induction is captured by the prior, and a computational theory should be as explicit as possible about the knowledge it assumes and how that knowledge is used. It has long been argued that different inductive contexts lead to quite different patterns of generalization behavior, but whether this is due to the operation of different kinds of knowledge, different mechanisms of reasoning, or both has not been so clear. We will argue that a single general-purpose Bayesian reasoning mechanism may be sufficient, by showing explicitly how to generate priors that can capture two important and very different kinds of domain knowledge and that can strongly predict people's judgments in appropriately different inductive contexts.

4. THE THEORY-BASED BAYESIAN FRAMEWORK

Our framework includes two components: a Bayesian engine for inductive inference, and a language for specifying relevant aspects of domain theories and using those theories to generate prior probability distributions for the Bayesian inference engine. The Bayesian engine reflects domain-general norms of rational statistical inference and remains the same regardless of the inductive context. Different domain theories may be appropriate in different inductive contexts, but they can often be formalized as instances of a single unifying scheme: a probabilistic process, such as diffusion, drift or transmission, defined over a structured representation of the relevant relations between categories, such as taxonomic or ecological relations.

4.1 The Bayesian Inference Engine

Assume that we are working within a finite domain containing n categories. We are interested in a novel property, Q, that applies to some unknown subset of these categories. Let H be the hypothesis space of all logically possible extensions for Q – the set of all possible subsets h of categories in the domain, each of which could a priori be the extension of the novel property. Since there are n categories, the number of hypotheses is 2^n. To each hypothesis we assign a prior probability $p(h)$, where $p(h)$ is the probability that h includes all and only the categories with property Q.

Suppose now that we observe X, a set of m labeled objects where the labels indicate whether each category in X has property Q. We want to compute $p(y \text{ has } Q|X)$, the probability that object y has property Q given the examples X. Summing over all hypotheses in H, we have

$$p(y \text{ has } Q|X) = \sum_{h \in H} p(y \text{ has } Q, h|X) \qquad (1)$$

$$= \sum_{h \in H} p(y \text{ has } Q|h, X) p(h|X). \qquad (2)$$

Now $p(y \text{ has } Q|h, X)$ equals one if $y \in h$ and zero otherwise (independent of X). Thus

$$p(y \text{ has } Q|X) = \sum_{h \in H: y \in h} p(h|X) \tag{3}$$

$$= \sum_{h \in H: y \in h} \frac{p(X|h)\, p(h)}{p(X)} \tag{4}$$

where the last step follows from Bayes's rule.

The numerator in Equation 4 depends on the prior $p(h)$, as well as on the likelihood $p(X|h)$, the probability of observing the labeled examples X given that h is the true extension of Q. The likelihood $p(X|h)$ should in general depend on the process assumed to generate the observations in X. Here, for simplicity we will assume that $p(X|h) \propto 1$ for all hypotheses consistent with X, and $p(X|h) = 0$ otherwise.[2] A hypothesis h for the extension of property Q is consistent with a set of labeled examples X if h includes all positively labeled categories in X and excludes all negatively labeled categories in X. Then Equation 4 is equivalent to

$$p(y \text{ has } Q|X) = \frac{\displaystyle\sum_{h \in H: y \in h,\, h \text{ consistent with } X} p(h)}{\displaystyle\sum_{h \in H: h \text{ consistent with } X} p(h)} \tag{5}$$

which is the proportion of hypotheses consistent with X that also include y, where each hypothesis is weighted by its prior probability $p(h)$. The probability of generalizing to y will thus be high to the extent that it is included in most of the high-prior-probability hypotheses that also include the observed examples X.

Other inferences can be formulated similarly. For example, the probability that all categories in a larger class Y (e.g., *all mammals*) have property Q

---

[2] More complex sampling models could be appropriate in other circumstances, and are discussed in Tenenbaum & Griffiths (2001) and Kemp & Tenenbaum (2003). For instance, an assumption that examples are randomly drawn from the true extension of Q might be particularly important when learning word meanings or concepts from ostensive examples (Tenenbaum & Xu, 2000; Xu & Tenenbaum, in press).

could be formalized as

$$p(Y \text{ has } Q|X) = \frac{\sum\limits_{h \in H : Y \subset h, h \text{ consistent with } X} p(h)}{\sum\limits_{h \in H : h \text{ consistent with } X} p(h)} \qquad (6)$$

Note that a Bayesian approach needs no special purpose rules for dealing with negative evidence or arguments with multiple premises. Once the prior distribution $p(h)$ and the likelihood $p(X|h)$ have been specified, computing the strength of a given argument involves a mechanical application of the norms of rational inference. Since we have assumed a simple and domain-general form for the likelihood above, our remaining task is to specify appropriate domain-specific prior probability distributions.

4.2 Theory-Based Priors

Generating the prior distributions used in Equations 5 and 6 appears to be a difficult problem – for either the cognitive modeler or the human reasoner. Somehow we need to specify 2^n numbers: $p(h)$ for each of the logically possible hypotheses h in H. We cannot simply assign all hypotheses equal prior probability; without any inductive biases, meaningful generalization would be impossible (Mitchell, 1997). Explicitly enumerating the priors for all 2^n hypotheses is also not an option. This would introduce far more degrees of freedom into the model than we could ever hope to test empirically. More importantly, it would fail to capture the most interesting aspect of these priors – that they are not just lists of numbers but rather the products of abstract systems of knowledge, or intuitive theories. Induction with different kinds of properties – such as anatomical features, behavioral tendencies, or disease states of animal species – will require different kinds of priors because we have qualitatively different kinds of knowledge that we bring to bear in those contexts. Our priors for induction can change when we learn new facts, but the biggest changes come not from statistical observations that might simply favor one hypothesis over another. Priors can change most dramatically, and can change globally across a large slice of the hypothesis space, when we acquire qualitative knowledge that alters our intuitive domain theories: when we learn about a new species with unexpected characteristics, such as whales or ostriches, or we learn something surprising about how various species might be related, such as that whales and dolphins are mammals, or we learn some new principle about how properties are distributed over species, such as that diseases tend to spread through physical contact or food.

The heart of our proposal is a way to understand formally how intuitive domain theories can generate the prior probabilities needed for induction. Two aspects of intuitive theories are most relevant for constructing priors for property induction: representations of how entities in the domain are related to each other, and processes or mechanisms operating over those relational structures that give rise to the distribution of properties over entities. To be concrete, we will assume that each of the n categories in a domain can be represented as a node in a relational structure, such as a directed or undirected graph. Edges in the graph represent relations that are relevant for determining inductive potential, such as taxonomic or causal relations among categories. Priors are generated by a stochastic process defined on this graph, such as a diffusion process, a drift process, or a noisy transmission process. These processes can be used to capture general beliefs about how properties of various types tend to be distributed over related categories in the domain. Once we have sufficiently characterized the relational structure and the stochastic generating process, that will fully specify the 2^n numbers in the prior. By choosing different kinds of structures and stochastic processes, we can capture different kinds of knowledge and account for qualitatively different patterns of inductive reasoning. In this chapter we describe and test two such models, one for reasoning about generic biological properties such as anatomical and physiological features, and another for reasoning about causally transmitted properties such as diseases.

4.2.1 A Theory For Generic Biological Properties, The prior distribution for default biological reasoning is based on two core assumptions: the *taxonomic principle* and the *mutation principle*. The taxonomic principle asserts that species belong to groups in a nested hierarchy, and more precisely, that the taxonomic relations among species can be represented by locating each species at some leaf node of a rooted tree structure. Tree-structured taxonomies of species appear to be universal across cultures (Atran, 1998), and they also capture an important sense in which species are actually related in the world: genetic relations due to the branching process of evolution. Outside of intuitive biology, tree-structured taxonomies play a central role in organizing knowledge about many systems of natural-kind and artifact categories (Rosch, 1978), as well as the meanings of words that label these categories (Markman, 1989; Tenenbaum & Xu, 2000).

The structures of people's intuitive taxonomies are liable to deviate from scientific phylogenies in non-negligible ways, since people's theories are based on very different kinds of observations and targeted towards predicting different kinds of properties. Hence we need some source of constraint besides

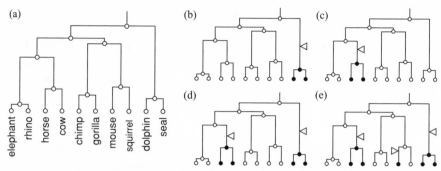

FIGURE 7.1. (a) A folk taxonomy of mammal species. (b–e) Examples of mutation histories.

scientific biology in order to generate the particular tree-structured taxonomy that our model will use. We have explored several different approaches to reconstructing taxonomic trees that best characterize people's intuitive theories. One possibility is to perform hierarchical clustering on people's explicit judgments of similarity for all pairs of species in the domain. Hierarchical clustering could also be applied to more implicit measures of psychological distance between species: for example, we could represent each animal using a set of behavioral and morphological features (e.g., "lives in water," "has a tail") and set the distance between two animals to be the distance between their feature vectors. We could also use more structured domain knowledge that might obviate the need for any bottom-up clustering. Both direct judgments of pairwise similarity and ratings of feature-category associations have been collected for many of the standard domains of animal species used in studying reasoning about generic biological properties (Osherson et al., 1990), and these data sets provide a convenient basis for comparing different modeling frameworks on equal grounds. Figure 7.1a shows a taxonomic tree that was reconstructed for ten mammal species, based on hierarchical clustering over a set of features collected by Osherson and colleagues (and slightly augmented as described later in Section 5.1).

Some simple and intuitive prior distributions $p(h)$ can be generated using the taxonomic principle alone. For instance, we could assign a uniform probability to each hypothesis corresponding to one of the nineteen taxonomic clusters (including singleton species) shown in the tree, and zero probability to all other sets of species. We call this the "strict-tree model." It corresponds roughly to some informal accounts of taxonomically driven induction (Atran, 1995), and it can qualitatively reproduce some important phenomena, such as diversity-based reasoning. Essentially this prior has also been used successfully to explain how people learn words that label taxonomic object categories.

But to see that it is not sufficient to explain biological property induction, compare the arguments *seals, squirrels* $\overset{T4}{\rightarrow}$ *horses* and *seals, cows* $\overset{T4}{\rightarrow}$ *horses*. The second appears stronger than the first, yet under the intuitive taxonomy shown in Figure 7.1, the strict-tree model assigns them both the same strength, since each set of premises is compatible with only one hypothesis, the set of all mammals.

The solution to this problem comes from realizing that in scientific biology, the assumption that every property is strictly confined to a single taxon is false. Properties arise randomly via mutations, and through a combination of chance and natural selection, two species may share a property even if it occurs in no common ancestor. Convergent evolution is particularly likely for survival-significant traits of interest to people (e.g., being warm-blooded, having an eye, being able to fly or swim, forming long-term monogamous pair bonds). A more veridical folk theory of generic biological properties should thus generate a prior that allows some probability (perhaps small) of a property occuring in two or more disjoint taxa.

To capture these patterns in how generic biological properties are distributed, our theory will assume that novel properties are generated by a mutation-like stochastic process defined over the tree structure specified by the taxonomic principle. We refer to this second assumption as the *mutation principle* and the Bayesian model of induction that uses the resulting prior as the "evolutionary model." Intuitively, we can imagine a property that arises at the root of the tree and spreads out towards the leaves. The property starts out with some value (on or off) at the root, and at each point in the tree there is a small probability that the property will mutate, or switch its value. Whenever a branch splits, both lower branches inherit the value of the property at the point immediately above the split, and mutations thereafter occur independently along the lower branches. For example, if a property is absent at the root of the tree in Figure 7.1a, but switches on at the two points marked in Figure 7.1d, then it would apply to just horses, cows, dolphins, and seals.

More formally, the mutation process is characterized by a single parameter λ, specifying the average rate at which mutations occur. Mutations are modeled as transitions in a two-state Markov chain defined continuously over the tree, with infinitesimal matrix $[-\lambda, \lambda; \lambda, -\lambda]$. The probability that two points in the tree separated by a branch of length t will have different values (present or absent) for a given property is then $\frac{1-e^{-2\lambda t}}{2}$. For simplicity we assume here that any property is equally likely to be present or absent at the tree root, and that mutations are equally likely in both directions (present $\rightarrow$ absent, absent $\rightarrow$ present), but more generally, prior knowledge about the nature or distribution of a feature could bias these probabilities. A *mutation history* for a property Q is an assignment of zero or more mutations to branches of the tree, together with a specification of the state of the property (present or absent) at the root of the tree.

The Markov mutation model allows us to assign a probability to any hypothetical mutation history for a property, based only on whether the property changes state between each pair of branch points on the tree. This is almost but not exactly what we need. Bayesian property induction requires a prior probability $p(h)$ that some novel property Q applies to any possible subset h of species. A mutation history for property Q induces a labeling of all leaf nodes of the tree – all species in the domain – according to whether Q is present or absent at each node. That is, each mutation history is consistent with exactly one hypothesis for Bayesian induction, but the mapping from mutation histories to hypotheses is many-to-one: many different mutation histories, with different probabilities, will specify the same distribution of a property Q over the set of species. We define the prior probability $p(h)$ that a new property Q applies to some subset h of species to be the sum of the probability of all mutation histories consistent with h. This prior (and all the resulting Bayesian computations) can be computed efficiently using belief propagation over the tree, as described more formally in Kemp, Griffiths, et al. (2004). For small trees, it can also be approximated by taking many samples from a simulation of the mutation process. We randomly generate a large number of hypothetical mutation histories with probability proportional to their likelihood under the Markov mutation model, by first choosing the property's state at the tree root and then following the causal direction of the mutation process down along all branches of the tree to the leaf nodes. We can estimate the prior $p(h)$ for each hypothetical labeling h of the leaf nodes as the frequency with which mutation histories consistent with h occur in this sample.

The prior generated by this mutation principle has several qualitative features that seem appropriate for our problem. First, unlike the strict-tree model described above, the mutation process induces a non-zero prior probability for any logically possible extension of a novel property (i.e., any of the 2^n hypotheses in the full hypothesis space H). The prior is "smooth" with respect to the tree: the closer two species lie in the tree, the more likely they are to share the same value for a novel property. Properties are more likely to switch on or off along longer branches (e.g., the mutation history in Figure 7.1b is more likely than in 7.1c). Hence $p(h)$ will be higher for properties that hold only for a highly distinctive taxonomic group of species, such as the aquatic mammals or the primates, than for properties that hold only for a less distinctive taxonomic group, such as the "farm animals" ($\{horses, cows\}$).

Multiple independent occurences of the same property will be rare (e.g., the mutation history in Figure 7.1b is more likely than in 7.1d, which is more likely than in 7.1e). Hence the prior favors simpler hypotheses corresponding to a single taxonomic cluster, such as {*dolphins, seals*}, over more complex hypotheses corresponding to a union of multiple disjoint taxa, such as the set {*dolphins, seals, horses, cows, mice*}. The lower the mutation rate λ, the greater the preference for strictly tree-consistent hypotheses over disconnected hypotheses. Thus this model captures the basic insights of simpler heuristic approaches to taxonomic induction (Atran, 1995) but embeds them in a more powerful probabilistic model that supports fine-grained statistical inferences.

Several caveats about the evolutionary model are in order. The mutation process is just a compact mathematical means for generating a reasonable prior for biological properties. We make no claim that people have conscious knowledge about mutations as specifically biological phenomena, any more than a computational vision model which appeals to an energy function claims that the visual system has explicit knowledge about energy. It is an open question whether the biological principles guiding our model are explicitly represented in people's minds or only implicitly present in the inference procedures they use. We also do not claim that a mutation process is the only way to build a prior that can capture generalizations about generic biological properties. The key idea captured by the mutation process is that properties should vary randomly but smoothly over the tree, so that categories nearby in the tree are more likely to have the same value (present or absent) for a given property than categories far apart in the tree. Other stochastic processes including diffusion processes, Brownian motion, and Gaussian processes will also capture this intuition and should predict similar patterns of generalization (Kemp & Tenenbaum, submitted). The scope of such "probabilistic taxonomic" theories is likely to extend far beyond intuitive biology: there may be many domains and contexts where the properties of categories are well described by some kind of smooth probability distribution defined over a taxonomic-tree structure, and where our evolutionary model or some close relative may thus provide a compelling account of people's inductive reasoning.

4.2.2 A Theory for Causally Transmitted Properties.

The evolutionary model in the previous section is appropriate for reasoning about many kinds of biological properties, and perhaps some kinds of nonbiological but still taxonomically distributed properties as well, but other classes of properties give rise to very different patterns of inductive generalization and will thus require differently structured priors. For instance, in some contexts inductive generalization will be asymmetric: the probability of generalizing a property from category A to category B will not be the same as the probability of generalizing the same property from B to A. Earlier we described one biological context where induction is frequently asymmetric: reasoning about disease properties, such as the probability that grizzly bears will have a disease given that salmon do, or vice versa. In this section we show how to capture this sort of inductive reasoning within our theory-based Bayesian framework.

The formal model we present could be appropriate for many properties whose distributions are governed by asymmetric causal relationships among categories, but for concreteness, we will assume that the domain comprises a set of species categories, and the novel property is a disease spread by predator-prey relations between species. Two abstract principles of an intuitive theory are relevant in this context; these principles are analogous to the taxonomic and mutation principles underlying the evolutionary model in the last section. First, a structured representation captures the relevant relations between entities in the domain: in this context, we posit a set of directed predator-prey relations. An example of such a food web is shown in Figure 7.4a. Second, a stochastic process defined over that directed-network structure generates prior probabilities for how novel properties are distributed over species: here, the process is designed to capture the noisy arrival and transmission of disease states.

As with the mutation process for generic biological properties presented above, we can describe this noisy-transmission process by explaining how to generate a single hypothetical property. If we draw a large sample of hypothetical properties by repeating this procedure many times, the prior probability for each hypothesis about how to generalize a particular novel property will be proportional to the number of times it appears in this sample. The transmission process has two parameters: b, the background rate, and t, the transmission probability. The first parameter captures the knowledge that species can contract diseases from causes external to the food web. For each species in the web, we toss a coin with bias b to decide whether that species develops the disease as a result of an external cause. The second parameter is used to capture the knowledge that diseases can spread from prey to predator up the food web. For each edge in the graph, we toss a coin with bias t to determine whether it is active. We stipulate that all species reachable by active links from a diseased animal also contract the disease. We refer to the Bayesian model using this prior as the "causal transmission model."

Figure 7.2 shows one possible outcome if we sample a property from the causal transmission process. We see that two of the species develop the disease

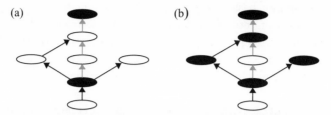

FIGURE 7.2. One simulated sample from the causal-transmission model, for the foodweb shown in Figure 7.4a. (a) Initial step showing species hit by the background rate (black ovals) and active routes of transmission (black arrows). (b) Total set of species with disease via background and transmission.

for reasons unrelated to the foodweb, and that four of the causal links are active (Figure 7.2a). An additional three species contract the disease by eating a disease-ridden species (Figure 7.2b). Reflecting on these simulations should establish that the prior captures two basic intuitions. First, species that are linked in the web by a directed path are more likely to share a novel property than species which are not directly linked. The strength of the correlation between two species' properties decreases as the number of links separating them increases. Second, property overlap is asymmetric: a prey species is more likely to share a property with one of its predators than vice versa.

Although the studies we will model here consider only the case of disease transmission in a food web, many other inductive contexts fit the pattern of asymmetric causal transmission that this model is designed to capture. Within the domain of biological species and their properties, the causal model could also apply to reasoning about the transmission of toxins or nutrients. Outside of this domain, the model could be used, for example, to reason about the transmission of lice between children at a day care, the spread of secrets through a group of colleagues, or the progression of fads through a society.

4.2.3 Common Principles of Theory-Based Priors. It is worth noting several deep similarities between these two theory-based Bayesian models, the evolutionary model and the causal transmission model, which point to more general aspects of our approach. In each case, the underlying intuitive theory represents knowledge on at least two levels of abstraction. The lower, more concrete level of the theory specifies a graph-structured representation of the relevant relations among species (taxonomic neighbors or predators), and a stochastic process that distributes properties over that relational structure, which is characterized by one or two numerical parameters controlling its degree of stochasticity. At a higher level, each theory specifies the *form* of the structure and stochastic process that are appropriate for reasoning about a certain domain of entities and properties: generic biological properties, such as anatomical and physiological attributes, are distributed according to a noisy mutation process operating over a taxonomic tree; diseases are distributed according to a noisy transmission process operating over a directed food web.

For a fixed set of categories and properties, the lower level of the theory is all we need to generate a prior for inductive reasoning. But the higher level is not just a convenient abstraction for cognitive modelers to talk about – it is a critical component of human knowledge. Only these abstract principles tell us how to extend our reasoning when we learn about new categories, or a whole new system of categories in the same domain. When European explorers first arrived in Australia, they were confronted with many entirely new species of animals and plants, but they had a tremendous head start in learning about the properties of these species because they could apply the same abstract theories of taxonomic organization and disease transmission that they had acquired based on their European experience. Abstract theories appear to guide childrens' conceptual growth and exploration in much the same way. The developmental psychologists Wellman and Gelman (1992) distinguish between "framework theories" and "specific theories," two levels of knowledge that parallel the distinction we are making here. They highlight framework theories of core domains – intuitive physics, intuitive psychology, and intuitive biology – as the main objects of study in cognitive development. In related work (Tenenbaum, Griffiths & Kemp, 2006; Tenenbaum, Griffiths, & Niyogi, in press), we have shown how the relations between different levels of abstraction in intuitive theories can be captured formally within a hierarchical probabilistic model. Such a framework allows us to use the same Bayesian principles to explain both how theories guide inductive generalization and how the theories themselves might be learned from experience.

Each of our theory-based models was built by thinking about how some class of properties is actually distributed in the world, with the aim of giving a rational analysis of people's inductive inferences for those properties. It is therefore not surprising that both the evolutionary model and the causal transmission model correspond roughly to models used by scientists in relevant disciplines – formalisms like the causal transmission model are used by epidemiologists, and formalisms like the evolutionary model are used in biological classification and population genetics. The correspondence is of course far from perfect, and it is clearest at the higher "framework" level of abstraction: constructs such as taxonomic trees, predator-prey networks, the mutation process, or the transmission process may in some sense be shared across intuitive theories and scientific theories, even while the specific tree or foodweb structures, or the specific mutation or transmission rate parameters, may differ in important ways.

Even though it may be imperfect and abstract, this correspondence between the world's structure and our models' representations provides an important source of constraint on our approach. If we were free to write down just any sort of probabilistic model as the source of a prior probability distribution, it would be possible to give a "rational analysis" of any coherent inductive behavior, but it is not clear how much explanatory value that exercise would have. By deriving priors from intuitive theories that at some deep level reflect the actual structure of the world, it becomes clearer why these priors should support useful generalizations in real-world tasks and how they might themselves be acquired by a rational learner from experience in this world. Our approach can be extended to other inductive contexts by formally specifying how the properties covered by those contexts are distributed in the world; Kemp and Tenenbaum (submitted) consider two other important contexts in addition to those discussed here.

Our primary goal here has been to characterize with the knowledge that guides generalization (theory-based priors) and the input-output mapping that allows this knowledge to be converted into judgments of inductive strength (Bayesian inference). Our work is located at the most abstract of Marr's levels – the level of computational theory (Marr, 1982) – and we make no commitments about the psychological or neural processes by which people make inductive judgments. Inference in both of our models can be implemented using efficient approximate methods that have appealing correlates in the traditional toolkit of cognitive processes: for instance, belief propagation over Bayesian networks, which can be seen as a kind of rational probabilistic version of spreading activation. We find it encouraging that efficient and psychologically plausible implementations exist for our models, but we are not committed to the claim that inference in these Bayesian networks resembles cognitive processing in any detailed way.

Finally, it is worth emphasizing that our models have not attempted to capture all or most of the content and structure of people's intuitive theories. We are modeling just those aspects of theories that appear necessary to support inductive reasoning about properties in fairly specific contexts. We are agnostic about whether people's intuitive theories contain much richer causal structures than those we attempt to model here (Carey, 1985), or whether they are closer to light or skeletal frameworks with just a few basic principles (Wellman & Gelman, 1992).

5. TESTING THE MODELS OF PROPERTY INDUCTION

We now describe two series of experimental tests for the theory-based Bayesian models introduced in the previous section. In each case, we consider multiple sets of inductive arguments whose strengths have been rated or ranked by human judges, and we compare these subjective argument strengths with the theoretical predictions of the models. We will also compare with several alternative models, including the classic similarity-coverage model and multiple variants within our Bayesian framework. The latter comparisons allow us to illustrate the distinctive importance of both ingredients in our approach: an appropriate representation of the relevant aspects of a domain's structure, and an appropriate probabilistic model for how properties of the relevant type are distributed over that structure.

5.1 Reasoning about Generic Biological Properties

We begin by looking at the classic datasets of Osherson, Smith, and their colleagues on inductive reasoning with generic biological properties. Five datasets will be considered. The two "Osherson" datasets are taken from Osherson et al. (1990). The "Osherson specific" set contains thirty-six two-premise arguments, of the form *gorillas, squirrels* $\longrightarrow$ *horses*. The conclusion category of each of these arguments is the same: *horses*. The two premise categories vary across arguments, but are always drawn from the set of ten mammal species shown in Figure 7.1. Various generic biological predicates are used across different arguments; in this section we drop references to the specific property assuming it is one of these generics. The "Osherson general" set contains forty-five three-premise general arguments, of the form *gorillas, squirrels, dolphins* $\longrightarrow$ *mammals*. The conclusion category of each of these arguments is always *mammals*, while the three premise categories again vary across arguments and are drawn from the set of ten mammal species shown in Figure 7.1. The three "Smith" data sets are similar, but they draw on different and fewer mammal categories (Smith et al., 1993).

We compare people's judgments of argument strength in these five datasets with the predictions of five computational models for induction with generic biological properties. Two are theory-based Bayesian models: the evolutionary model, in which the prior is generated by a mutation process defined on a taxonomic tree of species categories, and the strict-tree model, in which the prior is simply a uniform distribution over taxonomic clusters of species (without the possibility of a property arising in multiple disconnected branches of the taxonomy). Another model is inspired by Heit's proposal for a Bayesian analysis (see Section 3.3), in which the prior probability of a hypothesis is based on the number of familiar properties that can be retrieved from memory and that have the same extension as that hypothesis. We call this the "raw-feature model," because it embodies a prior that is based directly on raw experience, without the benefit of a structured domain theory that might help people to reason sensibly in cases that go substantially beyond their experience. The details of the raw-feature model are explained below. Finally, we consider two versions of the similarity-coverage model, MaxSim and SumSim, which respectively compute similarity to the set of premise categories in terms of the maximum or summed similarity to those categories (see Section 3.1).

In order to predict the strengths of arguments about a particular set of species, each of these models requires some way to represent people's prior knowledge about those species. We can compare the models on equal footing by grounding the knowledge representations for each model in a matrix of judged species-feature associations collected by Osherson and colleagues. Participants were given forty-eight familiar species and eighty-five familiar features (mostly anatomical or ecological properties, such as "has a tail" or "lives in water") and asked to rate the relative "strength of association" between each species and each feature. Participants gave ratings on a scale that started at zero and had no upper bound. In order to model the behavioral judgments described below, we supplemented these data with feature ratings for two additional species, *cows* and *dolphins*, to give a total of fifty species. We also substituted the judged features of *collies* for *dogs* (because *dogs* appeared as a premise category in some of the argument judgment tasks, but not in the feature rating task). Ratings were linearly transformed to values between 0 and 100, then averaged. Let F be the resulting 50×85 matrix of average species-feature associations. We also consider analogous binary matrices F_θ obtained by thresholding the average ratings at some level θ. Let $S(F)$ be a 50×50 matrix of species-species similarities, computed based on Euclidean distances between the two feature vectors in F representing each pair of species.

For evaluating the predictions of the SCM models, we used the entries of $S(F)$ to determine the necessary similarities between species. The taxonomic tree for the evolutionary and strict-tree models was constructed by running hierarchical agglomerative ("average linkage") clustering on $S(F)$, restricted to just the species categories involved in each experiment. The prior for the raw-feature model was defined from the thresholded species-feature matrices F_θ, inspired by the proposal of Heit (1998). (We treat the threshold θ as a free parameter of the model, to be optimized when fitting judgments of argument strength.) We assume that the features participants retrieve from memory correspond to the columns of F_θ, plus an additional feature corresponding to

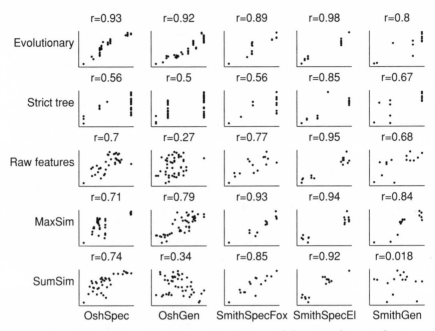

FIGURE 7.3. Comparing models of property induction with human judgments, for reasoning in a default biological context with generic anatomical or physiological properties. Each row of plots shows the performance of a single model over all data sets; each column shows the performance of all models over a single data set. In each plot, individual data points represent the strengths of individual inductive arguments. The *x*-value of each point represents the argument's predicted strength according to a given model, while the *y*-value represents the argument's subjective strength according to the mean judgments of human experimental participants.

all the animals. The prior $p(h)$ assigned to any hypothesis h for the extension of a novel property is proportional to the number of columns of F_θ (i.e., the number of familiar features) that are distributed as h specifies – that apply to just those categories that h posits. Hypotheses that do not correspond to any features in memory (any column of F_θ) receive a prior probability of zero.

All of these models (except the strict-tree model) include a single free parameter: the mutation rate in the evolutionary model, the balance between similarity and coverage terms in MaxSim and SumSim, or the feature threshold θ in the raw-feature model. Each model's free parameter was set to the value that maximized the average correlation with human judgments over all five datasets.

Figure 7.3 compares the predictions for all five of these models on all five datasets of argument strength judgments. Across these datasets, the predictions of the evolutionary model are better than or comparable to the best of the other models. This success provides at least some evidence that the model's core assumptions – a taxonomic-tree structure over species and a mutation-like distribution of properties over that tree – do in fact characterize the way people think and reason about generic biological properties. More revealing insights come from comparing the performance of the evolutionary model with that of the other models.

The strict-tree model captures the general trends in the data but does not predict people's judgments nearly as accurately as the evolutionary model. This is because, without the mutation principle, the strictly taxonomic hypothesis space is too rigid to capture the graded degrees of support that more or less diverse premise sets provide for inductive generalization. For example, in the Osherson-general experiment, the strict-tree model assigns the same probability (100%) to *cows, dolphins, squirrels* ⟶ *mammals* and *seals, dolphins, squirrels* ⟶ *mammals*, because in both cases the set of all mammals is the only hypothesis consistent with the examples. The evolutionary model correctly distinguishes between these cases, recognizing that the first premise set is better spread out over the tree and therefore provides better evidence that all mammals have the novel property. An intuitive explanation is that it feels very difficult to imagine a property that would be true of cows, dolphins, and squirrels but not all mammals, while it seems more plausible (if unlikely) that there could be some characteristic property of aquatic mammals (seals and dolphins) that might, for some unknown reason, also be true of squirrels or rodents, but no other animals. The mutation principle matches this intuition: the highly specific hypothesis {*seal, dolphin, squirrel*} can be generated by only two mutations, one on a very long branch (and thus relatively likely), while the hypothesis {*cows, dolphins, squirrels*} could arise only from three mutations, all on relatively short branches.

This problem with the strict-tree model is hardly restricted to the specific pair of arguments cited above, as can be seen clearly by the dense vertical groupings of datapoints on the right-hand side of the plots in Figure 7.3. Each of those vertical groupings corresponds to a set of arguments that are judged to have very different strengths by people but that all receive maximum probability under the strict-tree prior, because they are consistent with just the single hypothesis of generalizing to all mammals.

The raw-feature model is more flexible than the strict-tree model, but it is still not sufficient to capture the diversity effect, as can be seen by its dramatically worse performance on the datasets with general arguments. Consider the premise sets *dolphins, chimps, squirrels* and *dolphins, seals, horses*. It is difficult to think of anatomical or physiological properties that apply to all of the animals in the first set but only some of the animals in the second set. None of the features in our dataset is strongly associated with dolphins, chimps, and squirrels, but not also seals and horses. The raw-feature model therefore finds it hard to discriminate between these two sets of premises, even though it seems intuitively that the first set provides better evidence that all mammals have the novel property.

More generally, the suboptimal performance of the raw-feature model suggests that people's hypotheses for induction are probably not based strictly on the specific features that can be retrieved from memory. People's knowledge of specific features of specific animals is too sparse and noisy to be the direct substrate of inductive generalizations about novel properties. In contrast, a principal function of intuitive domain theories is to generalize beyond people's limited specific experiences, constraining the kinds of possible situations that would be expected to occur in the world regardless of whether they have been previously experienced (McCloskey et al., 1980; Murphy & Medin, 1985; Carey, 1985). Our framework captures this crucial function of intuitive theories by formalizing the theory's core principles in a generative model for Bayesian priors.

Taken together, the performance of these three Bayesian variants shows the importance of both aspects of our theory-based priors: a structured representation of how categories in a domain are related and a probabilistic model describing how properties are distributed over that relational structure. The strict-tree model incorporates an appropriate taxonomic structure over categories but lacks a sufficiently flexible model for how properties are distributed. The raw-feature model allows a more flexible prior distribution for properties, but lacking a structured model of how categories are related, it is limited to generalizing new, partially observed properties strictly based on the examples of familiar, fully observed properties. Only the prior in the evolutionary model embodies both of these aspects in ways that faithfully reflect real-world biology – a taxonomic structure over species categories and a mutation process generating the distribution of properties over that tree – and only the evolutionary model provides consistently strong quantitative fits to people's inductive judgments.

Turning now to the similarity-based models, Figure 7.3 shows that their performance varies dramatically depending on how we define the measure of similarity to the set of premise categories. MaxSim fits reasonably well, somewhat worse than the evolutionary model on the two Osherson datasets but comparably to the evolutionary model on the three Smith datasets. The fits on the Osherson datasets are worse than those reported by Osherson et al. (1990), who used direct human judgments of similarity as the basis for the model rather than the similarity matrix $S(F)$ computed from people's feature ratings. We used the species-feature associations here in order to compare all models (including the raw-feature model) on equal terms, but we have also compared versions of the evolutionary model and the similarity-coverage models using the similarity judgments of Osherson et al. (1990) to build the taxonomic tree or compute MaxSim or SumSim scores (Kemp & Tenenbaum, 2003). In that setting, too, the evolutionary model consistently performs at least as well as MaxSim.

SumSim is arguably the least successful model we tested. Its predictions for the strengths of general arguments are either uncorrelated with or negatively correlated with people's judgments. Although the good performance of MaxSim shows that a similarity-based model can describe people's patterns of inductive reasoning, the poor performance of SumSim calls into question the explanatory value of similarity-based approaches. As mathematical expressions, the SumSim and MaxSim measures do not appear very different, beyond the presence of a nonlinearity in the latter case. This nonlinearity turns out to make all the difference; it is necessary for similarity-based models to predict diversity-based inductive reasoning. Because the total inductive strength of an argument under SumSim is a linear function of the inductive strength associated with each premise category, the model assigns highest strength to arguments in which each of the premise categories would individually yield the strongest one-premise argument. This preference goes against diversity, because the categories that make for the best single-premise arguments tend to be quite similar to each other. For instance, unlike people, SumSim assigns a higher strength to *horses, cows, rhinos* $\longrightarrow$ *mammals* than to *horses, seals, squirrels* $\longrightarrow$ *mammals*, because the strength of a generalization from the individual premise categories *horses, cows,* or *rhinos* to *mammals* are some of the strongest in the domain – significantly higher than from less typical mammals such as *seals* or *squirrels*.

We can see why SumSim fails, but there is no principled a priori justification within the similarity-based paradigm for adopting the nonlinear MaxSim rather than the linear SumSim as a model of inductive generalization. The SumSim measure has if anything greater precedent in other similarity-based models of learning, categorization, and memory (Nosofsky, 1986; Kruschke, 1992; Hintzman et al., 1978). Osherson et al. (1990) do not attempt to justify the preference for MaxSim – it just seems to fit people's intuitions better in the particular task of property induction. That is fine as far as a descriptive model goes, but not very satisfying if one of our goals is to explain why people's intuitions work the way that they do.

In contrast, the theory-based Bayesian approach we have presented offers a principled and rational explanation for why people make the judgments that they do on these inductive reasoning tasks. People's judgments are approximately optimal, with respect to our evolutionary model that combines the inferential optimality of Bayesian principles with a prior based on how the properties of natural species are distributed in the real world. This rational approach can also explain why some Bayesian model variants fare better than others. The raw-feature and strict-tree models yield substantially poorer descriptive fits to human judgments, and each is based on a prior that neglects a key principle of how natural categories and properties are structured which the evolutionary model properly incorporates. Finally, our approach could explain why the most successful similarity-based models of induction work the way they do, and in particular, why they are based on the MaxSim mechanism rather than the more standard SumSim operation. In Kemp and Tenenbaum (2003) and Kemp, Griffiths, et al. (2004) we show that under certain conditions, MaxSim (but not SumSim) provides an efficient heuristic approximation to the ideal computations of the evolutionary Bayesian model. Hence at some level of analysis, and under certain circumstances, human inductive reasoning could be well described as a similarity-based computation – but which similarity-based computation that is, and why it works the way that it does, would still be best explained by an analysis in our theory-based Bayesian framework.

5.2 Reasoning about Causally Transmitted Properties

A second set of studies was intended to evaluate the descriptive power of the Bayesian causal-transmission model, our model for inductive reasoning about diseases and other causally transmitted properties, and also to show how different theory-based Bayesian models can be used to account for different patterns of inductive reasoning that arise with different kinds of properties.

We work with data from experiments by Shafto, Kemp, Bonawitz, Coley, and Tenenbaum (submitted) (see also Shafto et al., 2005). Participants were first trained to memorize the structure of the food webs shown in Figure 7.4. They were also familiarized with the correct taxonomic groupings for these species categories. After this initial training, participants were asked to judge the strength of inductive arguments about one of two kinds of properties: a disease property ("has disease D") or a genetic property ("has gene XR-23"). All arguments had a single premise and a specific conclusion, and the stimuli exhaustively explored all arguments of this form. That is, every pair of categories appeared as a premise-conclusion pair in some argument. Participants also provided pairwise similarity ratings between the species in each food web, and we again used hierarchical clustering to recover representations of people's taxonomic trees for these categories. The recovered

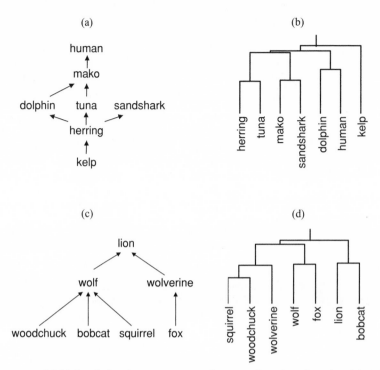

FIGURE 7.4. Multiple relational structures over the same domains of species. (a) A directed network structure capturing food web relations for an "island" ecosystem. (b) A rooted ultrametric tree capturing taxonomic relations among the same species. (c) A directed network structure capturing food web relations for a "mammals" ecosystem. (d) A rooted ultrametric tree capturing taxonomic relations among the same species.

taxonomies are shown in Figure 7.4. Free parameters for all models (the mutation rate in the evolutionary model, the background and transmission rates for the causal transmission model) were set to values that maximized the models' correlations with human judgments.

We hypothesized that participants would reason very differently about disease properties and genetic properties, and that these different patterns of reasoning could be explained by theory-based Bayesian models using appropriately different theories to generate their priors. Specifically, we expected that inductive inferences about disease properties could be well approximated by the causal-transmission model, assuming that the network for causal transmission corresponded to the food web learned by participants. We expected that inferences about genetic properties could be modeled by the evolutionary model, assuming that the taxonomic structure over species corresponded to the tree we recovered from participants' judgments. We also tested MaxSim

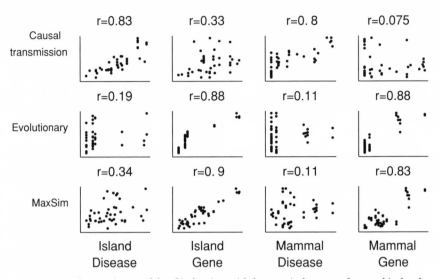

FIGURE 7.5. Comparing models of induction with human judgments, for two kinds of properties: disease properties and genetic properties. Both kinds of property-induction tasks were studied for two different systems of species categories, an "Island" ecosystem and a "Mammals" ecosystem, as shown in Figure 7.4. Plotting conventions here are the same as in Figure 7.3.

and expected that it would perform similarly to the evolutionary model, as we found for the previous set of studies.

Figure 7.5 shows that these predictions were confirmed. High correlations were found between the causal-transmission model and judgments about disease properties, and between the evolutionary model and judgments about genetic properties. Morever, we observed a double dissociation between property types and model types. The causal-transmission model correlates weakly or not at all with judgments about genetic properties, while there is no significant correlation between the evolutionary model and judgments about disease properties. This double dissociation is the clearest sign yet that when our Bayesian models fit well, it is not simply because they are using sophisticated general-purpose inference principles; their success depends crucially on using a theory-generated prior that is appropriately matched to the domain structure and inductive context.

The performance of MaxSim was also as hypothesized: highly correlated with inductive judgments about genetic properties (like traditional "blank" properties), but poorly correlated with judgments about disease properties when participants were familiar with relevant predator-prey relations. This result should not be surprising. It is well-known that similarity-based approaches have difficulty accounting for inductive reasoning beyond the context of generic biological properties, when some other relevant knowledge is available to people (Smith et al., 1993; Medin et al., 2003; Shafto & Coley, 2003). The usual interpretation of similarity's shortcomings expresses a general pessimism about computational models of commonsense reasoning: different kinds of properties or inductive contexts just call for fundamentally different approaches to reasoning, and cognitive scientists should not hope to be able to give a principled general-purpose account for all – or even a large class – of our everyday inductive inferences.

Our theory-based Bayesian framework offers a more optimistic view. We have separated out the general-purpose inferential mechanisms from the context-specific knowledge that guides those mechanisms, and we have introduced a potentially quite general way of modeling relevant aspects of contextual knowledge in terms of relational structures over categories and stochastic processes for generating distributions of properties over those structures. It is at least a start towards explaining more precisely how induction in different contexts operates, and how apparently quite different patterns of reasoning in different contexts or domains could be given a unifying and rigorous explanatory account.

6. THE GENERALITY OF BAYESIAN MODELS OF INDUCTION

Bayesian models have recently been shown to provide strong accounts of many core inductive capacities, not just the property induction tasks we consider here. Examples include Bayesian models of concept learning and categorization (Anderson, 1991; Tenenbaum, 2000), similarity judgment (Shepard, 1987; Tenenbaum & Griffiths, 2001), rule induction (Oaksford & Chater, 1994; McKenzie & Mikkelsen, 2000), word learning (Tenenbaum & Xu, 2000; Xu & Tenenbaum, in press), causal judgment and covariation assessment (Anderson, 1990; McKenzie, 1994; Griffiths & Tenenbaum, 2005; Steyvers et al., 2003), detection of suspicious coincidences (Griffiths & Tenenbaum, 2007) and predictions about the magnitudes or durations of everyday events (Griffiths & Tenenbaum, 2006). Yet the generality of Bayesian approaches has not gone unchallenged.

Over the last decade, Murphy and Ross (e.g., Murphy & Ross, 1994, this volume) have explored a set of natural inductive prediction tasks for which people's judgments often do not seem to follow Bayesian principles. In their studies, participants are presented with partial descriptions of objects or individuals and asked to predict other aspects of these entities. Murphy and Ross focus on cases where the partially described entity could belong to one of several mutually exclusive categories, each of which suggests different predictions about the properties to be predicted. For instance, a person walking up to a house could be either a real estate agent, a burglar, or a cable TV worker, and knowing that the individual belonged to one of those categories would make it seem more or less likely that he would examine the doors of the house. Murphy and Ross find that participants often base their predictions on only the single most probable category (given a partial entity description), rather than averaging the predictions of all categories weighted by their probability, as would be prescribed by a Bayesian analysis of prediction with category uncertainty (Anderson, 1991).

At first glance, these results might appear to be in conflict with our proposed Bayesian mechanism for property induction (in particular, Equations 5 and 6). However, important computational differences exist between our tasks and analyses and those of Murphy and Ross. In our models, we posit that learners implicitly consider a very large number of alternative hypotheses for how to generalize a novel property. These hypotheses need not – and in most cases, almost surely could not – be represented consciously and explicitly in people's minds. More fundamentally, the hypotheses in our models do not reflect mutually exclusive alternatives for categorizing an entity but rather mutually exclusive candidate extensions for a novel property. We use a Bayesian framework to model learners' uncertain beliefs about a property to be predicted – what subset of entities the property holds for – rather than uncertain beliefs about the categories that entities belong to. Each entity typically falls under many such hypotheses for the extension of a novel property, and which hypotheses an entity falls under is not in doubt; that is given by the structure of the learner's domain theory. The uncertainty in our tasks comes from providing incomplete information about the property to be predicted – participants are given only one or a few examples of entities that have the property – rather than from providing incomplete information about the entities over which predictions are to be made. Hence there is no direct tension between the Murphy and Ross findings and our work.

It remains an open question why human reasoning appears to incorporate uncertainty in a fully Bayesian fashion for some kinds of inductive inferences but not others. Murphy and Ross (Chapter 8 in this volume) suggest several possibilities, and they argue against explanations based on simple psychological processing factors such as the complexity or naturalness of the task. Another possibility that should be explored is a rational analysis that takes into account key computational differences in different inductive tasks – a "rational metanalysis," so to speak. Perhaps human reasoners are more likely to consider multiple alternative hypotheses in prediction tasks where doing so is more likely to lead to a substantial improvement in accuracy. Previous studies of Bayesian concept learning are consistent with this conjecture (Tenenbaum, 2000), but much more systematic investigation is required to assess the importance of this factor relative to others.

7. CONCLUSIONS AND OPEN QUESTIONS

Conventional models of induction focus on the processes of inference rather than the knowledge that supports those inferences. Inference mechanisms are typically given fully explicit and mathematical treatments, while knowledge representations are either ignored or boiled down to place-holders like a similarity metric or a set of features that at best only scratch the surface of people's intuitive theories. This focus probably stems from the natural modeler's drive towards elegance, generality, and tractability: the knowledge that supports induction is likely to be messy, complex, and specific to particular domains and contexts, while there is some hope that one or a few simple inference principles might yield insight across many domains and contexts. Yet this approach limits the descriptive power and explanatory depth of the models we can build, and it assigns a second-class status to crucial questions about the form and structure of knowledge. Our goal here is to return questions of knowledge to their appropriate central place in the study of inductive inference, by showing how they can be addressed rigorously and profitably within a formal Bayesian framework.

Every real-world inference is embedded in some context, and understanding how these different contexts work is critical to understanding real-world induction. We have argued that different contexts trigger different intuitive theories, that relevant aspects of these theories can be modeled as generative models for prior probability distributions in a Bayesian reasoning framework, and that the resulting theory-based Bayesian models can explain patterns of induction across different contexts. We described simple theories for generating priors in two different inductive contexts, a theory for generic biological properties such as genetic, anatomical, or physiological features of species, and a theory for causally transmitted properties such as diseases, nutrients, or knowledge states. We showed that Bayesian models based on a prior generated by each theory could predict people's inductive judgments for properties in the appropriate context, but not inappropriate contexts.

Intriguingly, both of these generative theories were based on principles analogous to those used by scientists to model analogous phenomena in real biological settings. In showing their success as descriptive models of people's intuitive judgments, we begin to provide an explanation for people's remarkable ability to make successful inductive leaps in the real world as the product of rational inference mechanisms operating under the guidance of a domain theory that accurately reflects the true underlying structure of the environment.

Of course, just specifying these two theory-based models is far from giving a complete account of human inductive reasoning. It will be a challenging long-term project to characterize the space of theories that people can draw on and the processes by which they are acquired and selected for use in particular contexts (see Shafto, Coley, & Vitkin, Chapter 5, this volume). Perhaps the most immediate gap in our model is that we have not specified how to decide which theory is appropriate for a given argument. Making this decision automatically will require a semantic module that knows, for example, that words like "hormone" and "gene" are related to the generic biological theory, and words like "disease" and "toxin" are related to the theory of causal transmission. How best to integrate some form of this semantic knowledge with our existing models of inductive reasoning is an open question.

We have discussed theories that account for inductive reasoning in two contexts, but it is natural and necessary to add more. Some of our ongoing work is directed towards developing and testing models beyond the tree- and network-based models described here. For example, in Kemp and Tenenbaum (submitted), we show how reasoning about properties such as "can bite through wire" can be modeled as Bayesian inference over a linear structure representing a dimension of strength, rather than a tree or a network representing taxonomic or foodweb relations (Smith et al., 1993). In other work, we are extending our approach to account for how multiple knowledge structures can interact to guide property induction; in particular, we are looking at interactions between networks of causal relations among properties and tree structures of taxonomic relations among species. Finally, in addition to broadening the scope of theory-based Bayesian models, we have begun more fundamental investigations into how these probabilistic theories can themselves be learned from experience in the world (Kemp, Perfors, & Tenenbaum, 2004) and how learners can infer the appropriate number and complexity of knowledge structures that best characterize a domain of categories and properties (Shafto et al., 2006). These problems are as hard to solve as they are important. Yet we believe we are in a position to make real progress on them – to develop genuine insights into the origins and nature of common sense – using models that combine the principles of Bayesian inference with structured knowledge representations of increasing richness and sophistication.

ACKNOWLEDGMENTS

This work has benefited from the insights and contributions of many colleagues, in particular Tom Griffiths, Neville Sanjana, and Sean Stromsten. Liz Bonawitz and John Coley were instrumental collaborators on the food web studies. JBT was supported by the Paul E. Newton Career Development Chair. CK was supported by the Albert Memorial Fellowship. We thank Bob Rehder for helpful comments on an earlier draft of the chapter.

References

Anderson, J. R. (1990). *The adaptive character of thought.* Hillsdale, NJ: Erlbaum.

Anderson, J. R. (1991). The adaptive nature of human categorization. *Psychological Review, 98*(3), 409–429.

Ashby, F. G., & Alfonso-Reese, L. A. (1995). Categorization as probability density estimation. *Journal of Mathematical Psychology, 39,* 216–233.

Atran, S. (1995). Classifying nature across cultures. In E. E. Smith & D. N. Osherson (Eds.), *An invitation to cognitive science* (Vol. 3) (pp. 131–174). MIT Press.

Atran, S. (1998). Folkbiology and the anthropology of science: Cognitive universals and cultural particulars. *Behavioral and Brain Sciences, 21,* 547–609.

Carey, S. (1985). *Conceptual change in childhood.* Cambridge, MA: MIT Press.

Gelman, S., & Markman, E. (1986). Categories and induction in young children. *Cognition, 23*(3), 183–209.

Goodman, N. (1972). Seven strictures on similarity. In *Problems and projects.* Indiana: Bobbs-Merrill.

Gopnik, A., & Meltzoff, A. (1997). *Words, thoughts, and theories.* Cambridge, MA: MIT Press.

Gopnik, A., & Schulz, L. (2004). Mechanisms of theory formation in young children. *Trends in Cognitive Sciences, 8,* 371–377.

Griffiths, T. L., & Tenenbaum, J. B. (2005). Structure and strength in causal induction. *Cognitive Psychology, 51,* 354–384.

Griffiths, T. L., & Tenenbaum, J. B. (2007). From mere coincidences to meaningful discoveries. *Cognition.*

Griffiths, T. L., & Tenenbaum, J. B. (2006). Optimal predictions in everyday cognition. *Psychological Science, 17*(9), 767–773.

Heit, E. (1998). A Bayesian analysis of some forms of inductive reasoning. In M. Oaksford & N. Chater (Eds.), *Rational models of cognition* (pp. 248–274). Oxford University Press.

Heit, E., & Rubinstein, J. (1994). Similarity and property effects in inductive reasoning. *Journal of Experimental Psychology: Learning, Memory, and Cognition, 20,* 411–422.

Hintzman, D. L., Asher, S. J., & Stern, L. D. (1978). Incidental retrieval and memory for coincidences. In M. M. Gruneberg, P. E. Morris, & R. N. Sykes (Eds.), *Practical aspects of memory* (pp. 61–68). New York: Academic Press.

Kemp, C., Griffiths, T. L., Stromsten, S., & Tenenbaum, J. B. (2004). Semi-supervised learning with trees. In *Advances in neural processing systems 16,* pp. 257–264. Cambridge, MA: MIT Press.

Kemp, C., Perfors, A., & Tenenbaum, J. B. (2004). Learning domain structures. In *Proceedings of the 26th annual conference of the Cognitive Science Society.* Mahwah, NJ: Erlbaum.

Kemp, C., & Tenenbaum, J. B. (2003). Theory-based induction. In *Proceedings of the 25th annual conference of the Cognitive Science Society.*

Kemp, C., & Tenenbaum, J. B. (submitted). Structured statistical models of inductive reasoning.

Kruschke, J. K. (1992). Alcove: An exemplar-based connectionist model of category learning. *Psychological Review, 99,* 22–44.

Markman, E. (1989). *Naming and categorization in children.* Cambridge, MA: MIT Press.

Marr, D. (1982). *Vision.* New York: W. H. Freeman.

McCloskey, M., Caramazza, A., & Green, B. (1980). Curvilinear motion in the absence of external forces: Naive beliefs about the motion of objects. *Science, 210*(4474), 1139–1141.

McKenzie, C. R. M. (1994). The accuracy of intuitive judgment strategies: Covariation assessment and Bayesian inference. *Cognitive Psychology, 26,* 209–239.

McKenzie, C. R. M., & Mikkelsen, L. A. (2000). The psychological side of Hempel's paradox of confirmation. *Psychonomic Bulletin and Review, 7,* 360–366.

Medin, D. L., Coley, J. D., Storms, G., & Hayes, B. K. (2003). A relevance theory of induction. *Psychological Bulletin and Review, 10,* 517–532.

Mitchell, T. M. (1997). *Machine learning.* McGraw-Hill.

Murphy, G. L. (1993). Theories and concept formation. In I. V. Mechelen, J. Hampton, R. Michalski, & P. Theuns (Eds.), *Categories and concepts: Theoretical views and inductive data analysis.* London: Academic Press.

Murphy, G. L., & Medin, D. L. (1985). The role of theories in conceptual coherence. *Psychological Review, 92,* 289–316.

Murphy, G. L., & Ross, B. H. (1994). Predictions from uncertain categorizations. *Cognitive Psychology, 27,* 148–193.

Nosofsky, R. M. (1986). Attention, similarity, and the identification-categorization relationship. *Journal of Experimental Psychology: General, 115,* 39–57.

Oaksford, M., & Chater, N. (1994). A rational analysis of the selection task as optimal data selection. *Psychological Review, 101,* 608–631.

Oaksford, M., & Chater, N. (Eds.) (1998). *Rational models of cognition.* New York: Oxford University Press.

Osherson, D., Smith, E. E., Wilkie, O., López, A., & Shafir, E. (1990). Category-based induction. *Psychological Review, 97*(2), 185–200.

Rips, L. J. (1975). Inductive judgements about natural categories. *Journal of Verbal Learning and Verbal Behavior, 14,* 665–681.

Rogers, T. T., & McClelland, J. L. (2004). *Semantic cognition: A parallel distributed processing approach.* Cambridge, MA: MIT Press.

Rosch, E. (1978). Principles of categorization. In E. Rosch & B. B. Lloyd (Eds.), *Cognition and categorization* (pp. 27–48). Hillsdale, NJ: Lawrence Erlbaum.

Shafto, P., & Coley, J. D. (2003). Development of categorization and reasoning in the natural world: Novices to experts, naive similarity to ecological knowledge. *Journal of Experimental Psychology: Learning, Memory, and Cognition, 29,* 641–649.

Shafto, P., Kemp, C., Baraff, E., Coley, J. D., & Tenenbaum, J. B. (2005). Context-sensitive induction. In *Proceedings of the 27th annual conference of the Cognitive Science Society.* Mahwah, NJ: Erlbaum.

Shafto, P., Kemp, C., Mansinghka, V., Gordon, M., & Tenenbaum, J. B. (2006). Learning cross-cutting systems of categories. In *Proceedings of the 28th annual conference of the Cognitive Science Society.* Mahwah, NJ: Erlbaum.

Shafto, P., Kemp, C., Bonawitz, E. B., Coley, J. D. & Tenenbaum, J. B. (submitted). Inductive reasoning about causally transmitted properties.

Shepard, R. N. (1987). Towards a universal law of generalization for psychological science. *Science, 237,* 1317–1323.

Silverman, B. (1986). *Density estimation for statistics and data analysis.* London: Chapman and Hall.

Sloman, S. A. (1993). Feature-based induction. *Cognitive Psychology, 25,* 213–280.

Smith, E. E., Safir, E., & Osherson, D. (1993). Similarity, plausibility, and judgements of probability. *Cognition, 49,* 67–96.

Steyvers, M., Tenenbaum, J. B., Wagenmakers, E. J., & Blum, B. (2003). Inferring causal networks from observations and interventions. *Cognitive Science, 27,* 453–489.

Tenenbaum, J. B. (2000). Rules and similarity in concept learning. In S. A. Soller, T. K. Leen, & K. R. Müller (Eds.), *Advances in neural processing systems 12* (pp. 59–65). Cambridge, MA: MIT Press.

Tenenbaum, J. B., & Griffiths, T. L. (2001). Generalization, similarity, and Bayesian inference. *Behavioral and Brain Sciences, 24,* 629–641.

Tenenbaum, J. B., Griffiths, T. L., & Kemp, C. (2006). Theory-based Bayesian models of inductive learning and reasoning. *Trends in Cognitive Sciences, 10*(7), 309–318.

Tenenbaum, J. B., Griffiths, T. L., & Niyogi, S. (in press). Intuitive theories as grammars for causal inference. In A. Gopnik & L. Schulz (Eds.), *Causal learning: Psychology, philosophy, and computation.* Oxford: Oxford University Press.

Tenenbaum, J. B., & Xu, F. (2000). Word learning as Bayesian inference. In *Proceedings of the 22nd annual conference of the Cognitive Science Society* (pp. 517–522). Hillsdale, NJ: Erlbaum.

Wellman, H. M., & Gelman, S. A. (1992). Cognitive development: Foundational theories of core domains. *Annual Review of Psychology, 43,* 337–375.

Xu, F., & Tenenbaum, J. B. (in press). Sensitivity to sampling in Bayesian word learning. *Developmental Science.*

8

Use of Single or Multiple Categories in Category-Based Induction

Gregory L. Murphy and Brian H. Ross

Uncertainty is a basic fact of life. Despite uncertainty, people must make predictions about the world. Will the car you are considering buying be reliable? Will you like the food you order? When you see an animal in the woods, what should you do? One source of information that reduces uncertainty is category membership. Although all Toyota Camrys are not exactly the same, they are similar enough that you can predict with some confidence that the new Camry you are considering will be reliable. Kansas City style barbecue ribs are not identical, but they taste more similar to one another than they do to roast chicken or "tofu surprise." Knowing the category of an entity therefore serves to reduce the uncertainty associated with it, and the category reduces uncertainty to the degree that the category members are uniform with respect to the prediction you want to make. This *category-based induction* is one of the main ways that categories are useful to us in everyday life.

Unfortunately, this reduction of uncertainty is limited by the uncertainty of category membership itself. If you go to the Toyota dealership and order a Camry, you can be close to 100% sure that your new car is going to be a Camry. But in many other situations, you cannot be 100% sure. Is the animal you see in the woods a squirrel, or was your glimpse too fleeting for you to rule out the possibility it was really a raccoon? Is the person you are dating honest? You know how you would react to a squirrel or an honest person, but when you are not sure if these things are in their respective categories, then you cannot be sure of their other properties.

The central issue we address is whether (and, if so, how and when) multiple categories are used in induction. If you are uncertain whether the animal is a squirrel or a raccoon, do you make a different prediction than if you are sure that the animal is a squirrel? Do you use what you know about both categories, or only one? For items that are not uncertain, but are members of multiple categories, the question is whether only one or a number of those categories are involved in the induction. If Alice is a physician and a mother, do you use your knowledge of both categories in making a prediction about her, or only one? If only one, how do you choose which one?

In a series of studies, we have looked at this problem from a number of angles, using naturalistic and artificial categories, manipulating uncertainty in a number of ways. The main questions we have asked are the following. (1) Do people change their inductions based on the certainty of an object's classification? (2) When people are not sure which of two categories an object is in, do they use both categories to make inductions? (3) What contextual or task variables moderate the effect of uncertainty? In particular, do people treat uncertainty differently depending on just how they make the judgment? (4) What happens when an entity is a member of multiple categories? Are all categories used, or only one of them?

This chapter presents an overview of our work in this area, attempting to integrate our findings from various paradigms with work of other researchers to provide a more complete account of how multiple categories are used in induction. These issues are important, because they get to the heart of what categories are used for. We need to know the categories of objects so that we can make predictions about properties that are not otherwise available to us. If categories could tell us only about visible properties of an object, they would not add any information to help direct our behavior towards the object. Thus, induction is central to category use. Finally, we believe that our results speak to important issues of the limits of reasoning. When people fail to use multiple categories, is it because they are unable to do so, because they don't understand the need to do so, or because of some performance problem? The answer will speak to issues of inductive processing more generally.

THE BASIC FRAMEWORK: HOW CATEGORIES *SHOULD* BE USED IN INDUCTION

In an important analysis, Anderson (1991) proposed that uncertainty about a category should be taken into account when making inductions about it. If you are not certain whether the strange fruit in front of you is an apple or a pear, then you should not be certain in predicting what it tastes like. Indeed, your prediction about the taste should be proportional to your belief in these two categories. If you are 90% sure it is an apple, then you can make a strong prediction that it will have an apple taste, but if you are only 55% sure, then you can make only a weak prediction. Anderson therefore suggested that when you make a prediction about an object, you access the categories that it might be in, and you assign it the properties of each category proportionally to its likelihood of being in that category (for more detail, see Anderson, 1991; Murphy & Ross, 1994). For example, if you are trying to predict whether this fruit will be mushy, you would estimate the likelihood that apples are mushy and that pears are mushy (and other fruits if they are also possible) and combine these likelihoods. Thus, this procedure entails that a category-based induction is made only to the degree that one is certain about the category; and if multiple categories are possible, then each is used proportionally to its likelihood.

This model appears normatively correct to us, and it is also consistent with later Bayesian approaches to classification and prediction (e.g., Heit, 2000; Tenenbaum 2000). However, following the general rule that anything that is normatively correct people do not actually do, we might well be skeptical of this proposal. And in fact, we have found consistent evidence that people do not in fact follow this rule, which we will summarize next.

Evidence from Natural Categories

Some of our research showing single-category induction has been conducted with real-world categories, taking advantage of people's prior knowledge of categories and properties. In one kind of experiment, we constructed scenarios in which entities had an uncertain classification. For example, we described a case in which an unfamiliar person walking up the driveway was likely to be a real estate agent (the primary category). (All the experiments reported here had multiple categories and induction properties, but we will mention only one example each, for the sake of exposition.) Depending on the condition, it was also possible, though less likely, that the person could be one of the following secondary categories – a burglar or cable TV worker. We then asked subjects who they thought the person most likely was and how likely they thought this person was to examine the doors of the house. Pretesting had shown that our subject population thinks that real estate agents and burglars both will pay attention to the doors of a house, but that a cable worker will not. Given the uncertainty about the person's identity, how should people make this prediction? If they are using both categories, they should be more certain that the unknown person will examine the doors when the secondary category is the burglar than when it is the cable TV worker. Because burglars confirm the prediction but cable TV workers do not, people's predictions should differ in the two cases. However, they do not in fact differ (Malt, Ross, & Murphy, 1995), even when considerable emphasis is laid on the uncertainty of the person's (or object's) classification (Ross & Murphy, 1996).

A different kind of experiment varied whether the initial categorization was described as being certain or uncertain. When it is certain, only one category should be used in the induction; when it is uncertain, both possible categories should be used. However, this manipulation also had no effect (Malt et al., 1995).

More recently, we used an analogous manipulation with pictures that were ambiguous between two different categories. By morphing two images, we were able to construct items like a peach-apple or a robin-blackbird (Murphy & Ross, 2005). Subjects were told to imagine that they were exploring an abandoned island to survey its flora and fauna. They were able to send samples of the objects they found to a lab for a quick analysis that would identify the most likely categories. The category list they were given mentioned either one or both of the categories. For example, for the peach-apple, they would be told either that it might be a peach or cherry or raspberry – or else it might be either a peach or apple or cherry or raspberry. Subjects were more certain about the object's identity in the first case than in the second (when the alternative category was mentioned as a likely possibility), yet this manipulation had no reliable effect on people's inductions.

Readers might well be thinking at this point, "Apparently, these guys cannot get any experiment to work. Everything they report is a null result." However, that is fortunately not the case. In the same experiments a number of reliable results showed that subjects were carefully reading the scenarios and were paying attention to the category information. However, rather than repeat those results here (which are not germane to the main theoretical issues), we will simply mention now that we later discuss results in which people *do* use multiple categories in induction, even with similar materials and questions. Thus, the null results of these studies are not due to dull subjects or insensitive measures, because positive results are possible, under some very specific conditions.

Evidence from Artificial Categories

Natural categories have the advantage that they are, well, natural, but they do not allow a precise manipulation of the probabilities of features within the categories. For better control, we have carried out many experiments using categories of geometric shapes (or other artificial stimuli). People first studied the categories. We then told subjects about a feature of another geometric stimulus (e.g., its shape) and asked them what category it most likely was in; then we asked them to make a prediction about one of its other features (e.g., its color or pattern). They also rated the probability that their answers were correct, a measure of inductive strength. Because subjects were allowed to examine the categories even while answering the questions, we were able to eliminate problems of learning and memory that might have influenced the results. Instead, people could directly see that the item's classification was uncertain (e.g., many triangles, but by no means all, were in one particular category), and they could also examine the distribution of features in order to make predictions. Thus, if they chose to use multiple categories to answer their questions, they could do so without great difficulty. But they did not.

For example, imagine that one category had a lot of triangles and also mostly solid black figures (see Figure 8.1). Depending on condition, other categories with some triangles also had some black items or else did not. In the first condition, people should be more confident in predicting that a new triangle would be black than in the second. That is, across secondary categories, there is evidence for the solid black feature in one condition but not the other. Yet, these two conditions did not differ (Murphy & Ross, 1994).

Again, this null result is not simply a matter of people's inattention to the categories. For example, when we varied the distribution of features *within* the critical category, it strongly influenced people's inductions (Murphy & Ross, 1994, 2005). That is, varying the number of solid black items in the triangle's most likely category changed people's judgments; varying the number of black items in other categories had no effect. Clearly, people were using one category rather than all the possible categories.

In a somewhat different design, we kept constant the predicted features but varied the certainty of the main category. For example, we reduced the number of triangles in the critical category so that people would be less certain that the triangle was in that category. Although this did in fact change their categorization certainty, it did not change their predictions. That is, people lowered their ratings that the triangle was in the category but did not lower their ratings that the triangle was black – even though this prediction should depend on the triangle being in the critical category (Murphy & Ross, 2005).

As a final note, researchers who hear about these studies often wonder whether asking what category the item is in is critical for obtaining these results. Perhaps explicitly choosing a category leads people to focus on that category. To address that question, one of our early experiments replicated the Figure 8.1 experiment but asked only about the property (Murphy & Ross, 1994, Expt. 2). This change did lead to an overall decrease in giving the property from the critical category (i.e., black), but the distribution of the number of black items in the other categories still had no effect on their certainty. Thus, the initial question does seem to get people to use the critical category more often, but does not influence whether they are likely to use more

Liz   Mary

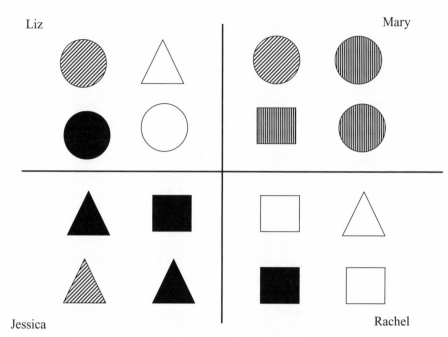

Jessica   Rachel

FIGURE 8.1. An example similar to the categories used in Murphy and Ross (1994), illustrating the main comparison of that set of studies. In one condition, subjects would be asked to predict the shading of a new triangle drawn by one of the children. Triangles were most often drawn by Jessica, so Jessica was the target category. Note that most of her drawings were black. Liz and Rachel also each drew a triangle, and they also drew black items. Thus, information from these categories might increase one's estimate that a new triangle would be black (if one used multiple categories). The control question might be to make a prediction about a new square. Rachel is most likely to have drawn a square, and most of her figures are empty. Mary and Jessica also drew squares but have no empty figures, and so the secondary categories do not strengthen this induction. Thus, if people were using multiple categories, their inductions of the first example (triangle-solid black) should be stronger than those in the second example (square-empty). But they are not.

than one category. Similarly, Murphy and Ross (2005, Expt. 3) repeated their experiment asking the categorization question *after* the induction question, so that it would not influence the induction judgment. The pattern of results was identical to the reverse order of questions.

EXPLANATIONS OF THE USE OF SINGLE CATEGORIES

Together, these experiments give surprisingly convincing evidence that people do not use multiple categories in making inductions. Even though we found that they were not certain in their initial categorization (either through rat-ings or else by observing considerable variance in that categorization across subjects), this uncertainty did not lower the certainty of their induction, nor did it make them attend to other categories that the item might have been in. One particularly striking aspect of these results is that on one question people might admit that they are not sure what category an item is in but on the next question they do not show any sign of this uncertainty on the induction using this category. It is as if these two judgments take place in compartmentalized phases. First one decides what category the object is in. Perhaps it is not certain, but the object seems most likely to be a robin. Then one makes an induction about the object, given that it *is actually* a robin. In this second phase, the uncertainty about the initial categorization has no effect – it is as if the uncertain categorization has been walled off and is now treated as if it were certain.

Why is this? One possibility is that people simply cannot carry out the computations necessary to use category uncertainty when making inductions. It is possible that keeping track of different categories, their properties, and their uncertainty is simply more than working memory can do. A second possibility is that people do not recognize the principle involved. That is, they may not realize that if you are uncertain about an object's identity, you should reduce the certainty of predictions about the object. This might be consistent with findings from the decision-making literature such as the lack of using base rates in making predictions. Just as people do not attend to the frequency of green cabs when deciding how likely it is that a green cab was involved in an accident (Tversky & Kahneman, 1980), they may not attend to how likely the object is to be a robin or blackbird when making a prediction about it.

However, neither of these possibilities has survived empirical testing. We have been able to find certain conditions in which people *are* sensitive to category uncertainty, which means that they must have the computational ability to use it in making decisions, and that they must understand the importance of using it, at least in the abstract. Ross and Murphy (1996) constructed a new induction question to test the limits of the earlier results. In our original work, for cases in which the real estate agent was the primary category, we used questions like "What is the probability that the man walking up the driveway will pay attention to the sturdiness of the doors on the house?" This is something that both real estate agents and burglars would do and cable TV workers would not (according to a norming study), yet the possibility that the person might be a burglar instead of a cable TV worker did not raise the rated probability of this property. In the new experiment, we made questions that were directly associated to the secondary category (a burglar, in this case), for example, "What is the probability that the man walking up the driveway will try to find out whether the windows are locked?" This activity is directly associated with burglars, whereas cable TV workers have little interest in windows. Our hypothesis was that in reading this question, subjects would be reminded of the possibility that the man might be a burglar. They might then increase their prediction (compared to the cable TV worker condition) as a result of being reminded of this category. And this is what happened: The predictions were 21% higher when a burglar was the secondary category than when a cable TV worker was.

Apparently, if the induction question makes people think of the secondary category, they can use information about that category in making their prediction. Perhaps using multiple categories in that question would raise people's awareness of the importance of considering secondary categories in general, and so they might use both categories to answer subsequent questions. But in fact, that did not happen. In two experiments, we found that when people answered the induction questions about properties associated to the secondary category, they seemed to be using two categories, but on subsequent questions about the same scenario (with unassociated properties), they reverted to using a single category (Ross & Murphy, 1996).

These results suggest the following, slightly informal explanation: If you hit people over the head with the fact that there are two possible categories, they can and do use both categories; if you don't hit them over the head, then they do not. This pattern of results shows that people do have the computational ability to deal with two categories (at least) and that they also can recognize the principle that both categories are relevant. But this ability and knowledge are put to work only in fairly circumscribed situations. As will be seen, the critical element in whether people do or do not use multiple categories seems to be whether the secondary category is brought to their attention *while* they are answering the question. If it is not, the general principle of hedging one's bets in uncertain cases (Anderson, 1991) does not seem strongly enough represented to cause people to use multiple categories.

Once again, we are left with the observation that classification seems to be a largely separate process from induction, even though they are logically strongly connected. One possible reason for this is that in many cases, the two are in fact done separately. We may classify entities without making an interesting induction about them: the squirrels on the lawn as we walk to work, the cars on the street, the trees in front of the house, the buildings, the people, the chairs in our office, and so on. We often do not need to make any predictions about the squirrels, trees, or chairs. And when we do make predictions, the prediction is often not category-based (e.g., to decide how to avoid something on your path, it is often more useful to know the object's size than its category). Furthermore, in many cases when we do make inductions, the category is certain. If we are worried about a dog prowling around the yard, we are likely not worried about whether it is a dog – that may be obvious. We are worried about what it might do. If we try to predict how our doctor will treat our condition, we do not worry about whether she is or is not really a doctor. We do not know exactly how often people are confronted with the situation in which something has an uncertain categorization and yet they attempt to make a prediction about it. Although we believe that induction with categorical uncertainty is a common event in an absolute sense, its relative frequency may be dwarfed by thousands of occasions in which categorization is clear or we do not draw an induction. Thus, when induction must be done when categories are uncertain, people may carry over habits from their experiences with certain categories.

We may be a bit better at dealing with uncertainty when we know almost nothing about the entity's categorization. For example, if we stop someone on the street to ask a question, we can have only a very vague idea of the person's profession or religion or hobbies. Under such circumstances, people take into account the uncertainty. In an experiment using the geometric figure categories, we placed one triangle (say) in all four categories and then asked people to make predictions about a new triangle. We obtained evidence that people used all four categories in this situation (see Murphy & Ross, 1994, for the details). We assume that the reason for this is that people have no preferred category in this situation and so cannot engage in the two-stage process we have described. That is, they could literally see that the triangle was equally likely to be in each of four categories and thus had no basis for picking one of the categories, and so they considered all four of them. However, this situation would be quite rare in real life, and we suspect that when there is only very weak evidence for a number of categories, people simply do not engage in category-based induction. That is, even if you believed profession is a good predictor of helpfulness, if you cannot tell what profession a stranger is likely to be in, you may not make a guess about his profession to predict his willingness to help you. Instead, you will simply not make the induction or will try to find another basis on which to make it.

However, even in situations where there is no clear reason that a category-based induction would help, people may use a single category that is brought to mind. Lagnado and Shanks (2004) described an interesting situation like this, using hierarchically organized categories of persons. They had two super-ordinate categories of readers of different types of newspapers, which we will just call A and B, each with two subcategories of particular newspapers. There were more readers of the newspapers in category A than of the newspapers in B, but one subcategory of B – let's call it B1 – was the most frequently read paper. Lagnado and Shanks taught subjects about the different categories by exposing them to exemplars and teaching them a property of each person (what party he or she voted for).

In their test problems, Lagnado and Shanks asked their subjects whether a randomly chosen person from this population was more likely to read the type of paper in A or B. Subjects generally guessed A, because of its greater frequency. Then they made a prediction about what party this random person voted for. They generally chose the party most voted for by A readers. On other trials, subjects were asked which of the subcategories a randomly chosen person was in (i.e., which particular paper they read). They usually guessed B1, which was the most frequently read paper subcategory, and then they predicted that the random person would choose the party most voted for by members of B1. However, this prediction was different from that made by the first set of subjects, because B1 members were somewhat unusual in their voting choices. What is very peculiar about this is that both subjects were given the exact same information about the person's category, namely, none: They were told that the person was randomly chosen and were not told any of the person's properties. However, by first guessing that the person might be in A or might be in B1, the subject then answered the second question using this likely category as the basis for the answer. That is, simply by *asking* (not telling) which specific or general category the person was in, Lagnado and Shanks changed their subjects' answers to the subsequent induction question.

What is striking about Lagnado and Shanks's demonstration is that with truly minimal evidence for what category something is in, subjects still used that category for making their predictions. Thus, their results are a striking demonstration that once people choose a category for an object, the uncertainty they experienced in classifying it has no further effect on induction.

This demonstration is important for evaluating the possibility we raised earlier that people may not understand the general principle of using multiple categories when categorization is uncertain. In our studies, subjects often rated category membership, and we could verify that it was uncertain; in Lagnado and Shanks's study, membership was clearly uncertain, because no information was given about the person at all. Thus, if people generally used this principle, they should have done so in these cases. Nonetheless, some of our other studies have shown that people do use multiple categories (Ross & Murphy, 1996). It may be that people "understand" the principle in some sense, but they do not actually put it to use in most cases. This is reminiscent of findings in cognitive development that children can put a principle into action when the task is easy or the application is obvious, but they do not follow the principle in more difficult conditions (e.g., Baillargeon, 1998). In our case, when the induction property itself brings up the alternative category (and when the subject has already identified the other category as most likely), both categories are together in working memory, and the person may realize the importance of using both of them. But when the question does not bring to mind an alternative category, only the selected category is in working memory, and the principle itself is not accessed. Presumably, people who make predictions for a living, such as weather forecasters, poker players, and the like, have more practice in dealing with their uncertainty and may be better at answering these questions. (Note to granting agencies: Anyone who would like to fund a case study of induction in poker playing, please contact the authors.)

CROSS-CLASSIFICATION

Multiple categories are important when an object's identity is uncertain. But multiple categories may be important in a different situation as well, namely, when an object has multiple "identities." We are not referring to a questionable personality disorder but to the fact that categories are cross-cutting. Rather than a single hierarchy in which every entity fits into exactly one category at a given level of specificity, categories are a hodge-podge of groupings with different bases, overlapping to various degrees. For example, within categories pertaining to people, there are classifications based on personality, size, ethnicity, profession, gender, sexual orientation, areas of interest and expertise, age, educational level, financial status, and so on. These categories are not all independent, but their bases may be quite different (e.g., gender vs. profession), and so they change the way that one thinks about the person being categorized. A large, outgoing forty-two-year-old Asian-American female accountant who is married, likes sewing and football, has a B.A. and M.B.A, and is upper-middle class is a member of a few dozen person categories. If you have to make a prediction about this person, how will you decide which category to use? Will you use just one? If so, how do you choose which category to use? Or will you use some or all of these categories? Research in social psychology has addressed this problem specifically for social categories and stereotypes (e.g., Macrae, Bodenhausen, & Milne, 1995; Nelson & Miller, 1995; Patalano, Chin-Parker, & Ross, 2006), and we have investigated it for object categories.

Cross-classification raises issues that are very analogous to those we considered in the multiple-categorization problems above. However, here the problem is not of uncertainty but of multiplicity. That is, we are not uncertain whether the person is female or an accountant – we know she is both.

Nonetheless, that does not mean that people will use both categories in making a prediction. If one category is more relevant than the others, then people tend to use that as the basis for prediction. For example, Heit and Rubinstein (1994) showed that when making inductions about a biological property from one animal to another, people had more confidence when the two animals were biologically related (e.g., were both mammals). However, when making inductions about a behavioral property, they were more confident when the two animals shared an ecological niche (e.g., were both ocean dwellers; also see Ross & Murphy, 1999). This selective use of relevant categories is not limited to adults. Kalish and Gelman (1992) found that preschool children made inductions about the physical properties of a new object based on its physical make-up (e.g., being made of glass) but made functional inductions based on the object's artifact category (e.g., being a knife) (though see Nguyen & Murphy, 2003).

This research shows that people make inductions at least partly based on their beliefs about whether the category supports induction of the property (see also Proffitt, Medin, & Coley, 2000). Thus, these beliefs provide one way of narrowing down the many categories that an object or person might belong to. Although Cheri may be a mother, this does not tell you what her highest educational degree is or whether she is wealthy. Thus, categories like mother may not be used in making these inductions about Cheri, whereas profession might be used. What is not so clear from these studies is what people do when multiple categories *are* relevant and potentially useful. The above studies were specifically designed so that different categories were differentially relevant, and so they could not answer this question. Therefore, we addressed this issue in a manner analogous to our previous work on multiple-category induction.

The problem with studying cross-classification is that we cannot as easily manipulate the categories experimentally, since learning complex cross-cutting categories would be rather difficult. Instead, we used real-world categories of food items, because we had already found that foods are very cross-classified (Ross & Murphy, 1999). For example, a bagel is a bread and a breakfast food. Because we were interested in induction, we created a novel predicate for each problem that we attributed to different categories (as in classic work on category-based induction such as Osherson, Smith, Wilkie, López, & Shafir, 1990; Rips, 1975). We showed subjects a table of different categories with these properties in them, which might include information such as breads contain chloride salts 55% of the time, and breakfast foods contain chloride salts 25% of the time. These were only two of the facts listed, so that subjects would not know which predicates were of special interest.

Then we asked the subjects to judge (among other things) what percentage of time a bagel had chloride salts. The question was whether they would use one of the categories (breads or breakfast foods) or both in arriving at an answer. We found (Murphy & Ross, 1999, Expt. 1) that the majority of subjects used only one category, but that a minority consistently used both categories in their induction. Thus, as in our earlier work on uncertain categorizations, it appeared that people had the ability to combine information from different categories but did not generally see the necessity of doing so. The choice to use multiple cross-cutting categories appeared to be a fairly high-level strategic decision.

Unfortunately, the story is a bit more complex. In later experiments, we simplified the display, presenting only the critical two categories (e.g., bread and breakfast food in the bagel example) and asking fewer questions. With these changes, the majority of people used both categories. Furthermore, when we constructed a version of this procedure using ambiguous categories (like the real estate agent/burglar cases considered in our previous work), we found that people again used multiple categories most of the time (see Murphy & Ross, 1999, for details).

These results complicate the picture slightly, but they can be explained in terms of the conclusions drawn earlier. In this series of studies, we presented the critical categories along with information about predicates (e.g., how often items in the category have chloride salts). This procedure had the effect of bringing to people's attention exactly the relevant categories and predicate. That is, the presentation format focused people on the information relevant to making the induction, removing other information that was not relevant, and so they accessed both categories. When the task did not focus people's attention on the critical categories (as in Experiment 1 of the series, when the critical categories were just two of four presented, and more questions were asked), they generally used only one category. Thus, these results are theoretically consistent with the very different manipulation of using a property associated to the category (as in the burglar–locked window example) – both serve the function of bringing an alternative category to the person's attention. Surprisingly (to us), we found almost identical results in this paradigm for the cross-cutting categories (like breakfast food/bagel) and uncertain categories. Thus, these results suggest that in cases where it is crucial to attend to different possible categories (e.g., medical decision making with uncertain diagnosis), explicitly presenting the categories and the relevant information may encourage people to make more accurate inductions.

Further work needs to be done on induction of cross-cutting categories. It is clear that people can choose which category is relevant when only one of them is related to the induction property (as in Heit & Rubinstein, 1994). It is also clear that people can and will use two cross-cutting categories when it is obvious that both are relevant, and the property information is easy to retrieve (as in Murphy & Ross, 1999). What is not so clear is what people do in more naturalistic situations in which the categories and induction feature are not explicitly presented. Unfortunately, this situation is exactly the one that is hardest to study, because it is difficult to identify and control the information known about each category. That is, to show use of multiple categories, we need to know the person's beliefs about each category so that we can tell whether he or she is relying on one or both of them. In the ambiguous-category case, we could control the categories by constructing scenarios in which different categories were mentioned. But in cross-classification, the item itself determines its categories, and we cannot make a bagel a dinner entree versus a breakfast food in different conditions. So, this topic is awaiting a clever idea for how to investigate it.

RECENT BAYESIAN APPROACHES

We end this chapter by considering some other cases in which it appears people are not basing their inductions on a single category, both to better understand the conditions under which single and multiple categories might be used and to extend our analysis of induction. A number of Bayesian approaches to categorization and inference have been proposed in the past decade, and they seem to come to a different conclusion about multiple category use. One notable example is the work of Joshua Tenenbaum (see Chapter 7 in this volume), who has shown very good fits of his Bayesian model to a task in which people generalize from known examples to novel ones. (See also Heit, 2000, for a different Bayesian model.) In one experiment (Tenenbaum, 1999), subjects viewed dots in a two-dimensional Cartesian grid that represented levels of insulin and cholesterol of healthy people. Subjects were asked to find the rectangle (i.e., the limits on both variables) that defined the healthy levels, based on these positive examples. Tenenbaum's model analyzes this situation as a collection of hypotheses about the range of healthy levels for each variable (e.g., perhaps 45 to 55 is the range for healthy insulin, or 43 to 55, or 46 to 60, etc.). Thus, if a subject received data for one variable showing healthy levels of 46, 52, 53, and 55, then hypotheses of 46 to 55, 45 to 55, 40 to 61, and so forth would all be consistent with the observed data. In making predictions about new data, the hypotheses consistent with the data were weighted so that more specific hypotheses were considered more likely. That is, hypotheses 46 to 55 and 40 to 60 would both be used in making predictions about a new item, but the first would be more heavily weighted than the second, because it is more specific. Tenenbaum (2000) reports a related experiment.

Tenenbaum found that both of these experiments were fit well by a Bayesian rule that considered each hypothesis, weighted by its likelihood. Assuming that the number ranges are like categories and the given data are like exemplars, his results suggest that people do after all use multiple categories in making predictions, just as Anderson (1991) said they should, contrary to our results in analogous situations.

What are we to make of this apparent contradiction? There are a number of differences between Tenenbaum's problems and the ones we have used in our experiments, and it is likely that many of them contribute to the (apparent) difference in results. One major difference is that our paradigm has focused on fairly fixed object categories, whereas the number ranges of Tenenbaum (1999) are rather ad hoc categories that do not have any independent existence. That is, the range 46 to 55 is considered only because it happens to include all the presented data points and not because there is any special coherence or similarity to this set of numbers. In contrast, our geometric shape categories were supposedly drawn by different children, were spatially separated, and had some family resemblance. Our natural categories, such as real estate agent or breakfast foods, were familiar categories that people use in everyday life. It is possible that only such entrenched categories show the bias for single-category use that we have found in most experiments.

Furthermore, it is possible that Tenenbaum's subjects are not considering each range of categories as an explicit category but instead are using a similarity metric comparing the novel data point to the presented data. Certainly, in doing this task, it does not seem that subjects are *consciously* considering "Is it 43 to 55 or 46 to 56 or 44 to 56 or 46 to 55 or. . . .?"(at least, we don't, when we try this task). However, in our experiments with a very small number of possible categories, we suspect that people are consciously choosing the category the item is in. Then, because we require them to provide an induction strength judgment, they must give a numerical response. This response may further encourage the use of a single category, since subjects must come up with an actual number, and that becomes increasingly difficult to do when the number of possible categories increases, each with different information in it. Although we do not have direct evidence that these factors account for the apparent differences in results, we do have some recent evidence that use of multiple categories depends on the experimental task, including the type of decision being made.

In a recent study with Michael Verde (Verde, Murphy, & Ross, 2005), we compared our past paradigm in which subjects provide probabilities as a measure of induction strength to a different paradigm in which we looked at speeded yes-no decisions, using reaction time (RT) as a measure of induction strength. Our reasoning was that if people are required to quickly make an induction about a novel item, they may be influenced by a number of categories that the item might be in. People may not be very good at segregating the information of different categories when pressured to make a prediction about an item. In order to test this possibility, however, we had to first teach the people the categories so that any activation of different categories would happen fairly automatically. If people had to consciously choose which categories to examine, as in all our previous work, they would probably follow a strategy that excluded all but the most likely category.

We will not describe the task in much detail here (see Verde et al., for a complete report). The basic design was somewhat like that shown in Figure 8.1, in which we asked people to make an induction about an item that was partially described. But rather than ask the subject to produce an answer, we presented the answer, and the subject confirmed or disconfirmed it. For example, if subjects had learned categories like Figure 8.1 (which we are reusing here just for simplicity), they might then have been given the item *triangle* followed a second later by *black,* which meant that they were to verify whether a new triangle was most likely to be black. In one condition, this judgment was consistent with the target category only, and in another, it was also consistent with a secondary category. If people responded more quickly in the second condition than the first, that would indicate that they were influenced by two categories rather than just one. And in fact, they did respond more quickly when the two categories were consistent, suggesting that both influenced the decision. (This result was not due to a speed-accuracy trade-off in that accuracy was as high or higher in the consistent condition.) Interestingly, when we used the exact same materials and asked people to provide probability ratings without time pressure, as in our past experiments, this effect disappeared. That is, we found evidence for multiple-category use in speeded RTs but not in explicit probability judgments with the exact same materials.

It may be that in certain kinds of decisions, multiple categories influence the speed or strength of an induction without necessarily influencing its outcome. To the degree that a secondary category is consistent with the decision suggested by the target category, that decision may be easier to make. However, when making numerical estimates or other deliberate judgments, people may use information from only one category to arrive at their answer.

The Verde et al. (2005) results also suggest a somewhat different way of thinking about the multiple-category issue. In Anderson's (1991) initial proposal, as well as in Tenenbaum's approach, an explicit calculation is done in which each category's induction is weighted by its likelihood in deriving the grand induction. Those proposals are intended as computational-level analyses rather than algorithmic hypotheses – that is, they are not claiming that people carry out these calculations in their heads to come up with the answer but instead are claiming that the information in different categories is somehow combined in making the induction. Our results with the speeded task suggest that spreading activation might be a possible mechanism under those circumstances. That is, when you are presented with a triangle, the categories with triangles are all activated to some degree, and the categories' other properties (green, blue, black, small) could in turn be activated proportionally. This is one way in which information from different categories could be combined without explicitly doing the Bayesian calculation.

But a more radical possibility is that the categories themselves are not actually involved in these predictions. Perhaps thinking about a triangle simply activates exemplars of the studied triangles, and their properties are thereby activated as well, without any category information being considered. In our early work with numerical judgments, it seemed clear that people were using categories, if only because their responses were often exactly the proportion of items in a category that had the given feature (Murphy & Ross, 1994). That is, if half of Category A items were solid black, many people responded 50% for their answer. Furthermore, varying properties *within* the target category had a reliable effect, and varying them *outside* the target category did not, showing again that subjects were paying close attention to the categories.

But we do not have this evidence for the speeded task, and this makes us wonder about similar situations both in experiments and the real world. For example, in Tenenbaum's numerical judgment task, we wonder if the tested number might simply activate the exemplars of the category (e.g., the healthy insulin levels) to varying degrees, leading to varying degrees of confidence in the induction. Such a mechanism might be able to account for the results without the introduction of the ad-hoc categories (46 to 55, 45 to 56, etc.). In a more naturalistic example, if you are walking in the woods and something brown and fast-moving starts to rustle in the brush to your left, your decision about whether to run away may be based on categories such as "bunny rabbit," "wolf," "coyote," "beaver," "deer," and so on, but it may also rely on a simpler association between the observed properties and an outcome (danger, in this case). That is, any brown, fast-moving exemplars associated with danger or its absence might influence your response now, regardless of their category membership. However, if you are able to identify the object's category membership in time ("it's only a duck"), then that information may control your induction even if other brown, fast-moving stimuli have had different properties (e.g., you have had bad experiences with coyotes sneaking up on you).

In short, in some cases, induction may be based not on category-level information at all but instead on remembered exemplars. Such inductions have many of the properties of inductions that Bayesian models such as Tenenbaum's and Anderson's have. That is, they would "weight" information from the most likely category most of all (because most of the exemplars would come from that category), and information from other categories would be weighted proportionally to their likelihood (based on the number of remembered exemplars from each category). But the induction itself might be somewhat different from the one envisioned in Anderson's model, where category-level information is the basis of induction. That is, if you identify the brown animal as a deer, then information about deer in general would be used in Anderson's model. In the exemplar-based approach we are considering, it might be only the properties of the particular remembered exemplars that affect the decision, and if the remembered exemplars are not very typical of their categories, then the prediction would deviate from a categorical induction.

A third possibility is that people might use both category and exemplar information in making the prediction. The activated properties provide some exemplar-based information that might combine with the category-level information, depending on the circumstances (time pressure, complexity of prediction, etc.). One can think of this combination as a type of specialization, where its usefulness depends on the consistency of category and exemplar-level information. It allows the greater statistical basis of the category to influence the decision but also allows sensitivity to the specifics of the item about which the prediction is made (see, e.g., Brooks, 1987; Medin & Ross, 1989; Murphy, 2002, for specificity effects). As Murphy and Ross (2005) argued, even when one makes category-based inductions, properties of the specific item involved may matter as well.

So far as we know, there has been no attempt to distinguish the exemplar-based and category-based induction processes for coherent categories. One reason for this is that in the classic category-based induction work, subjects are presented with entire categories and/or an undescribed exemplar. Consider the example, "If sparrows have sesamoid bones, what is the probability that eagles have sesamoid bones?" Here, only entire categories are mentioned. The questions asked by Rips (1975), Osherson et al. (1990), and the more recent work of Proffitt et al. (2000) all focus on category-level problems.

An important topic for future research, then, is to investigate how item-level and category-level information is used and integrated in making predictions

(Murphy & Ross, 2005). If you believe that dogs get sick from eating chocolate, will you change your prediction for a particularly robust, voracious dog who is known to eat any semi-edible garbage that it can grab? How about a yappy, pampered toy dog of weak disposition? Proffitt et al. (2000) make a strong argument that inductions are based on causal knowledge when it is available. The usual use of blank predicates is an attempt to eliminate such knowledge as a factor. But in everyday life, people do have beliefs about the predicates they make inductions about, and they also have knowledge about the specific individuals they are interested in (e.g., they can see the dog, they know their doctor, they have ridden in this car, and so on). The items are not unknown objects described only by their category name: "a dog," "a doctor," or "a car." So, to expand our understanding of induction further, we need to begin to address the interaction between category-based induction and individual-based induction.

CONCLUSION

In summary, we would often be better off if we considered multiple categories when making inductions about entities. When categorization is uncertain, our inductions ought to take our uncertainty into account. However, in a number of paradigms manipulating a number of variables, we have found that people generally do not spontaneously consider multiple categories when making inductions. Perhaps surprisingly, this does not appear to be due to unfamiliarity with the principle involved, as shortcomings in decision making often seem to be. Nor is the problem that people are not able to combine the predictions drawn from different categories. Instead, the problem appears to be a kind of production deficit in which the necessity of considering multiple categories does not occur to people except in situations that strongly bring the secondary categories to attention. When the property is associated to the secondary category, or when that category is presented in a way that is difficult to ignore (Murphy & Ross, 1999), people integrate information from multiple categories.

On the negative side, people's reluctance to spontaneously combine predictions from categories suggests that they will often make suboptimal predictions. But on the positive side, when the necessity for using multiple categories is brought to the fore, people are willing and able to use them. Thus, our results give some hope for improvement in category-based inductions in situations where those inductions are important. By presenting the secondary category prominently or asking just the right question, people can be encouraged to take multiple categories into account.

Finally, our most recent work suggests the possibility that performance in tasks that we think of as category-based induction may not necessarily be based on categories. Performance that seems to involve the use of multiple categories might be accomplished if people skip the categories entirely, relying on remembered exemplars. Although this is speculative, we see the possibility that people make use of both categories and exemplar information when making inductions to be an interesting possibility that also relates research on category-based induction to current work on classification.

AUTHORS´ NOTE

Please address all correspondence to Gregory L. Murphy, Department of Psychology, New York University, 6 Washington Place, 8th floor, New York, NY 10003; or email correspondence to gregory.murphy@nyu.edu.

References

Anderson, J. R. (1991). The adaptive nature of human categorization. *Psychological Review, 98*, 409–429.

Baillargeon, R. (1998). Infants' understanding of the physical world. In M. Sabourin, F. Craik, & M. Robert (Eds.), *Advances in psychological science*, Vol. 2: *Biological and cognitive aspects* (pp. 503–529). London: Psychology Press.

Brooks, L. R. (1987). Decentralized control of categorization: The role of prior processing episodes. In U. Neisser (Ed.), *Concepts and conceptual development: Ecological and intellectual factors in categorization* (pp. 141–174). Cambridge: Cambridge University Press.

Heit, E. (2000). Properties of inductive reasoning. *Psychonomic Bulletin & Review, 7*, 569–592.

Heit, E., & Rubinstein, J. (1994). Similarity and property effects in inductive reasoning. *Journal of Experimental Psychology: Learning, Memory, and Cognition, 20*, 411–422.

Kalish, C. W., & Gelman, S. A. (1992). On wooden pillows: Multiple classification and children's category-based inductions. *Child Development, 63*, 1536–1557.

Lagnado, D. A., & Shanks, D. R. (2003). The influence of hierarchy on probability judgments. *Cognition, 89*, 157–178.

Macrae, C. N., Bodenhausen, G. V., & Milne, A. B. (1995). The dissection of selection in person perception: Inhibitory processes in social stereotyping. *Journal of Personality and Social Psychology, 69*, 397–407.

Malt, B. C., Ross, B. H., & Murphy, G. L. (1995). Predicting features for members of natural categories when categorization is uncertain. *Journal of Experimental Psychology: Learning, Memory, and Cognition, 21*, 646–661.

Medin, D. L., & Ross, B. H. (1989). The specific character of abstract thought: Categorization, problem solving, and induction. In R. J. Sternberg (Ed.), *Advances in the psychology of human intelligence*, Vol. 5. Hillsdale, NJ: Erlbaum.

Murphy, G. L. (2002). *The big book of concepts*. Cambridge, MA: MIT Press.

Murphy, G. L., & Ross, B. H. (1994). Predictions from uncertain categorizations. *Cognitive Psychology, 27,* 148–193.

Murphy, G. L., & Ross, B. H. (1999). Induction with cross-classified categories. *Memory & Cognition, 27,* 1024–1041.

Murphy, G. L., & Ross, B. H. (2005). The two faces of typicality in category-based induction. *Cognition, 95,* 175–200.

Nelson, L. J., & Miller, D. T. (1995). The distinctiveness effect in social categorization: You are what makes you unusual. *Psychological Science, 6,* 246–249.

Nguyen, S. P., & Murphy, G. L. (2003). An apple is more than just a fruit: Cross-classification in children's concepts. *Child Development, 74,* 1783–1806.

Osherson, D. N., Smith, E. E., Wilkie, O., López, A., & Shafir, E. (1990). Category-based induction. *Psychological Review, 97,* 185–200.

Patalano, A. L., Chin-Parker, S., & Ross, B. H. (2006). The importance of being coherent: Category coherence, cross-classification, and reasoning. *Journal of Memory and Language, 54,* 407–424.

Proffitt, J. B., Coley, J. D., & Medin, D. L. (2000). Expertise and category-based induction. *Journal of Experimental Psychology: Learning, Memory, and Cognition, 26,* 811–828.

Rips, L. J. (1975). Inductive judgments about natural categories. *Journal of Verbal Learning and Verbal Behavior, 14,* 665–681.

Ross, B. H., & Murphy, G. L. (1996). Category-based predictions: Influence of uncertainty and feature associations. *Journal of Experimental Psychology: Learning, Memory, and Cognition, 22,* 736–753.

Ross, B. H., & Murphy, G. L. (1999). Food for thought: Cross-classification and category organization in a complex real-world domain. *Cognitive Psychology, 38,* 495–553.

Tenenbaum, J. B. (1999). Bayesian modeling of human concept learning. *Advances in Neural Information Processing Systems, 11,* 59–68.

Tenenbaum, J. B. (2000). Rules and similarity in concept learning. *Advances in Neural Information Processing Systems, 12,* 59–65.

Tversky, A., & Kahneman, D. (1980). Causal schemas in judgments under uncertainty. In M. Fishbein (Ed.), *Progress in social psychology* (pp. 49–72). Hillsdale, NJ: Erlbaum.

Verde, M. F., Murphy, G. L., & Ross, B. H. (2005). Influence of multiple categories on property prediction. *Memory & Cognition, 33,* 479–487.

9

Abductive Inference: From Philosophical Analysis to Neural Mechanisms

Paul Thagard

1. WHAT IS ABDUCTION?

In the 1890s, the great American philosopher C. S. Peirce (1931–1958) used the term "abduction" to refer to a kind of inference that involves the generation and evaluation of explanatory hypotheses. This term is much less familiar today than "deduction," which applies to inference from premises to a conclusion that has to be true if the premises are true. And it is much less familiar than "induction," which sometimes refers broadly to any kind of inference that introduces uncertainty, and sometimes refers narrowly to inference from examples to rules, which I will call "inductive generalization." Abduction is clearly a kind of induction in the broad sense, in that the generation of explanatory hypotheses is fraught with uncertainty. For example, if the sky suddenly turns dark outside my window, I may hypothesize that there is a solar eclipse, but many other explanations are possible, such as the arrival of an intense storm or even a huge spaceship.

Despite its inherent riskiness, abductive inference is an essential part of human mental life. When scientists produce theories that explain their data, they are engaging in abductive inference. For example, psychological theories about mental representations and processing are the result of abductions spurred by the need to explain the results of psychological experiments. In everyday life, abductive inference is ubiquitous, for example when people generate hypotheses to explain the behavior of others, as when I infer that my son is in a bad mood to explain a curt response to a question. Detectives perform abductions routinely in order to make sense of the evidence left by criminal activity, just as automobile mechanics try to figure out what problems are responsible for a breakdown. Physicians practice abduction when they try to figure out what diseases might explain a patient's symptoms. Table 9.1 summarizes the kinds of abductive inference that occur in various domains,

TABLE 9.1. *Abductive inference in five domains, specifying what needs to be explained and the kinds of hypotheses that provide explanations*

Domains	Targets to be Explained	Explanatory Hypotheses
science	experimental results	theories about structures and processes
medicine	symptoms	diseases
crime	evidence	culprits, motives
machines	operation, breakdowns	parts, interactions, flaws
social	behavior	mental states, traits

involving both targets that require explanation and the hypotheses that are generated to explain them. Abduction occurs in many other domains as well, for example, religion, where people hypothesize the existence of God in order to explain the design and existence of the world.

The next section will briefly review the history of the investigation of abduction by philosophers and artificial intelligence researchers, and discuss its relative neglect by psychologists. First, however, I want to examine the nature of abduction and sketch what would be required for a full psychological theory of it. I then outline a neurocomputational theory of abductive inference that provides an account of some of the neural processes that enable minds to make abductive inference. Finally, I discuss the more general implications of replacing logic-based philosophical analyses of human inference with theories of neural mechanisms.

Here are the typical stages in the mental process of abduction. First, we notice something puzzling that prompts us to generate an explanation. It would be pointless to waste mental resources on something ordinary or expected. For example, when my friends greet me with the normal "Hi," I do not react like the proverbial psychoanalyst who wondered "What can they mean by that?" In contrast, if a normally convivial friend responds to "Good morning" with "What's so good about it?", I will be prompted to wonder what is currently going on in my friend's life that might explain this negativity. Peirce noticed that abduction begins with puzzlement, but subsequent philosophers have ignored the fact that the initiation of this kind of inference is inherently emotional. Intense reactions such as surprise and astonishment are particularly strong spurs to abductive inference. Hence the emotional initiation of abductive inference needs to be part of any psychological or neurological theory of how it works. An event or general occurrence becomes a target for explanation only when it is sufficiently interesting and baffling. I know of no general experimental evidence for this claim, but Kunda, Miller, and Claire

(1990) found that surprise triggered causal reasoning in cases of conceptual combination.

Second, the mind searches for possible hypotheses that could explain the target. Sometimes, the search is easily completed when there is a prepackaged hypothesis waiting to be applied. For example, if you know that your friend Alice gets stressed out whenever she has a deadline to meet, you might explain her grumpy behavior by the conjecture that she has a project due. In more deeply puzzling cases, the search for an explanatory hypothesis may require a much longer search through memory, or even the use of analogy or other constructive processes to generate a highly novel hypothesis. This generation is what happens in science when a genuinely new theory needs to be developed.

Generation of a candidate explanatory hypothesis is the usual third stage of abductive inference. If one is epistemically lazy, abductive inference may end with the generation of a single candidate. But scientists and careful thinkers in general are aware of the perils of abductive inference, in particular that one should not accept an explanatory hypothesis unless it has been assessed with respect to competing hypotheses and all the available evidence. Philosophers call this fourth, evaluative stage of abductive reasoning *inference to the best explanation* (Harman, 1973; Thagard, 1988; Lipton, 2004). Ideally, the reasoner correctly decides that it is legitimate to infer a hypothesis because it really is the best explanation of all the available evidence. Thus, generation of an explanatory hypothesis blends into its evaluation.

Just as abduction originates with an emotional reaction, it ends with one, because formation and acceptance of explanatory hypotheses usually produce positive emotions. Gopnik's (1998) comparison of explanations with orgasms is exaggerated, but it is nevertheless important that finding an explanation for something puzzling is often very satisfying. Hence we can mark emotional satisfaction as the final stage of abductive inference, as shown in Figure 9.1. This diagram will be fleshed out substantially in later sections in terms of neurological processes. The result will be an account of abduction that goes far beyond the philosophical account that takes abduction to be a kind of inference of the form "q, if p then q, so maybe p." (Somebody once called this "modus morons.") To foreshadow, the main differences include not only the crucial involvement of emotion, but also the allowance that both targets and hypotheses can be multimodal rather than purely verbal representations. Moreover, I will contend that the relation between a target and an explanatory hypothesis is that the target phenomenon is caused by the factors invoked by the hypothesis, and that people's understanding of causality is inherently non-verbal because it is rooted in visual and kinesthetic perception. Hence abduction, instead of looking like a feeble-minded cousin of the deductive

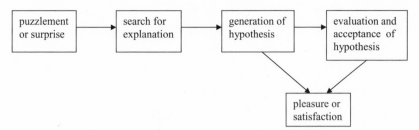

FIGURE 9.1. The process of abductive inference.

principle modus ponens, is actually a far richer and more powerful form of thinking.

2. ABDUCTION IN PHILOSOPHY, ARTIFICIAL INTELLIGENCE, AND PSYCHOLOGY

Although the term "abduction" emerged only in the nineteenth century, philosophers and scientists have been aware of inference to explanatory hypotheses at least since the Renaissance (Blake, Ducasse, and Madden, 1960). Some thinkers have been skeptical that a hypothesis should be accepted *merely* on the basis of what it explains, for example Isaac Newton, John Herschel, August Comte, and John Stuart Mill. But others, such as David Hartley, Joseph Priestley, and William Whewell have argued that such inference is a legitimate part of scientific reasoning. In the twentieth century, there are still philosophical skeptics about abduction (e.g., van Fraassen, 1980), but many others contend that abduction, construed as inference to the best explanation, is an essential part of scientific and everyday reasoning (Magnani, 2001; Psillos, 1999; Thagard, 1992, 1999, 2000).

The generation of explanatory hypotheses has also interested philosophers concerned with how scientific discoveries are made. Hanson (1958) tried to develop Peircean ideas into a "logic" of discovery. More recently, Darden (1991), Magnani (2001), and Thagard (1988) have examined cognitive processes that are capable of producing new hypotheses, including scientific theories. The work of Shelley (1996) and Magnani (2001) shows how abduction can involve visual as well as verbal representations, which is important for the multimodal theory developed in Section 3.

In the field of artificial intelligence, the term "abduction" is usually applied to the evaluation of explanatory hypotheses, although it sometimes also includes processes of generating them (Charniak and McDermott, 1985; Josephson and Josephson, 1994). AI models of abductive inference have primarily been concerned with medical reasoning. For example, the RED system takes as input descriptions of cells and generates and evaluates hypotheses about clinically significant antibodies found in the cells (Josephson and Josephson, 1994). More recently, discussions of causal reasoning in terms of abduction have been eclipsed by discussions of Bayesian networks based on probability theory, but later I will describe limitations of purely probabilistic accounts of causality, explanation, and abduction. Abduction has also been a topic of interest for researchers in logic programming (Flach and Kakas, 2000), but there are severe limitations to a characterization of abduction in terms of formal logic (Thagard and Shelley, 1997).

Some AI researchers have discussed the problem of generating explanatory hypotheses without using the term "abduction." The computational models of scientific discovery described by Langley, Simon, Bradshaw, and Zytkow (1987) are primarily concerned with the inductive generalization of laws from data, but they also discuss the generation of explanatory structure models in chemistry. Langley et al. (2004) describe an algorithm for "inducing explanatory process models," but it is clear that their computational procedures for constructing models of biological mechanisms operate abductively rather than via inductive generalization.

Psychologists rarely use the terms "abduction" or "abductive inference," and very little experimental research has been done on the generation and acceptance of explanatory hypotheses. Much of the psychological literature on induction concerns a rather esoteric pattern of reasoning, categorical induction, in which people express a degree of confidence that a category has a predicate after being told that a related category has the predicate (Sloman and Lagnado, 2005). Here is an example:

Tigers have 38 chromosomes.
Do buffaloes have 38 chromosomes?

Another line of research involves inductive generalizations about the behavior of physical devices (Klahr, 2000). Dunbar (1997) has discussed the role of analogy and other kinds of reasoning in scientific thinking in real-world laboratories. Considerable research has investigated ways in which people's inductive inferences deviate from normative standards of probability theory (Gilovich, Griffin, and Kahneman, 2002).

Experimental research concerning causality has been concerned with topics different from the generation of causal explanations, such as how people distinguish genuine causes from spurious ones (Lien and Cheng, 2000) and how knowledge of the causal structure of categories supports the ability to infer the presence of unobserved features (Rehder and Burnett, 2005). Social psychologists have investigated the important abductive task of *attribution,* in which people generate explanations for the behavior of others (Kunda, 1999; Nisbett and Ross, 1980). Read and Marcus-Newhall (1993) tested the applicability of Thagard's (1992) computational theory of explanatory coherence to the evaluation of social explanations. Generally, however, psychologists have had little to say about the mental mechanisms by which new hypotheses are formed and evaluated. My review of interdisciplinary research on abductive inference has been very brief, for I want to move on to develop a new neurocomputational theory of abduction.

3. NEURAL STRUCTURES

The structure of abduction is roughly this:

There is a puzzling target T that needs explanation.
Hypothesis H potentially explains T.
So, H is plausible.
H is a better explanation of T and other phenomena than competing hypotheses.
So H is acceptable.

It would be psychologically unrealistic, however, to assume, as philosophers and AI researchers have tended to do, that T and H must be sentences or propositions (the meanings of sentences). A broader view of mental representation is required.

As already mentioned, abductive inference can be visual as well as verbal (Shelley, 1996; Magnani, 2001). For example, when I see a scratch along the side of my car, I can generate the mental image of a grocery cart sliding into the car and producing the scratch. In this case both the target (the scratch) and the hypothesis (the collision) are visually represented. Other sensory modalities can also provide explanation targets. For example, in medical diagnosis the perception of a patient's symptoms can involve vision (rash), touch (swelling), sound (heart murmur), smell (infection), and even taste (salty, in patients with cystic fibrosis). An observant cook may similarly be prompted to generate hypotheses by various kinds of sensory experiments, asking such questions as "Why does the cheese have blue stuff on it?" (vision), "Why is the broccoli soggy?" (touch), "Why is the timer buzzing?" (hearing), "Why is the meat putrid?" (smell), and "Why is the soup so salty" (taste). Thus all of the senses can generate explanation targets that can initiate abductive inference.

It is an interesting question whether hypotheses can be represented using all sensory modalities. For vision the answer is obvious, as images and diagrams can clearly be used to represent events and structures that have causal effects. And the answer appears to be yes when one is explaining one's own behavior: I may recoil because something I touch feels slimy, or jump because of a loud noise, or frown because of a rotten smell, or gag because something tastes too salty. Hence in explaining my own behavior, my mental image of the full range of examples of sensory experiences may have causal significance. Applying such explanations of the behavior of others requires projecting onto them the possession of sensory experiences that I think are like the ones that I have in similar situations. For example, when I see people wrinkle up their noses in front of a garbage can, I may project onto them an experience similar to what I experience when I smell rotting garbage. In this case, my image of a smell is the olfactory representation of what I see as the cause of their behavior. Empathy works the same way, when I explain people's behavior in a particular situation by inferring that they are having the same kind of emotional experience that I have had in similar situations. For example, if a colleague with a recently rejected manuscript is frowning, I may empathize by remembering how annoyed I felt when a manuscript of mine was rejected, and my mental image projected onto the colleague constitutes a non-verbal representation that explains the frown. Of course, I may operate with verbal explanations as well, but these complement the empathetic ones. Hence there is reason to believe that abductive inference can be fully multimodal, in that both targets and hypotheses can have the full range of verbal and sensory representations. In addition to words, sights, sounds, smells, touches, and tastes, these can include emotional feelings, kinesthetic experiences such as feeling the body arranged in a certain way, and other feelings such as pain.

A narrowly verbal account of abduction such as those favored by logicians would clearly not be able to do justice to the multimodal character of abductive inference. But from a neurological perspective, there is no problem in postulating representations that operate in all relevant modalities. Let me define a neural structure as a complex <neurons, connections, spiking behaviors> that consists of a set of neurons, a set of synaptic connections among them, and a set of behaviors of individual neurons that specifies their patterns of spiking determined by the spiking behaviors of all those neurons to which they are connected. If the neurons are thought of as a dynamical system governed by a set of differential equations, then the spiking behaviors can be thought of as the state space of the system. In contrast to standard connectionist models of neural networks, it is important to specify the behavior of neurons as more than just patterns of activation, because there is evidence that spiking patterns can be both neurologically and computationally important (Eliasmith and Anderson, 2003; Maass and Bishop, 1999; Rieke et al., 1997).

On the plausible assumption that all mental representations are brain structures, we can conjecture that verbal and sensory representations are neural structures of the sort just described. Hence we can reconceptualize abduction neurologically as a process in which one neural structure representing the explanatory target generates another neural structure that constitutes a hypothesis. Two major problems need to be solved in order to construct a neurological model of abduction consistent with the flow chart presented earlier in Figure 9.1. The first is how to characterize the emotional inputs and outputs to the abductive process, that is, how to mark the target as puzzling and the hypothesis as satisfying. The second is how to represent the explanatory relation between the neurally represented target and hypothesis.

The first problem can be dealt with by supposing that emotions are also neural structures in the sense just defined. I do not mean to suggest that for each emotion there is a constrained set of neurons that encodes it. Emotions involve complex interaction among sensory processes involving bodily states, and cognitive processes involving appraisal of a person's situation (see Thagard, 2005, ch. 10). Hence the neural structure corresponding to an emotional experience is not a neuronal group situated in a particular brain area, but a complex of neurons distributed across multiple brain areas.

Now the question becomes: what is the relation between the neural structure for the explanation target and the neural structure for an emotion such as puzzlement? There are two possibly compatible answers involving different aspects of neural structure: connections and spiking behavior. The target neural structure may be interrelated with an emotional neural structure because some of the neurons in the first structure have direct or indirect synaptic connections with the second structure. Hence the two neural structures are part of a larger neural structure. Moreover, these interconnections may establish temporal coordination between the two neural structures, so that the spiking behavior of the target neural structure is synchronized or approximately coordinated with the spiking behavior of emotional neural structure. Through one or both of these means – physical connectivity and temporal behavior – the brain manages to mark the target as puzzling and in need of explanation. Similarly, the hypothesis can be represented by a neural structure which operates in any verbal or sensory modality, and which can be associated with a neural structure corresponding to the emotional experience of satisfaction or pleasure. Thus part of the flow chart in Figure 9.1 translates into the following neurological diagram, Figure 9.2. What remains to be investigated is the

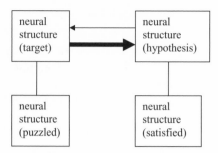

FIGURE 9.2. Abduction as a neural process.

relation of explanation and inference marked by the thin arrow. We need an account of explanation as a neurological process.

4. EXPLANATION AND CAUSALITY

Abductive inference is from a target to a hypothesis that explains it, but what is explanation? In philosophy and cognitive science, there have been at least six approaches to the topic of explanation (Thagard, 1992, pp. 118ff.). Explanations have been viewed as deductive arguments, statistical relations, schema applications, analogical comparisons, causal relations, and linguistic acts. All of these approaches have illuminated some aspects of the practice of explanation in science and everyday life, but the core of explanation, I would argue, is causality: a hypothesis explains a target if it provides a causal account of what needs to be explained. In medicine, a disease explains symptoms because the abnormal biological state that constitutes the disease produces the symptoms through biological mechanisms (Thagard, 1999). In ordinary social life, attributing a mental state such as an emotion explains a person's behavior because the mental state is the assumed cause of the behavior. In science, a theory explains phenomena such as the motions of the planets by providing the causes of such phenomena. Deductive, statistical, schematic, analogical, and linguistic aspects of explanation can all be shown to be subordinate to the fundamental causal aspect of explanation.

Hence the problem of describing the explanatory relation between hypotheses and targets is largely the problem of describing the causal relation between what neural structures for hypotheses represent and what neural structures for targets represent. To put it most simply, abduction becomes: T, H causes T, so maybe H, where H and T are not propositions but what is represented by neural structures. Hence it is crucial to give a philosophically and psychologically plausible account of causality.

The philosophical literature on causality is huge, but here is a quick summary of extant positions on the nature of causality:

1. Eliminativist: Causality is an outmoded notion no longer needed for scientific discourse.
2. Universalist: Causation is a relation of constant conjunction: the effect always occurs when the cause occurs.
3. Probabilistic: Causation is a matter of probability: the effect is more probable given the cause than otherwise.
4. Causal powers: the cause has a power to produce the effect.

Each of these positions is problematic. The eliminativist position runs afoul of the fact that talk of causal mechanisms still abounds in science. The universalist position is untenable because most causal relations are statistical rather than constant: infection by a mycobacterium causes tuberculosis, but many people infected by it never develop the disease. Similarly, the probabilistic position cannot easily distinguish between cases where a cause actually makes an effect more likely, as in infection by the mycobacterium, and cases where the effect is made more likely by some other cause. For example, the probability that people have tuberculosis given that they take the drug Isoniazid is much greater than the probability that they have tuberculosis, but this is because Isoniazid is a commonly prescribed treatment for the disease, not because it causes the disease. (See Pearl, 2000, for a broad and deep discussion of causality and probability.) People have an intuitive sense of the difference between causal and purely statistical relations. In part, this arises from an understanding of how mechanisms connect causes with their effects (see Section 7). But it also arises from a natural perceptual inclination to see certain kinds of occurrences as causally related to each other. This inclination does not depend on the postulation of occult causal powers that causes must have in relation to their effects, but on fundamental features of our perceptual systems.

Evidence that causal relations can be perceived comes from three kinds of psychological evidence: cognitive, developmental, and neurological. Michotte (1963) performed a large array of experiments with visual stimuli that suggest that adults have a direct impression of cause-effect relations: when people see an image of one ball moving into another that begins to move, the first ball is perceived to cause the second one to move. Such reactions are found even in young infants: Leslie and Keeble (1987) provided experimental evidence that even 27-week old infants perceive a causal relationship. Baillargeon, Kotovsky, and Needham (1995) report that infants as young as 2.5 months expect a stationary object to be displaced when it is hit by a moving object; by around

6 months, infants believe that the distance traveled by the stationery object is proportional to the size of the moving object. Thus at a very primitive stage of verbal development children seem to have some understanding of causality based on their visual and tactile experiences. According to Mandler (2004), infants' very early ability to perceive causal relations need not be innate but could arise from a more general ability to extract meaning from perceptual relationships. Whether or not it is innate, infants clearly have an ability to extract causal information that develops long before any verbal ability.

Recent work using functional magnetic resonance imaging has investigated brain mechanisms underlying perceptual causality (Fugelsang et al., 2005). Participants imaged while viewing causal events had higher levels of relative activation in the right middle frontal gyrus and the right inferior parietal lobule compared to those viewing non-causal events. The evidence that specific brain structures are involved in extracting causal structure from the world fits well with cognitive and developmental evidence that adults and children are able to perceive causal relations, without making inferences based on universality, probability, or causal powers. It is therefore plausible that people's intuitive grasp of causality, which enables them to understand the distinction between causal relations and mere co-occurrence, arises very early from perceptual experience. Of course, as people acquire more knowledge, they are able to expand this understanding of causality far beyond perception, enabling them to infer that invisible germs cause disease symptoms. But this extended understanding of causality is still based on the perceptual experience of one event making another happen, and does not depend on a mysterious, metaphysical conception of objects possessing causal powers. For discussion of the role of causality in induction, see Bob Rehder's Chapter 4 in this volume.

Now we can start to flesh out in neurological terms what constitutes the relation between a target and an explanatory hypothesis. Mandler (2004) argues that CAUSED-MOTION is an *image schema*, an abstract, non-propositional, spatial representation that expresses primitive meanings. Lakoff (1987) and others have proposed that such non-verbal representations are the basis for language and other forms of cognition. Feldman and Narayan (2004) have described how image schemas can be implemented in artificial neural systems. I will assume that there is a neurally encoded image schema that establishes the required causal relation that ties together the neural structure of a hypothesis and the neural structure of the target that it explains. We would then have a neural representation of the explanatory, causal relation between hypotheses and targets. This relation provides the abductive basis for the inferential process described in the next section.

The model of abductive inference sketched in Figures 9.1 and 9.2 has been implemented in a computer simulation that shows in detail how neural processes can generate emotional initiation and causal reasoning (Thagard and Litt, forthcoming). The details are too technical to present here, but the simulation is important because it shows how causal and emotional information distributed over thousands of artificial neurons can produce a simple form of abductive inference.

5. INFERENCE

On the standard philosophical view, inference is the movement from one or more propositions taken to be true to another proposition that follows from them deductively or inductively. Here a proposition is assumed to be an abstract entity, namely, the meaning content of a sentence. Belief and other mental states such as doubt, desire, and fear are all propositional attitudes, that is, relations between persons and propositions. An inference is much like an argument, which is the verbal description of a set of sentential premises that provide the basis for accepting a conclusion. Most philosophical and computational accounts of abductive inference have assumed this kind of linguistic picture of belief and inference.

There are many problems with this view. It postulates the existence of an infinite number of propositions, including an infinite number that will never be expressed by any uttered sentence. These are abstract entities whose existence is utterly mysterious. Just as mysterious is the relation between persons and propositions, for what is the connection between a person's body or brain and such abstract entities? The notion of a proposition dates back at least to Renaissance times when almost everyone assumed that persons were essentially non-corporeal souls, which could have some non-material relation to abstract propositions. But the current ascendancy of investigation of mental states and operations in terms of brain structures and processes makes talk of abstract propositions as antiquated as theories about souls or disease-causing humors. Moreover, philosophical theories of propositional belief have generated large numbers of insoluble puzzles, such as how it can be that a person can believe that Lewis Carroll wrote *Alice in Wonderland*, but not that Charles Dodgson did, when the beliefs seem to have the same content because Carroll and Dodgson are the same person.

Implicit in my account of abductive inference is a radically different account of belief that abandons the mysterious notion of a proposition in favor of biologically realistic ideas about neural structures. In short, beliefs are neural structures consisting of neurons, connections, and spiking behavior;

and so are all the other mental states that philosophers have characterized as propositional attitudes, including doubt, desire, and fear. This view does away with the metaphysical notion of a proposition, but does not eliminate standard mental concepts such as belief and desire, which are, however, radically reconstrued in terms of structures and processes in the brain (cf. Churchland, 1989).

This view of mental operations makes possible an account of the nature of inference that is dramatically different from the standard account that takes inference to operate on propositions the same way that argument operates on sentences. First, it allows for non-verbal representations from all sensory modalities to be involved in inference. Second, it allows inferences to be holistic in ways that arguments are not, in that they can simultaneously take into account a large amount of information before producing a conclusion. How this works computationally is shown by connectionist computational models such as my ECHO model of explanatory coherence (Thagard 1992). ECHO is not nearly as neurologically realistic as the current context requires, since it uses localist artificial neurons very different from the groups of spiking neurons that I have been discussing, but it at least shows how parallel activity can lead to holistic conclusions.

What then is inference? Most generally, inference is a kind of transformation of neural structures, but obviously not all such transformations count as inference. We need to isolate a subclass of neural structures that are representations, that is, ones that stand for something real or imagined in the world. Roughly, a neural structure is a representation if its connections and spiking behavior enable it to relate to perceptual input and/or the behavior of other neural structures in such a way that it can be construed as standing for something else such as a thing or concept. This is a bit vague, but it is broad enough to cover both cases where neural structures stand for concrete things in the world, for example, George W. Bush, and for general categories that may or may not have any members, for example, unicorns. Note that one neural structure may constitute many representations, because different spiking behaviors may correspond to different things. This capability is a feature of all distributed representations.

Accordingly, we can characterize inference as the *transformation of representational neural structures*. Inference involving sentences is a special case of such transformation where the relevant neural structures correspond to sentences. My broader account has the great advantage of allowing thinking that uses visual and other sensory representations to count as inference as well. From this perspective, abduction is the transformation of representational neural structures that produces neural structures that provide causal explanations.

This neural view of inference is open to many philosophical objections. It remains to be shown that neural structures have sufficient syntactic and semantic complexity to qualify as sentential representations. The syntactic problem is potentially solved by theories of neural combinatorics such as the tensor product theory of Smolensky (1990) which show how vectors representing neural activity can be combined in ways that capture syntactic structure. The semantic problem is potentially solved by providing more detail about how neural structures can relate to the world and to each other (Eliasmith, 2005). But much more needs to be said about what enables a neural structure to constitute a meaningful representation.

Another objection to my account of neural structures and inference is that it requires some way of specifying groups of neurons that are part of identifiable neural structures. In the worse case, one might be forced to conclude that there is only one neural structure in the brain, consisting of *all* the neurons with all their connections and spiking behaviors. This problem becomes especially acute in cases of inference that involve multiple kinds of verbal, perceptual, and emotional representation, which require that multiple brain areas be involved. In practice, however, the problem of isolating neural structures does not seem to be insurmountable. Neuroscientists often talk of groups, populations, or assemblies of neurons that are identifiable subsets of the 100 billion or so neurons that constitute an entire brain. Groups are identifiable because they have far more connections with each other than they do with neurons in other parts of the brain. Hence even though there is a great deal of interconnectivity in the brain, we can still identify groups of neurons with high degrees of connection to each other and spiking behaviors that enable them to constitute representations. So the view that inference is transformation of neural structures does not devolve into the much less precise claim that inference is just brain transformation.

Another philosophical objection to the neural theory of inference is that it is unduly narrow in that it does not apply to inferences by robots or by extraterrestrial beings with brains radically different from ours. My response is that I am only concerned here to provide a special theory of human inference and will leave the problem of developing a general theory of inference for the occasion when we actually encounter robots or aliens that are intelligent enough that we want to count what they do as inference. The general theory would consist of a broader account of a representational structure, <parts, relations, behaviors>, analogous to the <neurons, connections, spiking behaviors> of humans and other terrestrial animals. It is an open question what the degree of similarity will be between the mental mechanisms of human and non-human thinkers, if there are any of the latter.

6. EMOTIONAL INITIATION

I described earlier how abductive inference is initiated by emotional reactions such as surprise and puzzlement, but other forms of inference also have affective origins. The influence of emotions on decision making has often been noted (Damasio, 1994; Mellers et al., 1999; Thagard, 2001, 2006). But less attention has been paid to the fact that inferences about what to do are usually initiated by either positive or negative emotions. Decisions are sometimes prompted by negative emotions such as fear: if I am afraid that something bad will happen, I may be spurred to decide what to do about it. For example, a person who is worried about being fired may decide to look for other jobs. It would be easy to generate examples of cases where other negative emotions such as anger, sadness, envy, and guilt lead people to begin a process of deliberation that leads to a practical inference. More positively, emotions such as happiness can lead to decisions, as when someone thinks about how much fun it would be to have a winter vacation and begins to collect travel information that will produce a decision about where to go. Just as people do not make abductive inferences unless there is some emotional reason for them to look for explanations, people do not make inference about what to do unless negative or positive emotional reactions to their current situation indicate that action is required. In some cases, the emotions may be tied to specific perceptual states, such as when hunger initiates a decision about what to eat.

Deductive inference might be thought to be impervious to emotional influences, but there is neurological evidence that even deduction can be influenced by brain areas such as the ventromedial prefrontal cortex that are known to be involved in emotion (Houdé et al., 2001; Goel and Dolan, 2003). It is hard to say whether deduction is initiated by emotion, because I think it is rarely initiated at all outside the context of mathematical reasoning: readers should ask themselves when was the last time they made a deductive inference. But perhaps deduction is sometimes initiated by puzzlement, as when one wonders whether an object has a property and then retrieves from memory a rule that says that all objects of this type have the property in question. This kind of inference may be so automatic, however, that we never become aware of the making of the inference or any emotional content of it.

Analogical inference often involves emotional content, especially when it is used in persuasion to transfer negative affect from a source to a target (Blanchette and Dunbar, 2001; Thagard and Shelley, 2001). For example, comparing a political leader to Hitler is a common way of motivating people to dislike the leader. Such persuasive analogies are often motivated by emotional reactions such as dislike of a person or policy. Because I dislike the leader, I compare him or her to Hitler in order to lead you to dislike the leader also. Practical analogical inferences are prompted by emotions in the same way that other decisions are: I want to go on vacation, and remember I had a good time at a resort before, and decide to go to a similar resort. Analogical abductions in which an explanatory hypothesis is formed by analogy to a previous explanation are prompted by the same emotional reactions (surprise, puzzlement) as other abductive inferences.

Are inductive generalizations initiated by emotional reactions? At the least, emotion serves to focus on what is worth the mental effort to think about enough to form a generalization. As a social example, if I have no interest in Albanians, I will probably not bother to form a stereotype that generalizes about them, whereas if I strongly like or dislike them I will be much more inclined to generalize about their positive or negative features. I conjecture that most inductive generalizations occur when there is some emotion-related interest in the category about which a rule is formed.

It is unfortunate that no one has collected a corpus that records the kinds of inferences that ordinary people make every day. I conjecture that such a corpus would reveal that most people make a large number of practical inferences when decisions are required, but a relatively small number of inductive and deductive inferences. I predict that deduction is very rare unless people are engaged in mathematical work, and that inductive inferences are not very frequent either. A carefully collected corpus would display, I think, only the occasional inductive generalization or analogical inference, and almost none of the categorical inductions studied by many experimental psychologists. Abductive inferences generating causal explanations of puzzling occurrences would be more common, I conjecture, but not nearly as common as practical inferences generating decisions. If the inference corpus also recorded the situations that prompt the making of inferences, it would also provide the basis for testing my claim that most inference, including practical, abductive, inductive, analogical, and deductive, is initiated by emotions. For further discussion of the relation between deduction and induction, see Chapters 10 and 11 in this volume by Rips and Asmuth and by Oaksford and Hahn.

7. MECHANISMS

Some psychological research on inductive inference has pointed to the tendency of people to assume the presence of underlying mechanisms associated with categories of things in the world (Rehder and Burnett, 2005; Ahn, Kalish, Medin, and Gelman, 1995). Psychologists have had little to say about what mechanisms are, or how people use representations of mechanisms in their inferences. In contrast, philosophers of science have been productively addressing this issue, and the point of this section is to show the relevance of this understanding of mechanisms to the problem of abductive inference. The relevance is double, in that the neural structures I have been describing are clearly mechanisms, and abductive inferences often involve the generation or application of new hypotheses about mechanisms.

Machamer, Darden, and Craver (2000, p. 3) characterize mechanisms as "entities and activities organized such that they are productive of regular changes from start or set-up to finish or termination conditions." A mechanism can also be described as a system whose behavior produces a phenomenon in virtue of organized component parts performing coordinated component operations (Bechtel and Abrahamsen, 2005). I think these ways of describing mechanisms are mostly equivalent, and offer my own terminological variant of a mechanism as consisting of a complex <objects, relations, changes>, consisting of a set of objects (entities, parts) that have properties and physical relations to each other that cause changes to the properties of the objects and changes to the relations the objects have to each other and to the world. For example, a bicycle is a mechanism consisting of wheels, pedals, and other parts that are connected to each other, with regular changes to these parts and their relation to the world arising from external inputs such as a person pedaling and the internal organization of the machine. Similarly, a neural structure <neurons, connections, spiking behaviors> is clearly a mechanism where the objects are neurons, their relations are synaptic connections, and their changes are spiking behaviors. I conjecture that whenever people think of categories in terms of underlying mechanisms, they have something like the pattern of <objects, relations, changes> in mind. In human minds, mechanisms can be represented verbally, as in "the pedal is bolted to the frame," but visual and kinesthetic representations are also used in science and everyday thinking (Thagard, 2003). Neural structures as well as the inferences that transform them are clearly mechanisms, and mechanisms can be mentally represented by combinations of different sorts of neural structures.

I doubt that *all* abductive inference is based on representation of mechanisms, because abduction requires only a single causal relation, not full knowledge of a mechanism. If all I know about electric lights is that when you push the switch, the light comes on, then I can abduce from the fact that the light is on that someone pushed the switch. But such knowledge hardly constitutes awareness of a mechanisms because I know nothing about any interacting system of parts. However, when I do know a lot about an underlying mechanism, my abductive inferences can be much richer and more plausible. For example, an electrician who knows much about the objects that constitute a house's electrical systems (wires, switches, fuses, etc.) is in a much better position to explain the normal occurrences and breakdowns of the system. Similarly, a physician who is familiar with the biological mechanisms that operate in a patient's body can generate diagnoses about what might have gone wrong to produce various symptoms. The general structure of mechanism-based abductive inference is therefore:

Mechanism <objects, relations, changes> is behaving in unexpected ways.
So maybe there are unusual properties or relations of objects that are responsible for this behavior.

Mechanism-based abduction differs from the simple sort in that people making inferences can rely on a whole collection of causal relations among the relevant objects, not just a particular causal relation.

So far, I have been discussing abduction *from* mechanisms, in which representations of a mechanism are used to suggest an explanatory hypothesis about what is happening to the objects in it. But abductive inference is even more important for generating knowledge about how the mechanism works, especially in cases where its operation is not fully observable. With a bicycle, I can look at the pedals and figure out how they move the chains and wheels, but much of scientific theorizing consists of generating new ideas about unobservable mechanisms. For example, medical researchers develop mechanistic models of how the metabolic system works in order to explain the origins of diseases such as diabetes. Often, such theorizing requires postulation of objects, relations, and changes that are not directly observed. In such cases, knowledge about mechanisms cannot be obtained by inductive generalization of the sort that works with bicycles, but depends on abductive inference in which causal patterns are hypothesized rather than observed. This kind of abduction *to* mechanisms is obviously much more difficult and creative than abduction from already understood mechanisms. Often it involves analogical inference in which a mechanism is constructed by comparing the target to be explained to another similar target for which a mechanism is already understood. In this case, a mechanism <objects, relations, changes> is constructed by mapping from a similar one. For more on analogical discovery, see Holyoak and Thagard (1995, ch. 8).

In order to show in more detail how abductive inference can be both to and from mechanisms, it would be desirable to apply the neurocomputational model of abductive inference developed by Thagard and Litt (forthcoming). That model has the representational resources to encode complex objects and relations, but it has not yet been applied to temporal phenomena involving change. Hence neural modeling of inferences about mechanisms is a problem for future research.

8. CONCLUSION

In sum, abduction is multimodal in that can operate on a full range of perceptual as well as verbal representations. It also involves emotional reactions, both as input to mark a target as worthy of explanation and as output to signal satisfaction with an inferred hypothesis. Representations are neural structures consisting of neurons, neuronal connections, and spiking behaviors. In abduction, the relation between hypotheses and targets is causal explanation, where causality is rooted in perceptual experience. Inference is transformation of representational neural structures. Such structures are mechanisms, and abductive inference sometimes applies knowledge of mechanisms and more rarely and valuably generates new hypotheses about mechanisms.

Much remains to be done to flesh out this account. Particularly needed is a concrete model of how abduction could be performed in a system of spiking neurons of the sort investigated by Eliasmith and Anderson (2003) and Wagar and Thagard (2004). The former reference contains valuable ideas about neural representation and transformation, while the latter is useful for ideas about how cognition and emotion can interact. Thagard and Litt (forthcoming) combine these ideas to provide a fuller account of the neural mechanisms that enable people to perform abductive inference. Moving the study of abduction from the domain of philosophical analysis to the realm of neurological mechanisms has made it possible to combine logical aspects of abductive inference with multimodal aspects of representation and emotional aspects of cognitive processing. We can look forward to further abductions about abduction.

ACKNOWLEDGMENTS

I am grateful to Jennifer Asmuth, Aidan Feeney, Abninder Litt, and Douglas Medin for helpful comments on an earlier draft. Funding for research was provided by the Natural Sciences and Engineering Research Council of Canada.

References

Ahn, W., Kalish, C. W., Medin, D. L., & Gelman, S. (1995). The role of covariation versus mechanism information in causal attribution. *Cognition, 54,* 299–352.

Baillargeon, R., Kotovsky, L., & Needham, A. (1995). The acquisition of physical knowledge in infancy. In D. Sperber, D. Premack, & A. J. Premack (Eds.), *Causal cognition: A multidisciplinary debate* (pp. 79–116). Oxford: Clarendon Press.

Bechtel, W., & Abrahamsen, A. A. (2005). Explanation: A mechanistic alternative. *Studies in History and Philosophy of Biology and Biomedical Sciences, 36,* 421–441.

Blake, R. M., Ducasse, C. J., & Madden, E. H. (1960). *Theories of scientific method: The renaissance through the nineteenth century.* Seattle: University of Washington Press.

Blanchette, I., & Dunbar, K. (2001). Analogy use in naturalistic settings: The influence of audience, emotion, and goals. *Memory & Cognition, 29,* 730–735.

Charniak, E., & McDermott, D. (1985). *Introduction to artificial intelligence.* Reading, MA: Addison-Wesley.

Churchland, P. M. (1989). *A neurocomputational perspective.* Cambridge, MA: MIT Press.

Damasio, A. R. (1994). *Descartes' error.* New York: G. P. Putnam's Sons.

Darden, L. (1991). *Theory change in science: Strategies from Mendelian genetics.* Oxford: Oxford University Press.

Dunbar, K. (1997). How scientists think: On-line creativity and conceptual change in science. In T. B. Ward, S. M. Smith, & J. Vaid (Eds.), *Creative thought: An investigation of conceptual structures and processes* (pp. 461–493). Washington: American Psychological Association.

Eliasmith, C. (2005). Neurosemantics and categories. In H. Cohen & C. Lefebvre (Eds.), *Handbook of categorization in cognitive science* (Vol. 1035–1054). Amsterdam: Elsevier.

Eliasmith, C., & Anderson, C. H. (2003). *Neural engineering: Computation, representation and dynamics in neurobiological systems.* Cambridge, MA: MIT Press.

Feldman, J., & Narayan, S. (2004). Embodied meaning in a neural theory of language. *Brain and Language, 89,* 385–392.

Flach, P. A., & Kakas, A. C. (Eds.). (2000). *Abduction and induction: Essays on their relation and integration.* Dordrecht: Kluwer.

Fugelsang, J. A., Roser, M. E., Corballis, P. M., Gazzaniga, M. S., & Dunbar, K. N. (2005). Brain mechanisms underlying perceptual causality. *Cognitive Brain Research, 24,* 41–47.

Gilovich, T., Griffin, D., & Kahneman, D. (Eds.). (2002). *Heuristics and biases: The psychology of intuitive judgment.* Cambridge: Cambridge University Press.

Goel, V., & Dolan, R. J. (2003). Reciprocal neural response within lateral and ventral medial prefrontal cortex during hot and cold reasoning. *NeuroImage, 20,* 2314–2321.

Gopnik, A. (1998). Explanation as orgasm. *Minds and Machines, 8,* 101–118.

Hanson, N. R. (1958). *Patterns of discovery.* Cambridge: Cambridge University Press.

Harman, G. (1973). *Thought.* Princeton: Princeton University Press.

Holyoak, K. J., & Thagard, P. (1995). *Mental leaps: Analogy in creative thought.* Cambridge, MA: MIT Press/ Bradford Books.

Houdé, O., Zago, L., Crivello, F., Moutier, F., Pineau, S., Mazoyer, B., et al. (2001). Access to deductive logic depends on a right ventromedial prefrontal area devoted to emotion and feeling: Evidence from a training paradigm. *NeuroImage, 14,* 1486–1492.

Josephson, J. R., & Josephson, S. G. (Eds.). (1994). *Abductive inference: Computation, philosophy, technology.* Cambridge: Cambridge University Press.

Klahr, D. (2000). *Exploring science: The cognition and development of discovery processes.* Cambridge, MA: MIT Press.

Kunda, Z. (1999). *Social cognition.* Cambridge, MA: MIT Press.

Kunda, Z., Miller, D., & Claire, T. (1990). Combining social concepts: The role of causal reasoning. *Cognitive Science, 14,* 551–577.

Lakoff, G. (1987). *Women, fire, and dangerous things*. Chicago: University of Chicago Press.

Langley, P., Shrager, J., Asgharbeygi, N., Bay, S., & Pohorille, A. (2004). Inducing explanatory process models from biological time series. In *Proceedings of the ninth workshop on intelligent data analysis and data mining*. Stanford, CA.

Langley, P., Simon, H., Bradshaw, G., & Zytkow, J. (1987). *Scientific discovery*. Cambridge, MA: MIT Press/Bradford Books.

Leslie, A. M., & Keeble, S. (1987). Do six-month-old infants perceive causality? *Cognition, 25*, 265–288.

Lien, Y., & Cheng, P. W. (2000). Distinguishing genuine from spurious causes: A coherence hypothesis. *Cognitive Psychology, 40*, 87–137.

Lipton, P. (2004). *Inference to the best explanation* (2nd ed.). London: Routledge.

Maass, W., & Bishop, C. M. (Eds.). (1999). *Pulsed neural networks*. Cambridge, MA: MIT Press.

Machamer, P., Darden, L., & Craver, C. F. (2000). Thinking about mechanisms. *Philosophy of Science, 67*, 1–25.

Magnani, L. (2001). *Abduction, reason, and science: Processes of discovery and explanation*. New York: Kluwer/Plenum.

Mandler, J. M. (2004). *The foundations of mind: Origins of conceptual thought*. Oxford: Oxford University Press.

Mellers, B., Schwartz, A., & Ritov, I. (1999). Emotion-based choice. *Journal of Experimental Psychology: General, 128*, 332–345.

Michotte, A. (1963). *The perception of causality* (T. R. Miles & E. Miles, Trans.). London: Methuen.

Nisbett, R. E., & Ross, L. (1980). *Human inference: Strategies and shortcomings of social judgement*. Englewood Cliffs, NJ: Prentice Hall.

Pearl, J. (2000). *Causality: Models, reasoning, and inference*. Cambridge: Cambridge University Press.

Peirce, C. S. (1931–1958). *Collected papers*. Cambridge, MA: Harvard University Press.

Psillos, S. (1999). *Scientific realism: How science tracks the truth*. London: Routledge.

Read, S., & Marcus-Newhall, A. (1993). The role of explanatory coherence in the construction of social explanations. *Journal of Personality and Social Psychology, 65*, 429–447.

Rehder, B., & Burnett, R. C. (2005). Feature inference and the causal structure of categories. *Cognitive Psychology, 50*, 264–314.

Rieke, F., Warland, D., de Ruyter van Steveninick, R. R., & Bialek, W. (1997). *Spikes: Exploring the neural code*. Cambridge, MA: MIT Press.

Shelley, C. P. (1996). Visual abductive reasoning in archaeology. *Philosophy of Science, 63*, 278–301.

Sloman, S. A., & Lagnado, D. (2005). The problem of induction. In R. Morrison & K. Holyoak, J. (Eds.), *Cambridge handbook of thinking and reasoning* (pp. 95–116). Cambridge: Cambridge University Press.

Smolensky, P. (1990). Tensor product variable binding and the representation of symbolic structures in connectionist systems. *Artificial Intelligence, 46*, 159–217.

Thagard, P. (1988). *Computational philosophy of science*. Cambridge, MA: MIT Press/Bradford Books.

Thagard, P. (1992). *Conceptual revolutions*. Princeton: Princeton University Press.

Thagard, P. (1999). *How scientists explain disease.* Princeton: Princeton University Press.

Thagard, P. (2000). *Coherence in thought and action.* Cambridge, MA: MIT Press.

Thagard, P. (2003). Pathways to biomedical discovery. *Philosophy of Science, 70,* 235–254.

Thagard, P. (2005). *Mind: Introduction to cognitive science* (2nd ed.). Cambridge, MA: MIT Press.

Thagard, P. (2006). *Hot thought: Mechanisms and applications of emotional cognition.* Cambridge, MA: MIT Press.

Thagard, P., & Litt, A. (forthcoming). Models of scientific explanation. In R. Sun (Ed.), *The Cambridge handbook of computational cognitive modeling.* Cambridge: Cambridge University Press.

Thagard, P., & Shelley, C. P. (1997). Abductive reasoning: Logic, visual thinking, and coherence. In M. L. Dalla Chiara, K. Doets, D. Mundici, & J. van Benthem (Eds.), *Logic and scientific methods* (pp. 413–427). Dordrecht: Kluwer.

Thagard, P., & Shelley, C. P. (2001). Emotional analogies and analogical inference. In D. Gentner, K. H. Holyoak, & B. K. Kokinov (Eds.), *The analogical mind: Perspectives from cognitive science* (pp. 335–362). Cambridge, MA: MIT Press.

van Fraassen, B. (1980). *The scientific image.* Oxford: Clarendon Press.

Wagar, B. M., & Thagard, P. (2004). Spiking Phineas Gage: A neurocomputational theory of cognitive-affective integration in decision making. *Psychological Review, 111,* 67–79.

10

Mathematical Induction and Induction in Mathematics

Lance J. Rips[1] and Jennifer Asmuth

However much we may disparage deduction, it cannot be denied that the laws established by induction are not enough.

Frege (1884/1974, p. 23)

At the yearly proseminar for first-year graduate students at Northwestern, we presented some evidence that reasoning draws on separate cognitive systems for assessing deductive versus inductive arguments (Rips, 2001a, 2001b). In the experiment we described, separate groups of participants evaluated the same set of arguments for deductive validity or inductive strength. For example, one of the validity groups decided whether the conclusions of these arguments necessarily followed from the premises, while one of the strength groups decided how plausible the premises made the conclusions. The results of the study showed that the percentages of "yes" responses ("yes" the argument is deductively valid or "yes" the argument is inductively strong) were differently ordered for the validity and the strength judgments. In some cases, for example, the validity groups judged Argument A to be valid more often than Argument B, but the strength groups judged B inductively strong more often than A. Reversals of this sort suggest that people do not just see arguments as ranging along a single continuum of convincingness or probability but instead employ different methods when engaged in deductive versus inductive reasoning.

Earlier imaging evidence by Goel, Gold, Kapur, and Houle (1997) and by Osherson et al. (1998) had implicated separate brain regions when

[1] This paper was written while the first author was a Fulbright fellow at the Catholic University of Leuven, Belgium. We thank the Fulbright Foundation and the University for their support. We also thank Stella Christie, Mike Oaksford, Claes Strannegård, and the editors of this volume for comments and discussion of an earlier draft. Please send correspondence about this paper to Lance Rips, Psychology Department, Northwestern University, 2029 Sheridan Road, Evanston, IL 60208. Email: rips@northwestern.edu.

participants evaluated arguments for validity versus plausibility, and these earlier data had inspired our own experiment. All these results cast doubt on the view that there's a homogeneous "analytic" reasoning system responsible for correctly solving deductive and probabilistic problems.

But an incident that followed the proseminar alerted us that not everyone was buying into our reasoning distinctions. A faculty colleague who had attended the proseminar stopped us later and questioned whether deduction and induction were as distinct as we had claimed. Wasn't mathematical induction a counterexample to the separation between these two forms of reasoning? Mathematical induction is essential in many deductive proofs in mathematics, as any high school or college student knows. So how could induction and deduction be isolated subsystems if mathematicians freely used one to support the other?

At the time, we thought we had a perfectly good answer to our colleague's question. Mathematical induction is really nothing like empirical induction but is instead a deductive technique, sanctioned by the definition of the natural numbers (and certain other number systems). It's true that both types of "induction" often attempt to establish the truth of a generalization (*All cyclic groups are Abelian*; *All freshwater turtles hibernate*). So there is a loose analogy between them that might suggest labeling both "induction." But this is really no more than a case of ambiguity or polysemy. Mathematical induction in its usual form requires showing that the generalization holds of a base case (e.g., that the generalization is true for 0) and then showing that if the generalization is true for an arbitrary number k, it is also true for $k + 1$. Hence, by strict deductive reasoning, the generalization must be true for all natural numbers $(0, 1, 2, \dots)$. The conclusion of such a proof shares with all deductively valid conclusions the property that it is necessarily true or true in all possible worlds in which the givens are true.

A typical high school example of mathematical induction is the proof that the sum of the first n natural numbers is $\frac{1}{2} n (n + 1)$. Certainly this relationship holds when $n = 0$. If we assume that the relationship holds for the first k natural numbers (i.e., the sum of 0 through k is $\frac{1}{2} k (k + 1)$), then the sum of the first $k + 1$ numbers must be:

$$
\begin{aligned}
\sum_{i=0}^{k+1} i &= \frac{k(k + 1)}{2} + (k + 1) \\
&= \frac{k^2 + 3k + 2}{2} \\
&= \frac{(k + 1)(k + 2)}{2}
\end{aligned}
$$

The last expression is also of the form $\frac{1}{2}n(n+1)$. So this *sum formula* necessarily holds for all natural numbers.

By contrast, empirical induction leads to conclusions that are not necessarily true but only probably true, even when these conclusions involve mathematical relationships. For example, we might hope to establish inductively that people forget memories at a rate equal to $y = b - m\ln(t)$, where t is time since the remembered event and m and b are constants. To support such a conclusion, we might examine forgetting rates for many people and many event types and show that forgetting follows the proposed function in a convincing range of cases (Rubin & Wenzel, 1996). Even if the function fit the data perfectly, though, no one would suppose that the evidence established the conclusion as necessarily true. It's not difficult to imagine changes in our mental make up or changes in the nature of our everyday experience that would cause us to forget events according to some other functional form. The best we can hope for is a generalization that holds for people who are similar to us in causally important ways (see Heit's Chapter 1 in this volume for an overview of empirical induction).

We were able to convince our colleague that this line of thinking was correct. Or perhaps he was just too polite to press the point. In fact, we still believe that this standard answer isn't too far off the mark. But we also think that we dismissed our colleague's objection too quickly. One worry might be that the theoretical distinction between math induction and empirical induction is not as clear as we claimed. And, second, even if the theoretical difference were secure, it wouldn't follow that the psychological counterparts of these operations are distinct. In this chapter we try to give a better answer to the objection by examining ways that induction could play a role in mathematics. In doing so, we won't be presenting further empirical evidence for a dissociation between inductive and deductive reasoning. We will be assuming that the previous evidence we've cited is enough to show a difference between them in clear cases. Our hope is to demonstrate that potentially unclear cases – ones in which people reach generalizations – don't compromise the distinction (see Oaksford & Hahn, Chapter 11 in this volume, for a more skeptical view of the deduction/induction difference).

We consider first the relationship between math induction and empirical induction to see how deep the similarity goes. Although there are points of resemblance, we argue that there are crucial psychological differences between them. This isn't the end of the story, however. There are other methods of reaching general conclusions in math besides math induction, and it is possible that one of them provides the sort of counterexample that our colleague was seeking. One such method involves reasoning from an arbitrary case – what is called *universal generalization* in logic. Several experiments suggest that people sometimes apply this method incorrectly, and we examine these mistakes for evidence of a continuum between inductive and deductive methods. We claim, however, that although the mistakes show that people use inductive procedures when they should be sticking to deductive ones, they provide no evidence against a qualitative deduction/induction split.

Of course, we *won't* be claiming that there's no role for induction in mathematics. Both students and professional mathematicians use heuristics to discover conjectures and methods that may be helpful in solving problems (see Polya, 1954, for a classic statement on the uses of induction in mathematics). Our claim is simply that these inductive methods can be distinguished from deductive proof, a point on which Polya himself agreed: "There are two kinds of reasoning, as we said: demonstrative reasoning and plausible reasoning. Let me observe that they do not contradict each other; on the contrary they complete each other" (Polya, 1954, p. vi).

MATHEMATICAL INDUCTION AND UNIVERSAL GENERALIZATION

In their *The foundations of mathematics*, Stewart and Tall (1977) provide an example of a proof by induction similar to the one we just gave of the sum formula. They then comment:

Many people regard this as an 'and so on . . .' sort of argument in which the truth of the statement is established for $n = 1$; then, having established the general step from $n = k$ to $n = k + 1$, this is applied for $k = 1$ to get us from $n = 1$ to $n = 2$, then used again to go from $n = 2$ to $n = 3$, and so on, as far as we wish to go . . . The only trouble is that to reach large values of n requires a large number of applications of the general step, and we can never actually cover *all* natural numbers in a single proof of finite length. (p. 145)

This remark echoes Russell (1919, p. 21) in a similar context: "It is this 'and so on' that we must replace by something less vague and indefinite."

Perhaps this feeling of "and so on . . ." is what was bothering our colleague. If there is no more to a proof by induction than a sort of promissory note that we can keep going, then perhaps such a proof isn't much different from ordinary empirical induction. Just as we can't hope to enumerate all cases that fall under an inductive generalization in science, we can't hope to cover all natural numbers to which a mathematical generalization applies. Mathematical induction may only be able to give us a boost in confidence that the generalization holds in all cases, not an iron-clad proof.

Stewart and Tall (1977), however, offer a solution to show that mathematical induction is a rigorously deductive technique after all. "The way out of this dilemma is to remove the 'and so on . . .' part from the proof and place it squarely in the actual definition of the natural numbers" (p. 145). What follows in Stewart and Tall is an exposition of a variation on the Dedekind-Peano axioms for the natural numbers, with the following induction axiom:

(IAx) If $S \subseteq \mathbb{N}_0$ is such that $0 \in S$; and $n \in S \Rightarrow s(n) \in S$ for all $n \in \mathbb{N}_0$, then $S = \mathbb{N}_0$,

where S is a set, $\mathbb{N}_0$ are the natural numbers, and $s(\cdot)$ is the successor function (i.e., the function that yields $n + 1$ for any natural number n). For example, in the sample proof we gave earlier, S corresponds to the set of all natural numbers n such that the sum of 0 through n is $\frac{1}{2} n (n + 1)$, and the two parts of the proof correspond to the two clauses in (IAx). We first showed that 0 is in this set ($0 \in S$) and then that if n is in the set, so is $n + 1$ ($n \in S \Rightarrow s(n) \in S$). The conclusion is therefore that the sum formula is true for all natural numbers ($S = \mathbb{N}_0$). Since (IAx) is an axiom, this conclusion now has a kind of deductive legitimacy.[2]

Worry Number 1: The Justification of (IAx)

Stewart and Tall are right that (IAx) speaks to one sort of doubt about math induction. "And so on . . ." complaints about our proof of the sum formula could center around the fact that what's been demonstrated is a universal statement of the form: For all natural numbers n, if n satisfies the sum formula, so does $n + 1$. This generalization, together with the fact that 0 satisfies the formula, allows you to conclude by a modus ponens inference that 1 satisfies the formula:

($\forall n$) Sum-formula(n) $\supset$ Sum-formula($n + 1$).
Sum-formula(0).

Sum-formula(1).

This conclusion in turn allows you to make another modus ponens inference to 2:

($\forall n$) Sum-formula(n) $\supset$ Sum-formula ($n + 1$).
Sum-formula(1).

Sum-formula(2).

---

[2]   Use of math induction as a proof technique was, of course, well established before the introduction of (IAx) as a formal axiom. Medieval Arabic and Hebrew sources use implicit versions of math induction to prove theorems for finite series and for combinations and permutations (Grattan-Guinness, 1997). According to Kline (1972, p. 272), "the method was recognized explicitly by Maurolycus in his *Arithmetica* of 1575 and was used by him to prove, for example, that $1 + 3 + 5 + \cdots + (2n - 1) = n^2$."

And so on. In general, this *modus ponens* strategy requires k modus ponenses to conclude that k satisfies the sum formula, and it will be impossible to reach the conclusion for all natural numbers in a finite number of steps. (IAx) sidesteps this worry by reaching the conclusion for all n in one step. However, putting the "and so on . . . " idea "squarely in the actual definition of the natural numbers," as Stewart and Tall suggest, isn't a very comforting solution if this means hiding the "and so on . . . " pea under another shell. What justifies such an axiom?

There are several ways to proceed. First, we could try to eliminate the "and so on . . . " doubt by showing that (IAx) is inherently part of people's thinking about the natural numbers and, in this sense, is "squarely in" their definition. According to this idea, any kind of intuitive understanding of these numbers already allows you to conclude in one go that if 0 is in S and if $k + 1$ is in S whenever k is, then all natural numbers are in S. This is close to Poincaré's (1902/1982) view. Although he acknowledged that there is "a striking analogy with the usual procedures of [empirical] induction," he believed that mathematical induction "is the veritable type of the synthetic *a priori* judgment." By contrast with empirical induction, mathematical induction "imposes itself necessarily, because it is only the affirmation of a property of the mind itself" (pp. 39–40). Thus, any attempt to found math induction on a formal axiom like (IAx) can only replace an idea that is already intuitively clear with one that is more obscure. Goldfarb (1988) points out that the psychological nature of math induction was irrelevant to the goals of those like Frege, Hilbert, and Russell, who were the targets of Poincaré's critique (see Hallett, 1990, for debate about these goals). But perhaps Poincaré's theory is sufficient to settle specifically psychological doubts. Another possibility, one more consistent with Frege's (1884/1974) and Russell's (1919) viewpoint, is that (IAx) is the result of a principle that applies in a maximally domain-general way and is thus a precondition of rationality. We'll look more closely at the source of this generality in just a moment in examining Frege's treatment of (IAx).

We favor a view in which math induction is inherent in the concept of the natural numbers – whether this is specific to the natural-number concept or is inherited from more general principles – and this view preserves a crisp distinction between deductive and inductive reasoning. But can we really rule out the possibility that the "and so on . . ." doubt is a symptom of a true intermediate case? Maybe (IAx) merely plasters over a gap like that in ordinary induction – the "and so on . . ." gap that is left over from the modus ponens strategy.

One thing that seems clear is that in actually applying math induction – for example, in our use of it to prove the sum formula – the modus ponens strategy is never performed. In our original proof, for instance, we didn't (explicitly or implicitly) grind through the first few steps of the strategy (from 0 to 1 to 2...) before concluding that the sum formula is true for all n. So the way in which the modus ponens strategy gives us reason to believe in math induction must be indirect. Perhaps by reflecting on the modus ponens strategy, we somehow come to see that this strategy is unnecessary and that we can use the short-cut math induction procedure in its place. But if this is true, it can't be the *success* of the modus ponens strategy that convinces us, since this strategy is an infinite process that is never completed. We don't learn math induction from the modus ponens strategy in the usual generalizing or transferring sort of way. Instead, it must be our realizing that the modus ponens strategy could *potentially* yield the right result under some idealized conditions (e.g., infinite time and other resources) that persuades us that math induction will work. If we push further and ask what's responsible for such a realization, however, the answer seems to lead right back to our understanding of the structure of the numbers themselves. At best, the modus ponens strategy plays a mediating role in reminding us of a property of the natural number system but provides no independent justification.

Why is (IAx) inherent in the number concept? One way to see this comes from Frege's (1984/1974) treatment of math induction. (The modernized version that follows is from Quine, 1950, chap. 47. A somewhat similar attempt appears in Dedekind, 1888/1963, especially Theorems 59 and 89.) We can think of the natural numbers as a set that contains 0 and that contains all immediate successors of each of its members. Such a set, however, could contain other objects besides numbers. It could also contain, for example, Frege's hat, since Frege's hat does not have a successor. What we need to define the natural numbers is a minimality rule that says that the natural numbers are the *smallest* set containing 0 and containing all immediate successors of its members. Put slightly differently, the natural numbers are the elements that belong to all such sets, including the set containing only 0 and the successors of (the successors of...) 0. This definition of the natural numbers appears in (1):

(1) $n \in \mathbb{N}_0 \leftrightarrow (\forall u)((0 \in u \,\&\, (\forall k)(k \in u \supset s(k) \in u)) \supset n \in u)$,

where $\mathbb{N}_0$ is the set of natural numbers and $s(\cdot)$ is the successor function, as before.

From this definition, mathematical induction follows, just as Stewart and Tall (1977) claimed. For suppose S is a set that fulfills the two conditions on (IAx), as in (2):

(2) $0 \in S \,\&\, (\forall k)(k \in S \supset s(k) \in S)$.

If n is a natural number, (3) then follows from the definition in (1):

(3) $(\forall u) ((0 \in u \mathbin{\&} (\forall k) (k \in u \supset s(k) \in u)) \supset n \in u)$,

and in particular (i.e., by instantiating u to S):

(4) $(0 \in S \mathbin{\&} (\forall k) (k \in S \supset s(k) \in S)) \supset n \in S$.

It then follows by modus ponens from (2) and (4) that $n \in S$. Hence, every natural number is an element of S.

Frege's method helps to bring out what's important about (IAx) as a part of the natural-number concept. In using (IAx) to prove a theorem, as we did with the sum formula, we take an "insider's view" of the number system in which its familiar properties are already in place. For these purposes, (IAx) is the usual tool we pick up in high school algebra. But to see the role that (IAx) plays in the definition of the natural numbers – the reason that it appears among the Dedekind-Peano axioms – we need to adopt an "outsider's view." From this perspective, (IAx) is a kind of closure principle. It says, in effect, that nothing can be a natural number that isn't either 0 or a successor of (a successor of ...) 0. This is the importance of the minimality constraint we've just looked at. For these purposes, we could substitute for (IAx) other rules that have equivalent effects, given the rest of the axioms – rules that may seem less artificial and less similar to empirical induction. An example is the Least-Number Principle (see Kaye, 1991) that we can spell out in a way that can be compared to (IAx):

(LNP) If $S \subseteq \mathbb{N}_0$ and $n \in S$, then there is an $m \in S$ such that for all $k < m$, $k \notin S$.

In other words, if S is a nonempty set of the natural numbers, there's a smallest number in S. For other number systems, other types of math induction may be required (see, e.g., Knuth, 1974).

Worry Number 2: The Justification of (UG)

But there could be another hang up about proofs like the example we gave for the sum formula. As part of the proof of this formula, we showed that for any particular k, if k satisfies the sum formula then so does $k + 1$. The second sort of doubt is whether this is enough to prove that the same is true for *all* natural numbers. Clearly, (IAx) is completely powerless to quell this second kind of doubt. The axiom requires us to show that $n \in S$ entails $s(n) \in S$ for *all* natural numbers n, and this is precisely where the second sort of doubt arises.

This kind of doubt surfaces in some psychological treatments of math induction. For example, in one of the very few empirical studies on this topic, Smith (2002, p. 6) cites a definition similar to (IAx) and then goes on to remark, "The definition secures a generalization (universalization). The reference in the premises is to a property true of *any* (some particular) number. But the reference in the conclusion is to *any* number whatsoever, any number at all. Note that the term *any* is ambiguous here since it covers an inference from some-to-all." The word *any* does not, in fact, appear in the definition that Smith cites. The relevant clause is " . . . and if it is established that [the property] is true of $n + 1$ provided it is true of n, it will be true of all whole numbers." But what Smith seems to mean is that the proof is a demonstration for some particular case, k and $k + 1$, whereas the conclusion is that the property is true for all natural numbers n. Similarly, in discussing earlier work by Inhelder and Piaget, Smith states:

[mathematical induction] runs from what is shown to be true of a specified number *n* (*n'importe quel nombre*) and what in that case is also shown to be true of its successor (*n* + 1) to a conclusion about any number whatsoever (*nombre quelconque*). It is just such an inference which is at issue in mathematical induction and it was Inhelder and Piaget's (1963) contention that their evidence showed that children were capable of this type of reasoning (p. 23).

The inference that Smith is pointing to, however, is not a feature of math induction per se but of the universal generalization that feeds it. Universal generalization, roughly speaking, is the principle that if a predicate can be proved true for an arbitrary member of a domain, it must be true for all members. A formal statement of this rule can be found in most textbooks on predicate logic. We have adapted slightly the following definition from Lemmon (1965):

(UG) Let $P(e)$ be a well-formed formula containing the arbitrary name e, and x be a variable not occurring in $P(e)$; let $P(x)$ be the propositional function in x which results from replacing all and only occurrences of e in $P(e)$ by x. Then, given $P(e)$, UG permits us to draw the conclusion $(\forall x)P(x)$, provided that e occurs in no assumption on which $P(e)$ rests.

For example, when we proved that the sum formula holds for $k + 1$ if it holds for k, we used no special properties of k except for those common to all natural numbers. In this sense, k functioned as an arbitrary name. Hence (by universal generalization), for all natural numbers n, the sum formula holds of $n + 1$ if it holds for n. This generalization is needed to satisfy the second condition of (IAx), but it is also needed to supply the major premises for the modus ponens strategy and, of course, for much other mathematical reasoning. The confusion between (IAx) and (UG) is an understandable one. We could rephrase (IAx) in a way that refers to an arbitrary case: if S is a subset of the natural numbers, if 0 is an element of S, and if whenever an arbitrary natural number k is in S so is $k + 1$, then S includes all natural numbers. This rephrasing is valid, but it combines (IAx) and (UG) in a way that obscures their separate contributions.

(UG), like (IAx), may seem to lend deductive legitimacy to what looks at first like empirical induction. Unlike the case of (IAx), though, there's not much temptation to see this rule as sanctioning a kind of induction-by-enumeration. Informal use of mathematical induction seemed to fall short because it required an infinite number of modus ponens inferences, and (IAx) was introduced to avoid this. But the informal use of universal generalization in mathematics doesn't have the same kind of "and so on..." gap. Once we've shown that P is true for an arbitrary element e, we needn't apply this result to get $P(0)$, $P(1)$, $P(2)$, and so on. In general, informal universal generalization (e.g., in the proof of the sum formula) doesn't raise the same kind of sophisticated issues about the nature of proof that informal use of math induction does (although it does take some sophistication to formulate (UG) correctly for a logic system, as the definition from Lemmon, 1965, suggests).

Instead, the worry about (UG) stems from its similarity to an inductive heuristic in which you generalize from a specific number. (Kahneman and Tversky's [1972] representativeness heuristic is a related example in the context of probability estimation.) In the case of the sum formula, for instance, it's clearly not mathematically kosher to proceed like this:

Let's pick an arbitrary number, say, 7.
Simple calculations show that $0 + 1 + 2 + 3 + 4 + 5 + 6 + 7 = 28$ and $1/2 \times 7 \times (7 + 1) = 28$.
Hence, $\sum i = 1/2\, n\, (n + 1)$.

An example of this sort may increase your confidence that the sum formula is true, but it doesn't produce a deductively valid proof. However, there's an intuitive kinship between this pseudo-proof and the earlier correct proof of the sum formula. The phrase *arbitrary number* captures this kinship, since it can mean either a specific number that we select in some haphazard way or it can mean a placeholder that could potentially take any number as a value. Sliding between these two meanings yields an inductive, example-based argument, on one hand, and a deductively valid (UG)-based proof, on the other. For the sum formula, it's the difference between the argument from seven that we just gave and the correct argument with k.

(UG) is pervasive in mathematics, in part because most algebraic manipulations depend on it. Variables like k turn up everywhere, not just in the context of mathematical induction. Thus, confusion about the nature of variables is apt to have wide-spread consequences and blur the distinction between inductive arguments and deductive proof. We consider the empirical evidence for this confusion in the next section, including actual pseudo-proofs from students that are quite similar to our argument from seven. We then return to the issue of whether this evidence shows that the difference between deduction and induction in math is merely one of degree.

INDUCTION IN MATHEMATICS

In Smith's (2002) study of children's arithmetic, the key question to participants was: "If you add any number [of toys] at all to one pot and the same number to the other, would there be the same in each, or would there be more in one than in the other?" A correct answer to this question seems to depend on the children realizing that for all numbers x and quantities m and n, $x + m = x + n$ if and only if $m = n$. In the experiment, m and n are the initial quantities of toys in the pots ($m = n = 0$ in one condition of the study, and $m = 1$ and $n = 0$ in another). It is certainly possible to prove this principle using (IAx), but it is far from clear that this is the way children were approaching the problem. Reasoning along the lines of (UG) would mean going from "for arbitrary k, $(m + k = n + k)$ if and only if $(m = n)$" to the above conclusion for all x. But again it is unclear that this is how children went about answering this question. Among the children's justifications that Smith quotes on this problem, the only one that directly suggests (UG) is "I'm putting like a number in the orange pot and a number in the green pot, and it's got to be the same."

There is plenty of reason, however, to suspect that children in this experiment were using specific examples to justify their decisions. Some simply cited a specific number, for example, "If you added a million in there, there would be a million, and if you added a million in there, there would be a million," or "it would be just a million and six in there and a million and six in there." Others gave a more complete justification but also based on a specific number of items: "If we started putting 0 in there and 1 in there, and then adding 5 and 5, and so it wouldn't be the same – this would be 5 and 6." Instead of the (UG) strategy of thinking about an arbitrary addition, these children seem to generalize directly from a particular number, such as 5 or 1,000,006, to all numbers. The numbers may be selected arbitrarily but they aren't capable of denoting any natural number in the way (UG) requires. It is possible, of course, that these children were using a correct general strategy and simply citing specific cases to aid in their explanations, but the experiments we are about to review suggest than even college students evaluate "proof by specific examples" as a valid method.

Variations on this kind of instance-based strategy are probably common in mathematics. One traditional way of thinking about this is that people use these strategies as heuristics to suggest the right generalization before they apply more rigorous mathematical methods to produce a genuine proof. This is similar to the distinction from Polya (1954) that we mentioned earlier (see, also, Thagard's Chapter 9 on abduction in this volume). There might be a "context of discovery" in which such informal methods are appropriate, and a "context of justification" where only proof-based methods such as (IAx) and (UG) apply. We were once given the advice that you should try to prove a theorem only when you were 95% sure it was right. This advice separates neatly the informal, confidence-based aspect of mathematics from its formal, proof-based side. So does the usual classroom advice to experiment with different values to find a formula before you try to prove it with (IAx).

But whatever validity the discovery/justification division has in mathematics, it is clear that students do not always honor it. Even when asked to prove a proposition (so that justification is required), students often produce what look to be instance-based strategies. We give some examples here from experiments on college students and then try to draw some implications about the relation between induction and deduction in math contexts.

Algebra

Asking college student to prove simple propositions in number theory often results in "proof by multiple examples," such as the following one (Eliaser, 2000):

Show that every odd multiple of 5 when squared is not divisible by 2.
Proof:
 Odd multiples of 5: 5, 15, 25 . . .
 $5^2 = 25 \rightarrow$ not divisible by 2.
 $15^2 = 225 \rightarrow$ not divisible by 2.
 Therefore shown.

In the experiment from which we took this excerpt, Northwestern University undergraduates had to prove a group of simple statements, half of which had a universal form, like the one above, requiring an algebraic proof. Although nearly all these students were able to use algebra (as they demonstrated in a post test), only 41% initially employed it in proving universal propositions. Instead, 33% used multiple examples (as in the sample "proof") and 17% used single examples.

Of course, students may not always see the right proof strategy immediately and may fall back on examples instead. For instance, the students may not remember or may not know how to set up a problem that requires representing the parity of a number (i.e., that all even numbers have the form $2x$ and all odd ones $2x + 1$). But this doesn't seem to be the whole story behind the students' dismal performance. In a second study, Eliaser (2000) gave potential proofs to a new group of undergraduates and asked them to rate the quality of the proof on a four-point scale from "shows no support" to "completely proves." The "proofs" included single-example, multiple-example, and algebraic versions. But despite the fact that students didn't have to produce their own proofs and only had to evaluate the proofs of others, they nevertheless rated multiple-example pseudo-proofs higher than either single-example or (correct) algebraic proofs, for universal claims, such as the one about odd multiples of 5.

Depressing performance of a similar kind comes from a study of students who were training to be elementary math teachers (Martin & Harel, 1989). These students rated proofs and pseudo-proofs for two number-theoretic statements (e.g., If a divides b and b divides c, then a divides c). The pseudo-proofs included a typical example (e.g., "12 divides 36, 36 divides 360, 12 divides 360") and an example with a big, random-looking number:

Let's pick any three numbers, taking care that the first divides the second, and the second divides the third: 49 divides 98, and 98 divides 1176. Does 49 divide 1176? (*Computation shown to left.*) The answer is yes.

The pseudo-proofs also included an instantiation of the more general, correct proof:

Take 4, 8, and 24. 4 divides 8, which means that there must exist a number, in this case 2, such that $2 \times 4 = 8$. 8 divides 24, which means there must exist a number, in this case 3, such that $3 \times 8 = 24$. Now substitute for 8 in the previous equation, and we get $3 \times (2 \times 4) = 24$. So we found a number ($3 \times 2$), such that $(3 \times 2) \times 4 = 24$. Therefore, 4 divides 24.

Students rated these pseudo-proofs, along with other pseudo- and correct proofs on a scale from 1 (not considered a proof) to 4 (a mathematical proof). If we take a rating of 4 to be an endorsement of the argument as a proof, then 28% endorsed the correct proof, 22% the instantiated pseudo-proof, 39% the specific example, and 38% the big random-looking example.

Geometry

Students' use of example-based proof strategies isn't limited to algebra. It's a common classroom warning in high school geometry that students shouldn't draw general conclusions from the specific cases that they see in the diagrams accompanying a problem. Diagrams represent one way in which the givens of a problem could be true, not all possible ways. Despite these warnings, students do generate answers to test questions based on single diagrams.

Evidence on this point comes from a study by Koedinger and Anderson (1991). This study presented students with yes/no questions about geometric relationships, accompanied by one of two diagrams. For example, one problem asked, "If $\angle BCD = \angle ACD$, must $\overline{AB} \perp \overline{CD}$?" The two possible diagrams for this problem appear as Figures 10.1a and 10.1b. For half the problems the correct answer was "yes," as in this example. The remaining problems had "no" as the correct answer, for instance, "If $\overline{AC} = \overline{CB}$, must $\overline{AB} \perp \overline{CD}$?" The two possible diagrams for this problem are Figures 10.1c and 10.1d. For each of these pairs of problems, the given information and the conclusion were true of one diagram (Figures 10.1a and 10.1c) and were false of the other (Figures 10.1b and 10.1d). Individual participants saw only one of the possible diagrams per problem.

The results showed that students were usually able to get the right answer: they were correct on about 68% of trials. For problems where the correct answer was "yes" (so that a proof was possible), the students performed more accurately when the corresponding proof was easy than when it was difficult, suggesting that they were attempting such a proof. Nevertheless, they tended to be swayed by the diagrams: they made more "yes" responses in all conditions when the diagram pictured the given information and the conclusion (as in Figures 10.1a and 10.1c) than when it didn't (Figures 10.1b and 10.1d). Koedinger and Anderson take this pattern of results to mean that the students were attempting to find a proof but were using the diagram as a backup inductive strategy if no proof was forthcoming (a "modified misinterpreted necessity model" in the jargon of reasoning research; see Evans, Newstead, & Byrne, 1993).

Further evidence that students rely on diagrams for inductive support comes from one of our own studies of non-Euclidean geometry. In this experiment, we gave participants a short introduction to hyperbolic geometry, which differs from Euclidean geometry by the following *hyperbolic axiom*: for any given line ℓ and point p not on ℓ, there are multiple lines through p parallel to ℓ. The participants then solved a number of problems in the new geometry while thinking aloud. Figure 10.2 illustrates one such problem. To avoid confusing participants about the meaning of *parallel*, we substituted the nonsense term *cordian*, which we defined according to the hyperbolic axiom. For the problem in Figure 10.2, we told participants that lines ℓ and m are

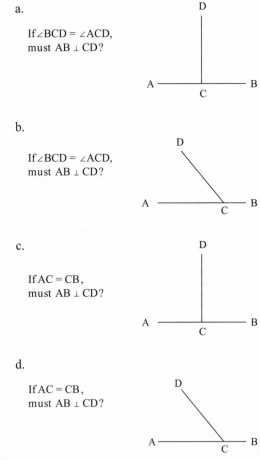

a.

If ∠BCD = ∠ACD,
must AB ⊥ CD?

b.

If ∠BCD = ∠ACD,
must AB ⊥ CD?

c.

If AC = CB,
must AB ⊥ CD?

d.

If AC = CB,
must AB ⊥ CD?

FIGURE 10.1. Stimulus problems from a study of geometry problem solving (adapted from Koedinger and Anderson, 1991, Figure 2).

cordian, that ∠BAC and ∠BDC were 90° angles, and asked them to decide whether triangle ABC was congruent to triangle DCB.[3]

---

[3] If the two triangles ABC and DCB are congruent, corresponding angles of these triangles must also be congruent. In Figure 10.2, ∠BAC and ∠CDB are given as congruent, but what about the pair ∠DCB and ∠ABC and the pair ∠BCA and ∠CBD? In Euclidean geometry, the congruence of each of these pairs follows from the fact that alternate interior angles formed by a transversal and two parallel lines are congruent. In hyperbolic geometry, however, the alternate interior angles formed by a transversal and two parallel ("cordian") lines are not congruent. For example, in Figure 10.2, ∠ABC and ∠DCB are both the alternate interior angles formed by the cut of transversal BC across parallel lines ℓ and m. But because these corresponding angles cannot be proved congruent, neither can the two triangles.

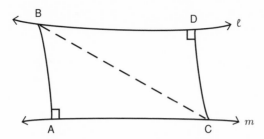

FIGURE 10.2. Stimulus problem for a study of non-Euclidean geometry.

Diagrams for non-Euclidean problems are apt to be misleading. Although there are several conventions for drawing such diagrams (such as the one adopted in Figure 10.2; see Greenberg, 1993), they can nevertheless suggest Euclidean relationships that don't hold in the non-Euclidean domain. Participants quickly recognize this difficulty, but they still fall back on the appearance of a diagram. The following transcript is from a participant working on the problem in Figure 10.2:

Must be true, ABC is congruent to DCB. If ∠BAC is 90, must they be congruent? It does not mention a line will diverge, so how can I judge how far apart these lines will be at any given point, since they're curving? Angle ABD is split, maybe in half, if you dissect it, it appears as though it's dissected . . . I have no information about the angles ACD or ABD. I must assume that there can be less than 360° [in a quadrilateral]. That the angle B could be equal to angle C. Angle B equals angle ACD. Therefore, if those angles are equal, and the line joining them is drawn, angle ABC is equal to angle DBC. Okay. The dotted line will be line *q*. Line segment *q* bisects angle ABD. . . . Angle, angle, angle . . . theorem states that ABD is congruent with – ABC is congruent with DCB. Must be true? Yes.

Although this participant seems initially unsure of the angle relationships, he or she is gradually seduced by the appearance that ∠ABD and ∠ACD are equal and that the dashed line bisects both these angles.

Implications

These examples show that people sometimes use inductive strategies where deductive methods are necessary. More surprisingly, people sometimes evaluate the inductive methods more favorably than the correct deductive ones. We can explain the first of these findings on the assumption that people resort to inductive methods when they run out of deductive ones – either because no proof is possible or because they can't find one – as Koedinger and Anderson (1991) propose. But the evaluation results make it likely that this isn't the whole story. Why do people find inductive pseudo-proofs better than true proofs when they're able to assess them directly?

The answer may lie in the relative complexity of the true proofs versus the inductive lures. Examples are likely to be easier to understand than proofs, especially if the proofs are lengthy. Similarly, there's a difference in concreteness between proofs with individual numbers and those with arbitrary names (i.e., mathematical variables) in algebra. Geometry diagrams also have a concreteness advantage over the proofs that refer to them. Even among correct deductive proofs, we evaluate the simpler, more elegant ones as superior to their more complex competitors, and it is possible that students' incorrect evaluations are a more extreme version of the same tendency.

Explanations along these lines do no harm to the thesis that deductive and inductive reasoning make use of qualitatively different mechanisms. These explanations take the induction/deduction difference for granted and account for students' errors on the basis of factors, such as complexity or abstractness, that swamp deductive methods or make them seem less attractive. We know of no experimental results that can eliminate these explanations. But it's also interesting to consider the possibility of a more continuous gradient between inductive and deductive strategies. One proposal along these lines might be based on the idea that people search for increasingly nonobvious counterexamples to an argument or theorem. If they are unable to find any counterexamples, either because there are none or because the individuals can no longer hold enough examples in working memory, they declare the argument valid. In the case of algebra, we can imagine students first choosing a specific number that the problem suggests and that meets the theorem's givens. For example, in the problem mentioned earlier of showing that the squares of odd multiples of 5 are not divisible by 2, the participant began by verifying that 5^2 is not divisible by 2. If the first instance does not yield a counterexample, the students try another (e.g., $(3 \times 5)^2$) until they either discover a counterexample or run out of working-memory resources. In the case of geometry, students might first verify that the conclusion is true of the diagram that appears with the problem. They may then consider new diagrams of their own in the same search for counterexamples.

In the present context, one difficulty with this line of thinking, however, is that it doesn't account for Koedinger and Anderson's (1991) evidence that students also attempt to apply a separate deductive strategy and resort to diagrams only when the first strategy fails. The counterexample hypothesis predicts instead that students should begin by considering the given diagram, look for other diagrams that might falsify the conclusion, and end by accepting the theorem as valid if it correctly applies to all the diagrams they have examined. In addition, there is a theoretical problem. In the case of a universal proposition – such as the sum formula that applies to all natural numbers – there's no endpoint at which you can stop and be sure that no counterexamples will be found. There will always be additional numbers that have features other than the ones you've so far considered. Rather than provide a continuum between inductive and deductive reasoning, this strategy never provides more than weak inductive support. Of course, the fact that a pure counterexample strategy is inadequate as an explanation of the data doesn't mean that there aren't other methods intermediate between induction and deduction that may be more reasonable. But we know of no convincing cases of this type.

Another way to put this point is to say that there is no number or diagram that is "completely arbitrary" in a way that could prove a universal proposition. "Each number has its own peculiarities. To what extent a given particular number can represent all others, and at what point its own special character comes into play, cannot be laid down generally in advance" (Frege, 1884/1974, p. 20). The sort of arbitrariness that does prove such a proposition – and that (UG) demands – is a matter of abstractness, not randomness or atypicality. Arbitrariness in the latter sense drives you to more obscure cases as potential counterexamples. But the sort of arbitrariness that is relevant to proving a universal proposition pulls in the opposite direction of inclusiveness – an instance that could potentially be any number.

SUMMARY AND CONCLUSION

We now have a more complicated answer to give to our colleague. Our original response was that mathematical induction is a deductive technique with a confusing name. When people use math induction to prove a theorem, they aren't using induction and they aren't sacrificing deductive validity; the theorem is still necessarily true, just as with other standard proof techniques. Although there is debate about the role of probabilistic proofs in mathematics (see Fallis, 1997) – methods that truly are inductive – math induction isn't such a method.

But while we still think this is correct, math induction does loosely resemble empirical induction. From a formal point of view, there is a tension between math induction and the usual constraint that proofs be finite. Math induction seems to rely on an infinite process of iterating through the natural numbers – the modus ponens strategy that we discussed earlier. From a psychological point of view, of course, no such infinite process is remotely possible. It's this gap that creates the similarity with empirical induction, since in both cases the conclusion of the argument seems beyond what the premises afford. An induction axiom like (IAx) makes up for this gap in formal contexts, but why is math induction a deductively correct proof tool if it can't be backed up by the infinite iteration it seems to require?

We've argued elsewhere (Rips, Bloomfield, & Asmuth, 2007) that math induction is central to knowledge of mathematics: it seems unlikely that people could have correct concepts of natural number and other key math objects without a grip on induction. Basic rules of arithmetic, such as the associative and commutative laws of addition and multiplication, are naturally proved via math induction. If this is right, then it's a crucial issue how people come to terms with it. We've tried to argue here that the analogy we've just noted – enumeration : conclusion by empirical induction :: modus ponens strategy : conclusion by math induction – is misleading. Math induction doesn't get its backing from the modus ponens strategy. Rather the modus ponens strategy plays at most a propaedeutic role, revealing an abstract property of the natural number system that is responsible for the correctness of math induction. It is still possible, of course, that math induction picks up quasi-inductive support from its fruitfulness in proving further theorems, but in this respect it doesn't differ from any other math axiom.

Although we think that math induction doesn't threaten the distinction between deductive and inductive reasoning, there is a related issue about generalization in math that might. Math proofs often proceed by selecting an "arbitrary instance" from a domain, showing that some property is true of this instance, and then generalizing to all the domain's members. For this universal generalization to work, the instance in question must be an abstraction or stand-in (an "arbitrary name" or variable) for all relevant individuals, and there is no real concern that such a strategy is not properly deductive. However, there's psychological evidence that students don't always recognize the difference between such an abstraction and an arbitrarily selected exemplar. Sometimes, in fact, students use exemplars in their proofs (and evaluate positively proofs that contain exemplars) that don't even look arbitrary but are simply convenient, perhaps because the exemplars lend themselves to concrete arguments that are easy to understand. In these cases, students are using an inductive strategy, since the exemplar can at most increase their confidence in the to-be-proved proposition.

It's no news, of course, that people make mistakes in math. And it's also no news that ordinary induction has a role to play in math, especially in the context of discovery. The question here is whether these inductive intrusions provide evidence that the deduction/induction split is psychologically untenable. Does the use of arbitrary and not-so-arbitrary instances show that people have a single type of reasoning mechanism that delivers conclusions that are quantitatively stronger or weaker, but not qualitatively inductive versus deductive? We've considered one way in which this might be the case. Perhaps people look for counterexamples, continuing their search through increasingly arbitrary (i.e., haphazard or atypical) cases until they've found such a counterexample or have run out of steam. The longer the search, the more secure the conclusion. We've seen, however, that this procedure doesn't extend to deductively valid proofs; no matter how obscure the instance, it will still have an infinite number of properties that prohibit you from generalizing from it. It is possible to contend that this procedure is nevertheless all that people have at their disposal – that they can never ascend from their search for examples and counterexamples to a deductively adequate method. But although the evidence on proof evaluation paints a fairly bleak picture of students' ability to recognize genuine math proofs, the existence of such proofs shows they are not completely out of reach.

References

Dedekind, R. (1963). The nature and meaning of numbers (W. W. Beman, Trans.). In *Essays on the theory of numbers* (pp. 31–115). New York: Dover. (Original work published 1888.)

Eliaser, N. M. (2000). What constitutes a mathematical proof? *Dissertation Abstracts International, 60 (12)*, 6390B. (UMI No. AAT 9953274)

Evans, J. St. B. T., Newstead, S. E., & Byrne, R. M. J. (1993). *Human reasoning.* Hillsdale, NJ: Erlbaum.

Fallis, D. (1997). The epistemic status of probabilistic proofs. *Journal of Philosophy, 94*, 165–186.

Frege, G. (1974). *The foundations of arithmetic* (J. L. Austin, Trans.). Oxford, England: Blackwell. (Original work published 1884.)

Goldfarb, W. (1988). Poincaré against the logicists. In W. Aspray & P. Kitcher (Eds.), *History and philosophy of modern mathematics* (pp. 61–81). Minneapolis: University of Minnesota Press.

Goel, V., Gold, B., Kapur, S., & Houle, S. (1997). The seats of reason? An imaging study of deductive and inductive reasoning. *NeuroReport, 8*, 1305–1310.

Grattan-Guinness, I. (1997). *The Norton history of the mathematical sciences.* New York: Norton.

Greenberg, M. J. (1993). *Euclidean and non-Euclidean geometries* (3rd ed.). New York: Freeman.

Hallett, M. (1990). Review of *History and philosophy of modern mathematics. Journal of Symbolic Logic, 55*, 1315–1319.

Kahneman, D., & Tversky, A. (1972). Subjective probability: A judgment of representativeness. *Cognitive Psychology, 3*, 430–454.

Kaye, R. (1991). *Models of Peano arithmetic.* Oxford, England: Oxford University Press.

Kline, M. (1972). *Mathematical thought from ancient to modern times.* Oxford, England: Oxford University Press.

Knuth, D. E. (1974). *Surreal numbers.* Reading, MA: Addison-Wesley.

Koedinger, K. R., & Anderson, J. R. (1991). Interaction of deductive and inductive reasoning strategies in geometry novices. *Proceedings of the Thirteenth Annual Conference of the Cognitive Science Society, 780*–784.

Lemmon, E. J. (1965). *Beginning logic.* London: Nelson.

Martin, W. G., & Harel, G. (1989). Proof frames of preservice elementary teachers. *Journal for Research in Mathematics Education, 20,* 41–51.

Osherson, D., Perani, D., Cappa, S., Schnur, T., Grassi, F., & Fazio, F. (1998). Distinct brain loci in deductive versus probabilistic reasoning. *Neuropsychologia, 36,* 369–376.

Poincaré, H. (1982). *Science and hypothesis* (G. B. Halsted, Trans.). In *The foundations of science.* Washington, DC: University Press of America. (Original work published 1902.)

Polya, G. (1954). *Induction and analogy in mathematics.* Princeton, NJ: Princeton University Press.

Quine, W. V. (1950). *Methods of logic* (4th ed.). Cambridge, MA: Harvard University Press.

Rips, L. J. (2001a). Two kinds of reasoning. *Psychological Science, 12,* 129–134.

Rips, L. J. (2001b). Reasoning imperialism. In R. Elio (Ed.), *Common sense, reasoning, and rationality* (pp. 215–235). Oxford, England: Oxford University Press.

Rips, L. J., Bloomfield, A., & Asmuth, J. (2007). *Number sense and number nonsense.* Manuscript submitted for publication.

Rubin, D. C., & Wenzel, A. E. (1996). One hundred years of forgetting. *Psychological Review, 103,* 734–760.

Russell, B. (1919). *Introduction to mathematical philosophy.* New York: Dover.

Smith, L. (2002). *Reasoning by mathematical induction in children's arithmetic.* Amsterdam: Pergamon.

Stewart, I., & Tall, D. (1977). *The foundations of mathematics.* Oxford, England: Oxford University Press.

11

Induction, Deduction, and Argument Strength in Human Reasoning and Argumentation

Mike Oaksford and Ulrike Hahn

Recently researchers in the psychology of reasoning seem to be lining up on two sides of a divide. On the one hand, some view human inference to be sensitive to the deductive relationships between propositions (e.g., Johnson-Laird & Byrne, 1991, 2002; Rips, 1994). For example, the natural language sentence *birds fly* can be encoded as the logical proposition that *if x is a bird, then x flies*. It is a matter of pure deductive logic that *if this proposition is true*, then when someone comes to learn that *Tweety is a bird*, they should conclude that *Tweety can fly*. That is, this inference is simply an instantiation of the logical rule of *modus ponens*:

$$\frac{p \to q, \, p}{\therefore \, q} \tag{1}$$

This inference schema reads that if the propositions above the line are true, then it can be inferred that the propositions below the line are true. If people endorse this inference maximally, then it would seem that they are sensitive to the *deductive correctness* of this argument.

On the other hand, there are those who believe that in evaluating an argument like this people are more sensitive to *inductive strength* than deductive correctness. On some accounts (Oaksford & Chater 2007; Oaksford & Chater, 2003a–d; Oaksford, Chater, & Larkin, 2000), what matters is what probability the premises, *if x is a bird, then x flies* and *Tweety is a bird*, confer on the conclusion. If one identifies the inductive strength of the conditional with the conditional probability of things flying given they are birds, then the transfer of inductive strength to the conclusion is particularly straightforward.[1] One

---

[1] Inductive strength, as applied to arguments, is interpreted as the probability of the conclusion given the premises (see also Rips, 2001). A rational calculation of this probability requires that the individual propositions that make up the premises can also be assigned inductive strengths, here interpreted as probabilities.

simply uses the categorical premise *Tweety is a bird*, $P(\text{Tweety is a bird}) = 1$, to conditionalize on the conditional premise. So if the inductive strength of the conditional is .9, that is $P(x\,flys|x\,is\,a\,bird) = .9$, then the inductive strength of the conclusion that *Tweety can fly* is also .9.

"*Inductive* strength" (Skyrms, 1975) is an appropriate description because on this account one's degree of belief in the conditional, $P(if\,x\,is\,a\,bird,\,then$ $x\,flys)$, is $P(x\,flys|x\,is\,a\,bird)$, which can be calculated from the evidence for (birds that fly) and against (birds that don't fly) the hypothesis that *if x is a bird, then x flys*. Of course *inductive* strength or *argument strength* (Rips, 2001) does not have to be established by enumerative induction. For example, the strength of someone's belief that the train they are about to board stops at the destination to which they want to travel but to which they have never travelled before is based on their confidence in the railway guard who told them to board the train and not on past inductions from having boarded the train before.

Why have some researchers proposed that people assess arguments in putatively deductive tasks by appeal to inductive strength? The reasons are theoretical and empirical. Empirically, there is much evidence that people do not respond on a variety of tasks in a way that is consistent with a standard logical account. For example, according to standard logic, if people understand the task correctly, that is, they interpret the premises as true, then they should always endorse the conclusion that *Tweety can fly* in the above argument. In many tests of this hypothesis using abstract materials, where, for example, participants are asked to judge inferences like *modus ponens*, endorsement rates are indeed very high (see Schroyens & Schaeken, 2003, for a meta-analysis). However, when real world material is used, endorsement rates can be much lower, that is, significantly less than 1 (e.g., Oaksford et al., 2000). Moreover, other inferences which participants should always endorse according to standard logic, for example, *modus tollens*:

$$\frac{p \rightarrow q, \neg q}{\therefore \neg p} \tag{2}$$

are always endorsed at much lower rates. One interpretation of these phenomena is that for these inferences people are assessing inductive strength, on the assumption that the proportion of people endorsing an inference is a reflection of the underlying subjective degree of belief that people have about the conditional (Evans & Over, 2004).

Theoretically, one good reason to believe that people should not be particularly sensitive to deductive relations is that standard logic is *monotonic*; in other words the *law of strengthening the antecedent* holds that is,

$$\frac{p \to q}{\therefore (p \wedge r) \to q} \tag{3}$$

However, it seems that for most inferences that people are likely to encounter in their everyday lives, this logical law fails.[2] For example, *if x is a bird, then x flys* does *not* entail that *if (x is a bird and x is an Ostrich), then x flys*. As the logical standard against which *deductive correctness* is normally assessed in psychology is *monotonic*, that is strengthening of the antecedent is valid, perhaps people should not be sensitive to deductive relations. Non-monotonicity is the *sine qua non* of inductive reasoning. That is, each observation, *bird A can fly, bird B can fly, and so forth* can be viewed as a premise in the inductive argument to the conclusion that *birds fly*. However, this conclusion can be defeated (logically) by the observation of one non-flying bird. Thus the observation that most everyday arguments seem to be non-monotonic seems to suggest that they are mainly assessed for *argument strength*, as for these arguments deductive correctness may be unattainable.

Rips (2001a, b; 2002; see also Rips [this volume] for further discussion) has argued that trying to make inductive strength do service for deductive correctness (Oaksford & Chater, 1998, 2001) or trying to make deductive correctness do service for inductive strength (Johnson-Laird, 1994; Johnson-Laird, Legrenzi, Girotto, Legrenzi, & Caverni, 1999) is misguided, and he refers to these attempts as *reasoning imperialism*. In this chapter, we argue that our position is not an imperialist one. Rather, it is that *while people may well be capable of assessing deductive correctness when explicitly asked to, this is rarely, if ever, their focus of interest in evaluating an argument*. Thus we will conclude that inductive strength is probably more important in determining people's behaviour than deductive correctness even on putative deductive reasoning tasks. However, despite our emphasis on inductive strength, we still think that deductive relations, or structure, may be crucial to human inference, as we point out in Section 4.

In Section 1, we begin by examining Rips' (2001) own evidence and arguments for a clear distinction between these two ways of evaluating inferences. We argue (i) that the data are perhaps not as convincing as they may first seem, (ii) that establishing the claim of sensitivity to deductive correctness can not be established by examining isolated inferences but only for a whole

---

[2] This can be readily established by a simple thought experiment. Think of any conditional statement about the everyday world you like and see how easy it is to generate exceptions to the rule (see also Chater & Oaksford, 1996).

logic, (iii) that the generality of a concept of a logical system makes it difficult to refute the claim that people are sensitive to deductive relations in *some* logic, but (iv) that given (ii), it is clear that people probably *should* not be sensitive to standard deductive validity because it leads to many paradoxes.

In Section 2, we move on to look at conditional inference, as in the examples of *modus ponens* and *modus tollens* above. Here we argue that an account based on *probability logic* (Adams, 1975, 1998) which uses an account of inductive strength resolves many of the paradoxes observed for standard deductive validity and moreover provides a better account of the data. We also show that inductive processes, that is, updating beliefs in the light of evidence by Bayesian revision, may be directly involved in drawing conditional inferences because of possible violations of what is called the *rigidity condition* for *Jeffrey conditionalization*. We also evaluate the inductive strength of some conditional argument forms. In particular, we show that people may judge some conditional reasoning fallacies as being as strong as a deductively correct inference.

Finally, we show in Section 3 how some very similar proposals address informal argument fallacies, for example, *the argument from ignorance, circularity,* and *the slippery slope argument*. That is, invoking the concept of argument or inductive strength can resolve the paradox of why some instances of informal argument fallacies seem perfectly acceptable and capable of rationally persuading someone of a conclusion.

The theme of this paper could be characterized as an attempt to demonstrate that an account of argument strength helps resolve many paradoxes and *fallacies* in reasoning and argumentation. A *logical paradox* (see Section 1.2 on the paradoxes of material implication) is usually taken to mean an example of a logically valid inference, for which there seem to be instances that are considered obviously unsound.[3] Following logicians like Adams (1975, 1998), we suggest that this may be because these inferences are *inductively weak*. To commit a *logical fallacy* is to endorse an argument that is not logically valid. What is paradoxical about the logical fallacies is that there seem to be many for which there are instances that seem to be perfectly good arguments. Indeed this point extends to a whole range of what are typically called *informal*

---

[3] There is a potentially important distinction between valid but unsound inferences with true premises and inferences with false premises that are unsound. It has been argued (Ferguson, 2003) that the defeasibility revealed by violations of strengthening the antecedent is not problematic because the violations are instances where the premises are strictly false, for example, it is known that not all birds fly. However, the paradoxes of material implication, as we will see, seem to be instances where not only is the inference intuitively unsound, but the premises are also considered true.

reasoning fallacies in logic text books (e.g., Copi & Cohen, 1990). Although people have been warned against committing these fallacies since Aristotle's *Sophistical refutations*, examples continue to crop up that seem like perfectly convincing arguments. We suggest that a probabilistic notion of argument strength allows instances of fallacies that are convincing to be distinguished from instances that are not convincing.

The upshot of all these arguments is not to deny that people possess some understanding of deductive validity, but rather to establish that in determining human inferential behaviour, argument strength is the more central concept. Thus, in the conclusion, we point out, by considering some recent approaches in AI, that without some structure it would not be possible to appropriately transmit inductive strengths from the premises to the conclusions of complex arguments. Consequently, deductive correctness and inductive strength should be seen as working together rather than as independent systems.

1. TWO SYSTEMS OF REASONING

If deductive correctness and inductive strength are psychologically one and the same thing, then it would be expected that deductive correctness should track inductive strength. However, when people are asked to rate inferences for deductive correctness or inductive strength, they do not seem to be treating deductive correctness simply as at the extreme end of a scale of inductive strength. Rips (2001) had participants categorize arguments as deductively correct or not and as inductively strong or not. The arguments fully crossed deductive correctness with causal consistency. If deductive correctness were simply the extreme end of the scale of inductive strength, then there should be a monotone relationship between these judgements. However, this relationship was violated in Rips' data. This was revealed by a cross-over interaction. Participants judged deductively correct but causally inconsistent arguments to be deductively correct more often than they judged them to be inductively strong. However, participants judged deductively incorrect but causally consistent arguments to be inductively strong more often than they judged them to be deductively correct.

Rips (2001, 2002) interprets these results as arguing against *reasoning imperialism*, that is, the tendency to generalise either the *inductive-strength* view or the *deductive-correctness* view outside their proper domains. So, for example, proponents of the probabilistic view (e.g., Oaksford & Chater, 1998, 2001) seem to regard most inference as reflecting a probabilistic judgement, that is, they seem to endorse inductive strength as the sole measure of an inference. Similarly, proponents of mental-models theory (Johnson-Laird, 1994, 1999) adopt a logical approach to inductive inference and probability judgement. Assessing probabilities or inductive strength is based on the proportion of possible states of the world, or "mental models," in which a proposition is true.

We first observe that although we have argued for the importance of inductive strength in assessing arguments in the past, this has usually been as a corrective to the commonly held view that it was all deduction. The possibility that people have mechanisms for evaluating deductive correctness has been conceded in several places. For example, Chater and Oaksford (1999) argued that in syllogistic reasoning, while possible conclusions may be generated by probabilistic heuristics, these may then be tested by processes that assess deductive correctness.

However, in a recent paper (Oaksford & Chater, 2002) we posed the question, "How much deduction is there?" and our response, after surveying several possible ways of answering this question, was "very little". It is important to bear in mind that our concerns have always been with the kinds of inferences that people could be expected to routinely perform in their everyday lives. *Thus while people may well be capable of assessing deductive correctness when explicitly asked to, this is rarely, if ever, their focus of interest in evaluating an argument* – unless they are mathematicians or logicians.

We argue that Rips (2001) does not provide a strong test of whether deductive correctness and inductive strength dissociate. We concentrate on two cases. The first is the case of a deductively incorrect but inductively strong argument, where we argue that the case for a dissociation is weak. This is because the materials for this case did not provide any plausible logical structure. The second is the case of a deductively correct but inductively weak argument, where we argue that there is a much stronger case for a dissociation. However, it could not be observed because of the restricted range of arguments used.

1.1 Deductively Incorrect and Inductively Strong Arguments

We assume the standard of deductive correctness intended by Rips (2001) is standard truth-functional propositional logic, as can be found in most undergraduate texts (e.g., Enderton, 1972). As we will argue in the next section, this choice is important, but it goes uncommented on in Rips (2001). The case where the dissociation was at its most extreme in Rips (2001) was the deductively incorrect but causally consistent cases, for example

Car X10 runs into a brick wall (4)
Car X10 stops

The premise above the line does not logically entail the conclusion below the line, but the probability of the conclusion given the premise is high because it is causally consistent. In constructing the deductively incorrect but causally consistent cases, Rips (2001) used four inference forms, *modus ponens* (*if p then q, p*, therefore *q*), conjunctive syllogism (*not*[*p and q*], *p*, therefore *not q*), disjunctive syllogism (*p or q, not p*, therefore *q*), and conjunction elimination (*p and q*, therefore *q*). The example in (4) was explicitly presented as the deductively incorrect but causally consistent case for *modus ponens*. The deductively correct and causally consistent case included the major premise, *if Car X10 runs into a brick wall, then Car X10 stops.*

The premises in examples like (4) *have no logical structure*, at least not at the propositional level that we are considering. So invocations such as, "Considering just the form of the sentences (and not their specific content), does this form ensure that if the sentences above the line are true so is the sentence below the line?" (Rips, 2001, p. 131)[4] seem misplaced – the sentences above the line do not have any "form" relevant to answering this question. Nonetheless, around *35% of participants rated these cases as deductively correct*, which was well above chance. This level of error did not change when participants were asked this question in two slightly different ways, which emphasised certainty rather than form. However, regardless of the question posed, this level of error seems too high to support the claim that people are sensitive to logical form.

In Rips (2001) the critical deductively incorrect and causally consistent cases were constructed for the other inference forms, except in the case of *conjunction elimination*,[5] in the same way as for *modus ponens* (Rips *personal communication*). That is, the major premise of the deductively correct and causally consistent case was left out. Considering how these cases could have been constructed, while retaining some logical structure in the premises, suggests an alternative explanation for the strong differentiation between judgements of deductive correctness and causal consistency for these cases. Let us take conjunctive syllogism as an example. Rips's (2001) paper gives the impression that these cases were constructed with the same substitution instances for *p* and *q*. However, this would have the consequence that the deductively correct and causally consistent case is actually causally inconsistent:

Not(*Car X10 runs into a brick wall and Car X10 stops*)   (5)
Car X10 runs into a brick wall
Car X10 does not stop

---

4 This question is also highly ambiguous as not even experts agree on the "form" of English sentences. So exactly what participants understood from this instruction is unclear.

5 For conjunction elimination, p and q therefore q, the following argument form was used as the logically incorrect and causally consistent case, p therefore p and q. That is, rather than omit a major premise a conjunct was removed again, leading to an unstructured premise.

Consequently, Rips (2001) replaced *Car X10 stops* with *Car X10 speeds on*. The conclusion is then that *Car X10 does not speed on*, which is causally consistent with the minor premise. Constructing the deductively incorrect but causally consistent case, while retaining some logical structure, could be achieved by using the premises in (5) but reversing the polarity of the conclusion, that is, *Car X10 stops*. The problem about (5), even with this substitution, is that the major premise seems to express a causally inconsistent proposition. One of the other facts about *Car X10* that seems to have to be true when it hits a wall is that it stops, but the major premise denies this (assuming that there is only one *Car X10* and that the two conjuncts are indexed to the same space-time location). Similar arguments apply for *modus ponens* and *disjunctive syllogism*. These considerations suggest that including some logical structure for the deductively incorrect but casually consistent cases would appear to have to introduce some level of causal inconsistency.

Despite the absence of logical structure for the deductively incorrect and causally consistent cases in Rips (2001), 35% of these arguments were judged deductively correct. We believe that a proper test of the hypothesis would have to involve using materials like (5) but with the reversed polarity conclusion for the deductively incorrect but causally consistent cases. We suspect that the additional structure may lead to *more* judgements of deductive correctness while the presence of a causally inconsistent major premise may lead to *fewer* judgements of causal consistency. The combined effect would be to reduce the gap between these two types of judgements found by Rips (2001, see also Heit & Rotello, 2005[6]). In sum, the way the deductively incorrect but causally consistent cases were constructed seems to beg the question against the unitary view. Thus, we don't interpret the existing evidence using the Rips (2001) paradigm as convincing evidence against a unitary view.

In this section we have concentrated on arguments that are deductively incorrect but inductively strong and argued that these may be more closely aligned than Rips (2001) might lead one to expect. In the next section, we concentrate on arguments that are deductively strong but inductively weak.

---

[6] Heit and Rotello (2005) used similar materials to Rips (2001) but used abstract material (Experiment 1) and analysed their results using signal detection theory. The results were similar to Rips (2001). Heit and Rotello's (2005) Experiment 2 used quantified statements where class inclusion (all birds have property A, therefore robins have property A) was respected or violated (premise and conclusion inverted). While these results are interesting, our feeling is that they tell us most about the semantics/pragmatics of the words "necessary" and "plausible," where it has been known for some time that they don't neatly carve up some underlying probability scale (see Dhami & Wallsten, (2005); Rapoport, Wallsten, & Cox, 1987; Wallsten, Budescu, Rapoport, Zwick, & Forsyth, 1986).

1.2 Deductively Correct and Inductively Weak Arguments

Rips (2001) also provides *a priori* arguments for why, when the probability of the conclusion given the premise is 1, the argument is not necessarily deductively correct – although if it is deductively correct this probability must be 1. We now suggest that some deductively correct arguments may actually have an inductive strength of 0. Moreover, we argue that this is appropriate because they are universally agreed to be poor arguments.

Sensitivity to deductive correctness can't really be assessed by asking participants to evaluate just a few inferences. Deductive systems come as packages and prescribe a whole range of inferences while proscribing others. This point raises two questions. First, what is the deductive system that provides the standard of deductive correctness in Rips's (2001) experiments? Second, given this system, for how many inferences licensed by that system do deductive correctness and inductive strength dissociate? Clearly if it is only for a few inferences, then the imperialist thesis is not threatened very much.

In the last section, we assumed that the standard of deductive correctness intended in Rips (2001) was standard propositional logic. However, Rips's (1994) PSYCOP system is slightly different[7] but shares most properties with standard logic. In particular, standard propositional and predicate logic and Rips's (1994) system are truth conditional and truth functional. That is, the meaning of a simple proposition, p, is equivalent to the conditions that make it true in the world. The meaning of more complex propositions, for example, p *and* q, is a function of the truth values of the constituent propositions, that is, p *and* q is true only when both p is true and q is true, otherwise it is false. However, the study of *deductive logic* and thus what we mean by "deductive correctness" goes beyond this truth-functional core.

The concept of a deductive logic is very general. We can regard a logic as a pair $\langle L, \models \rangle$ consisting of a language L and a consequence relation $\models$ (Scott, 1971). All pairs of formulae (or sequences of formulae) such that $\phi \models \varphi$ define the consequence relation. Two questions arise about the resulting logic – (1) can a procedure be defined for deriving φ from ϕ? and (2) is there an efficient implementation of that procedure once defined? Any pair of formulae (or sequences of formulae) such that $\phi \models \varphi$ define a deductively correct inference *with respect to that language and to that consequence relation*. Thus the concept of deductive correctness is a *relative* concept, although in the psychology of reasoning only standard truth-functional logic is usually intended when an argument is described as deductively valid or "correct."

---

[7] Not all inferences with conditionals licensed by standard logic are provable in Rips's (1994) system, but all inferences provable in Rips system are classically valid.

Some deductive systems preserve the truth-functional core, for example, systems of *modal* logic (Hughes & Cresswell, 1968), but some systems abandon parts of it for some connectives. In particular, in most interesting systems of *conditional logic* (Nute, 1984; Bennett, 2003) the conditional is not truth functional (Lewis, 1973; Stalnaker, 1968), and in some it is neither truth functional nor truth conditional (Adams, 1975, 1998). Indeed, looked at from a *dynamic* perspective (see next section), the Adams conditional *can be meaningfully assessed only for inductive strength*. The general point is that the question of whether people are sensitive to "deductive correctness" is much more difficult to answer than Rips (2001) suggests. There are many possible logics, many of which are yet to be explored. One could never exclude the possibility that one of these will map perfectly onto people's judgements of deductive correctness.

Nonetheless, one thing we can be reasonably sure of is that people are unlikely to regard deductive correctness *in standard logic* as a particularly intuitive or useful way to assess arguments. Rips (2001) only used inference patterns from the truth-functional core of standard logic and avoided any of the more complex arguments involving conditionals, that is, only *modus ponens* was used. However, there are a range of arguments involving conditionals that are deductively correct according to standard logic. It can only really be argued that people are sensitive to deductive correctness in standard logic, if they judged *all* of these arguments to be deductively correct. However, the psychology of deductive reasoning has shown that human deductive reasoning performance rarely matches up to standard logic. In mental models and mental logic, the deviations are then explained at the performance level, that is, resource limitations on working memory exclude our ability to assess some inferences. This means that the question has always been one of degree—do people conform to standard logic *enough* to argue that they are sensitive to deductive correctness in this logic? Rips (2001) uses very simple deductive arguments to argue for an affirmative answer. However, as we now show, there are equally simple deductively correct arguments in standard logic that people certainly *should* not endorse.

For example, here are two argument forms that are simple, one-premise, deductively correct inferences in standard logic:

$$\frac{\neg p}{\therefore p \to q} \quad \frac{q}{\therefore p \to q} \tag{6}$$

If the material conditional of standard logic is regarded as the proper interpretation of the conditional of everyday language, then either argument form can lead to conclusions like *if the moon is made of cheese, then Tony Blair is*

Prime Minister. This is because in standard logic the material conditional is true if the antecedent is false or the conclusion is true. So in both cases, if the premise is true – the moon is not made of cheese or Tony Blair is Prime Minister – then the conclusion must also be true. We doubt that anyone would judge these as deductively correct. These are the *paradoxes of material implication,* and unless people endorse these inferences as deductively correct, it can not be claimed that people are sensitive to standard deductive validity for the conditional.

We now suggest that the reason why the arguments in (6) are paradoxical is that, despite being deductively correct, they are inductively weak. That is, the mismatch with argument strength explains their paradoxical nature and also confirms that it is argument strength that is the dominant factor in evaluating arguments. In the introduction, we proposed identifying the probability of a conditional with the conditional probability, that is,

$$P(p \rightarrow q) = P(q|p), \text{ where } P(p) > 0 \qquad (7)$$

Edgington (1991) refers to (7) as simply "The Equation." $P(q|p)$ is given by the *Ratio formula* (Bennett, 2003, proposed this name; "$\wedge$" is the logical symbol for *and*):

$$P(q|p) = \frac{P(p \wedge q)}{P(p)} \qquad (8)$$

The Ratio formula suggests that people should "believe $p \rightarrow q$ to the extent that you think that $p \wedge q$ is nearly as likely as p" (Edgington, 1991, p. 189). So when $P(p) = 0$, you should not accept $p \rightarrow q$, as $P(q|p)$ is 0 or undefined (see Bennett, 2003). Thus if $P(p) = 0$, then the inferences in (7) should be regarded as maximally inductively weak, as either $P(\text{conclusion}|\text{premises}) = 0$ or they can't be assigned an inductive strength at all (see Bennett, 2003). Thus, the paradoxes of material implication are deductively correct but inductively weak. Our guess is that for these conditional inferences, judgements of deductive correctness would track inductive strength. Moreover, given their paradoxical nature, they *should* track inductive strength.

In this section, we have argued that the claim that people are sensitive to deductive correctness is difficult to assess given the generality of the concept of a logical system. We pointed out that there were several *conditional logics,* most of which, unlike standard logic, are not truth functional. These systems define a range of inferences that are deductively correct. We argued that only if people judged them all as deductively correct could it be argued that people are sensitive to deductive correctness for the conditional for that logic. We then examined the paradoxes of material implication. It seems unlikely that people would regard these as deductively correct, and that is why they are regarded as *paradoxes*. However, these turned out to be inductively weak, which explains their paradoxical status.[8]

In the next section, we explore psychological accounts of the conditional more fully. In particular, we look at recent accounts of the psychological data based on Adams's (1975, 1998) *probability conditional*. Following some recent proposals (Oaksford, 2005), we suggest that not only are conditionals assessed for inductive strength in psychological experiments, but inductive learning processes may also be invoked in assessing conditional inferences. We also evaluate the inductive strength of the conditional arguments usually investigated in the psychology of reasoning.

2. CONDITIONAL INFERENCE

Along with many other researchers (e.g., Anderson, 1995; Chan & Chua, 1994; George, 1997; Liu, 2003; Liu, Lo, & Wu, 1996; Politzer, 2005; Stevenson & Over, 1995), we have recently been arguing for an account of conditional inference based on inductive strength (Oaksford & Chater 2007; Oaksford & Chater, 1998, 2001, 2003a–d; Oaksford, Chater, & Larkin, 2000). The main assumption underlying this approach, as we discussed in the introduction and in the last section, is that the probability of a conditional is the conditional probability, that is, see (7) above. This assumption is at the heart of Adams's (1975, 1998) account of the *probability conditional*. However, in that account the Ratio formula (8) is not definitional of conditional probability. People's understanding of $P(q|p)$ is given by the subjective interpretation provided by the *Ramsey test*. As Bennett (2003) says:

> The best definition we have [of conditional probability] is the one provided by the Ramsey test: your conditional probability for q given p is the probability for q that results from adding $P(p) = 1$ to your belief system and conservatively adjusting to make room for it (p. 53).

The Ratio formula indicates that in calculating the probability of the everyday conditional, all that matters are the probabilities of the true antecedent cases, that is, $P(p \wedge q)$ and $P(p \wedge \neg q)[P(p) = P(p \wedge q) + P(p \wedge \neg q)]$. This contrasts immediately with standard logic where the probability of a conditional is given by the probability of the cases that make it true, that is, $P(p \rightarrow q) = P(\neg p) + P(p, q)$. Evans et al. (2003) and Oberauer and Wilhelm (2003) have confirmed that people interpret the probability of the

---

[8] Although, as we discuss later (in the paragraph before Section 2.1), this is not the only possible response. In some non-classical logics, the paradoxes are also not valid inferences.

conditional as the conditional probability and not the probability suggested by standard logic.

(7) has the important consequence that the *probability conditional* is not truth functional and it is not truth conditional either, that is, conditionals are not propositions that can have a truth value. If they were propositions, then asking about their probability, $P(p \to q)$, would be equivalent to asking about the probability that $p \to q$ is *true*. But from (7), $P(p \to q) = P(q|p)$, and so the question being asked is what is the probability that $q|p$ is true. However, "$q|p$" is not a claim about the world, that is, it doesn't make sense to ask whether this is true or false. According to the Ramsey test, this expression relates to a mental process, not a fact about the world that could be true or false.[9]

If indicative conditionals do not have truth values, then it would seem impossible to define any valid inferences that follow from them. An inference is classically valid if the *truth* of the premises guarantees the *truth* of the conclusion. However, while classical validity is therefore impossible for arguments involving conditionals, they may possess another virtue, *probabilistic validity* or *p-validity*. Adams (1975) discovered that most classically valid arguments also possess a property that can best be formulated using the concept of *uncertainty*. The uncertainty of a proposition p, $U(p)$, is simply $1 - P(p)$. The property he discovered was that for many "*classically valid argument*[s] *the uncertainty of the conclusion cannot exceed the sum of the uncertainties of the premises*" (Bennett, 2003, p. 131). That is,

$$\text{If } p_1 \dots p_n \text{ entail } q, \text{ then } U(q) \le \sum_{i=1}^{n} U(p_i) \qquad (9)$$

Adams (1975) calls an argument fulfilling this condition *p-valid*. Arguments containing indicative conditionals, while not candidates for classical validity, may be *p*-valid and so can be evaluated on that basis.

---

[9] These considerations place constraints on the way conditionals can be embedded in truth-functional compound sentences (Lewis, 1976). However, there is linguistic evidence that the constraints on embeddings recommended by the probability conditional may be reflected in natural languages (Bennett, 2003). Bennett (2003) argues that this linguistic fact seems to disarm some of the strongest criticisms of the Equation due to Lewis (1976).

This thesis may also seem to violate intuitions that conditionals such as "if a steam roller runs over this teacup, it will break" and "if Lincoln visited Gettysburg, then he delivered a speech there" are determinately true. The issues highlighted by examples like these relate to how conditionals and the predicate "true" are used in natural language. It is possible that the teacup does not break (as it is made of titanium, i.e., it just bends a bit). Moreover, only someone who knew Lincoln gave the Gettysburg address would be in a position to affirm this conditional, but, given this knowledge, why would they ever have grounds to assert this conditional? "True" might also be used in natural language to mean a probability infinitesimally different, but still different, from 1 (Pearl, 1988).

All p-valid arguments are classically valid, but not all classically valid arguments are p-valid. For example, as we have seen, the paradoxes of material implication (6) are not p-valid, that is, they can be inductively weak. Strengthening of the antecedent (3) also turns out not to be p-valid. Although it makes sense to assign a high probability to *if Tweety is a bird, then Tweety can fly*, because most birds fly, anyone would assign a very low probability, that is, 0, to *if Tweety is a bird and Tweety is one second old, then Tweety can fly* (how old Tweety is can be adjusted to produce probabilities for the conclusion that are greater than 0). Thus the uncertainty of the conclusion, that is, 1, is greater than the uncertainty of the premise – it is an inductively weak argument. So the probability conditional is defeasible or *non-monotonic* at its very foundation.

P-validity holds for an argument form or schemata. For example, if it is p-valid, there can be no instances where (9) is violated. Inductive strength applies to particular arguments, that is, content matters. So for example, if "*is one second old*" were replaced with "*is green*," then this instance of strengthening the antecedent might be viewed as inductively strong.[10] Strengthening of the antecedent nonetheless is not p-valid because (9) does not hold for all instances of this inference, that is, (9) does not hold in all models of the premises. An instance of a p-valid inference may also be inductively weak. For example, in a *modus ponens* inference, someone may be maximally uncertain about whether *birds fly* and whether *Tweety is a bird*, that is, the probability of both premises is .5. As we will see later, the probability of the conclusion is therefore .25. That is, although (9) is not violated, this is an inductively weak argument, that is, the probability of the conclusion given the premises is low.

However, when it comes to conditionals, p-validity is perhaps not that interesting a concept, that is, it is useful only in the *static* case of fixed probability distributions. Conditionals in probability logic can also be looked at *dynamically*, that is, they allow people to update their beliefs (prior probability distributions) given new information. So if a high probability is assigned to *if x is a bird, x flys*, then on acquiring the new information that *Tweety is a bird*, one's degree of belief in *Tweety flys* should be revised to one's degree of belief in *Tweety flys given Tweety is a bird*, that is, my degree of belief in the conditional. So using P_0 to indicate *prior* degree of belief and P_1 to indicate *posterior* degree of belief, then:

$$P_1(q) = P_0(q \mid p), \text{ when } P_1(p) = 1. \tag{10}$$

---

[10] Although as "is green" seems totally irrelevant to the whether birds fly, this argument feels circular, that is, the conclusion is just a restatement of the premises. We look at argumentative fallacies, like circularity, in relation to an account of argument strength in Section 4.

This is exactly the formulation we used in the introduction to the chapter to illustrate evaluating an argument for inductive strength.

One possible consequence of moving to an account of the conditional that avoids the problems for standard logic, that is, the paradoxes, is an account of conditional inference based on inductive strength. This is not a necessary consequence of avoiding the paradoxes, as there other systems of conditional logic. For example, the Stalnaker conditional (Stalnaker, 1968), which is based on possible worlds, avoids the paradoxes but is not always consistent with the equation. Nonetheless, as we now show, an account based on inductive strength seems to resolve some fundamental issues in the psychology of conditional reasoning. Moreover, such an account may incorporate inductive processes (Oaksford & Chater 2007). Finally, there are relevant data that allow us to briefly compare two different accounts of inductive strength that appear in Rips (2001) and to which we have recently made appeal.

2.1 Inferential Asymmetries and Inductive Processes in "Deductive" Reasoning

Oaksford and Chater (2007) recently showed how the account of conditional inference based on inductive strength (Oaksford, Chater, & Larkin, 2000) was compatible with the dynamic view of inference in probability logic (Adams, 1998). Along with *modus ponens* (MP) and *modus tollens* (MT), psychologists have also investigated two other inference forms that are truth-functional fallacies, *denying the antecedent* (DA) and *affirming the consequent* (AC):

$$\frac{p \to q, \neg p}{\neg q}\text{(DA)} \quad \frac{p \to q, q}{p} \tag{AC}$$

The problem with applying the scheme for dynamic updating by conditionalization to inferences other than *modus ponens* is that the premises all involve the conditional *if p then q*. However, the appropriate conditional probability for, say, the categorical premise of a *modus tollens* inference, $P(\neg q) = 1$, to conditionalize on is $P(\neg p | \neg q)$, but the premises of this inference do not entail a value for this conditional probability.

Oaksford et al.'s (2000) solution to this problem was to assume that people's prior world knowledge included estimates of the prior marginal probabilities, $P_0(p)$ and $P_0(q)$. Oaksford & Chater (2007) then showed how with $P_0(q|p) = a$, $P_0(p) = b$ and $P_0(q) = c$, these probabilities entail relevant conditional probabilities for all four inferences:

MP $\quad P_1(q) = P_0(q|p) = a$ $\tag{11}$

DA $\quad P_1(\neg q) = P_0(\neg q | \neg p) = \dfrac{1 - c - (1 - a)b}{1 - b}$ $\tag{12}$

$$\text{AC} \quad P_1(p) = P_0(p|q) = \frac{ab}{c} \tag{13}$$

$$\text{MT} \quad P_1(\neg p) = P_0(\neg p|\neg q) = \frac{1 - c - (1 - a)b}{1 - c} \tag{14}$$

Equations (11) to (14) show the posterior probabilities of the conclusion of each inference, assuming the posterior probability of the categorical premise is 1. By using Jeffrey conditionalization, these cases can be readily generalized to when the probability of the categorical premise is less than 1. For example, for MP, assuming $P_1(p) = d$:

$$\text{MP} \ P_1(q) = P_0(q|p)P_1(p) = ad \tag{15}$$

(15) actually represents a lower bound on the posterior probability, with the upper bound at $ad + 1 - d$.

In studies investigating all four inferences, a significant asymmetry has been observed between *modus ponens* (1) and *modus tollens* (2), with (1) being endorsed considerably more than (2). Moreover, *affirming the consequent* is endorsed more than *denying the antecedent*. In most other psychological accounts, this latter asymmetry is explained as an instance of the asymmetry between (1) and (2) on the assumption that some people believe that *if p then q* pragmatically implicates its converse, *if q then p*. Oaksford, Chater, and Larkin (2000; Oaksford & Chater, 2003a, b) showed that as long $P_0(q|p)$ is less than 1, then (11) to (14) can generate these asymmetries. The precise magnitude of the asymmetries depend on the particular values of $P_0(q|p)$, $P_0(p)$, and $P_0(q)$.

However, no values of these probabilities are capable of generating the empirically observed magnitudes of the MP–MT and AC–DA asymmetries – the best fit values underestimate the former and overestimate the latter. Oaksford & Chater (2007) argued that this is related to perceived failures of what is called the *rigidity assumption* for conditionalization, which is that

$$P_1(q|p) = P_0(q|p) \tag{16}$$

This assumption is implicit in (15). This means that learning that the categorical premise has a particular posterior value does not alter the conditional probability. However, consider the following example for MT, where the conditional premise is *if you turn the key the car starts* and the categorical premise is *the car does not start*. What is odd about the assertion of the categorical premise is that it seems informative only in a context where the car was expected to start, and the only way one would normally expect a car to start was if the key had been turned. Consequently, the assertion of the categorical premise raises the possibility of a counterexample to the conditional.

In several recent approaches to conditional inference (e.g., Schroyens, Schaeken, & Handley, 2003; Quinn & Markovits, 2002), after reaching a tentative conclusion based on a mental-models representation, people search for a possible counterexample in long-term memory. If they find one, then they do not draw the inference. Oaksford & Chater (2007) proposed a probabilistic version of this account for *modus tollens*, where an initially high estimate of $P_0(q|p)$ is revised down by Bayesian revision on a single counterexample to derive a revised lower estimate for $P_0(q|p)$, $P_0^R(q|p)$. It is this value that is then used in (14) to calculate the relevant conditional probability to conditionalize on. A similar revision is not hypothesised to occur for MP, as this inference directly provides the appropriate conditional premise to conditionalize on.

How should the probability of the conditional be updated? Oaksford and Chater (2007) assumed that people's degree of belief in a conditional is determined by the evidence that they possess for a dependency between p and q and the evidence that they have that p and q are independent. The equation states that the degree of belief in the conditional, that is, the hypothesis that there is a dependency between p and q, should be equal to $P_0(q|p)$. Hence the degree of belief in the independence hypothesis is $1 - P_0(q|p)$. In the independence hypothesis $P_0(q|p) = P_0(q)$. Someone's new degree of belief in the conditional and consequently their revised estimate of $P_0(q|p)$, that is, $P_0^R(q|p)$, is the probability of the dependence model given the occurrence of a p, $\neg q$ case. This can be calculated by simple Bayesian revision. For example, assume that $P_0(q|p) = .97$ (as in a recent meta-analysis [Schroyens & Schaeken, 2003]), which is also the prior degree of belief assigned to the hypothesis of a dependency between p and q (by equation 7). A prior degree of belief of .03 is therefore assigned to the independence hypothesis. Then, assuming that $P_0(p) = .5$ and $P_0(q) = .6$, so in the independence hypothesis $P_0(q|p) = .6$, on updating, $P_0^R(q|p) = .71$. The revision is quite marked because a counterexample is so much more likely in the independence than in the dependence model. Moreover, using this value in (14), the conditional probability for MT, and so $P_1(\neg p)$, is .64. This revision process considerably increases the magnitude of the MP–MT asymmetry. Without the revision process, MP endorsement should be 97% and MT, 96.25%, that is, they should be endorsed in almost equal proportion. However, after revision the asymmetry is considerably greater, with MT endorsements falling to 64%.

In Schroyens and Schaeken's (2003) account, the retrieval of a possible counterexample falsifies the conditional and so means that the inference can not be valid. In the present *inductive* account the possibility of a counterexample revises one's degree of belief in the conditional by Bayesian updating, which in turn reduces the posterior degree of belief in the conclusion. Oaksford and Chater (2007) generalise this account to DA and AC and show how it provides a much better account of the MP–MT and AC–DA asymmetries. For example, using the same figure as in the above example, AC should be endorsed at 59% and DA at 51%. In sum, evaluating conditional inferences for inductive strength rather than deductive correctness gets round paradoxical problems for the standard logic of the conditional. Moreover, it provides a better account of the data by invoking inductive processes of Bayesian updating to cope with rigidity violations.

2.2 Measures of Argument Strength Applied to Conditional Inference

Rips (2001) actually introduces two different concepts of inductive strength, both of which Hahn, Oaksford, and Corner (2005) looked at independently as measures of *argument strength* to apply to reasoning fallacies more generally (see Section 3). The measure that features in the bulk of Rips's (2001) paper is the probability of the conclusion given the premises. However, in a footnote (Rips, 2001, p. 128, footnote 1), he considers another measure of argument strength:

$$Argument\ Strength = \frac{P(conclusion|premises) - P(conclusion)}{1 - P(conclusion)} \qquad (17)$$

This measure, which is called *conditional agreement* (Bishop, Feinberg, & Holland, 1975), has the advantage that it looks at the *change* in the probability of the conclusion brought about by the premises and scales this by how far someone needs to go to be convinced of the conclusion. As Rips (2001) observes, it is important to have a measure like this because otherwise arguments where the premises are irrelevant to the conclusion would not be assigned 0 argument strength but would be as strong as the prior probability of the conclusion.

In this section we apply different measures of argument strength to some data from a meta-analysis of conditional inference (Schroyens & Schaeken, 2003). This analysis consists of the data from sixty experiments on conditional inference conducted over the last thirty years and reports the frequency of endorsement of the MP, DA, AC, and MT inferences.[11] Recently, Oaksford and

---

[11] These studies all involved abstract material. Consequently, it could be argued that people have no prior beliefs to bring to bear. However, the conversational pragmatics of the situation, where the conditional is asserted, immediately suggest, via the Ratio formula, that $P_0(q|p)$ is high and so $P_0(p)$ is non-zero. In modelling these data Oaksford & Chater (2007) only assumed that $P_0(p)$ is maximally uncertain, that is, .5. Moreover, in general we believe that prior knowledge is always bought to bear analogically even on abstract materials, that is, perhaps only a small subset

Chater (2007) fitted the probabilistic model based on inductive strength, outlined in the last section, to the data from this meta-analysis. The observed probability of drawing each of the four inferences provides the measure of $P(conclusion|premises)$. The best-fit model parameters provide estimates of $P(conclusion)$, that is, the prior marginal probabilities, $P_0(p)$ and $P_0(q)$.

One theme that has emerged so far is the theoretical possibility that people may regard a particular instance of an inferential fallacy to be nonetheless inductively strong. In particular, they may regard them as being as inductively strong as some valid inferences. Rips's (2001) data does not address this issue because, as we have seen, his deductively incorrect arguments were not instances of classical logical reasoning fallacies, that is, the premises contained no relevant logical structure. By applying these measures of argument strength to these data, we can assess whether this possibility is observed empirically. But first, we introduce a problem for the measure of argument strength in (17) and introduce a measure that may get round it.

As a measure of argument strength, (17) has some counterintuitive properties. Consider an argument that moves someone from having a very low degree of belief in a conclusion, $P(conclusion) = .01$, to complete uncertainty, $P(conclusion) = .5$. Intuitively, this argument is stronger than one that moves someone from a high degree of belief in a conclusion, $P(conclusion) = .9$, to an even higher degree of belief in a conclusion, $P(conclusion) = .99$. However, according to (17), the argument strength of the former is .495, while that of the latter is .9. That is, counterintuitively, the second argument is by far the stronger of the two.

There are many different measures that might be useful as an index of argument strength, probably as many as there are indices of deviations from independence, that is, $P(conclusion|premises) = P(conclusion)$, of which Hattori and Oaksford (in press) recently counted at least forty. Hahn et al. (2005) suggested that the *likelihood ratio* may be a better measure of argument strength. The likelihood ratio maps the prior odds onto the posterior odds and so can also be calculated from $P(conclusion|premises)$ and $P(conclusion)$:

$$Likelihood\ Ratio = \frac{P(conclusion|premises)(1 - P(conclusion))}{P(conclusion)(1 - P(conclusion|premises))} \qquad (18)$$

Using (18) with the previous example, the argument strength of the first argument, taking someone from .01 to .5, is 93, whereas the argument strength of the second argument, taking someone from .9 to .99, is 11. So the likelihood ratio matches intuition in judging the first argument to be stronger than the

of exemplars of conditional relationships are accessed to provide rough and ready estimates of some of relevant parameters.

second. However, as the degree of conviction gets closer to 1 in the second argument, then this measure may reverse this pattern. Nonetheless, as long as non-extreme values are assumed, this measure seems to capture intuition. Hahn et al. (2005) mention some other advantages of the likelihood ratio but, like Rips (2001), do not attempt to decide the issue of which is the best measure, although they suggest that argument strength may be better viewed as a bi-dimensional concept, with $P(conclusion|premises)$ as one dimension and change, perhaps measured by the likelihood ratio, as the second.

What happens when these measures are used to estimate argument strength for the data from Schroyens and Schaeken's (2003) meta-analysis? In these data, the three measures, $P(conclusion|premises)$, conditional agreement (17), and the likelihood ratio (18), diverged on the ordering of argument strength over the four inferences. $P(conclusion|premises)$ is simply the endorsement rate of each inference in the data. Estimates of the prior probability of the conclusion, $P(conclusion)$, were derived from fitting the model in (11) to (14) to the data. For $P(conclusion|premises)$ the average ordering was MP (.97 [SD = .03]) > MT (.72[.14]) > AC (.60[.19]) > DA (.54[.17]), which agreed with the likelihood ratio, MP (2572 [3822]) > MT (3.69[2.78]) > AC (2.48[2.56]) > DA (2.26[1.17]). The extreme values of the likelihood ratio for MP occurred because for several experiments all participants endorsed this inference, which meant $P(conclusion|premises)$ was in the extreme range. Conditional agreement led to DA being ranked as a stronger argument than AC: MP (.92 [.13]) > MT (.44[.28]) > DA (.26[.23]) > AC (.21[.38]). That there is some disagreement about the strengths of the different arguments suggests that there is scope for experimental investigations discriminating between different accounts of argument strength. Participants would need to be asked not just how much they endorse the conclusion *but by how far the premises had altered their prior beliefs*, alternatively their prior beliefs, given the pragmatics of the task (see footnote 2) could be measured.

Are there experiments where the fallacies, AC or DA, are arguments as strong or stronger than the logically valid inferences? We concentrate on the relationship between the fallacies and MT because of the revision strategy we discussed above, where MP is evaluated with respect to $P_0(q|p)$, whereas MT and the fallacies are evaluated with respect to $P_0^R(q|p)$. According to the likelihood ratio, for 25% of the experiments, AC or DA was as strong or stronger than MT. The other two measures agreed on this analysis for all but one study. It could be argued that this pattern could arise because these are studies for which Oaksford and Chater's (2007) probabilistic model provides poor fits, and so the estimates of the prior marginal probabilities are inaccurate. This argument has some initial plausibility. However, two of the experiments had the poorest fits to the data and were technically outliers. With these experiments removed, the fit, measured by the co-efficient of variation R^2, did not differ significantly between the studies where AC or DA were stronger than MT (mean $R^2 = .92$, SD $= .07$) and the rest (mean $R^2 = .93$, SD $= .08$), $t(56) = .57$, $p = .57$.

It could also be argued that these results are not surprising because in other theories, like mental models (Johnson-Laird & Byrne, 2002) or versions of mental logic (Rips, 1994), AC can be drawn more often than MT. In these theories, this happens if the task rule is interpreted as a bi-conditional, in which case all four inferences are valid. However, *if p then q* does not logically entail *if and only if p then q*. Moreover, the simple alphanumeric stimuli used in the experiments in Schroyens and Schaeken's (2003) meta-analysis do not provide an appropriate context for the bi-conditional interpretation. Consequently, if people do interpret the rules in this way, they are still in error. There are some studies for which DA is drawn at least as often, if not more often, than MT, although, within a study, we doubt whether this effect was ever significant. This data can be interpreted as showing that some logical reasoning fallacies are regarded as at least as strong as deductively correct inferences (although the data is also consistent with the interpretation that people erroneously assume that the conditional implicates its converse). In the probabilistic account we introduced in the last section, DA can be endorsed more than MT when $P_0(p)$ is greater than $P_0(q)$, which is probabilistically consistent as long as $P_0(q|p)$ is not too high.

In this section, we have discussed alternative accounts of argument strength to which we think people may be sensitive. However, the appropriate experiment to judge between appropriate measures has not been conducted. This is because in standard conditional reasoning experiments, people are asked to judge only their absolute rate of endorsement of the conclusion, which is a function of both the prior, $P(conclusion)$, *and* the amount of change, $P(conclusion|premises) - P(conclusion)$, brought about by an argument. However, the analysis in this section did not show much discrimination between a measure of change, the likelihood ratio, and $P(conclusion|premises)$. This will require experiments where change is explicitly addressed and where people are not just asked *how much do you endorse a conclusion?* but also *how good an argument is it for you?*

We also observed that there are experiments where the argument strength associated with a reasoning fallacy was as high as that associated with a deductively correct inference. This is at least suggestive of a rather extreme dissociation between deductive correctness and argument strength that goes beyond that observed by Rips (2001). In Rips's data, no deductively incorrect argument was evaluated as of similar inductive strength to a deductively correct argument. Moreover, Rips's (2001) deductively incorrect arguments were not instances of logical reasoning fallacies. If people are genuinely sensitive to deductive correctness, it might have been hoped that they would have a facility to detect reasoning fallacies and so always evaluate them as significantly weaker than a deductively correct argument (although see Massey, 1981). In the next section, we show how we have recently used the concept of argument strength to provide a new analysis of a range of what have been called *informal reasoning fallacies*. These analyses extend our proposal that while people may well be capable of assessing deductive correctness when explicitly asked to, this is rarely, if ever, their focus of interest in evaluating an argument.

3. ARGUMENT STRENGTH AND INFORMAL REASONING FALLACIES

Fallacies, or arguments that seem correct but aren't, for example, DA and AC, have been a longstanding focus of debate. Catalogues of reasoning and argumentation fallacies originate with Aristotle and populate books on logic and informal reasoning to this day. The classic tool brought to the analysis of fallacies such as the argument from ignorance is formal logic, and it is widely acknowledged to have failed in providing a satisfactory account. Testament to this is the fact that fallacies figure in logic textbooks under the header of "informal reasoning fallacies" (see, e.g., Hamblin, 1970) – an acknowledgement of the inability to provide a sufficient formal logical treatment. In particular, logical accounts have proved unable to capture the seeming exceptions to fallacies that arise with simple changes in content that leave the structure of the argument unaffected. This suggests that either it is not formal aspects of fallacies that make them fallacious, or else that the relevant formal aspects are not being tapped into by classical logics.

Oaksford and Hahn (2004; see also Hahn & Oaksford, 2005; Hahn, Oaksford, & Bayindir, 2005; Hahn, Oaksford, & Corner, 2005) provide evidence of such variation and put forward an alternative, Bayesian account: individual arguments are composed of a conclusion and premises expressing evidence for that conclusion. Both conclusion and premises have associated probabilities which are viewed as expressions of subjective degrees of belief. Bayes's theorem then provides an update rule for the degree of belief associated with the conclusion in the light of the evidence. *Argument strength*, then, on this account is a function of the degree of prior conviction, the probability of evidence, and the relationship between the claim and the evidence, in particular how much more likely the evidence would be if the claim were true. That is, as in discussing conditional inference, different instances of argumentative fallacies may vary in argument strength, conceived of as the probability of the conclusion given the premises.

We now illustrate this approach by appeal to a particular informal reasoning fallacy: the argument from ignorance.

3.1 The Argument from Ignorance

A classic informal argument fallacy, which dates back to John Locke, is the so-called argument from ignorance, or *argumentum ad ignorantiam.*

Ghosts exist, because nobody has proven that they don't. (19)

This argument does indeed seem weak, and one would want to hesitate in positing the existence of all manner of things whose non-existence simply had not been proven, whether these be UFO's or flying pigs with purple stripes. However, is it really the general structure of this argument that makes it weak, and if so what aspect of it is responsible? Other arguments from negative evidence are routine in scientific and everyday discourse and seem perfectly acceptable:

This drug is safe, because no one has found any side effects. (20)

Should all arguments from negative evidence be avoided, or can a systematic difference between the two examples be recognized and explained?

A Bayesian account can capture the difference between (19) and (20) as we show below. Moreover, it can capture the difference between positive and negative evidence which allows one to capture the intuition that the positive argument (21) is stronger than the negative argument (22):

Drug A is toxic because a toxic effect was observed (positive argument). (21)

Drug A is not toxic because no toxic effects were observed (negative argument, i.e., the argument from ignorance). (22)

Though (22) too can be acceptable where a legitimate test has been performed, that is,

If drug A were toxic, it would produce toxic effects in legitimate tests.
Drug A has not produced toxic effects in such tests.
Therefore, A is not toxic.

Demonstrating the relevance of Bayesian inference for negative versus positive arguments involves defining the conditions for a legitimate test. Let e stand for an experiment where a toxic effect is observed and $\neg e$ stands for an experiment where a toxic effect is not observed; likewise let T stand for the hypothesis that the drug produces a toxic effect and $\neg T$ stand for the alternative hypothesis that the drug does not produce toxic effects. The strength of the argument from ignorance is given by the conditional probability that the hypothesis, T, is false given that a negative test result, $\neg e$, is found, $P(\neg T | \neg e)$. This probability is referred to as negative test validity. The strength of the argument we wish to compare with the argument from ignorance is given by positive test validity, that is, the probability that the hypothesis, T, is true given that a positive test result, e, is found, $P(T | e)$. These probabilities can be calculated from the sensitivity ($P(e | T)$) and the selectivity ($P(\neg e | \neg T)$) of the test and the prior belief that T is true ($P(T)$) using Bayes's theorem. Let n denote sensitivity, that is, $n = P(e | T)$, l denote selectivity, that is, $l = P(\neg e | \neg T)$, and h denote the prior probability of drug A being toxic, that is, $h = P(T)$, then,

$$P(T | e) = \frac{nh}{nh + (1 - l)(1 - h)} \tag{23}$$

$$P(\neg T | \neg e) = \frac{l(1 - h)}{l(1 - h) + (1 - n)h} \tag{24}$$

Sensitivity corresponds to the "hit rate" of the test and 1 minus the selectivity corresponds to the "false positive rate." There is a trade-off between sensitivity and selectivity which is captured in the receiver-operating characteristic curve (Green & Swets, 1966) and which plots sensitivity against the false positive rate (1 – selectivity). Where the criterion is set along this curve will determine the sensitivity and selectivity of the test.

Positive test validity is greater than negative test validity as long as the following inequality holds:

$$h^2(n - n^2) > (1 - h)^2(l - l^2) \tag{25}$$

Assuming maximal uncertainty about the toxicity of drug A, that is, $P(T) = .5 = h$, this means that positive test validity, $P(T | e)$, is greater than negative test validity, $P(\neg T | \neg e)$, when selectivity (l) is higher than sensitivity. As Oaksford and Hahn (2004) argue, this is often a condition met in practice for a variety of clinical and psychological tests. Therefore, in a variety of settings, positive arguments are stronger than negative arguments.[12]

Oaksford and Hahn (2004) also provide experimental evidence to the effect that positive arguments such as (21) are indeed viewed as more convincing than their negative counterparts under the conditions just described. The evidence from their experiment further shows that people are sensitive to manipulations in the amount of evidence (one versus fifty studies or tests) as predicted by the account. Finally, participants in their experiment displayed sensitivity to the degree of prior belief a character in a dialogue initially displayed toward the conclusion, as the Bayesian account predicts. This finding captures the "audience dependence" of argumentation assumed in the rhetorical research tradition (e.g., Perelman & Olbrechts-Tyteca, 1969).

Hahn, Oaksford, and Bayindir (2005) generalised this account to other versions of the argument from ignorance. One might still query whether the account just outlined amounts to a satisfactory treatment of the argument from ignorance. This is because the textbook example of the ghosts (19) differs from Oaksford and Hahn's (2004) experimental materials in one, possibly important way. The argument for ghosts involves not only negative evidence, but also a flip in polarity between evidence and conclusion: negative evidence is provided to support the *positive* existence of something. In other words the inference is of the form

$$not \text{ proven } (not \text{ exist}) \rightarrow \text{exist} \tag{26}$$

as opposed to merely

$$not \text{ proven } (\text{exist}) \rightarrow not \text{ exist} \tag{27}$$

The examples in Oaksford and Hahn (2004) arguably have the structure in (27), not the structure in (26). But it may be the opposite polarity case (26) that constitutes the true fallacy of the argument from ignorance.

Classical logic licenses an inference from $not(not\ p)$ to p, but not the inference underlying (26) which might be rendered as

$$not \text{ says } (not\ p) \rightarrow p \tag{28}$$

This is because when one has not said "*not p*," one can either have said "*p*" or not spoken about "*p*" at all. For example, in an argument one might defend oneself with the claim "I didn't say you were rude," which could be true either because one had specifically claimed the opposite or because one had not

---

[12] This means that people's criterion is set such that positive evidence counts more for a hypothesis than negative evidence counts against it.

mentioned rudeness at all. So maybe nothing at all can be inferred in such cases?

Hahn, Oaksford, and Bayindir (2005) established that (28) can be regarded as a strong argument by using a form of the argument from ignorance based on *epistemic closure* which is related to the negation-as-failure procedure in artificial intelligence (Clark, 1978). The case can be made with an informal example: imagine your colleagues at work are gathering for a staff picnic. You ask the person organizing the picnic whether your colleague Smith is coming, to which you receive the reply that "Smith hasn't said that he's not coming." Should this allow you to infer that he is in fact coming, or has he simply failed to send the required reply by e-mail? Your confidence that Smith will be attending will vary depending on the number of people that have replied. If you are told that no one has replied so far, assuming Smith's attendance seems premature; if by contrast you are told that everyone has replied, you would be assured of his presence. In between these two extremes your degree of confidence will be scaled: the more people have replied the more confident you will be. In other words, the epistemic closure of the database in question (the e-mail inbox of the organizer) can vary from no closure whatsoever to complete closure, giving rise to corresponding changes in the probability that *not says* (*not p*) does in fact suggest that *p*.

Hahn, Oaksford, and Bayindir's (2005) experiments confirmed that people are sensitive to variations in the epistemic closure of a database and that this affects their willingness to endorse argument like (28). Moreover, in their data, it was found that arguments like (28) can be regarded as even stronger than the standard negative evidence case (27). Therefore, as our example suggested, there would seem to be nothing in the structure of arguments like the Ghosts example that make them inherently unacceptable.

The real reason we consider negative evidence on ghosts to be weak, that is, why (19) is a weaker argument than (20), is because of the lack of sensitivity (ability to detect ghosts) we attribute to our tests as well as our low prior belief in their existence. That is, the weakness of this argument is due to the probabilistic factors that affect the strength of the argument, that is, $P(conclusion|premises)$. Hahn and Oaksford (2006) have shown how this account generalises to other inferential fallacies, such as circularity and the slippery slope argument.

In summary, in this section we have shown how the concept of argument strength can resolve the problem of why some instances of informal argument fallacies nonetheless seem like perfectly acceptable arguments that should rationally persuade an audience of the conclusion. This is the same problem that we investigated in microcosm in the section on conditional inference.

4. CONCLUSIONS

Rips (2001, 2002) suggested that recent proposals in the psychology of deductive reasoning seem to imply *reasoning imperialism*. That is, proponents of the view that people evaluate even deductive arguments for inductive or argument strength are interpreted as seeing no role for deductive correctness (e.g., Oaksford & Chater, 1998). Moreover, some researchers seem to be committed to the opposite point of view that deductive correctness can provide an account of inductive strength (Johnson-Laird, 1994; Johnson-Laird, Legrenzi, Girotto, Legrenzi, & Caverni, 1999). While we can not reply for the latter imperialists, we have attempted to reply for the former. However, as we have pointed out, we do not view ourselves as arguing for an imperialist position, and in concluding we will point out why. But first we summarise what we hope has been learnt from this discussion.

We first addressed Rips's (2001) paper. We showed that the data are perhaps not as convincing as they may first seem, because the examples of deductively incorrect and inductively strong arguments had no logical structure and yet up to 35% of participants identified them as deductively correct. Moreover, we argued that establishing the claim of sensitivity to deductive correctness can be established only for a whole logic and not by examining isolated inferences. We therefore looked at some other simple inferences that are valid in propositional logic, the implicit standard in Rips (2001), and showed that some are paradoxical, that is, they lead to intuitively unacceptable conclusions. That is, one would not want to reason according to this standard. We diagnosed the problem as a mismatch between argument strength and deductive correctness – if argument strength can be low for a deductively correct argument, it may be viewed as paradoxical. This is *prima facie* strong evidence for the primacy of argument strength.

We then looked at conditional inference in particular. We showed that *probability logic* (Adams, 1998) uses an account of inductive strength which resolves many of the paradoxes observed for standard deductive validity. Moreover, we showed how a dynamic view of inference in probability logic is consistent with Oaksford et al's. (2000) probabilistic account. This account also provides a better account of the data by invoking inductive processes of updating beliefs in the light of possible counterexamples. The possibility of counterexamples arises because of possible violations of the *rigidity condition* for conditionalization. We also evaluated the inductive strength of some conditional argument forms and showed that people judge some conditional reasoning fallacies to be as strong as a deductively correct inference. This should not be possible according to the account Rips defends based on standard logic where all deductively correct inferences must have maximal argument strength, that is, $P(conclusion|premises) = 1.$[13]

We finally showed that the concept of argument strength can be applied much more generally to the informal argument fallacies, such as the argument from ignorance, to resolve the paradox of why some instances of these fallacies seem perfectly acceptable and capable of rationally persuading someone of a conclusion. This again provides a strong argument for the centrality of argument strength in human reasoning and argumentation.

However, as we said in the introduction to the chapter, the upshot of all these arguments is not to deny that people possess some understanding of deductive validity, but rather to establish that in determining human inferential behaviour, argument strength is the more central concept. In AI knowledge representation, technical problems in developing tractable non-monotonic logics that adequately capture human inferential intuitions has provided the impetus for the development of alternative approaches that explicitly include some measure of the strength of an argument (Gabbay, 1996; Fox, 2003; Fox & Parsons, 1998; Pollock, 2001; Prakken & Vreeswijk, 2002). It is this inclusion that provides these systems with their nice default properties. These systems often address uncertainty and argument strength qualitatively rather than use the probability calculus. In some accounts (e.g., Pollock, 2001) argument strengths are assumed to range from 0 to ∞, whereas in others they are treated as qualitative categories with varying numbers of bins, for example, ++ , +, −, − − (Fox & Parsons, 1998; see also some of the work reviewed in Prakken & Vreeswijk, 2002). In the latter case, argument strengths can combine like multivalued truth tables. Some of these rules for combining qualitative argument strengths are consistent with the probability calculus (Fox & Parsons, 1998). One important aspect of these approaches is that most use logical entailment to determine whether a proposition is relevant to another proposition and so can transmit an element of argument strength from one to the other. These accounts illustrate an important fact that to build practical systems that track argument strength across complex arguments requires some account of structure.

These systems also raise other interesting questions that reasoning researchers probably need to address. For example, some of these systems are not consistent with the probability calculus. The reason is the apparently

---

[13] The reason this is not the case in probability logic is that the moment the Equation is accepted, one is outside the realm of classical or standard logic, in which the probability of a conditional is $P(\neg p) + P(p, q)$.

commonsense principle embodied in *Theophrastus's rule*: the strength that a chain of deductively linked arguments confers on the conclusion can not be weaker than the weakest link in the chain (Walton, 2004). This is a condition that can not be guaranteed by the probability calculus. Examples that seem to conform to Theophrastus' rule but not to the probability calculus have persuaded Walton (2004) and, for example, Pollock (2001) that a third form of reasoning should be countenanced in addition to deductive and inductive/statistical reasoning, that is, *plausibilist* reasoning.

In argumentation theory, it is well recognized that many fallacies are fallacies of relevance. For example, the *argumentum ad misericordiam*, that is, the appeal to pity, may be *relevant* to arguments about, for example, whether to make charitable donations despite the lack of a logical connection. This suggests that accounts of argumentative relevance that rely purely on logical consequence are unlikely to do justice to the concept of relevance required by a theory of informal argument. Similar arguments have been made with respect to relevance logics (Anderson & Belnap, 1970). The concept of relevance goes beyond logical entailment, even *relevant* entailment. For example, it is relevant to whether an animal has palpitations that it has a heart, but this is due to the causal structure of the world, not the logical relations between propositions (Oaksford & Chater, 1991; Veltman, 1986). In sum, existing theories of argumentation that transmit plausibilities via logical consequence relations may not capture all the ways in which relevance relations are established in argument. Possible alternatives include *informational relevance* in Bayesian networks (Pearl, 1988). However, such *networks* also rely on *structure* to get around the unconstrained nature of general probabilistic reasoning.

The relevance of these AI approaches to human cognition could be questioned. However, these attempts to provide computational accounts of reasoning processes do place constraints on the computations that must underpin human reasoning in the brain. The constraint on which they are unambiguous is that basing an account of inference on argument strength, probabilistic or not, is going to require an account of structure, logical or not. Consequently, given that most practical systems currently use logical entailment to transmit argument strengths, it seems best to view these notions as cognitively complementary. This view has the consequence that while most judgements of the acceptability of an argument are based on argument strength, people must also be sensitive to the deductive relations between propositions in order to appropriately transmit them in a passage of reasoning. Thus even if there are dissociable brain regions dedicated to deduction and induction (Goel, Gold, Kapur, & Houle, 1997; Osherson, Perani, Cappa, Schnur, Grassi, & Fazio,

1998), deductive correctness and inductive strength should generally be seen as working together rather than as independent systems.

References

Adams, E. W. (1975). *The logic of conditionals.* Dordrecht: Reidel.

Adams, E. W. (1998). *A primer of probability logic.* Stanford, CA: CSLI Publications.

Anderson, A. R., & Belnap, N. D. (1975). *Entailment: The logic of relevance and necessity,* Vol. 1, Princeton: Princeton University Press.

Anderson, J. R. (1995). *Cognitive psychology and its implications.* New York: W. H. Freeman.

Bennett, J. (2003). *A philosophical guide to conditionals.* Oxford: Oxford University Press.

Bishop, Y. M. M., Feinberg, S. E., & Holland, P. W. (1975). *Discrete multivariate analysis.* Cambridge, MA: MIT Press.

Chan, D., & Chua, F. (1994). Suppression of valid inferences: Syntactic views, mental models, and relative salience. *Cognition, 53,* 217–238.

Chater, N., & Oaksford, M. (1996). The falsity of folk theories: Implications for psychology and philosophy. In W. O'Donohue & R. F. Kitchener (Eds.), *The philosophy of psychology* (pp. 244–256). London: Sage Publications.

Chater, N., & Oaksford, M. (1999). The probability heuristics model of syllogistic reasoning. *Cognitive Psychology, 38,* 191–258.

Clark, K. L. (1978). Negation as failure. In H. Gallaire & J. Minker (Eds.), *Logic and databases* (pp. 293–322). New York: Plenum Press.

Copi, I. M., & Cohen, C. (1990). *Introduction to logic* (8th Ed.). New York: Macmillan Press.

Dhami, M. K., & Wallsten T. S. (2005). Interpersonal comparison of subjective probabilities: Towards translating linguistic probabilities. *Memory and Cognition, 33,* 1057–1068.

Edgington, D. (1991). The matter of the missing matter of fact. *Proceedings of the Aristotelian Society, Suppl. Vol. 65,* 185–209.

Evans, J. St. B. T., & Over, D. E. (2004). *If.* Oxford: Oxford University Press.

Evans, J. St. B. T., Handley, S. J., & Over, D. E. (2003). Conditionals and conditional probability. *Journal of Experimental Psychology: Learning, Memory, & Cognition, 29,* 321–335.

Enderton, H. (1972). *A mathematical introduction to logic.* New York: Academic Press.

Fox, J. (2003). Probability, logic and the cognitive foundations of rational belief. *Journal of Applied Logic, 1,* 197–224.

Fox, J., & Parsons, S. (1998). Arguing about beliefs and actions. In A. Hunter and S. Parsons (Eds.), *Applications of uncertainty formalisms (Lecture notes in artificial intelligence 1455)* (pp. 266–302). Berlin: Springer Verlag.

Gabbay, D. (1996). *Labelled deduction systems.* Oxford: Oxford University Press.

George, C. (1997). Reasoning from uncertain premises. *Thinking and Reasoning, 3,* 161–190.

Green, D. M., & Swets, J. A., (1966). *Signal detection theory and psychophysics.* New York: Wiley.

Hahn, U., & Oaksford, M. (2006). A Bayesian approach to informal argument fallacies. *Synthese, 152,* 207–236.

Hahn, U., Oaksford, M., & Bayindir, H. (2005). How convinced should we be by negative evidence? In B. Bara, L. Barsalou, and M. Bucciarelli (Eds.), *Proceedings of the 27th Annual Conference of the Cognitive Science Society* (pp. 887–892), Mahwah, NJ: Lawrence Erlbaum.

Hahn, U., Oaksford, M., & Corner, A. (2005). Circular arguments, begging the question and the formalization of argument strength. In A. Russell, T. Honkela, K. Lagus, & M. Pöllä, (Eds.), *Proceedings of AMKLC'05, International Symposium on Adaptive Models of Knowledge, Language and Cognition* (pp. 34–40), Espoo, Finland, June 2005.

Hamblin, C. L. (1970). *Fallacies.* London: Methuen.

Hattori, M., & Oaksford, M. (in press). Adaptive non-interventional heuristics for covariation detection in causal induction: Model comparison and rational analysis. *Cognitive Science.*

Heit, E., & Rotello, C. M. (2005). Are there two kinds of reasoning? In B. Bara, L. Barsalou, & M. Bucciarelli (Eds.), *Proceedings of the 27th Annual Conference of the Cognitive Science Society* (pp. 923–928). Mahwah, NJ: Lawrence Erlbaum.

Hughes, G. E., & Cresswell, M. J. (1968). *An introduction to modal logic.* London: Methuen.

Johnson-Laird, P. N., & Byrne, R. M. J. (1991). *Deduction.* Hove, Sussex: Lawrence Erlbaum.

Johnson-Laird, P. N., & Byrne, R. M. J. (2002). Conditionals: A theory of meaning, pragmatics, and inference. *Psychological Review, 109,* 646–678.

Johnson-Laird, P. N., Legrenzi, P., Girotto, V., Legrenzi, M. S., & Caverni, J. P. (1999). Naive probability: A mental model theory of extensional reasoning. *Psychological Review, 106*(1), 62–88.

Lewis, D. (1973). *Counterfactuals.* Oxford: Blackwell.

Lewis, D. (1976). Probabilities of conditionals and conditional probabilities. *Philosophical Review, 85,* 297–315.

Liu, I. M. (2003). Conditional reasoning and conditionalisation. *Journal of Experimental Psychology: Learning, Memory, & Cognition, 29,* 694–709.

Liu, I. M., Lo, K., & Wu, J. (1996). A probabilistic interpretation of "If-then." *Quarterly Journal of Experimental Psychology, 49A,* 828–844.

Massey, G. J. (1981). The fallacy behind fallacies. *Midwest Studies in Philosophy, 6,* 489–500.

Nute, D. (1984). Conditional logic. In D. Gabbay & F. Guenthner (Eds.), *Handbook of philosophical logic,* Vol. 2 (pp. 387–439). Dordrecht: Reidel.

Oaksford, M., & Chater, N. (1991). Against logicist cognitive science. *Mind & Language, 6,* 1–38.

Oaksford, M., & Chater, N. (1994). A rational analysis of the selection task as optimal data selection. *Psychological Review, 101,* 608–631.

Oaksford, M., & Chater, N. (1996). Rational explanation of the selection task. *Psychological Review, 103,* 381–391.

Oaksford, M., & Chater, N. (1998). *Rationality in an uncertain world: Essays on the cognitive science of human reasoning.* Hove, Sussex: Psychology Press.

Oaksford, M., & Chater, N. (2001). The probabilistic approach to human reasoning. *Trends in Cognitive Sciences, 5,* 349–357.

Oaksford, M. & Chater, N. (2002). Commonsense reasoning, logic and human rationality. In R. Elio (Ed.), *Common sense, reasoning and rationality* (pp. 174–214). Oxford: Oxford University Press.

Oaksford, M., & Chater, N. (2003a). Computational levels and conditional reasoning: Reply to Schroyens and Schaeken (2003). *Journal of Experimental Psychology: Learning, Memory, & Cognition, 29,* 150–156.

Oaksford, M., & Chater, N. (2003b). Conditional probability and the cognitive science of conditional reasoning. *Mind & Language, 18,* 359–379.

Oaksford, M., & Chater, N. (2003c). Modeling probabilistic effects in conditional inference: Validating search or conditional probability? *Revista Psychologica, 32,* 217–242.

Oaksford, M., & Chater, N. (2003d). Probabilities and pragmatics in conditional inference: Suppression and order effects. In D. Hardman & L. Macchi (Eds.), *Thinking: Psychological perspectives on reasoning, judgment and decision making* (pp. 95–122). Chichester, UK: John Wiley & Sons.

Oaksford, M., & Chater, N. (2003e). Optimal data selection: Revision, review and re-evaluation. *Psychonomic Bulletin & Review, 10,* 289–318.

Oaksford, M., & Chater, N. (2007). *Bayesian rationality: The probabilistic approach to human reasoning.* Oxford: Oxford University Press.

Oaksford, M., Chater, N., & Larkin, J. (2000). Probabilities and polarity biases in conditional inference. *Journal of Experimental Psychology: Learning, Memory & Cognition, 26,* 883–899.

Oaksford, M., & Hahn, U. (2004). A Bayesian approach to the argument from ignorance. *Canadian Journal of Experimental Psychology, 58,* 75–85.

Oberauer, K., & Wilhelm, O. (2003). The meaning of conditionals: Conditional probabilities, mental models, and personal utilities. *Journal of Experimental Psychology: Learning, Memory, & Cognition, 29,* 321–335.

Osherson, D., Perani, D., Cappa, S., Schnur, T., Grassi, F., & Fazio, F. (1998). Distinct brain loci in deductive vs. probabilistic reasoning. *Neuropsychologica, 36,* 369–376.

Pearl, J. (1988). *Probabilistic reasoning in intelligent systems: Networks of plausible inference.* San Mateo, CA: Morgan Kaufman.

Perelman, C., & Olbrechts-Tyteca, L. (1969). *The new rhetoric: A treatise on argumentation.* Notre Dame, IN: University of Notre Dame Press.

Politzer, G. (2005). Uncertainty and the suppression of inferences. *Thinking and Reasoning, 11,* 5–34.

Pollock, J. L. (2001). Defeasible reasoning with variable degrees of justification. *Artificial Intelligence, 133,* 233–282.

Prakken, H., & Vreeswijk, G. A.W. (2002). Logics for defeasible argumentation. In D. M. Gabbay & F. Guenthner (Eds.), *Handbook of philosophical logic,* 2nd ed., Vol. 4 (pp. 219–318). Dordrecht: Kluwer Academic Publishers.

Quinn, S., & Markovits, H. (2002). Conditional reasoning with causal premises: Evidence for a retrieval model. *Thinking and Reasoning, 8,* 179–19.

Rapoport, A., Wallsten, T. S., & Cox, J. A. (1987). Direct and indirect scaling of membership functions of probability phrases. *Mathematical Modelling, 9,* 397–417.

Rips, L. J. (1994). *The psychology of proof.* Cambridge, MA: MIT Press.

Rips, L. J. (2001a). Two kinds of reasoning. *Psychological Science, 12,* 129–134.

Rips, L. J. (2001b). Reasoning imperialism. In R. Elio (Ed.), *Common sense, reasoning, and rationality* (pp. 215–235). Oxford University Press.

Rips, L. J. (2002). Reasoning. In H. F. Pashler (Series Ed.) and D. L. Medin (Vol. Ed.), *Stevens' handbook of experimental psychology: Vol. 2. Cognition* (3rd Ed.). New York: Wiley.

Schroyens, W., & Schaeken, W. (2003). A critique of Oaksford, Chater, and Larkin's (2000) conditional probability model of conditional reasoning. *Journal of Experimental Psychology: Learning, Memory, & Cognition, 29,* 140–149.

Schroyens, W. J., Schaeken, W., & Handley, S. (2003). In search of counter-examples: Deductive rationality in human reasoning. *Quarterly Journal of Experimental Psychology, 56A,* 1129–1145.

Scott, D. (1971). On engendering an illusion of understanding. *The Journal of Philosophy, 68,* 787–807.

Skyrms, B. (1975). *Choice and chance* (2nd Ed.). Belmont, CA: Wadsworth.

Stalnaker, R. C. (1968). A theory of conditionals. In N. Rescher (Ed.), *Studies in Logical Theory* (pp. 98–113). Oxford: Blackwell.

Stevenson, R. J., & Over, D. E. (1995). Deduction from uncertain premises. *Quarterly Journal of Experimental Psychology, 48 A,* 613–643.

Veltman, F. (1985). Logics for conditionals. PhD. Thesis, Faculteit der Wiskunde en Natuurwetenschappen, University of Amsterdam.

Wallsten, T. S., Budescu, D. V., Rapoport, A., Zwick, R., & Forsyth, B. (1986). Measuring the vague meanings of probability terms. *Journal of Experimental Psychology: General, 115,* 348–365.

Walton, D. N. (2004). *Relevance in argumentation.* Mahwah, NJ: Lawrence Erlbaum.

12

Individual Differences, Dual Processes, and Induction

Aidan Feeney

In this chapter I hope to demonstrate that answering the question "*who* does *what* in reasoning experiments?" can also help us answer fundamental questions about the nature of thought. Because it is nearly always the case that some experimental participants display phenomena of interest and others don't, almost every experiment run by cognitive psychologists produces data on individual differences. But, as most psychologists do not wish to take differences between their participants as the starting point of their investigations, individual differences tend to be ignored. Thus, the means that experimental psychologists report when they describe their data abstract across differences between individuals, with only the standard deviation or standard error indicating the extent to which participants varied in their responses. In this chapter I will address what the study of differences between individuals might tell us about a range of issues in inductive reasoning, including what constitutes a good inference, what processes underlie induction, and how induction differs from deduction.

My primary focus will be on the general question of how individual-differences data support dual-process theories of thinking (Evans & Over, 1996; Stanovich, 1999; Sloman, 1996). Dual-process theories have been applied to deduction, decision making, and induction. I will outline the dual-process approach and describe evidence in its favour, paying particular attention to individual differences. I will also describe how individual-differences methodology has been used to arbitrate between different normative accounts of specific thinking tasks (see Stanovich & West, 1998b, c). With this background covered I will consider what individual differences might tell us about category-based induction. In particular, what can the method tell us above and beyond more standard experimental methods about people's inductive reasoning abilities? Does the method have anything to say about how a dual-process approach might be applied to induction across categories? And can it inform the debate about the normative status of inductive phenomena? I will describe the results of two studies designed with these questions in mind.

I will conclude with a consideration of other questions about induction to which the individual-differences methodology might help provide some answers. I will briefly describe a recent study designed to investigate who is susceptible to inductive reasoning fallacies, that is, judgements about the strength of inductive arguments that depart from the prescriptions of some normative theory of induction. In addition, I will consider recent claims about dissociations between induction and deduction (Rips, 2001; Rips and Asmuth, Chapter 10, this volume; Oaksford and Hahn, Chapter 11, this volume; Heit & Rotello, 2005). I will outline a dual-process perspective on this dissociation and argue that an individual-differences approach allows one to test the dual-process account. First, however, as dual-process theories of thinking have motivated much of the individual differences work I will describe, it is important to review them in some detail here.

DUAL-PROCESS THEORIES OF THINKING

It is now a relatively common claim that there are two types of thinking. Roughly speaking, these types correspond to an intuitive mode of thought and a more analytic way of thinking. Recently, there have been at least three attempts to put this claim on a sound theoretical footing (Evans & Over, 1996; Sloman, 1996; Stanovich, 1999; for recent reviews see Evans, 2003, and Osman, 2005). All versions of the theory agree that one type of thinking is fast, associative, and automatic while the other is slow, rule-based, and, to some degree at least, controlled. I will refer to the first of these types of thinking as Type 1 and to the second as Type 2. All three theories claim that the two types of thinking overlap and that they are not confined to any particular thinking task. For this reason the distinction between types of reasoning is orthogonal to the philosopher's distinction between induction and deduction (Sloman, 1996; but see Oaksford and Hahn, Chapter 11, this volume; and Rips and Asmuth, Chapter 10, this volume). They also agree that when engaged in the same thinking task, the systems can produce conflicting responses. Sloman enumerates a range of thinking tasks where he claims that conflicting responses are available. These range from Tversky and Kahneman's (1983) conjunction fallacy to the case of belief bias in syllogistic reasoning (see Evans, Barston, & Pollard, 1983). Evans and Over (1996) and Stanovich (1999) explicitly claim that the second type of thinking calls on working memory resources and hence is likely to be predicted by measures of cognitive ability.

As Sloman equates Type-2 thinking with symbol manipulation, this claim is implicit in his account.

Given that claims about the existence of dual processes are almost always contentious, I will briefly review the evidence most often cited to support dual-process claims about thinking. Conveniently for the purposes of this overview, the task used to measure belief bias in syllogistic reasoning (Evans, Barston, & Pollard, 1983) has been explored using a variety of methodologies and participants. In the syllogisms used in belief bias tasks, participants are presented with two quantified premises and are asked to verify a conclusion provided by the experimenter. For example:

All beekeepers are artists   Argument 1
All artists are archers
Therefore, all beekeepers are archers

Participants are presented with syllogisms whose conclusions either necessarily follow or do not follow from the premises and which are believable or unbelievable given background knowledge. A believable and logically valid problem taken from Evans et al. (1983) is as follows:

No police dogs are vicious   Argument 2
Some highly trained dogs are vicious
Therefore, some highly trained dogs are not police dogs

Problem 3 is an unbelievable invalid problem taken from the same experiment.

No millionaires are hard workers   Argument 3
Some rich people are hard workers
Therefore, some millionaires are not rich people

Evans and colleagues found main effects of logic and of conclusion believability in their study. That is, participants were more likely to accept conclusions that were either believable or logically necessary given the premises. Furthermore, they showed that the results were not due to the existence of separate groups of logical and belief-based responders in their sample. Sometimes individual participants responded on the basis of belief and sometimes on the basis of what was necessarily true. This is one of the best examples of thinking tasks that give rise to conflicting responses (see Sloman, 1996). That is, Type-1 and Type-2 processes produce different answers in competition with one another. Sometimes the Type-1 answer is accepted whereas on other occasions the Type-2 response overcomes the Type-1 response.

There are a number of lines of investigation that support the dual-process interpretation of Evans et al.'s results. For example, Gilinsky and Judd (1994) showed that susceptibility to effects of belief on conflict problems increases with age. This makes sense if logical or Type-2 thinking is associated with working memory and IQ, both of which decline as we get older (e.g., Hasher & Zacks, 1988; Horn & Cattell, 1967). In another line of investigation it has been shown that susceptibility to belief bias on conflict problems may be reduced by stressing the concept of logical necessity in the instructions (Evans, Allen, Newstead, & Pollard, 1997). This result is predicted because of the controlled nature of Type-2 thinking processes. Further evidence for the dual-process interpretation comes from a recent study by Evans and Curtis-Holmes (2005) using a speeded response paradigm (for a related use of this paradigm see Shafto, Colony, and Vitkin, Chapter 5 this volume). When participants were required to make a speeded response, they were more susceptible to the effects of belief in conflict problems. To summarise then, responses based on Type-1 processes are primary, but responses based on Type-2 processing can dominate if participants are instructed to suppress Type-1 outputs, if they have sufficient time for the slower Type-2 processes to operate, or if they are young.

Before proceeding it is worthwhile to consider two other recent sources of particularly compelling evidence. Goel and Dolan (2003) have reported the results of an MRI study of belief bias in which they found very strong evidence for separate types of thinking. When participants gave belief-based responses on conflict problems, researchers observed increased activation in ventral medial prefrontal cortex (VMPFC). When these same participants gave logical responses on conflict problems, the researchers observed increased activation in right inferior prefrontal cortex. Goel and Dolan argue that VMPFC is associated with the effects of beliefs in reasoning (see also Adolphs, Tranel, Bechara, Damasio, & Damasio, 1996), whereas activation in inferior prefrontal cortex is due to the inhibition of a response based on Type-1 thinking processes in favour of a Type-2 or logical response. The notion that inhibition is important to logical reasoning is further supported by some data on children's reasoning reported by Handley, Capon, Beveridge, Dennis, and Evans (2004). These authors found that scores on the conflict index in children aged ten years were correlated with performance on a task designed to measure ability to inhibit a prepotent response. Children who were more likely to respond logically had higher inhibitory control. Both of these studies suggest the existence of two systems for reasoning, one of which is dominant and whose effects must be suppressed by the other.

Handley et al.'s study is interesting in the current context because it employed an individual-differences methodology. However, the individual-differences variable measured was response inhibition and, although there is currently considerable interest in the relationship between measures of inhibition and working memory (see Kane & Engle, 2003), there has been little other work on inhibition and thinking. By far the most popular individual differences variable to have been employed by researchers interested in dual-process theories of thinking is general cognitive ability. It is to a review of the literature on cognitive ability and thinking that I will now turn.

INDIVIDUAL DIFFERENCES IN COGNITIVE ABILITY AND THINKING

In a series of papers, Keith Stanovich and his colleagues have described the results of a large-scale research program designed to investigate the relationship between cognitive ability and thinking. For the most part using SAT scores as an indicator of ability, these researchers have investigated which tasks are predicted by ability and which are not. This program of research is notable because of the range of deductive, decision-making, and (to some extent) inductive tasks it has investigated. It is motivated by two arguments, the first of which is that individual-differences studies allow one to test dual-process theories of thinking. Explicit in Evans and Over's and Stanovich's formulation of the theory (and implicit in Sloman's) is the claim that Type-2 processes are subject to capacity limitations whereas Type-1 processes are not. Thus, on tasks where Type-2 processes are required in order for the normatively correct answer to be produced, participants who are lower in cognitive resources will tend to perform more poorly than those who are high in cognitive resources.

There are a number of lines of work in the literature linking IQ measures to general cognitive constraints. First, performance on intelligence tests is held to be constrained by basic cognitive abilities. For example, Carpenter, Just, and Shell (1990) gave an account of individual differences in the series-completion problems used in Raven's Progressive Matrices test. Their account implicated variations in the ability to induce abstract relations and the ability to coordinate goals in working memory as the basis for individual differences. In support of this account, Unsworth and Engle (2005) have recently shown that individual differences in working memory predict performance on Raven. Although other evidence (e.g., Fry & Hale, 1996) suggests that processing speed mediates the relationship between memory and IQ, nonetheless there is very good evidence for relationships between constraints on basic cognitive abilities and performance on tests of ability. As SAT scores are known to be very closely related to IQ (Frey & Detterman, 2004), it is reasonable to conclude that the same constraints limit SAT performance.

According to Stanovich (1999), the finding that correct performance on certain tasks, but not others, is associated with SAT scores lends support to the suggestion that there are at least two types of thinking and that each is involved to different extents in the accomplishment of a variety of thinking tasks. Stanovich (1999, pg. 143) claims that large differences in performance due to cognitive ability will be found only for thinking tasks that engage both systems. When a thinking task engages the associative system only, then no difference will be observed. In addition, individual differences are more likely to be found when the systems produce conflicting responses.

Stanovich illustrates this argument with reference to performance on deontic and indicative versions of Wason's selection task (see Stanovich & West, 1998b). In the selection task participants are presented with a conditional rule that is said to govern a set of instances. In standard indicative versions of the task, the rule governs what is printed on each side of sets of cards. For example, "If there is an A on one side of the card (p), then there is a 3 on the other side (q)." Participants are shown four cards. On the visible sides are printed an A (p), an L (not-p), a 3 q), and a 7 (not-q). Participants are asked which card or cards need to be turned over to test the rule. Deontic versions of the selection task concern what should or ought to be done. Most often, they concern social laws, obligations, or permissions. For example, "If someone is drinking alcohol in a bar (p) then they must be over 18 (q)". Printed on the visible side of the cards in this example might by "Beer" (p), "Coke" (not-p), "21" (q), and "16" (not-q).

One of the earliest findings in the literature on the indicative selection task (see Wason, 1966) was that people tended not to select the cards that could falsify the rule (the p and the not-q cards in the example above). However, when deontic content is included (see Johnson-Laird, Legrenzi, & Legrenzi, 1972), people regularly select the falsifying cases. There are many explanations of why people behave differently on the indicative and deontic tasks (see Cheng & Holyoak, 1985; Cosmides, 1986; Manktelow & Over, 1991; Oaksford & Chater, 1994). Stanovich argues that most explanations suggest that people's selections on the deontic task are not determined by conscious, analytic reasoning but by largely unconscious, heuristic processes. Correct responding on the indicative task, on the other hand, requires that the analytic system overcome the unconscious associative system which, in most participants, is responsible for the selection of those cards that match the items in the rule.

If Stanovich is right, then correct performance on the indicative task should be associated with cognitive ability whereas correct performance on the deontic task should not. Stanovich and West (1998b) confirmed this prediction. They found clear evidence that people who reported higher SAT results were more likely to select the potentially falsifying cards on the indicative selection task. There was much less evidence for such an association on the deontic task. Broadly similar results have been reported by Newstead,

Handley, Harley, Wright, and Farrelly (2004), who also found that whether associations between ability and performance on deontic and indicative tasks are found depend on the ability range of the participants sampled.

The second argument that Stanovich uses to motivate the individual-differences approach relates to what counts as the correct normative response on any particular task. There has been substantial debate about which is the correct normative account of tasks as varied as Kahneman and Tversky's (1983) Linda problem and Wason's selection task (see Cohen, 1981; Oaksford & Chater, 1994). Stanovich and West (1998b, c) argued that an association between cognitive ability and certain patterns of performance on these tasks might favour one normative account over another (see also Cohen, 1981). For example, Oaksford and Chater (1994) have recast Wason's selection task as one of deciding which card or cards is likely to be most informative. From a Bayesian perspective, given certain assumptions about the probability of items mentioned in the conditional rule, it turns out that the most informative cards on the indicative task are the p and q cards. Oaksford and Chater argue that their Bayesian reanalysis of the task is closer to a correct normative analysis than is the Popperian notion of falsification, which claims that the "correct" solution is to select the p and not-q cards.

To arbitrate between these competing normative accounts, Stanovich and West looked for associations between cognitive ability and the tendency to select cards in accordance with each of these distinct normative approaches. They found that more able participants were more likely to select the falsifying cards than were the less able participants. Less able participants, on the other hand, were more likely to select the p and q cards. Stanovich concludes that the individual-differences data suggest that from a normative point of view, it is more appropriate to think about the indicative selection task as one requiring falsification rather than decisions about expected information gain. Of course this argument may not always hold. For example, if one happens to sample from the bottom of the range of ability scores, then the most able participants in a particular sample may very well perform in non-normative ways on a particular thinking task (see Newstead et al., 2004). However, if one consistently finds, across a range of samples and abilities, that the most able participants consistently favour one response over another, then this lends support to the claim that the response favoured by these participants is the one that is normatively correct.

Unfortunately, although Stanovich and colleagues have investigated a number of phenomena (including belief bias), very little data has been published on the relationship between inductive reasoning and general cognitive ability. One exception is work by Stanovich and West (1998a) on a task where participants make a decision in the face of conflicting evidence comprised of a vivid testimonial from a friend and a statistical summary of the experiences of a number of people (see also Jepson, Krantz, & Nisbett, 1983; Fong, Krantz, & Nisbett, 1986). This task satisfies Stanovich's (1999) conditions for the observation of an association between intelligence and normatively correct responses. This is because in order to resist a response based on the vivid single case, Type-2 processes are required to decontextualise the problem. A response based on the vivid non-statistical information is likely to be delivered by context-sensitive Type-1 processes. Stanovich and West (1998a) report correlations of .33 and .38 between the tendency to resist the effects of the salient single case in favour of the statistical evidence and a composite measure of thinking ability. This association suggests that sensitivity to evidence quality in inductive reasoning is related to cognitive ability and hence reflects the operation of Type-2 thinking processes.

INDIVIDUAL DIFFERENCES AND INDUCTION: THE CASE OF DIVERSITY

What might an individual-differences approach tell us about category-based induction where people are asked about their willingness to project a (usually) blank property from members of one or more premise categories to members of another conclusion category? One potential use of the methodology is to explore the diversity effect (see Heit, Chapter 1, this volume; Shafto, Coley, & Vitkin Chapter 5, this volume). Consider Arguments 4 and 5 below.

> Tigers have property X   Argument 4
> Cows have property X
> All mammals have property X

> Tigers have property X   Argument 5
> Lions have property X
> All mammals have property X

Participants are said to be sensitive to evidential diversity if they prefer arguments based on dissimilar rather than similar premise categories. Because the premises in Argument 4 concern more diverse categories than do the premises in Argument 5, Argument 4 is said to be stronger than Argument 5. As we will see, an individual-differences approach may be useful in approaching normative and psychological questions about diversity.

The Normative Argument for Diversity

Although there is general agreement that, all else being equal, diverse evidence is strong evidence, it has been difficult to formally prove this intuition to be true. As a consequence there has been disagreement in the literature about whether diversity is a sound normative principle for inductive reasoning. Sensitivity to diversity is advocated by a range of philosophers of science (Nagel, 1939; Carnap, 1950; Hempel, 1966), and in the psychological literature the soundness of diversity is assumed in a variety of models (see Osherson et al., 1990; Sloman, 1993; Heit, 1998). In addition, a variety of Bayesian justifications for its soundness have been offered (see Howson & Urbach, 1989).

However, Bayesian accounts of diversity have been called into question (Wayne, 1995; for a reply see Myrvold, 1995), and arguments against the generality of a diversity principle have been made by Lo, Sides, Rozelle, and Osherson (2002) and by Medin, Coley, Storms, and Hayes (2003). Medin et al. have demonstrated a number of exceptions to diversity (for an experimental reappraisal of one of these exceptions see Heit & Feeney, 2005). Other exceptions to diversity include those found in cross-cultural work comparing Itzaj-Mayan Indians to North American students. Although the students displayed sensitivity to diversity (see López, Atran, Coley, Medin, and Smith, 1997), members of the Itzaj tribe did not. Proffitt, Coley, and Medin (2000) showed that some tree experts do not show strong diversity effects when reasoning about trees. Reviewing all of this work, Heit, Hahn, and Feeney (2005) have argued that these exceptions to diversity do not invalidate the diversity principle. Instead, they may involve the sensible use of background knowledge beyond simple similarity information when evaluating arguments. Knowledge about diversity is but one of many sources of knowledge that might be used to evaluate inductive inferences.

Heit et al.'s attempt at reconciliation notwithstanding, there is clearly some disagreement about the normative status of the diversity principle. In some ways (but not in others), this disagreement parallels the normative debates we encountered when considering Stanovich's individual-differences approach to thinking. Below I will describe two individual-difference studies that apply Stanovich's logic to the diversity effect. These studies examined whether there is a positive correlation between sensitivity to evidential diversity and cognitive ability. If such a correlation were to be observed, then, by Stanovich's argument, we would have additional reason to believe that, all things being equal, sensitivity to diversity is a normatively sensible strategy.

Dual-Process Predictions

Using an individual-differences approach to study diversity will also enable us to give preliminary consideration to how a dual-process view might be applied to category-based induction. Certainly, at least one theory of induction makes clear dual-process predictions. Sloman – a dual-process theorist – has also put forward an important account of category-based induction called the feature-based model (FBM) (Sloman, 1993). According to this model, category-based induction is explicable without the need to assume a stable category structure. In the FBM the premises of an argument are encoded by training a connectionist network to associate the property to be projected with the features of the categories in the premises. Argument strength is determined by the amount of activation of the target property in the presence of the conclusion category. The greater the featural overlap between premise and conclusion categories, the stronger the argument. In this approach, diverse premises lead to associations with a wider variety of features and hence are more likely to lead to strong activation of the target property in the presence of the conclusion category. This similarity-based model is associative in nature. It claims that category-based induction is achieved by Type-1 processes and, therefore, that the tendency to be sensitive to evidential diversity should not be associated with a measure of cognitive ability. However, Sloman (1996) has made the point that although a feature-based process may be pre-eminent in category-based induction, rule-based or Type-2 processes may also play a role. Furthermore, under certain conditions, relationships between categories do affect judgements of inductive strength (see Experiment 4, Sloman, 1998). Individual-differences studies allow us to test the strong predictions of the FBM. Any indication of a significant association between ability and sensitivity to diversity would suggest that, contrary to the predictions of the FBM, Type-1 and Type-2 processes may be involved in the evaluation of category-based inductive arguments.

It is somewhat more difficult to see how dual-process theory might map onto other theories of category-based induction. For example, according to Osherson and colleagues' Similarity-Coverage Model (SCM), the strength of a category-based inductive argument is determined by the similarity of the categories in the premises to the category in the conclusion and the degree to which the categories in the premises cover the superordinate category that includes all categories mentioned in the argument (Osherson, Smith, Wilkie, López, & Shafir, 1990). It is the coverage component of the model that accounts for diversity effects. The coverage measure is the average maximum similarity between the categories in the premises and instances of the superordinate category that come to mind when assessing the argument. As diverse categories in the premises are likely to be similar to a wider variety of instances from the superordinate, the coverage measure in the model tends to be elevated by the presence of diverse premise categories. This model is different from the FBM because it assumes the existence of a stable category structure. It also predicts that for arguments like 6 and 7, where the conclusion category is specific rather than general, in order to display sensitivity to diversity, people must generate the lowest level superordinate category that contains the categories in the premises and the conclusion.

Bears have property X   Argument 6
Gorillas have property X
Tigers have property X

When the conclusion in the argument is general, however, as it is in Argument 4, then people do not have to generate a covering category.

Bears have property X   Argument 7
Mice have property X
Tigers have property X

The need to generate a covering category has been implicated by López, Gelman, Gutheil, and Smith (1992) as an important factor in the development of category-based induction. Lopez et al. found developmental trends where sensitivity to diversity emerged for general arguments before specific arguments. An individual-differences study will allow for an alternative test of Lopez's argument. If generating a covering category is an additional source of difficulty, then sensitivity to diversity for specific arguments should be related to cognitive ability. In addition, we should observe less sensitivity to diversity when the conclusion category is specific rather than general. Perhaps we might also expect to observe a weaker relationship between sensitivity to diversity and ability with specific conclusions, as only the most able people in any sample may display such sensitivity at above chance levels.

The relevance account of category-based induction (Medin, Coley, Storms, & Hayes, 2003) attributes diversity effects to participants' hypotheses about the nature of the blank feature. Although they focus on the roles played by causal and environmental knowledge in producing exceptions to diversity, when no such knowledge is available, participants will use the degree of similarity between the categories in the premises to guide their hypothesis formation. Dissimilar categories lead to hypotheses that the feature is general and hence highly projectible, whereas similar categories lead to hypotheses about specific and hence non-projectible features (see also Heit, 1998).

The relevance account appears to give no grounds for dual-process predictions in its current form. However, the relevance theory of linguistic pragmatics (Sperber & Wilson, 1986/1995), upon which the relevance account is based, uses logical rules for non-demonstrative inference (see Sperber & Wilson, 1995, chapter 2). Thus, people work out the implications of an utterance by deriving deductive conclusions from assumptions made available by the context and what is explicated by the utterance. For such an approach to be applied to category-based induction, it is likely that people would have to explicitly represent principles of inductive inference and draw inferences about what follows from those rules and information in the utterance. For example, given dissimilar premise categories, people might infer that the blank property is general and, based on this interim conclusion and the further premise that general properties are highly projectible, might conclude that members of the category in the conclusion are also likely to possess the property. Certainly the relevance account of induction is not committed to such a thorough application of relevance theory. Nonetheless, under such an application category-based induction might come to have a rather explicit or Type-2 character, and one might predict that sensitivity to an inductive principle such as diversity would be associated with cognitive ability.

Finally, Heit (1998) has offered a Bayesian account of induction pitched at a computational rather than an algorithmic level. As a computational-level account specifies what the goals of people's cognition should be (see Marr, 1982), the Bayesian account might make the simple prediction that if there are differences in people's sensitivity to diversity, then they should be predicted by ability. If there is variability in the extent to which people attain their cognitive goals, then people higher in cognitive capacity should be more likely to attain them.

Some Recent Evidence

In both of the studies to be described here (for a more complete description see Feeney, in press), I presented participants with a series of category-based inductive arguments and the AH4 (Heims, 1968), a test of cognitive ability previously used to study individual differences in induction (see Newstead et al., 2004). The test has verbal/numerical and spatial components, each of which has sixty-five items and is administered separately under timed conditions.

In the first study 100 students at the University of Durham were presented with 48 inductive arguments. Half of these had general conclusions and half had specific conclusions. Half of the items were designed to measure sensitivity to diversity. The other items were control items designed to examine monotonicity effects and will not be described here. There were twelve pairs of diversity items. One item in each pair concerned similar premise categories, while the other concerned dissimilar premise categories. One of the categories in the pair always remained the same. For example, in one pair the diverse argument concerned hippos and hamsters, while the non-diverse argument concerned hippos and rhinos. All of the arguments concerned blank premises such as Property X or Property B. Participants' task was to indicate on a percentage scale the extent to which they thought the conclusion was supported by the premises. For the purposes of statistical analyses I counted the number of pairs where the strength rating for the diverse argument was stronger than for the non-diverse argument.

There are two analyses of interest here. In the first I examined whether overall, participants were sensitive to diversity at a rate greater than chance. I found significant diversity effects for arguments with general conclusions (sensitivity in 58% of trials) but not for arguments with specific conclusions (sensitivity in 46% of trials). In general, people do not appear to be highly sensitive to premise diversity when evaluating arguments. The fact that they were significantly less sensitive for arguments with specific conclusions, $t(99) = 4.05$, $p < .001$, lends some support to the claim made by Lopez et al. that the generation of a superordinate category for arguments with a specific conclusion is an extra source of difficulty.

The mean AH4 score for this study was 95.6 (S.D. = 14.4). This is close to the norm for this kind of sample (mean 96.4, S.D. = 15.01). When the reasoning data were collapsed across conclusion type, there was a significant association between AH4 score and sensitivity to diversity ($r = .27$, $p < .01$). This association was significant when items with general conclusions were considered on their own ($r = .27$, $p < .01$). However, when items with specific conclusions only were analysed, the association between AH4 scores and sensitivity to diversity was no longer significant ($r = .16$, $p > .1$). Closer analysis of response patterns revealed that not one participant displayed diversity for all six pairs of arguments with specific conclusions, whereas ten participants displayed maximum sensitivity in the general condition. The requirement to generate a superordinate covering category seems to have rendered sensitivity to diversity very difficult for the vast majority of participants in this sample

In a second study I achieved greater control over our experimental materials than I did in the first. In the first study I used different materials for the diversity-specific and diversity-general conditions. In the second study I used the same materials for each condition. One-hundred-and-fifteen students at the University of Durham completed the AH4 and thirty-six reasoning problems. Eighteen of these problems concerned monotonicity and will not be discussed here. The set of thirty-six problems was composed of six sets of six. Each set of six employed the same five mammal categories, three of which were premise categories (mice, dolphins, squirrels), one of which was a specific conclusion category (dogs), and one a general conclusion category (I used mammal for all six problem sets). For the specific and general diverse items, two taxonomically dissimilar mammal categories were presented in the premises (mice, dolphins), whereas for the non-diverse items two taxonomically similar items were presented (mice, squirrels). Problems were presented in one of four different random orders.

Once again I found that sensitivity to diversity was significantly greater than chance for arguments with general conclusions (59%) but not for arguments with specific conclusions (52%). The significant difference in sensitivity to diversity due to conclusion type, $t(114) = 2.96$, $p < .005$, is further support for the claim that the requirement to generate a covering category interferes with diversity-based reasoning.

Although the raw diversity findings from this study are similar to those obtained in Study 1, there are differences in the individual-differences data. Mean performance on the AH4 was 106.3 (S.D. $= 10.65$). There are two things to note about this result. First, it is significantly greater than the norm for a sample of university students (mean $= 96.4$; S.D. $= 15.01$). As different degree courses have different academic entry requirements, the difference between the mean AH4 scores observed in these studies is most likely due to the degree course from which the sample for each study was drawn. Second, the standard deviation of the mean for this sample is considerably smaller than the normal standard deviation. Accordingly, all of the correlation coefficients reported below will be adjusted for truncated variance.

When the reasoning data were collapsed across conclusion type, I observed a significant association between sensitivity to diversity and AH4 scores (r(adj) $= .28$, $t < .005$). The association between reasoning performance and ability is significant when arguments with general conclusions are considered on their own (r(adj) $= .23$, $p < .02$) and when arguments with specific conclusions are considered on their own (r(adj) $= .25$, $p < .01$).

Interpreting the Data

These two studies have produced evidence that bears on theories of inductive reasoning, specific claims about the normative basis for the diversity effect, and on the general claim that there are two types of thinking. First, the finding that people tend not to be sensitive to premise diversity when the conclusion is specific suggests that Lopez et al. may be correct in their prediction that having to generate a covering category is a source of difficulty in induction. However, whereas Lopez et al. made their prediction for children's reasoning, our finding concerns the reasoning of university undergraduates.

An examination of overall sensitivity to diversity across both studies might tempt one to argue that people never reliably generate the covering category and, therefore, to conclude that evidence for the diversity effect with specific conclusions has been overstated. However, the individual-differences analysis of Study 2 allowed us to observe a significant association between cognitive ability and sensitivity to diversity in specific arguments. Although we did not find evidence for such an association in Study 1, we appear to have sampled a higher part of the distribution of ability scores in Study 2. As Newstead et al. (2004) have demonstrated in the case of the selection task, whether an association is observed between ability and performance on difficult thinking tasks often depends on the nature of the sample. In a high ability sample, those who are highest in ability tend to be sensitive to premise diversity with specific conclusions. This appears to support the prediction that the requirement to generate a covering category is an additional source of difficulty in induction. Sensitivity to diversity under these circumstances appears to be relatively rare.

The association that we observed between sensitivity to diversity and intelligence, by Stanovich's normative argument, provides some evidence that, all things being equal, sensitivity to diversity is normatively sound. One concern about this argument relates to the point in the previous paragraph: in any particular study whether certain effects are found to be associated with cognitive ability will depend on the make-up of the sample. In Study 1 we found an association between sensitivity to diversity and ability. However, the sample in Study 1 was of average ability. It was possible that, for the higher ability sample in Study 2, no association would be found. Although we did find a relationship in Study 2, a failure to do so would have been very problematic for the normative argument. In principle, it is always possible that an association will not be found with a sample that is of higher average ability than the current sample. For this reason, the normative argument is strongest for those phenomena that have been tested by a number of studies across a range of abilities.

Our data also have implications for dual-process theories. In particular, they have implications for the prediction made by the FBM that category-based induction is achieved as a result of Type-1 processes and may be modelled wholly in associationist terms (Sloman, 1993). We have seen here that individual differences in cognitive ability predict sensitivity to diversity. Associations such as this one are taken by dual-process theorists to indicate that Type-2 processes are at play. In this case, such a conclusion is problematic for the FBM. Type-2 processes might be involved in the diversity effect because people may explicitly represent principles of inductive reasoning. Upon noticing that the categories in the premises are dissimilar, people may bring to mind the principle that diverse evidence leads to strong inductive inferences. This possibility has also been suggested by McDonald, Samuels, and Rispoli (1996) and, as we noted earlier, is consistent with certain applications of relevance theory to category-based induction.

Finally, there are two ways in which category-based inductive phenomena generally, and the diversity effect specifically, differ from other reasoning and decision-making phenomena studied by dual-process theorists. First, category-based phenomena require people to draw on their extensive knowledge of categories in the world. It is possible, therefore, that our individual-differences findings may be due to people high in cognitive ability having richer representations of categories than people lower in ability. This would mean that their associative systems had more effective knowledge bases to make inferences over, leading to greater sensitivity to diversity. Whilst this counter-explanation does not apply to other dissociations between Type-1 and Type-2 processes, it is an important one in this context. However, in the case of diversity, this counter-explanation seems to boil down to the unlikely possibility that some undergraduate students have insufficient featural knowledge to distinguish similar from dissimilar mammals.

Second, Stanovich (1999) argues that associations between cognitive ability and performance on particular tasks will be strongest when different responses are cued by Type-1 and Type-2 processes. As sensitivity to diversity is predicted by the associative account (Sloman, 1993) and a range of other more rule-based accounts (e.g., Osherson et al., 1990; Heit, 1998), the task we have employed here is, in this respect, unlike other tasks previously used to dissociate types of thinking. Nonetheless, we have observed significant associations between sensitivity to diversity and cognitive ability. This observation suggests that sensitivity to diversity is more likely when there is greater involvement of Type-2 processes.

OTHER APPLICATIONS OF THE APPROACH

As we have seen, the individual-differences paradigm may be very useful in helping us to answer questions about diversity. There are a range of other questions raised in other chapters of this book to which the approach might usefully be applied. Some of these questions concern normative issues, whilst others are more psychological.

Normative Issues

There exist several cases in the literature on induction where the findings predicted by a particular normative account are not observed, or, alternatively, phenomena are observed that are not predicted by the normative account.

Consider Murphy and Ross's (Chapter 8, this volume) description of data from inductive tasks involving uncertain categorisation that appear to be inconsistent with a rational analysis. For example, Murphy, Malt, and Ross (1995) asked participants to say how likely an individual described as walking towards a house would be to check the sturdiness of the doors of the house. In one condition the individual was either an estate agent or a cable TV repairman. In another he was either an estate agent or a burglar. In both conditions the individual was most likely to be an estate agent. Because pretests had shown that people believe that burglars would be more likely to check the doors than a TV repairman, participants should have rated more highly the likelihood that the uncategorized individual will check the windows when there is a possibility that he is a burglar. However, in this experiment and many others involving abstract as well as concrete materials, the alternative category made no difference to people's likelihood judgements.

A related demonstration concerns people's inductive inferences based on cross-classifiable categories such as "bagel" which may be classified as a bread or a breakfast food. Here, Ross and Murphy (1999) find that although a majority of participants rely on just one of the categories when evaluating the likelihood that a target will possess some property, a minority take both possible classifications into account.

These findings pose a problem for Bayesian accounts of induction because they suggest that people are, in certain respects, poor Bayesians. However, as Murphy and Ross remark in their chapter, their problems resemble some of the problems, such as the taxi-cab problem, used by Kahneman and Tversky to study decision making. Just as Ross and Murphy find that increasing the relevance of the alternative category increases people's tendency to take it into consideration, so Kahneman and Tversky observed that making the base rate causally relevant increased the rate at which it played a role in people's judgements. Stanovich and West (1998a) have demonstrated an association between cognitive ability and base rate neglect so that the most able participants in a sample are less likely to ignore the base rate. A similar question may be asked about induction under uncertainty. Will the tendency to ignore the alternative category be predicted by ability? Perhaps Murphy and Ross's means hide predominantly high ability participants who take the alternative into account. This may be especially true of the cross-classification studies where a minority take both classifications into account. Perhaps this minority tend to be highest in ability. If so, then we would have a situation, similar to that which pertains in several other areas of high-level cognition (for a review see Stanovich, 1999), where only a minority of participants behave in accordance with the norm for the task. Because those participants tend to be the most able, the observation of non-normative behaviour overall is less problematic.

Another example of an experimental effect that is not predicted by Bayesian accounts of induction is the conjunction fallacy (Medin et al., 2003), where adding categories to the conclusion causes the argument to become stronger. Medin et al. observed two types of conjunction fallacy. The conjunction fallacy by property reinforcement is observed when the addition of a second category to the conclusion of an argument causes the feature shared by the categories in the argument to become more relevant. For example, Medin et al. observed that the argument from chickens to cows and pigs was stronger than that from chickens to cows or from chickens to pigs. Medin et al. account for this finding by suggesting that the environment shared by members of all three categories becomes more available when all three are present in the argument. The causal conjunction fallacy occurs when the addition of an extra category to the conclusion causes the causal relationship between the categories in the argument to become relevant. Thus, the argument from grain to mice and owls is stronger than that from grain to mice or from grain to owls. Of course, in probabilistic terms this is non-normative because the probability of a conjunction of events can never be higher than the probability of either one of the conjuncts.

Again, it may be the case that these fallacies are resisted by participants who are highest in ability. Indeed, Stanovich and West found an association between ability and resistance to the conjunction fallacy in Kahneman and Tversky's famous Linda problem, where many participants estimate it to be more likely that Linda is a feminist bankteller than that she is a bankteller. As has been the case with other types of thinking, an individual-differences approach may very well resolve apparent discrepancies between average behaviour and the predictions of normative or computational-level analyses.

A recent study of category-based induction by Feeney, Shafto, and Dunning (in press) applied the individual-differences approach to both types of conjunction fallacy. One-hundred-and-thirty participants completed the AH4 and thirty-six category-based arguments. Half of these arguments were designed to test susceptibility to the conjunction fallacy by property reinforcement and the other half to test susceptibility to the causal conjunction fallacy. The eighteen property reinforcement arguments consisted of six items, each comprised of three arguments. One of the arguments in each item concerned all three categories, with one category in the premise and the other two in the conclusion. The conclusion of the other two arguments concerned one or the other of the conclusion categories from the first argument. These single-conclusion category arguments were randomly labelled A or B. Each of the corresponding six causal items also contained a three-category argument and a pair of two-category arguments. Following Medin et al. the categories in the three-category arguments always made up a causal chain. For example, grain, mice, and owls may share a property because mice eat grain and owls eat mice. Accordingly, because grain is closer to mice in this chain than it is to owls, we labelled one type of single-conclusion argument Close (in this example, grain to mice) and the other (grain to owls) as Distant.

Our data contained clear evidence for the existence of a conjunction fallacy in category-based induction. Preliminary analysis revealed that participants were susceptible to the fallacy by property reinforcement on 47% of trials and to the causal version of the fallacy on 53% of trials. We split our participants into low and high ability groups. The mean overall score on the AH4 was 94.57 (S.D. = 14.32). The mean score for the low ability group was 83.09 (S.D. = 11.00), whilst the mean score for the high ability group was 105.70 (S.D. = 5.88). For the property reinforcement materials, an ANOVA on ratings of inductive strength revealed a significant interaction between ability and number of conclusions in the argument. However, the equivalent interaction from the analysis of strength ratings for the causal materials did not approach significance. The means in these interactions are shown in Figure 12.1, where it may be seen that the high ability participants did not tend to distinguish between two-conclusion category and one-conclusion category property reinforcement arguments, whereas participants lower in ability did. Figure 12.1 also shows that all participants, regardless of ability, tended to respect causal distance in their ratings of argument strength. So, for example, the argument from grain to mice was rated stronger than that from grain to owls. In fact, participants were more likely with these materials to respect causal distance than they were to commit the causal conjunction fallacy.

The results are intriguing. First of all, because the conjunction fallacy by property reinforcement is not observed in more able participants, our results suggest that it may be relatively unproblematic for Bayesian accounts (see Heit, 1998) of category-based induction. However, both high and low ability participants were equally likely to commit the causal conjunction fallacy and to respect causal distance in their ratings of argument strength. The causal conjunction fallacy remains, therefore, problematic for Bayesian accounts of induction. Causal knowledge appears to be very compelling when people are evaluating inductive arguments. In this respect our results are similar to those reported by other researchers who have shown the pre-eminence of causal information in induction (see Rehder & Hastie, 2001; Rehder, this volume).

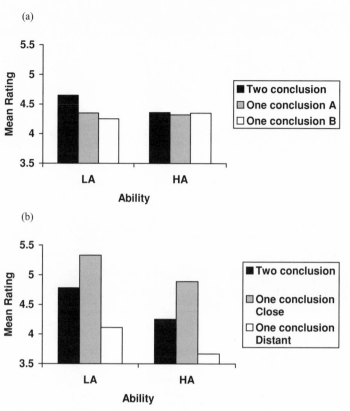

FIGURE 12.1. Interaction between Ability and Conclusion Type from Feeney, Shafto, and Dunning (in press).

The Relationship between Induction and Deduction

The final issue to which we will briefly apply the individual-differences method is the distinction made by philosophers between deductive or necessary inferences and inductive or plausible inferences. One important question about this distinction is whether it corresponds to a psychological dissociation between the two types of reasoning. There are a variety of views on this issue. One view is that induction and deduction are achieved by the same processes (see Johnson-Laird, Legrenzi, Girotto, Legrenzi, and Caverni, 1999). Another view is that there is a clear dissociation between induction and deduction (see Rips, 2001). Support for this view comes from an experiment by Rips (2001; see also Heit & Rotello, 2005) where participants were asked to evaluate the same set of inferences under inductive or deductive instructions. There were four types of inference: valid and causally strong; valid but causally weak;

TABLE 12.1. *Examples of the materials used by Rips (2001) to demonstrate a dissociation between induction and deduction*

Valid Strong	Valid Weak	Invalid Strong	Invalid Weak
If Car #10 runs into a brick wall it will stop.	If car #10 runs into a brick wall it will speed up.		
Car #10 runs into a brick wall.	Car #10 runs into a brick wall.	Car #10 runs into a brick wall.	Car #10 runs into a brick wall.
-------------------	-------------------	-------------------	-------------------
Car #10 will stop.	Car #10 will speed up.	Car #10 will stop.	Car #10 will speed up.

invalid but causally strong; invalid and causally weak. An example of each of these inferences is to be seen in Table 12.1. For valid but causally weak and invalid but causally strong problems, Rips observed an interaction such that the former were rated stronger than the latter under deductive instructions, whereas under inductive instructions this pattern was reversed. Rips argued that this finding constitutes a psychological dissociation between induction and deduction.

A dual-process view, on the other hand, is that although there are distinct psychological processes for thinking, these processes do not map onto induction and deduction (see Sloman, 1996). According to a dual-process view, both Type-1 and Type-2 processes may be involved to a greater or lesser extent in any thinking task, inductive or deductive. When participants distinguish between deductive and inductive reasoning instructions, they do so because they have explicit knowledge about the difference between concepts such as necessity and plausibility, and, given different instructions, Type-2 processes allow them to apply different standards for evaluating arguments.

Support for the dual-process view comes from an experiment by Feeney, Dunning, and Over (in preparation) where eighty-one students from the University of Durham completed a subset of Rips's problems under induction conditions. Their task was to decide whether the conclusion of each argument was plausible given the information in the premises. Causal strength and validity were independently manipulated, and participants saw four arguments of each type. They circled "strong" if they thought that the argument was plausible and "not strong" if they thought that it was implausible. As with other studies described in this chapter, participants in this study completed the AH4. Their mean score was 94.40 (S.D. = 12.94). We carried out a median split on our data by cognitive ability. The mean score of the forty-one participants in the low ability group was 84.24 (S.D. = 8.20), whilst

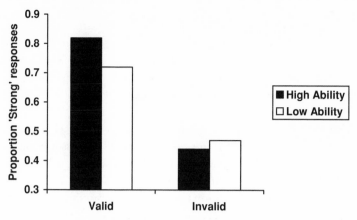

FIGURE 12.2. Means involved in the interaction between Ability and Validity from Feeney, Dunning, and Over (in submission).

the mean score of the forty participants in the high ability group was 104.8 (S.D. = 7.42).

A 2(Ability) × 2 (Validity) × 2(Strength) mixed design ANOVA on the proportion of plausible judgements in each condition revealed significant main effects of Validity, $F(1, 79) = 114.59$, MSe = .07, $p < .001$, and of Strength, $F(1, 79) = 172.45$, MSE = .06, $p < .001$. Whilst the interaction between Ability and Strength was non-significant, $F(1, 79) = 1.05$, MSE = .06, $p > .3$, Ability did interact significantly with Validity, $F(1, 79) = 5.14$, MSE = .07, $p < .03$. The means involved in this interaction are presented in Figure 12.2, where it may be seen that high ability participants judge a greater proportion of valid arguments to be strong than do low ability participants, and they judge a greater proportion of invalid arguments to be "not strong" than do low ability participants.

It is clear from Figure 12.2 that overall, logical validity plays an important role in people's judgements of inductive strength. However, what is most striking is that validity plays a greater role in the judgements of participants high in cognitive ability than in the decisions made by participants lower in ability. These results are consistent with the claim that inductive judgements are mediated by two types of process. One type of process is sensitive to content and context, whereas the other is sensitive to structure. The first type of process underlies effects of belief in reasoning, but because it does not depend on cognitive capacity, effects of belief do not interact with cognitive ability. The second type of process underlies our sensitivity to logical validity. Because it is dependent on cognitive capacity, sensitivity to logical validity in this study interacts with cognitive ability.

CONCLUSIONS

In this chapter I have described how results from studies using the individual-difference method have informed recent dual-process theorising about thinking. I have shown how the method may provide valuable insights into the processes involved in induction. For example, sensitivity to evidential diversity is associated with cognitive ability and, in the presence of a specific conclusion, is almost impossible for all but the most able participants. These results suggest that the diversity effect is not explicable in wholly associationist terms and that the generation of a covering category is, as appears to be predicted by the SCM, an extra source of difficulty in induction. The method also appears useful in testing Bayesian accounts of inductive reasoning and dual-process accounts of the relationship between induction and deduction.

Individual differences are but one of several methods for testing models of induction, and as a consequence, individual-differences studies are unlikely to lead to the formulation of an entirely novel theory of induction. However, as the range of approaches described in this volume attests, there is currently a broad range of theories of induction formulated at a number of levels of explanation. One might argue that currently the field does not need new theories so much as it does evidence with which to discriminate between existing theories and approaches. Individual-differences studies are likely to be a rich source of discriminating evidence.

AUTHOR NOTE

Please address correspondence to Aidan Feeney, Applied Psychology, University of Durham Queen's Campus, Thornaby, Stockton-on-Tess TS17 6BH, United Kingdom, Email: aidan.feeney@durham.ac.uk

References

Adolphs, R., Tranel, D., Bechara, A., Damasio, H., & Damasio, A. R. (1996). Neuropsychological approaches to reasoning and decision-making. In A. R. Damasio (Ed.), *Neurobiology of decision-making*. Berlin: Springer-Verlag.

Carnap, R. (1950). *Logical foundations of probability*. Chicago: University of Chicago Press.

Carpenter, P. A., Just, M. A., & Shell, P. (1990). What one intelligence test measures: A theoretical account of processing in the Raven Progressive Matrices test. *Psychological Review, 97*, 404–431.

Cheng, P. W., & Holyoak, K. J. (1985). Pragmatic reasoning schemas. *Cognitive Psychology, 17*, 391–416.

Cohen, L. J. (1981). Can human irrationality be experimentally demonstrated? *Behavioral & Brain Sciences, 4*, 317–370.

Cosmides, L. (1989). The logic of social exchange: Has natural selection shaped how humans reason? Studies with the Wason selection task. *Cognition, 31*, 187–276.

Evans, J. St. B. T. (2003). In two minds: Dual process accounts of reasoning. *Trends in Cognitive Sciences, 7*, 454–459.

Evans, J. St. B. T., Barston, J. L., & Pollard, P. (1983). On the conflict between logic and belief in syllogistic reasoning. *Memory & Cognition, 11*, 295–306.

Evans, J. St. B. T., & Curtis-Holmes, J. (2005). Rapid responding increases belief bias: Evidence for the dual process theory of reasoning. *Thinking and Reasoning, 11*, 382–389.

Evans, J. St. B. T., Newstead, S. E., Allen, J. L., & Pollard, P. (1994). Debiasing by instruction: The case of belief bias. *European Journal of Cognitive Psychology, 6*, 263–285.

Evans, J. St. B. T., & Over, D. E. (1996). *Rationality and reasoning.* Hove, UK: Psychology Press.

Feeney, A. (in press). How many processes underlie category-based induction? Effects of conclusion specificity and cognitive ability. *Memory & Cognition.*

Feeney, A., Dunning, D. & Over, D. E. (in preparation). Reason distinctions: An individual differences study.

Feeney, A., Shafto, P., & Dunning, D. (in press). Who is susceptible to conjunction fallacies in category-based induction? *Psychonomic Bulletin & Review.*

Fong, G. T., Krantz, D. H., & Nisbett, R. E. (1986). The effects of statistical training on thinking about everyday problems. *Cognitive Psychology, 18*, 253–292.

Frey, M. C., & Detterman, D. K. (2004). Scholastic assessment or g? The relationship between the Scholastic Assessment Test and general cognitive ability. *Psychological Science, 15*, 373–378.

Fry, A. F., & Hale, S. (1996). Processing speed, working memory, and fluid intelligence: Evidence for a developmental cascade. *Psychological Science, 7*, 237–241.

Gilinsky, A. S., & Judd, B. B. (1994). Working memory and bias in reasoning across the life-span. *Psychology and Aging, 9*, 356–371.

Goel, V., & Dolan, R. J. (2003). Explaining modulation of reasoning by belief. *Cognition, 87*, B11–B22.

Handley, S. J., Capon, A., Beveridge, M., Dennis, I., & Evans, J. St. B. T. (2004). Working memory and inhibitory control in the development of children's reasoning. *Thinking and Reasoning, 10*, 175–195.

Hasher, L., & Zacks, R. T. (1988). Working memory, comprehension, and aging: A review and a new view. *The Psychology of Learning and Motivation, 22*, 193–225.

Heim, A. W. (1967). *AH4 group test of intelligence* [Manual]. London: National Foundation for Educational Research.

Heit, E. (1998). A Bayesian analysis of some forms of inductive reasoning. In M. Oaksford & N. Chater (Eds.), *Rational models of cognition* (pp. 248–274). Oxford: Oxford University Press.

Heit, E., & Feeney, A. (2005). Relations between premise similarity and inductive strength. *Psychonomic Bulletin and Review, 12*, 340–344.

Heit, E., Hahn, U., & Feeney, A. (2005). Defending diversity. In W. Ahn, R. Goldstone, B. Love, A. Markman, & P. Wolff (Eds.), *Categorization inside and outside of the laboratory: Essays in honor of Douglas L. Medin* (pp. 87–99). Washington DC: American Psychological Association.

Heit, E., & Rotello, C. (2005). Are there two kinds of reasoning? *Proceedings of the Twenty-Seventh Annual Conference of the Cognitive Science Society* (pp. 923–928). Mahwah, NJ: Erlbaum.

Hempel, C. G. (1966). *Philosophy of natural science.* Englewood Cliffs, NJ: Prentice Hall.

Horn, J. L., & Cattell, R. B. (1967). Age differences in fluid and crystallized intelligence. *Acta Psychologica, 26*, 107–129.

Howson, C., & Urbach, P. (1993). *Scientific reasoning: The Bayesian approach.* Chicago: Open Court.

Jepson, C., Krantz, D. H., & Nisbett, R. E. (1983). Inductive reasoning: Competence or skill? *Behavioral and Brain Sciences, 6*, 494–501.

Johnson-Laird, P. N., Legrenzi, P., Girotto, V., Legrenzi, M., & Caverni, J.-P. (1999). Naive probability: A mental model theory of extensional reasoning. *Psychological Review, 106*, 62–88.

Johnson-Laird, P., Legrenzi, P., & Legrenzi, S. (1972). Reasoning and a sense of reality. *British Journal of Psychology, 63*, 395–400.

Kane, M. J., & Engle, R. W. (2003). Working memory capacity and the control of attention: The contributions of goal neglect, response competition, and task set to Stroop interference. *Journal of Experimental Psychology: General, 132*, 47–70.

Lo, Y., Sides, A., Rozelle, J., & Osherson, D. (2002). Evidential diversity and premise probability in young children's inductive judgment. *Cognitive Science, 26*, 181–206.

López, A., Atran, S., Coley, J. D., Medin, D. L., & Smith, E. E. (1997). The tree of life: Universal and cultural features of folkbiological taxonomies and inductions. *Cognitive Psychology, 32*, 251–295.

López, A., Gelman, S. A., Gutheil, G., & Smith, E. E. (1992). The development of category-based induction. *Child Development, 63*, 1070–1090.

McDonald, J., Samuels, M., & Rispoli, J. (1996). A hypothesis assessment model of categorical argument strength. *Cognition, 59*, 199–217.

Malt, B. C., Ross, B. H., & Murphy, G. L. (1995). Predicting features for members of natural categories when categorization is uncertain. *Journal of Experimental Psychology: Learning, Memory, and Cognition, 21*, 646–661.

Manktelow, K. I., & Over, D. E. (1991). Social roles and utilities in reasoning with deontic conditions. *Cognition, 39*, 85–105.

Marr, D. (1982). *Vision.* San Francisco: W. H. Freeman & Co.

Medin, D. L., Coley, J., Storms, G., & Hayes, B. K. (2003). A relevance theory of induction. *Psychonomic Bulletin & Review, 10*, 517–532.

Murphy, G. L., & Ross, B. H. (1999). Induction with cross-classified categories. *Memory & Cognition, 27*, 1024–1041.

Myrvold, W. C. (1995). Bayesianism and diverse evidence: A reply to Andrew Wayne. *Philosophy of Science, 63*, 661–665.

Nagel, E. (1939). *Principles of the theory of probability.* Chicago: University of Chicago Press.

Newstead, S. E., Handley, S. J., Harley, C., Wright, H., & Farrelly, D. (2004). Individual differences in deductive reasoning. *Quarterly Journal of Experimental Psychology, 57*, 33–60.

Oaksford, M., & Chater, N. (1994). A rational analysis of the selection task as optimal data selection. *Psychological Review, 101*, 608–631.

Osherson, D. N., Smith, E. E., Wilkie, O., López, A., & Shafir, E. (1990). Category-based induction. *Psychological Review, 97*, 185–200.

Osman, M. (2004). An evaluation of dual-process theories of reasoning. *Psychonomic Bulletin & Review, 11*, 988–1010.

Proffitt, J. B., Coley, J. D., & Medin, D. L. (2000). Expertise and category-based induction. *Journal of Experimental Psychology: Learning, Memory, and Cognition, 26*, 811–828.

Rehder, B., & Hastie, R. (2001). Causal knowledge and categories: The effects of causal beliefs on categorization, induction, and similarity. *Journal of Experimental Psychology: General, 130*, 323–360.

Rips, L. J. (2001). Two kinds of reasoning. *Psychological Science, 12*, 129–134.

Ross, B. H., & Murphy, G. L. (1999). Food for thought: Cross-classification and category organization on a complex real-world domain. *Cognitive Psychology, 38*, 495–553.

Sloman, S. A. (1993). Feature-based induction. *Cognitive Psychology, 25*, 231–280.

Sloman, S. A. (1996). The empirical case for two systems of reasoning. *Psychological Bulletin, 119*, 3–22.

Sperber, D., & Wilson, D. (1986/1995). *Relevance: Communication and cognition.* Oxford: Basil Blackwell.

Stanovich, K. E. (1999). *Who is rational? Studies of individual differences in reasoning.* Mahwah, NJ: Erlbaum.

Stanovich, K. E., & West, R. F. (1998a). Individual differences in rational thought. *Journal of Experimental Psychology: General, 127*, 161–188.

Stanovich, K. E., & West, R. F. (1998b). Cognitive ability and variation in selection task performance. *Thinking and Reasoning, 4*, 193–230.

Stanovich, K. E. & West, R. F. (1998c). Individual differences in framing and conjunction effects. *Thinking and Reasoning, 4*, 289–317.

Tversky, A., & Kahneman, D. (1983) Extensional vs. intuitive reasoning: The conjunction fallacy in probability judgment. *Psychological Review, 90*, 293–315.

Unsworth, N., & Engle, R. W. (2005). Working memory capacity and fluid abilities: Examining the correlation between Operation Span and Raven. *Intelligence, 33*, 67–81.

Wason, P. (1966) Reasoning. In B. Foss (Ed.), *New horizons in Psychology* (pp. 135–151). Harmondsworth: Penguin.

Wayne, A. (1995). Bayesianism and diverse evidence. *Philosophy of Science, 62*, 111–121.

13

Taxonomizing Induction

Steven A. Sloman

The chapters in this book offer a variety of perspectives on induction. This is not shocking, as inductive problems are both fundamental and unsolvable. They are fundamental in that organisms must solve them in order to know most of the things about their environment that they cannot observe directly, like what's around the next corner or what to expect from that woolly mammoth over there. They are unsolvable in that uncertainty cannot be eliminated. However we define induction, as discussed in Heit's Chapter 1, it involves conclusions that we cannot be sure about. There seems to be general agreement with Hume's (1748) conclusion that no logic of justification for inductive inference is possible.

Despite the variety of perspectives, the chapters revolve around three central themes concerning, respectively, the prevalence of induction, how to carve up the space of inductive inferences, and the role of causality. I will briefly discuss each in turn.

1. THE PREVALENCE OF INDUCTION

The consensus in these essays is that most of the conclusions that people come to have an inductive basis and that little human reasoning is well-described as deductive. Indeed, the brunt of Oaksford and Hahn's Chapter 11 is that probabilistic inference is the dominant mode of human reasoning, a claim echoed by Heit and by Thagard (Chapter 9).

Even the Rips and Asmuth Chapter 10 leaves the reader with the impression that deductive reasoning is exceptional. Rips and Asmuth make a strong argument that inductive proofs in math have the strength of deductive inference, that they are deductive proofs in disguise. The existence of deductive proofs entails the existence of deductive reasoning, so the existence of mathematicians and logicians proves that human beings are capable of deductive inference. But in the course of their argument, Rips and Asmuth review a lot of evidence that students find deductive proofs hard to generate and that they confuse them with demonstrations via examples. Their data give the impression that nonexperts rarely rely on deductive inference.

The authors seem to agree that reasoning is either inductive or deductive. Heit, Oaksford and Hahn, and Rips and Asmuth all make this dichotomy explicit. So does Thagard, who views abduction as a species of induction because both involve uncertain conclusions. On this view, if little reasoning is deductive, then almost all reasoning is inductive.

The field of psychology at large seems to agree with this conclusion. Less and less work is being done on how people make deductive inferences. One of the central players in that line of work has concluded that logic is rarely a reasonable standard to evaluate human reasoning and that most reasoning is pragmatic and probabilistic (Evans, 2002). With the exception of Johnson-Laird (2005), this seems to be a widely held view.

Of course, the claim that most reasoning is inductive is not terribly strong. If we follow Skyrms (2000) in holding that an inductive argument is merely one in which the conclusion is not necessary given the premises (see Heit's chapter), we are left with a vast number of argument forms and types. The set of inductive arguments includes those that seem almost deductively valid (if Houdini could hold his breath for fifteen minutes, then he could hold his breath for fifteen minutes and one second), arguments that are exceptionally weak (lobster is expensive today, therefore lobster was expensive in the 17th century), causal arguments (A causes B and A occurred, therefore B probably occurred), abductions (see Thagard's chapter), and many more. Is there one big homogeneous space of inductive arguments, or can they be grouped in meaningful ways? This is the second theme of the book.

2. IS INDUCTIVE REASONING ONE THING OR MANY?

This question can refer to a normative issue, whether there is more than one system for justifying inductive leaps, or a descriptive issue, whether there are natural fault lines that distinguish different modes or systems that people use to make inductive inferences. I address the normative issue very briefly and then focus on the major topic of this book, the descriptive issue.

Normative Criteria

The implicit claim in Tenenbaum, Kemp, and Shafto (Chapter 7), made explicitly by Oaksford and Hahn, is that there is a single normative model of induction, a criterion for justification defined in Bayesian terms as probabilistic support for a conclusion. Bayesian theory provides a way to maintain a coherent set of beliefs by providing a rule to update the probability that is assigned to beliefs in the face of new data. This rule has the virtue that, in the case of repeated events, the updated probabilities converge to the long-run relative frequency of the event.

I will not take issue with Bayesianism, though others have (see Howson & Urbach, 1993, for a discussion). But I will point out that even if this view is right, the conclusion that induction has a single set of normative criteria does not immediately follow, because probabilistic support comes in varieties. Different senses of probability can be distinguished. One common distinction is between an extensional type that measures the inherent unpredictability of events such as the randomness of a coin toss, referred to as "aleatory uncertainty," and the type of probability that refers to degree of ignorance or "epistemic uncertainty," like the degree of confidence that you assign to your answer to a trivial pursuit question (before looking it up). Randomness in the world and lack of certainty in a judgment have different sources. Randomness is a property of events in the world independent of the judge and uncertainty a property of a mental state of the judge. They also present different obstacles to prediction. Randomness generally refers to a principled and fixed limit on the accuracy of prediction, whereas uncertainty can be reduced with more knowledge or expertise.

Having such different sources and prospects, these two forms of probability appear to provide quite different forms of justification. The fact that they both can be updated via a common equational form (Bayes's rule) is not a very deep commonality. Bayes's rule requires models of its terms, both its prior belief and likelihood terms (see Tenenbaum et al., Chapter 7 for an explanation of what these terms refer to). Neither of these is trivial. Tenenbaum et al. offer a sophisticated theory of the source of prior beliefs, that is, how people generate a space of hypotheses and assign probability to them. Likelihoods require a model that spells out how each hypothesis expects data to be generated in order to provide, for every hypothesis, a probability assignment for every possible pattern of data. These models can have very different forms and make different assumptions depending on the kind of probability at issue. Thus the criteria for inductive justification that they provide are fundamentally different for sufficiently distinct problems.

Moreover, the aleatory/epistemic distinction is not the only important one. Tenenbaum et al. discuss the variety of different relational structures that are necessary for the range of problems that people encounter. To illustrate, they propose one type of relational structure for the biological domain (a hierarchical one). A different type would be required to count days of the week (a periodic one). That choice and all others influence the normative model used in the final analysis. So, again, the argument for a single normative criterion for inductive inference still needs to be made.

That question is not at the heart of this book; this book is really concerned with the psychological/cognitive scientific question of how people actually reason inductively, not how they should or whether they are justified. Although descriptive and normative models are related conceptually in many ways, they must be evaluated in entirely different ways. Descriptive models must be evaluated according to their ability to describe behavior; normative models must be evaluated according to their ability to accurately describe what is right and what is wrong. The distinction has been muddied however by the development of the "rational analysis" school of cognitive science (Oaksford & Chater, 1998), as exemplified by the Tenenbaum et al. chapter.

On Computational Models

Tenenbaum, Kemp, and Shafto offer a valuable perspective on induction, one that they claim is a *computational-level model* of human induction. Is their model normative, identifying whether behaviors are well designed to achieve their users' goals, or descriptive, identifying which behaviors will be produced? When Marr (1982) introduced the concept of a computational model, he intended it as a functional description of what an organism is trying to accomplish, the problems it faces, as opposed to the strategies it uses to accomplish them (an algorithmic model) or how those strategies are realized in a physical system (an implementational model).

A computational model in Marr's sense is neither normative nor descriptive. It is not normative in that it merely characterizes a problem without specifying whether or not that is the right problem to solve. The characterization might be correct or incorrect, but either way nothing is implied about whether the organism's thought or behavior is effective or not. A computational theory is not descriptive because it is a representation of a problem in the world, not necessarily anything that an organism does or even knows about at any level. A computational theory of nest building by an ant colony describes a problem that no single ant is trying to solve. The solution is an emergent property of the behavior of a large number of ants blind to any larger purpose. Similarly, a computational model of human induction, like the Bayesian model suggested by Tenenbaum et al., is an abstract representation of a problem. Solving that problem, or just trying to, does not require that people have access to that computational representation. People do not need to know Bayes's rule in order to make inductions in a way that approximates or is consistent with it.

The model is not descriptive unless it takes a stand on how the computation is performed or how well people conform to the constraints it imposes. In other words, the normative/descriptive distinction becomes relevant when we assess how well the organism is doing at achieving its goals as represented by the computational model. If it wants gummy bears and it gets gummy bears, then its behavior is normatively appropriate. How it goes about getting gummy bears is a descriptive question. In the domain of induction, a normative theory would prescribe how to obtain an optimal solution to the problem. The only reason to compare that optimal solution to what people do, a comparison important to Tenenbaum et al., is to see if the normative theory is also descriptive. If it is, then people are rational and we have a rational model of behavior. If it is not, then we remain without a descriptive theory.

Positing that a normative theory is also descriptively adequate is certainly reasonable, but it is known to be false in general. Dozens of demonstrations of fallacious reasoning, including the conjunction fallacy (Tversky & Kahneman, 1983), some cases of base-rate neglect (Barbey & Sloman, in Press), and many others (Gilovich, Griffin, & Kahneman, 2002), all show that people, for good or for bad, do not always behave according to normative principles when reasoning inductively.

A lot can be and has been learned about how the mind works by examining the hypothesis that people are normative. However, this research strategy can also lead to confusion on both sides of the normative/descriptive divide. One kind of error occurs when a normative theorist thinks his or her theory is descriptively adequate when it is not. A complementary error occurs when a descriptive theorist fails to consider ways in which people make mistakes. Worse, empirical methodologies are sometimes used that are designed to hide human error. This can only interfere with the development of both descriptive and prescriptive theory.

Descriptive Models

The most pertinent question for this book is whether human inductive reasoning occurs in one or more fundamentally different ways. The chapters offer several ways of cutting the pie:

NO CUT. Oaksford and Hahn argue for a single method of making inductive inferences, one that conforms to Bayesian inference. They show that a range of judgments about the strength of an inductive inference is consistent with

Bayesian tenets. This broadly supports the stance of Tenenbaum, Kemp, and Shafto.

The strength of this proposal is its breadth. It offers a conception that covers induction in all its forms and, unlike any other model, proposes a method that is both mathematically well-defined and highly flexible in its ability to adjust to all forms of relational knowledge. A danger of this approach is that with great flexibility comes great freedom to fit all patterns of data, both real and imagined. Theoretical power is a curse when it comes to demonstrating the empirical value of a model because it allows the model to wrap itself around any potential result, even those not found.

BY DOMAIN. Tenenbaum et al.'s suggestion that different relational structures are used with different kinds of arguments motivates their effort to spell out how different relational structures are chosen and applied to particular arguments based both on prior domain knowledge and specific facts presented within an argument. So, although they propose an overarching formal relation that applies to all inductive inference, they believe that the way the relation is applied depends on domain-specific relational structure. Inductions about biological relations are supported by fuzzy hierarchical knowledge about biological taxonomy. Inductions about the spread of diseases are supported by knowledge of the causal relations that govern interactions between predators and their prey. Tenenbaum et al. propose that there are also other relational structures for induction.

The proposal is impressive in its coverage and potential for generating domain-specific theories. The danger of this approach is a particular case of the concern about Bayesianism stated earlier: It opens the possibility of multiplying relational structures, each shaped to fit a specific study. Presumably, relational structures are not independent entities but are generated on the basis of basic principles. For instance, biological hierarchies can be grounded in one or another causal model: The hierarchy might emerge from a causal analysis of how biological entities function, top-down from causal beliefs about evolutionary processes, or in some other way. In fact, it might be that once the causal model that grounds the hierarchy is spelled out, the hierarchy itself will turn out to be superfluous. Inductions might be mediated directly by causal knowledge (see Hayes, Chapter 2, for a related point).

The fact that some relational structure can be used along with Bayesian principles to successfully fit data on induction does not provide indisputable evidence that people use that relational structure to reason. The relational structure may serve as a proxy for some other kind of knowledge that might not be domain specific, like causal knowledge.

SIMILARITY VERSUS CAUSAL KNOWLEDGE. Several chapters argue that people use similarity relations to make inductions when no other useful information is available but use causal knowledge when they can (Shafto, Coley, & Vitkin; Rehder; Blok, Osherson, & Medin). This idea can be traced to Quine (1970), who argued that natural kinds are classified using an innate sense of similarity of objects to one another until a conceptual theory becomes available to replace the unanalyzed similarity construct. Theoretical knowledge often becomes available to the child through learning; it becomes available to scientists as their field of study matures.

Hayes points out that distinctions among similarity, causal, and categorical reasoning tend to be ecologically invalid. Similarity is generally an indicator of categorical relations, and categories cohere only by virtue of causal structure. So the norm in the real world is that cues tied to the various strategies are highly intercorrelated and mutually supportive. Experimenters have managed to construct situations that disentangle the cues, but such situations might eliminate people's ability to do what they are especially good at, namely, to combine different kinds of convergent information. Nevertheless, people are at times faced with objects and events that they cannot analyze in any depth. Sometimes, an object or event is so new that one is limited to a superficial analysis that affords comparison only by similarity and not by unobservable attributes like causal structure. I had this experience recently in Portugal when a barnacle was put on my lunch plate, apparently a delicacy. All I could do was remark on its striking superficial properties (properties quite unrelated to eating lunch). Admittedly, even in this case of ignorance and surprise I was able to infer that what I was looking at was in some way related to organic matter. Hayes is fundamentally correct that induction is guided not by one sort of cue or another, but by a desire to explain why categories have properties (Sloman, 1994), and this gives the various reasoning strategies the common goal of making inferences in a way that respects the latent structure of an object.

ASSOCIATIVE VERSUS DELIBERATIVE REASONING. Feeney argues in his Chapter 12 that induction is mediated by two different systems of reasoning (Evans & Over, 1996; Stanovich, 1999; Sloman, 1996), one governed by associative principles and the other more deliberative, rule-based, and dependent on working memory capacity. His evidence comes from a couple of studies of individual differences showing that participants who score higher on a test of intelligence demonstrate more sensitivity to the diversity principle, the principle that multiple pieces of evidence for a conclusion are strong to the degree that the pieces are diverse (dissimilar). On the assumption that more intelligent people can allocate deliberative reasoning resources more effectively than less intelligent people but that everyone is equally capable of associative reasoning, this suggests that sensitivity to diversity emerges from deliberative effort, not associative reasoning, an idea previously championed by McDonald, Samuels, and Rispoli (1996).

Sloman (1998) also argued for a dual-system model of induction but on an entirely different basis. In that paper, I report several experiments showing an inclusion similarity phenomenon, namely, that people will make inductions proportional to similarity even when doing so neglects transparent categorical relations between premise and conclusion. For example, people did not always judge

> Every individual body of water has a high number of seiches.
> Therefore, every individual lake has a high number of seiches.

to be perfectly strong even when they agreed that a lake is a body of water. Moreover, they judged

> Every individual body of water has a high number of seiches.
> Therefore, every individual reservoir has a high number of seiches.

to be even weaker (again even when they agreed that the premise category includes the conclusion category), presumably because reservoirs are less typical bodies of water than lakes. These kinds of judgments fall out of an associative model of reasoning: People made their judgments based on similarity or some kind of feature-based analysis, not on the basis of categorical knowledge.

But if the latent categorical premise was made explicit,

> All reservoirs are bodies of water.
> All bodies of water have a high number of seiches.
> All reservoirs have a high number of seiches.

then everyone judged the argument perfectly strong. By turning the argument into an explicit syllogism, people were induced to use a strategy that is highly sensitive to categorical relations. My argument in 1998 was that this strategy is deliberative and not merely associative because, unlike associative knowledge, it depends on an explicit categorical relation and leads to certainty in the conclusion.

INTENDED MEANING VERSUS KNOWLEDGE-BASED INFERENCE. Most of the discussion in this book assumes that inductions take place through a cognitive process mediated by knowledge. But several authors note that the communicative context of induction might also influence people's inductions.

Communicative context affects induction in a couple of ways. For one, induction can be influenced by the semantics of a language. Medin and Waxman point out that asymmetries in children's inferences first pointed out by Carey (1985) can be explained this way. Carey found that young children were more willing to project an unfamiliar part from humans to dogs than from dogs to humans. One interpretation of Medin and Waxman is that "human" is an ambiguous term, implying on one hand "animal of human form" and, on the other hand, "non-animal entity." They suggest that arguments in the human to dog direction could suggest the more inclusive animal sense of "human," whereas arguments in the dog to human direction could suggest the less inclusive non-animal sense. This would explain the observed asymmetry by appealing to different intended meanings of a word.

Induction can also be influenced by pragmatic considerations. Feeney and Shafto, Coley, and Vitkin mention that many of the conclusions we draw are given to us or at least guided by people around us. We seek expertise everywhere. Even experimenters might be deemed experts so that the format of the arguments they present might be treated as suggesting appropriate conclusions. For instance, Medin, Storms, Coley, and Hayes (2003) suggest that some monotonicities and nonmonotonicities have a pragmatic basis. If told that grizzly bears have a property, you might be willing to conclude that it is more likely that squirrels have the property than you thought beforehand. But if told that three different kinds of bear have the property (grizzlies, polar bears, and black bears say), then you might conclude that the experimenter is trying to tell you something about what kind of thing has the property and therefore that it seems more likely that only bears do. This is a plausible inference on the assumption that the experimenter is picking categories so as to be informative, that is, that the choice of premises is pragmatically driven.

However, it is also a reasonable inference from the assumption that categories are being randomly chosen from the set of things that have the property. If a wide range of mammals had the property, then it is very unlikely that three bears would be randomly chosen; they would be much more likely to be chosen if only bears had the property. In other words, some pragmatic effects might reflect sampling assumptions that people make about how premises and conclusions are chosen (Tenenbaum & Griffiths, 2001). However, there is evidence that people find arguments with more premises stronger regardless of what they are told about sampling procedures (Fernbach, 2006). This fact contradicts both the sampling and the pragmatic inference theories.

CATEGORICAL VERSUS NON-CATEGORICAL INFERENCE. Murphy and Ross (Chapter 8) demonstrate convincingly that in their experimental paradigm people tend to focus on a single category, neglecting alternative categories. The observation that people focus on only a single possibility and neglect alternatives converges with other category research (Lagnado & Shanks, 2003), as well as research showing that people tend to focus on only a single causal model when troubleshooting (Fischhoff, Slovic, & Lichtenstein, 1978), when making probability judgments (Dougherty, Gettys, & Thomas, 1997), and when engaged in various forms of deductive inference (Johnson-Laird, 2005).

Tenenbaum (1999) found that a model that posits that people make inductions by weighting each category-hypothesis in a Bayesian manner fits human data fairly well. Such a model assumes that people consider multiple categories in induction. To account for this inconsistency with their findings, Murphy and Ross suggest that people are not even using categories in Tenenbaum's task but rather relying on associations between attributes and the new property. This is precisely the theoretical issue that separates Osherson, Smith, Wilkie, & Shafir (1990) similarity-coverage model of induction from Sloman's (1993) feature-based model. The notion of coverage in the similarity-coverage model is category coverage, the degree to which premise categories cover the lowest-level category that includes all premise and conclusion categories. This notion requires that people have a category hierarchy available and that the determination of category membership is an explicit part of the inductive process. The feature-based model also has a notion of coverage – feature coverage – the extent to which the features (properties or attributes) of the premise categories cover the features of the conclusion category. No hierarchical category knowledge is assumed.

Murphy and Ross are right that the question of whether people use categories is prior to the question of how many categories people consider. It may be that relatively little induction is mediated by categorical knowledge at all. Indeed, Sloman's (1998) data suggest that hierarchical knowledge is considered only when it is made explicit. After all, so many other kinds of knowledge are available to mediate induction such as similarity comparisons and causal knowledge. This observation supports Tenenbaum et al.'s insight that categorical knowledge is only one kind of relational structure and that one of the key problems of induction is how to choose from and deploy a variety of different relational structures.

ABDUCTION VERSUS OTHER FORMS OF INDUCTION. Thagard observes the generality of the process of abduction and notes that, while it can be construed as a form of induction in that it involves uncertain conclusions, it is distinguished in the process of reasoning that it entails. The critical element of abduction according to Thagard is the process of explanation that it entails.

Belief changes following an abductive process pertain to explanations of ob-servations. Explanations earn belief according to the quality of their account of observations.

Thagard is surely right that abductive processes have been neglected in cognitive theory (though see Lombrozo, in press). But the importance of explanation is not limited to abduction. It is known to be just as central to other inductive forms. Explanations frequently mediate induction by selecting relevant features (Sloman, 1994; Sloman & Wisniewski, 1992). To decide if property A should be projected from category X to category Y, people explain why category X has property A and evaluate whether that explanation would pertain to category Y. Should the property of being hard to see at night be projected from Black Labradors to Blond Labradors? Presumably not as Black Labs are invisible because of their color and that color is not shared by Blond Labs. Explaining why Black Labs have the property is a critical part of the inductive inference.

3. CAUSALITY

Although the chapters in this collection offer a variety of perspectives on how to distinguish inductive forms, a theme common to many chapters is the central role played by causal knowledge in inductive inference. Hayes focuses on the role of causal relations in guiding people to make inferences based on causally relevant properties rather than causally irrelevant ones. Shafto et al. and Feeney provide strong evidence that people reason with causal relations when they have sufficient knowledge. Rehder offers a causal model of inductive inference. Tenenbaum et al. claim that causal structure is an important type of relational structure for inference. Thagard argues that causality is the core of explanation, and that explanation is the heart of the abductive inferences that he discusses.

These authors are all in one way or another echoing Hume (1748), who argued that inductive inferences are parasitic on causal beliefs (cf. Sloman & Lagnado, 2005). As regards the psychology of induction, the jury is out about whether all inductive inferences have a causal basis or whether only some do. As many of the chapters attest, the evidence is overwhelming that other prin-ciples also apply to particular inductive inferences. Some inferences clearly appeal to similarity and others to categorical relations (Murphy & Ross). But it might be that these other relations are just proxies for causal structure. Objects that are more similar tend to share more causal roles, so similarity provides a heuristic basis for making causally appropriate inferences. Hadjichristidis et al. (2004) show that people's inferences are proportional to a property's causal centrality but only to the extent that the objects are similar. This suggests that people treat similarity as a cue for the extent to which objects share causal structure. And when similarity conflicts with causal relations, causality wins (Hayes).

Category knowledge serves as a proxy for causal structure in a couple of senses. First, some categories are defined by their role in a causal relation. The category of "brown things" is the set of things that cause light to reflect off of them such that visual systems perceive brown. The category of "goals in a hockey game" is the set of events that consist of an outcome that gives a hockey team a point. Second, more complex categories are also associated with causal roles, frequently multiple causal roles. For instance, the set of objects that we call "automobile" tend to participate in causal roles involving transportation of people, systems of steering and acceleration, expensive repairs, and so forth.

The most direct explanation for how an induction is made is not necessarily causal. But there might be a causal explanation at some level operating in the background to motivate the relational structure used to make the inductive inference in every case.

4. A TAXONOMIC PROPOSAL

The range of topics covered by the chapters in this book exposes the point that Shafto et al. make explicitly: People use a variety of strategies and frames for assessing inductive strength in everyday life. Strategies seem to be arrayed along a series of levels that require progressively more conceptual effort and provide progressively more justifiable responses. The hierarchy conforms to the trade-off between cognitive effort and cognitive effect that determines relevance (Wilson & Sperber, 2004). At the bottom of the ladder, induction makes use of rough guesses and, at the top, involves deliberation including construction and calculation:

Most effort, most justifiable:	Set theoretic frames (including categorical)
Some effort, moderate justifiability:	Causal models
Least effort, least justifiable:	Associative strategies (correlational; similarity)

The bottom level involves pattern recognition (Sloutsky & Fisher, 2004). Objects that have a particular pattern have some property; therefore objects with similar patterns have that property. If I know a particular kind of mushroom is poisonous, then I avoid all mushrooms that look like it unless I have more specific information to help me along. But if I have causal knowledge to deploy, and I have the time and motivation to deploy it, then I can do better. For instance, if I can identify the poison-relevant attributes of the mushroom, or if I can figure out from the first mushroom where the poison resides and how to get rid of it, or if I can use the first mushroom to obtain some kind of chemical imprint of the poison, then I can use that new information to generalize to new mushrooms. I can use a causal model to draw a more specific and more certain conclusion about a novel object (Sloman, 2005). This requires more effort, but the greater specificity and certainty offers a bigger payoff.

However, causal knowledge is not perfect and causal relations might all be probabilistic (Pearl, 2000), so in some cases one can do better than by using a causal model. For instance, if in addition to causal knowledge, I know that 99% of the mushrooms in the area are poisonous, I would be unlikely to risk eating the mushroom under any circumstances. This third kind of inference is set theoretic in the sense that it involves a representation or a calculation over a set of objects (all the mushrooms in the area). Lagnado and Sloman (2004) argue that thinking about sets involves an outside view of a category in terms of its extension as a set of instances, and that such thinking requires special effort. People find it easier to think about categories from the inside, in terms of their properties and relations among those properties. In the context of induction, the distinction can be seen most clearly in the inclusion fallacy of Shafir, Smith, and Osherson (1990):

Robins have sesamoid bones.
Therefore, all birds have sesamoid bones.

versus

Robins have sesamoid bones.
Therefore, all penguins have sesamoid bones.

Most people judge the first argument stronger, although it cannot be if you believe that all penguins are birds. The first argument entails that penguins as well as all other birds have the property; the second that only penguins do. So the second argument must be stronger, and this is obvious once you see the category inclusion relation between penguins and birds – a relation among sets. But most people do not consider that relation until it is pointed out to them or made transparent in some other way. This kind of thinking generally involves the greatest effort, especially without cues to aid it along, but it offers the biggest payoff. In this case, it affords certainty about the stronger argument.

The first level of the hierarchy is clearly associative and the top level is clearly not. This is consistent with Feeney's evidence that some inferences are made intuitively and others involve deliberative processing. Some dual-process models (Sloman, 1996) imply that we always engage in associative reasoning at some level, that is, that the similarity-based response is always available. In order to engage in deliberative processing, we need to take whatever cues we can from language, perception, or elsewhere in order to construct an effective organizational frame.

Beyond dual processes, the proposed framework is consistent with other ideas suggested in this book. It is consistent with the idea that people use similarity if a causal model is not available as long as no set-theoretic alternative is. One set-theoretic alternative is a category hierarchy, and Murphy and Ross's evidence that people rely on a single category when making inductions may reflect a constraint on how people think about sets. The proposal is also consistent with Tenenbaum et al.'s proposal that people use a variety of relational schemes that are individually appropriate for different inferences. But the proposal does entail that we cannot reduce every inductive inference that people make to a single inferential model, unless we choose a model – like unconstrained Bayesian inference – that is so general that it does not have predictive power. To successfully predict human induction, the next generation of models will have to respect this variety in inductive procedures.

ACKNOWLEDGMENTS

This work was funded by NSF Award 0518147. It has benefited greatly from the comments of Aidan Feeney, Evan Heit, and especially Phil Fernbach.

References

Barbey, A. K., & Sloman, S. A. (2006). Base-rate respect: From ecological rationality to dual processes. *Behavioral and Brain Sciences.*

Dougherty, M. R. P., Gettys, C. F., & Thomas, R. P. (1997). The role of mental simulation in judgments of likelihood. *Organizational Behavior and Human Decision Processes, 70*, 135–148.

Evans, J. St. B. T. (2002). Logic and human reasoning: An assessment of the deduction paradigm. *Psychological Bulletin, 128*, 978–996.

Evans, J. St. B. T., & Over, D. E. (1996). *Rationality and reasoning.* Hove, UK: Psychology Press.

Fernbach, P. M. (2006). Sampling assumptions and the size principle in property induction. *Proceedings of the Twenty-Eigth Annual Conference of the Cognitive Science Society,* Vancouver, Canada.

Fischhoff, B., Slovic, P., & Lichtenstein, S. (1978). Fault trees: Sensitivity of estimated failure probabilities to problem representations. *Journal of Experimental Psychology: Human Perception and Performance, 4*, 330–344.

Gilovich, T., Griffin, D., & Kahneman, D. (2002). *Heuristics and biases: The psychology of intuitive judgment.* Cambridge: Cambridge University Press.

Hadjichristidis, C., Sloman, S. A., Stevenson, R. J., Over, D. E. (2004). Feature centrality and property induction. *Cognitive Science, 28*, 45–74.

Howson, C., & Urbach, P. (1993). *Scientific reasoning: The Bayesian approach.* Second edition. Open Court, Chicago.

Hume, D. (1748). *An enquiry concerning human understanding.* Oxford: Clarendon.

Johnson-Laird, P. (2005). Mental models and thought. In K. Holyoak & R. Morrison (Eds.), *The Cambridge handbook of thinking & reasoning,* pp. 185–208. New York: Cambridge University Press.

Lagnado, D. A., & Shanks, D. R. (2003). The influence of hierarchy on probability judgment. *Cognition, 89*, 157–178.

Lagnado, D., & Sloman, S. A. (2004). Inside and outside probability judgment. D. J. Koehler & N. Harvey (Eds.), *Blackwell handbook of judgment and decision making,* pp. 157–176. Oxford, UK: Blackwell Publishing.

Lombrozo, T. (in press). The structure and function of explanations. *Trends in Cognitive Science.*

Marr, D. (1982). Vision: A computational investigation into the human representation and processing of visual information. New York: W. H. Freeman and Company.

McDonald, J., Samuels, M., & Rispoli, J. (1996). A hypothesis assessment model of categorical argument strength. *Cognition, 59*, 199–217.

Oaksford, M., & Chater, N. (Eds.) (1998). *Rational models of cognition.* Oxford, UK: Oxford University Press.

Osherson, D.N., Smith, E. E., Wilkie, O., Lopez, A., & Shafir, E. (1990). Category-based induction. *Psychological Review, 97*, 185–200.

Quine, W. V. (1970). Natural kinds. In N. Rescher (Ed.), *Essays in honor of Carl G. Hempel,* pp. 5–23. Dordrecht: D. Reidel.

Shafir, E., Smith, E., & Osherson, D. (1990). Typicality and reasoning fallacies. *Memory and Cognition, 18*, 229–239.

Skyrms, B. (2000). *Choice and chance: An introduction to inductive logic.* (Fourth edition). Belmont, CA: Wadsworth.

Sloman, S. A. (1994). When explanations compete: The role of explanatory coherence on judgments of likelihood. *Cognition, 52*, 1–21.

Sloman, S. A. (1996). The empirical case for two systems of reasoning. *Psychological Bulletin, 119*, 3–22.

Sloman, S. A. (1998). Categorical inference is not a tree: The myth of inheritance hierarchies. *Cognitive Psychology, 35*, 1–33.

Sloman, S. A., & Lagnado, D. (2005). The problem of induction. In K. Holyoak & R. Morrison (Eds.), *The Cambridge handbook of thinking & reasoning,* pp. 95–116. New York: Cambridge University Press.

Sloman, S. A., & Wisniewski, E. (1992). Extending the domain of a feature-based model of property induction. *Proceedings of the Fourteenth Annual Conference of the Cognitive Science Society,* Bloomington, IN.

Sloutsky, V. M., & Fisher, A. V. (2004). Induction and categorization in young children: A similarity-based model. *Journal of Experimental Psychology: General, 133,* 166–188.

Stanovich, K. E. (1999). *Who is rational? Studies of individual differences in reasoning.* Mahwah, NJ: Erlbaum.

Tenenbaum, J. B. (1999). Bayesian modeling of human concept learning. In M. Kearns, S. Solla, & D. Cohn (Eds.), *Advances in neural information processing systems 11,* pp. 59–65. Cambridge: MIT Press.

Tenenbaum, J. B., & Griffiths, T. L. (2001). Generalization, similarity and Bayesian inference. *Behavioral and Brain Sciences, 24,* 629–640.

Tversky, A., & Kahneman, D. (1983). Extensional versus intuitive reasoning: The conjunction fallacy in probability judgment. *Psychological Review, 90,* 293–315.

Wilson, D., & Sperber, D. (2004). Relevance theory. In L.R. Horn & G. Ward (Eds.), *The handbook of pragmatics,* pp. 607–632. Oxford, UK: Blackwell Publishing.

Index